A Systemic
Theory of
Democracy

A Systemic Theory of Democracy

Towards the Democratic Diagnosis
of Political Systems

Victor Sanchez-Mazas

General management: Lucas Giossi
Editorial liaison officer: Loraine Chappuis
Editorial and sales management: Sylvain Collette and May Yang.
Promotion and distribution: Manon Reber
Production manager: Christophe Borlat
Editorial: Alice Micheau-Thiébaud and Jean Rime
Graphic design: Kim Nanette
Accounting: Daniela Castan
Logistics: Émile Razafimanjaka

Cover illustration: Vassily Kandinski, 1923, *Circles in a Circle*, Philadelphia Museum of Art

First edition 2024
Épistémé. Lausanne
Épistémé is an imprint of the foundation of the Presses polytechniques
et universitaires romandes.
ISBN 978-2-88915-648-1, print version
ISBN 978-2-8323-2286-4, ebook version (pdf), doi.org/10.55430/8034VSMVA01

Table of contents

Introduction

Politics is a complex matter. Some people don't know much about it, some don't seem to care, and others even claim to be "against it." Some contend that they understand how it works and how it should work, and perhaps a few really do. However, despite all these disparate understandings of the political reality, most people conceive of it as an abstraction, a simplification of political complexity: *the system*. If you ask people how they define politics or what they think about it, it is likely that the term "system" (or a related concept such as "society") will appear in the first few sentences of their answers. Somehow, the broad spectrum of political ideas can be over-simplified by adding a verb to the noun "system": keep the system, reform the system, change the system, fight the system, and even destroy the system. While these verbs mark some positional differences regarding the political reality, the noun "system" represents a shared or unquestioned understanding of what this political reality basically is. The meaning of "system" appears to be self-evident, and most people (including politicians and academics) often employ this abstraction as if it were unproblematic; an undisputable common reference. This book starts from the premise that *democracy is a complex system*. It contends that by investigating the complexity of what a system is in general, we can better locate the distinctiveness of what *democratic systems* are and could be. This book interrogates what democracy is if we take it as a complex system, what it could be, and how to transform it.

Deliberative and democratic systems

The idea of democracy *as a system* has often, if not always, been more or less silently endorsed (or at least presupposed) by most democratic scholars, whether they are normatively or empirically oriented. After all, the main object of democratic scholarship is this complex political whole that we commonly label (yet diversely conceive of) as *democracy*. After long focusing on specific deliberative venues (typically mini-publics), deliberative democracy's systemic turn (Parkinson & Mansbridge 2012; Dryzek 2009) has undoubtedly brought back an explicit emphasis on the systemic dimension. *Deliberative systems* now qualify a distinct and dominant approach to deliberative democracy. Originating from the deliberative model of democracy, the systemic turn was also applied to the *representative* system (Rey 2023) or adopted by authors calling to bypass models' boundaries and instead focus on the overall *democratic* system (Warren 2017; Saward 2021). During this progressive reshaping (or at least reframing) of democratic theory, much effort has been dedicated, of course, to discussing the deliberative and/or democratic qualities of political systems. In addition, much has been said about *why* deliberative democracy should be understood as a complex whole, made of the interaction of its parts.

The systemic turn in deliberative democracy advocates for a shift from the *micro*-focus characterizing its preceding institutional/empirical phase (Owen & Smith 2015: 2114). During this stage of the deliberative paradigm, the emphasis was indeed placed on the real-world applications of its philosophical grounds and normative prescriptions. This crucial endeavor of empirical applicability mainly drove scholars' attention towards traditional or innovative venues that were or could be made maximally deliberative; randomly selected mini-publics are typical examples of the spotlight on deliberative forums. However, the academic focus on the deliberative quality of discrete instances (through notably the development of measurement tools such as the DQI, Steenbergen et al. 2003) blurred to some extent the importance of "the interdependence of sites within a larger system" (Mansbridge et al. 2012: 1). The systemic approach instead argues that *connections* between sites have important impacts on their deliberative quality. Moreover, the attention given to the deliberative potential of specific venues occulted the fact that the deliberative quality also (if not primarily) qualifies broad systems (i.e., "deliberative democracy") and can be conceived of as an *emergent* phenomenon (Parkinson 2018). Accordingly, the interplay between the multiple elements composing complex political systems can "summatively" produce deliberative systems (ibid.). In essence, the systemic turn in deliberative democracy reorients the question of deliberative quality to the larger scale of democratic *systems*.

The major motivation for the systemic shift was broadly to reconcile the normative ideals of deliberative democracy with the practical constraints and complexity of real-world politics. This reconciliation requires the acknowledgment that no single deliberative institution, even innovative or allegedly ideal ones (such as citizens' assemblies), can suffice to enact or even improve the legitimacy of the *entire* system (Parkinson 2012: 170). In addition, taken as a system, deliberative democracy provides the opportunity to answer its inherent problem of scale, according to which it is practically impossible to have venues that are both deliberative and democratic. By adopting a *distributed* vision of the deliberative ideal, the systemic approach does not require each deliberative norm to be present at the same time and in the same venue. Indeed, a deliberative system can have some highly participative venues and others fostering good deliberation. Moreover, the systemic approach enables the normative inclusion of non-deliberative forms of communication (e.g., rhetoric), conceiving them as potentially beneficial for the system as a whole, and thus ending the need for conceptual stretching of what deliberation is (Steiner 2008; Bächtiger et al. 2010). The systemic approach to deliberative democracy enlarges the scope of what might beneficially contribute to a deliberative democratic system, by a revalorization of democratic practices and institutions such as vote, protest, partisan media, and experts forums (Mansbridge et al. 2012). With such important conceptual amendments, the model of deliberative democracy can bypass some of its major shortcomings and open itself towards other democratic models and perspectives.

A substantial proportion of deliberative systems' literature has also been dedicated to discussing *how* deliberative democracy should be conceived as being a system. Several features have been advanced as characterizing deliberative democracy as a system, including a functional division of labor, the distinction of different components or parts of the system, the connections or couplings between these parts, and the distribution of deliberative and democratic expectations across the system. However, less effort has been deployed so far to further discuss the *articulation* of these features in a systematic framework (with the exceptions of Bächtiger & Parkinson 2019; and beyond the deliberative model, Warren 2017 and Saward 2021). As the systemic approach to deliberative democracy can be labelled as an "emerging orthodoxy" (Boswell & Corbett 2017), the variety of existing accounts reveals differing pictures of the content and shape of a deliberative democratic system. I suggest that these differences of conceptions are provoked, except by diverse normative presuppositions, by different understandings of the *systemic* dimension, that is *how* deliberative democracy is a system.

The depiction of deliberative democracy as a system is generally taken as an enlightening metaphor (see Parkinson 2016). It expresses the complexity of the interplay between countless elements. As Parkinson (2018: 432) puts it, "democracy can only be a multiple act, multiple stage, and multiple actor drama." After deliberativists' long focus on specific institutional venues as the embodiment of deliberative democracy (particularly parliaments and mini-publics), the merit of the systemic approach is that it reintroduces the distinction between two levels of analysis: the parts and the whole (Parkinson 2018; 2020). While the labelling of the whole has been firmly settled in the concept of *system*, the related term of *society* has also been advanced, with much less success so far[1] (Dryzek 2011). Besides system or society as enlightening metaphors for the complexity of the whole, other metaphors are also used to describe the multiplicity of its constitutive parts: spaces, arenas, spheres, venues, stages, steps, moments. Apart from a diversity of labels, these categories are also filled with different contents. The *relationships* between these parts, whether transmissions (Dryzek 2009; 2010) or couplings (Mansbridge et al. 2012; Hendriks 2016; Boswell et al. 2016), are also conceived in different veins. These substantial differences, far from being only terminological variations, persist due to a lack of both conceptual development and mutual confrontation.

The use of these metaphors is indeed enlightening. They have made a wonderful case for a systemic *return*. They have opened new horizons for normative theorizing with the development of related approaches, including notably Warren's (2017) problem-based approach to democracy and Saward's (2021) framework for democratic design. They have also reoriented some of the empirical work towards the investigation of the functioning of whole deliberative democratic systems, instead of single institutional venues (Curato 2015; O'Flynn & Curato 2015; Beste 2016; Bächtiger & Parkinson 2019; Parkinson et al. 2020). Finally, they have deeply inspired the design and assessment of democratic innovations, both within academia (Jonnson 2015; Dean, Boswell & Smith 2020; Saward 2021; Jäske & Setälä 2020) and outside it (Burall 2015; OECD 2020).

---

[1] See Dryzek (2011) on the terms *system* and *society* and Dryzek (2017) on the term *polity*. I suggest that the term *system* is preferable to *society*, since the latter is more encompassing and includes all types of social systems. Systems, on the contrary, are limited within boundaries. Moreover, the *distinction* between systems allows us to discuss *interactions* between them; an analytical possibility not provided by society. I discuss the meaning of *systems* and *society* in Chapter 3.

But the *metaphorical* depiction of deliberative democracy as a system, characterized by a functional division of labor, has also potentially contributed to a lack of engagement with the complex functioning of such a system. Since its main founding accounts (Dryzek 2009; Mansbridge et al. 2012), only a few major contributions propose articulated elements of a theory of deliberative democratic systems (Bächtiger & Parkinson 2019) or of democratic systems *tout court* (Warren 2017; Saward 2021). Yet the complexity of such systems (greatly increased if we consider a margin of contextual and temporal variability of their shape) demands more theoretical investigation. I will argue that several issues remain unsatisfactorily answered or simply undiscussed. For instance, how can we observe, map, and distinguish deliberative and/or democratic systems? What analytical lens do we use when selecting empirical realities to be normatively assessed? Are our analytical categories silently presupposing normative expectations? Are these categories sensitive to contexts or do they portray a rigid picture of what deliberative and/or democratic systems can and/or should be? And ultimately, what are the normative criteria that drive the assessment of the relative merits of different systems, from where do they emerge, and how should we apply these to empirical realities? This book tackles such fundamental issues about the theoretical architecture of democratic systems.

Democratic theorizing, perspectival lenses, and normativity

The (re-)emphasis on the systemic dimension in democratic theory has emerged within the deliberative model of democracy, mainly because it was a positive and arguably necessary reaction to its own shortcomings. Nonetheless, probably due to the predominance of the deliberative model within contemporary democratic theory, the importance of the "system as a whole" has also fueled debates beyond the paradigmatic boundaries of deliberative democracy. Several authors call for a broader discussion on *democratic systems* (Warren 2017; Saward 2021; Dean et al. 2019; Asenbaum 2022a). To start with, Warren makes a strong case against models-thinking in democratic theory: "A strategy that encourages us to center our thinking on an ideal typical feature of democracy, such as deliberation or elections, and then to overextend the claims for that feature" (2017: 39). Targeting in particular the deliberative model, he sees this strategy as dominant within democratic theory, but as one that now hampers its healthy development. Against deliberativists' alleged narrowness, and welcoming the newly systemic focus, Warren forcefully reminds us that Habermas's depiction of deliberative democracy (1996) was "less a 'models' than a systems approach" (ibid.: 41). In a similar vein, Saward (2021: 4) questions the firm yet artificial separation between the models of democracy, often resulting in a kind of self-sufficiency that prevents productive cross-fertilization between these sealed and opposing models. Regarding the deliberative model in particular, Saward wonders, despite the systemic turn's openness towards non-deliberative features as necessary for democracy, "why is it not the democratic system, rather than the deliberative system, that is the focus?" (ibid.: 22). After all, it is precisely the point of the systemic turn that systems that are deliberative *and* democratic cannot be made of "deliberation all the way down," as Thompson noted (2008: 513). If, as acknowledged by its proponents, deliberative democratic systems require non-deliberative features such as voting or bargaining, why would "deliberative" remain the prominent normative horizon for democratic systems *tout court*? Put otherwise, why would a complex democratic system made of multiple elements, deliberation among them, still be labelled as deliberative? And, more importantly, why would non-deliberative elements such as voting be assessed in terms of their *deliberative* contribution to the system?

The case against the deliberative model is powerful. At the time of writing, I am not aware of a defense from deliberativists on this front. But the seminal contribution of Bächtiger & Parkinson suggests an answer: "Democracy is certainly possible without much deliberation, but we believe that a democracy with a deliberative timbre is a better one" (2019: 157). If we endorse this belief, the primacy of deliberativeness within the normative core of democratic systems does indeed make sense, as does the prominence of the normative ideal of *deliberative democratic systems*. I don't contend that this belief is misplaced (I hold it myself to some extent), only that it is very consequential (and potentially misleading) as a *starting assumption* for the investigation of the complexity and versatility of democratic systems. Indeed, this belief, the deliberative model as a whole, and any other model of democracy (agonistic, electoral, participatory, etc.), are what I call *perspectival lenses*. As Saward (2019: 1) suggests "what we see as important in democratic theory depends on the lenses we look through."

As I understand perspectival lenses, these are latent presuppositions that we hold (sometimes unconsciously) or assumptions that we choose to make (more or less explicitly) when investigating a social phenomenon such as democracy. These perspectival lenses can be made of conceptual semantics, analytical categories, normative expectations, or a sound theoretical articulation of all these, as is the model of deliberative democracy. They can relate to the principles at the normative core of democracy, to the institutions that (must) constitute it, and to the examples that come to mind when referring to existing democracies (or to those that pop-up when pointing at non-democracies). Perspectival lenses can also operate at a deeper level, by reproducing assumptions on the contextual possibility of democracy and the extent of its potential variability. They are unavoidable when observing a social phenomenon, thus I don't believe one can tackle the complexity of democracy without endorsing *some* perspectival lenses. There are no neutral lenses that would bring clarity without perspectival bias, no external viewpoint that escapes being a particular perspective. Of course, every lens leads to a different picture. That is why it is crucial to carefully choose the ones we endorse and *justify* this choice.

In his discussion of democratic theorizing, Saward employs the following description of the process of *theorizing* (in contrast with *theory* as an outcome): "[It involves] finding a perspective or 'lens' through which a problem should be viewed and an invitation to see the problem in a new or revised way" (Hammond 2018 in Saward 2019: 7). Accordingly, lenses are not only tools to observe something with more clarity, but also a way of seeing it differently. The choice of different lenses can *challenge* existing views. The perspectival lenses I choose to endorse here are precisely meant to challenge presuppositions: my own presuppositions of course, and ultimately those at play in the current state of the literature. The aim to challenge existing assumptions of democratic theory and possibly open new roads of thinking about democracy motivates the following choice of perspectival lenses.

The matter I tackle throughout this work is how we can conceptualize and analyze *democracy as a system* and what challenges and opportunities for democratic theory and practice this attempt would provide. As I argue in the next two chapters, the answers to those questions are not as straightforward as may appear at first sight. Among the existing answers, the deliberative systems approach and the resulting debates on democratic systems didn't go far enough, I claim, in the endorsement of this systemic perspective. Moreover, the broad initial focus on *deliberative* systems begins with a very strong yet contested *normative* assumptions on what democratic systems should look like. This is not a problem, but rather a consequential choice of perspective: from the beginning it determines possible answers. Instead I would prefer to start this discussion by being more agnostic on the normative horizon of democratic systems,[2] as I try to be on most relevant assumptions.

This starting agnosticism enables two accounts to be included in the same discussion – both the theoretical accounts that emerge from the model of deliberative democracy, which emphasize the deliberative quality, and the accounts that have democratic systems *tout court* as a normative horizon, in which the deliberative quality is only one among other democratic expectations. What's more, it offers a genuine opportunity to make original proposals on the appropriate theoretical and normative articulation of democracy and deliberation. *Must, can,* or *should* democracy be deliberative? Does it make sense at all to speak of deliberative systems? Although these questions might allow this investigation to make novel insights, they are not its main aim. Despite the emergence of the systemic turn within the model of deliberative democracy, this is not research *about* deliberative systems, but on democracy as a system, yet it draws important resources *from* the literature on deliberative systems.

While I reject the analytical lens of the deliberative model (and of any model of democracy), I also resist a recent suggestion to go "beyond deliberative systems" by endorsing "a multiperspectival approach" (Asenbaum 2022a: 89). For Asenbaum, the charge against single models is relevant, but the alternative advanced by its proponents is unsatisfactory. On his understanding, what he labels the *pragmatist* approach (attributed mainly to Warren 2017 and Saward 2021) involves theorizing democracy at "a meta level outside any particular perspective" (ibid.). The problem is, he contends, that this leads theorizing democracy into a "norm-free zone," with "a lack of normative clarity" (ibid.). Instead, he suggests that a constant shift between

---

[2]   Saward (2021: 27) argues that starting with a models' perspective "sidesteps or downplays democracy's potential for versatility and multiplicity." As this book aims to explore democracy's complexity and variability as a system, I consider it crucial not to restrict at the outset its normative horizon into the "straightjacket" (ibid.) of a theoretical model, despite its great qualities and the fact that this discussion emerged from it in the first place.

multiple perspectives (in his example, deliberative, participatory, ago-nistic, and transformative models of democracy) would "[overcome] the narrowness of single models while at the same time affording rich normativity" (ibid.). This approach is sure to be useful to broaden the scope beyond each model's focus, as each of these models captures essential elements of democratic systems. Shifting between the per-spectives of several models can indeed bring to light the multiplicity and diversity of democratic features. While the varying perspectives of these models contest each other, I suggest that the challenging poten-tial of such a multiperspectival approach is quite limited (and relies exclusively on perspectives *internal* to democratic theory). Anoth-er strategy might prove much more effective at challenging the core assumptions of democratic systems.

Before describing and defending this promising strategy in its own right, I want to support the broad approach to democratic theoriz-ing that Asenbaum labels as *pragmatist,* as both strategies share com-monalities (2022a). Sidestepping the models' perspectives can indeed be considered "stepping back onto a meta level" (ibid. 88). From my understanding, that means both raising the theoretical abstraction in order to discuss core features of democratic systems and switching the focus towards what Saward (2021: xv) describes as "second-order mod-elling," that is, the theoretical framework from which first-order mod-els of democracy can emerge. For my present purpose of investigating the core architecture of democratic systems, both moves appear use-ful (if not necessary). The problem is, according to Asenbaum (without justifying his assertion), that such a move entails a loss of normativity. I am not sure it does, nor that it would necessarily be an issue.

First of all, there is a major difference between endorsing a nor-mative *model* such as the deliberative one and laying down normative *assumptions* to work with (possibly stemming from multiple demo-cratic models and even from perspectives outside democratic theory). Second, one can do major democratic theorizing without endorsing a normative model. For instance, Warren' seminal work (2017) does not endorse a normative model but still makes a few powerful (yet minimal) assertions on the normative core of democracy. Third, dem-ocratic theorizing is possible without the purpose of making norma-tive claims at all. One can indeed work on the conceptual clarification of essentially contested terms or propose an analytical framework for the comparison of democratic practices, as Warren does. Fourth, not endorsing a normative perspective does not mean having no perspective at all. For instance, Saward (2021) tackles the complexity of democracy through the external and challenging perspective of *design*. Finally, if normative positioning is crucial in many contributions to democratic theory, democratic theorizing can sometimes benefit from "largely setting it aside or delaying its treatment" (Saward 2019: 4). Indeed, since the relevance of normative positions depends largely on the empirical assumptions we employ to ground them, delaying our normative claims and grounding them explicitly on what we take as social reality can actually help us develop more nuanced and complex normative positions.

These remarks are meant to justify the strategy that I adopt for the treatment of democratic systems: I do not endorse a normative model (or several) of democracy; and I do not posit normative premises to start with. Instead, since I am interested in the complexity of democratic systems, I interrogate the object of democracy from the external perspective of *systems*. Put differently, my perspectival lens in this book is a *systemic perspective* on democracy. The following analysis takes the concept of system as its entry point and as its orientation towards the understanding of *democratic* systems.[3]

Systemic lens and systems theory

Engaging with the complexity of *systems in general* could prove insightful in order to develop a systematic theoretical framework of *democratic systems* in particular. As Dean, Rinne, and Geissel note, "the conceptual groundwork for a democratic systems approach is in its infancy" (2019: 42). Of course, the broad common features of the systemic approach to democracy are clear by now. Moreover, some conceptual "building blocks" of such a framework have been proposed and tentatively articulated (Warren 2017; Dean et al. 2019; Bächtiger & Parkinson 2019; Saward 2021). Yet, this work is still very much in progress. I suggest

---

[3] By putting "systems" at the heart of my reflection on democratic systems, I do not mean that it is the only nor the best way to investigate democracy's complexity. Some choose other entry points and perspectival lenses. Among them, *pragmatism* shares affinities with systems theory, in particular the centrality of problem-solving and of incremental improvement through experimentation. Indeed, several major authors from the debate on democratic systems claim to endorse a *pragmatic approach* (Fung 2012; Warren 2017; and Saward 2021 to some extent). This perspective is certainly fruitful for generating interesting insights regarding democracy's complexity, as is the focus on systems theory.

that this process could be profoundly enriched by giving greater attention to the *systemic* dimension.

To look through a systemic lens could be insightful. As contemporary societies grow increasingly more complex, with the development of social media and new technologies (e.g., blockchain and artificial intelligence), along with the emergence of powerful actors of a new kind (e.g., Big Tech and SpaceX), and in the face of global challenges such as the environmental crisis or tenacious pandemics, democracies are also experiencing profound internal challenges and transformations (e.g., populism, conspiracy theories, post-truth politics). The systemic metaphor can push us to consider that democracies as *systems* are going through systemic changes,[4] in relation and in reaction to mutations of *other systems* such as the mass media or the globalized economy. The depiction of democracy as a system indeed reminds us that it is itself "embedded in a political economy, in an administrative system, in a culture, in ideologies, power relations, and interests" (Parkinson 2012: 171). The systemic lens could then be helpful, for instance, in uncovering connections (or lack thereof) among and within these systems, and in provoking new insights on what is actually problematic and generating innovative solutions accordingly. The framework of systems could also, after all, serve as a conceptual common denominator to discuss the relationships of democracy with other social systems (e.g., economy, law, religion, education, science, mass media, etc.). However, observing democracy as a system is not straightforward. It is not self-evident to understand what a system actually is. Consequently, in order to investigate democracy though a systemic lens, we need further resources to substantiate this lens and give it a genuine systemic perspective.

An obvious option exists: systems theory. The widespread use of the pivotal terms *systems* and *functions* in the deliberative/democratic systems' literature resonates loudly with the long tradition of systems theory. Although Dean et al. (2019: 42) contend that the systemic approach to democracy has "coupled systems theory with normative democratic theory," a sound engagement between these two traditions has not occurred yet. I suggest that the development of a theory of democratic systems would strongly benefit from critically reengaging

---

4   See Papadopoulos (2012) for a discussion on the global transformations of political systems that (should) constitute the context for the advancement of deliberative democracy.

with systems theory. Indeed, as a scientific tradition whose aim was precisely to "put the pieces together," often within a grand theory of society, systems theory could be helpful to inspire and justify some conceptual articulations of an overarching theoretical core of democratic systems.

Reengaging with systems theory nevertheless requires a great deal of caution. Democratic theorists appear reluctant to do it effectively because of an understandable discomfort with the contentious intellectual past of the concepts of "system" and "functions." For instance, the manifesto of deliberative democracy's systemic turn explicitly distances itself from "old style functionalism" (Mansbridge et al. 2012). In the same vein, Mansbridge, who first coined in 1999 the term of *deliberative system*, expressly warns us against a mechanistic understanding of systems (2019). Warren (2017) stresses the burdensome baggage of functionalism in the history of social sciences and its "conventional" death several decades ago. Moreover, he also warns us of the absence of individual and collective agency in systems theory and its de facto support of conservative ideologies through its insistence on maintenance and stability. For this reason, he makes a call to define systems "more contingently" (ibid. 43). Similarly, Curato et al. (2019: 111) points out systems theory's propensity towards reification of the system's elements and its pathologizing of societies that fail to conform to these elements. Instead, the systemic perspective on democracy should, according to them, foster disruption and "[provide] foundations for emancipation against domination." Finally, Warren (2017: 43) highlights the important lack of normative bite of *functions* as conceived by systems theory, and suggests conceptualizing democratic functions "more normatively." As such, Warren's quasi-oxymoron of "normative functions" is offered as an alternative to the alleged shortcomings of systems theory, yet one that illustrates the significant tension in combining normative/critical aspirations with a systemic perspective.

That being said and cautions being heard, the helping hand of systems theory should not necessarily be discarded so fast. One can legitimately wonder whether the strict and widespread rejection of systems theory in social and political sciences in general, and democratic theory in particular, does not entail "throwing the baby out with the bathwater." Indeed, even if the criticisms highlighted above are fully justified, perhaps not everything from systems theory deserves to be thrown into the dustbin of the history of social sciences. Furthermore, the fact that democratic theorists claim to endorse a systemic perspective and resort abundantly to the concepts of systems theory indicates that they might need *something* from systems theory. Perhaps they could rely on systems theory with minor adaptations for their normative purposes, maybe they should instead take systems theory as a constructive antagonist. But I suggest that they cannot *ignore it* as they have so far; instead, they should *confront it*.

Such a confrontation could alert us, democratic theorists, to the challenges and opportunities that we might encounter now that we attempt to think of democracy *as a system*. Indeed, I contend that democratic theorists would benefit from explicitly displaying what they are departing from if they wish to build a theory of democratic *systems*, where "systems" is not only an illuminating metaphor, but a central operative concept. To be sure, I do not mean that using system as a metaphor is worthless, not at all. Rather, I consider that, *in addition* to the metaphorical use, it is also useful, and perhaps necessary, to use system as a central operative concept to make sense of the complexity of democratic systems. In my opinion, the concept of system is more than an enlightening metaphor: it is a complex conceptual apparatus necessary to make sense of the complexity of the social world. For this reason, to read democracy through a systemic lens would cast light on a significant part of the complexity of democracies, or so I will argue. To be clear, systems theory is taken here as an external perspective challenging core issues of democratic theory. Systems theory is thus used here as a tool for the development of democratic theory. This book discusses the architecture of democratic systems, with the help of systems theory; it is not *about* systems theory, nor does it target an audience of systems theorists but of democratic theorists, and it aims to contribute to the debate on democratic systems.

Democracy as a system

This book takes seriously the idea that *democracy is a system*. It aims to sketch a picture of what democracy would look like if were taken as a complex system. By placing system at the core of this analysis, I am aiming to provide a challenging viewpoint on democracy. By observing democracy from a *systemic perspective*, novel and critical insights could emerge, or so I hope to demonstrate in the following work. Finally, the following discussion is attempting to contribute, through both its flaws and its strengths, to the overall development of a *theory of democratic systems.*

This is a journey through the complexity of democracy. Its point of departure is clear: the strong foundations of the model of deliberative democracy, and the challenges and opportunities provided by its systemic turn. Regarding the challenges, they revolve around the difficulty in articulating, in a consistent and systematic theoretical framework, the diverse constitutive features of deliberative/democratic systems: *a functional division of labor, the distinction of different parts of the system, the connections between these parts, and the distribution of deliberative and/or democratic expectations across the system.* This difficulty is illustrated by the co-existence, without much explicit confrontation, of a few major accounts of deliberative/democratic systems that share both commonalities and differences. Broadly speaking, they converge on the above-mentioned features of "systemness" but diverge in their conceptualizations and specific contents. Two main sources of variability are identified as pivotal: the extent of context-sensitivity of these accounts and the relative importance given to deliberative *or* democratic expectations. Moreover, most of these accounts are structured on the distinction between two "layers": one the one hand, what deliberative/democratic systems are made of, and on the other hand, what characterizes their normative orientation. This two-fold structure of a conceptualization of systems emerges, I would suggest, from the attempt to reconcile normative theorizing with empirical constraints and possibilities of real-world politics. This conceptual structure and the features of systemness highlighted above constitute the *core* of existing theories of deliberative/democratic systems. It is that conceptual core, at this level of abstraction, that this research investigates and attempts to clarify. Framed in systemic terms, I target the "latent structures" of existing theories of democratic systems. This research tentatively thematizes, criticizes, reconceptualizes, and rearticulates these in a comprehensive and consistent framework. This is the challenge of this book: to develop a conceptual system that makes sense of the complexity of democratic systems.

The systemic turn in deliberative democracy brought with it crucial opportunities. It was probably a mutation that was necessary to redirect deliberative democracy from its misleading focus on micro institutional design and its tendency towards conceptual stretching. Yet, it also (re-)opens new horizons for empirical research and concrete democratic innovation, scaling-up the crucial questions of measurement, comparative assessment, and design. Although some seminal works took this opportunity within the model of deliberative democracy (André Bächtiger & John Parkinson's *Mapping and Measuring Deliberation*), others endorsed the systemic perspective outside/beyond its original emergence from the deliberative model (Mark Warren's *Problem-Based Approach to Democratic Theory*; Michael Saward's *Democratic Design*). All of these major contributions stress how the refocus on the "big picture" of democracy enables multiple democratic *possibilities*. From there, these seminal pieces respectively suggest how to measure, comparatively assess, and design diverse instantiations of the democratic ideal. In order to develop guidelines and tools towards these aims, the authors go back to the conceptual and normative *core* of (deliberative) democratic systems and provide original conceptual frameworks of what (deliberative) democracy is and what it is composed of. These frameworks are not only allegedly suited to their respective aims of measuring, assessing, or designing, but also supposedly "correct" in their own right as theoretical depictions of democracy.

The contrasting of these frameworks, firstly between them, and secondly their confrontation with the apparatus of systems theory, aims to foster this debate regarding the conceptual and normative core of democracy. This is the first and main task of this book. However, it does so by being motivated to contribute, not primarily to the tasks highlighted above (measuring, assessing, and designing), but particularly to another and complementary opportunity that I see offered by the systemic perspective: to *diagnose* the specific democratic problems of political systems.

Context-sensitive diagnosis

If (deliberative) democratic systems can take multiple forms that are still recognizably democratic, their architecture can then endorse multiple forms and be composed of different elements. If one accepts this broad assumption, one recognizes with Saward that "democracy is not one size-fits-all" (2003: 169), and thus that democratic arrangements can vary *to some extent*. It is evident that not anything goes; the democratic ideal is uniquely distinct. But it is far from clear to what extent democratic arrangements can fluctuate, and what must remain common to all of these in order to preserve their genuine democratic character. The theorization of democratic systems, analytically speaking, is the depiction of commonalities along differences (i.e., some elements are present in every system) and differences within commonalities (i.e., these common elements can nevertheless take variable forms). If one accepts the multiplicity of democratic forms, the issue of *context-sensitivity* becomes a central concern for the theorization of democratic systems. It is indeed essential to understand which elements of the system are sensitive or not to contextual variations occurring between different systems and within the same system. This sensitivity to contextual variations must be integrated in the conceptual tools that we deploy to describe and assess democratic systems.

What would *context* mean in a systemic perspective? A context expresses the limitation of a reality under investigation; it refers to a specific system in its environment. I will argue that putting *systems* at the core of the analysis provides a clear common lens to observe the specificities of political contexts. The systemic lens gives us the ability to describe political contexts along common possibilities of differences, rather than fixed ascriptions of what they could and should look like. In particular, I will demonstrate how the systemic perspective enables a conceptualization of democratic systems that combines the commonality of broad goals (political functions) with the variability of both democratic *means* (as practices) and democratic *ends* (as particular regulations of political functions through different democratic principles). This conceptual picture portrays the possibility of conceiving democratic systems as made of different practices articulating different democratic principles within different systemic architectures, while still remaining recognizably yet distinctively *democratic*.

In that sense, the theoretical framework of democratic systems suggested in this research is *context-sensitive to an explicitly limited extent*. It provides a way to describe contexts along similar lines and argues that any political context must *at least* be described along common possibilities of difference (e.g., the internal distinction of politics from administration). It is thus a "thin" and minimal depiction of political contexts as systems. It leaves open the opportunity of adding potential differences to which the analysis of political contexts should be critically sensitive, such as historical and cultural backgrounds. The context-sensitive framework of democratic systems developed here is restricted to the contextual description of actual political realities along common systemic lines: the external and internal differentiation of the political system, its external and internal connections, its operative organizations and processes (pictured through spatial and sequential representations), their specific criteria of inclusion, and the democratic principles enacted by the practices shaping them.

From and beyond this description, *diagnosis* aims to uncover the specific problems faced by political systems, in order to orient these towards specific democratic solutions. The leading assumption is that while democracy as a whole is under threat in the twenty-first century, and that most democracies are enduring profound challenges and risks of democratic backsliding, the problems they face are largely context-specific, so are the possible solutions to these problems. As Fung (2012: 609) puts it, "the reality of collective decision-making falls far short of the democratic ideal in countless ways." Diagnosis aims to target the variability, both across political contexts and across time, of democratic shortcomings and challenges. The systemic perspective encourages us to consider problems at the systemic level, not in isolation. As Mansbridge et al. (2012: 4) suggest, "a systemic approach allows us to see more clearly where a system might be improved." It can help problematize political features not solely in themselves, but regarding how they unfold in broader systemic architecture, considering the potential connections and compensatory/undermining relationships between multiple political venues.

My goal is to propose the grounds for a systematic framework serving to identify and describe problems along similar lines. Such a framework focuses on diagnosis *as a process*, instead of diagnoses or general problems *as outcomes* of this process. It aims to problematize democratic issues through shared analytical lenses and frame them in common terms. Its ambition is to detect the specific democratic deficits of political systems *systematically, explicitly, comprehensively*, and *reflexively*. Moreover, following Rainer Forst's normative theory of justification, I suggest that the task of diagnosis derives from the democratic necessity of justification and critique of existing political structures. Therefore, the diagnosis of political problems in democratic terms is itself a pivotal democratic task, to be tackled by people themselves in diagnosing the problems of *their* political systems, in *their* terms, and with their *own* democratic sensibilities and priorities. As such, the diagnosis of democracies is also and ultimately *democratic diagnosis*. The diagnostic framework proposed here aims to contribute to the enhancement of both *academic* diagnostic capacities, through the elaboration of methodological tools to lead empirical diagnosis of political contexts, and *democratic* diagnosis opportunities, through the development and improvement of democratic venues to identify the problems faced by specific political contexts. Crucially, both paths need to be undertaken; the diagnostic framework developed in this book only suggests *one* common route that leads to this crossroad.

Plan of the book

In short, this book critically engages with the systemic turn in democratic theory, extracting and discussing the main questions to be answered for the sake of building a systemic theory of democracy (Chapters 1 and 2); it reengages with systems theory in general and regarding political systems in particular in order to provide insights on how to answer these questions (Chapters 3 and 4); it turns towards Forst's conceptions of power and justification to ground a normative horizon for democracy (Chapter 5); it answers the initial set of questions by rearticulating the insights from systems theory and Forst's normative theory in a consistent framework of democratic systems (Chapter 6); and finally, it discusses how this framework could be useful for diagnosing specific democratic problems (Chapter 7).

Chapter 1 introduces the systemic turn in deliberative democracy, stressing first the centrality of the issue of context-sensitivity in the construction of systemic frameworks and second the commonality of a dual structure that I label "descriptive and normative layers." It displays and contrasts the two main accounts of deliberative systems: Dryzek's deliberative capacities approach (2009; 2010) and Parkinson & Mansbridge's manifesto for the systemic turn in deliberative democracy (2012). By highlighting both their commonalities and differences, the chapter extracts six main questions that need to be investigated further to open the black box of deliberative/democratic systems and then articulated into a comprehensive and consistent whole in order to develop a systemic theory of democracy.

Chapter 2 opens the black box of deliberative/democratic systems, by discussing in detail each of the six questions identified in Chapter 1. It answers these questions by relying on the most recent literature on deliberative/democratic systems, with a particular emphasis on three seminal works (Warren 2017; Bächtiger & Parkinson 2019; Saward 2021).

It concludes with the need to reengage with systems theory in order to answer these questions with a genuine systemic approach.

Chapter 3 undertakes a critical rereading of systems theory, with a natural emphasis on its main contributor, Niklas Luhmann. It starts from systems theory's epistemological and ontological assumptions, continues with the broad sketching of the general functioning of systems, and then outlines in detail the specificities of the functioning of *social* systems. It concludes by a discussion on systems theory particular and limited conception of normativity and agency. This paves the way for a systemic conceptualization of *political* systems, which constitutes a common ground for envisioning democracy's distinctiveness.

Chapter 4 displays the Luhmannian sociological understanding of political realities, by emphasizing the challenges posed by the predominance of contingency within it. It depicts the distinctiveness of political systems along the lines of processes of external and internal differentiation, rather than relying on fixed "essences" of the political reality. It concludes with the relevance and usefulness of Luhmann's sociological framework to map and describe political systems with a common lens putting *functions* at their core, but also stresses its lack of normative bite for the assessment of their democratic quality.

Chapter 5 thus operates a deviation from the Luhmannian paradigm on the grounds of the concept of power. It suggests that, more than Habermas's account, Forst's conceptualization of noumenal power as embedding reasons/justifications provides a fruitful route towards the specification of the normative distinctiveness of democratic systems. Forst's descriptive account is connected to his normative theory, with at its core the "right to justification" and the criteria of reciprocity and generality. These are taken as normative compasses to navigate context-specific democratic continuums, operating as criteria for the minimal justifiability of democratic arrangements and for the trade-offs between democratic norms.

Chapter 6 sketches my own reconstruction of a theory of democratic systems on the grounds developed in previous chapters. It does so by taking an original position on each of the six questions posed in Chapter 1. The first part of the chapter presents and discusses the analytical distinctions necessary for observing and detecting with a common lens the specificities of concrete political systems. From the commonality of political systems, a list of ten democratic *preconditions* is drawn up and framed in purely systemic terms. The second part focuses on the construction of a flexible normative layer that articulates political *functions*, democratic *practices*, and democratic *norms*. It lays the theoretical grounds for the application of this normative layer within a diagnostic tool for the identification of specific democratic problems. It concludes on the place of deliberation as a practice and as a democratic principle in this conceptual framework, by suggesting that despite its justified theoretical prominence, the deliberative ideal would maintain its sharp critical potential if it remained analytically distinct from other democratic principles and was not taken as *the* democratic end.

Chapter 7 argues for the need and usefulness of developing a framework for the context-sensitive diagnosis of democratic problems. It suggests that democratic problems and solutions are specific to the democratic continuum on which the political system under analysis is positioned. Through questions to be asked in a chronological sequence, the chapter lays the grounds for possible developments of diagnosis capacities, both for academic inquiries and for citizens themselves. It concludes on the necessity for democratic systems to develop citizens' capacities and institutional venues for *democratic diagnosis*.

1 | Systems in democratic theory

Democracy can only be a multiple act, multiple stage, and multiple actor drama, no matter what adjective precedes it. Just as life emerges from the complex interplay of non-living units, or as a song is made up of elements which are not themselves 'song,' so deliberative democracy is a complex and dynamic pattern of human practices which are not themselves deliberative democracy. (Parkinson 2018: 432)

The aim of Chapters 1 and 2 is to present and discuss how systems have been conceived by democratic theorists up to now, before turning in Chapters 3 and 4 to a critical reengagement with systems theory. The progressive reintroduction of the idea of *democracy as a system* has so far focused on its democratic and deliberative qualities. What makes a political system democratic (and/or deliberative) is obviously the ultimate question for democratic theorists, and the final aim of this book is indeed to propose an original answer to this question. However, it is precisely to better answer it that something else must *first* be investigated. Indeed, in order to argue in favor of some features of a deliberative/democratic system and their articulation, I suggest that it is essential to clarify what thinking in systemic terms entails.

Most of the impetus for the idea of deliberative/democratic systems comes from the specific aspects of a system, such as the division of labor, the interdependence and connections among parts of the system, the complementarity among elements, and so on. These features of *systemness* are relative to (social) systems in general and not particular to democracy. Through the theoretical debates over democracy, and especially deliberative democracy, these features of systemness have (re-)emerged over the past two decades, progressively and from diverse sources, often as detached pieces, to finally become crystalized as a distinct approach to democracy. I must insist at the outset that I am deeply sympathetic with this approach, and it is exactly for this reason that I attempt here to contribute to its development. Chapters 1 and 2 are thus not a *critique* of the systemic approach to democracy, but rather *a careful and critical reading* with a specific purpose: to uncover the existing conceptualizations of deliberative and democratic *systems*. Therefore, Chapter 1 retraces the literature over deliberative democratic systems in order to extract their different characteristics and to highlight the issues we encounter when we attempt to articulate them. Chapter 2 discusses these issues in detail through a contrasting of the major accounts of deliberative/democratic systems.

Methodologically speaking, I do not start this discussion on systems and systemness with a conceptual scheme, based on consensual definitions of what systems are. Indeed, I am completely putting aside for now any definition of systems. I am instead relying on democratic theorists endorsing the systemic approach to clarify what "systems" means *for them*. Of course, this is necessarily drawn from my own interpretation of their publications on the matter. This methodological strategy could be framed as *interpretive close reading*.

This chapter tracks the systemic turn in deliberative democracy, from the first mention of a deliberative system and starting intuitions of distribution and sequencing, to its explicit consolidation as a distinct approach with two dominant models: John Dryzek's deliberative capacities approach (2009; 2010) and John Parkinson & Jane Mansbridge's *Deliberative Systems: Deliberative Democracy at the Large Scale* (2012). After highlighting the issue of context-sensitivity in the construction of models of (deliberative) democratic systems, I display these two models and discuss in detail their descriptive and normative layers. I conclude this chapter by detailing the different questions to be answered for the construction of a systemic theory of democracy, questions to which I present the main existing answers in Chapter 2.

The systemic turn in deliberative democratic theory

The question of democracy is by essence a concern with a broad and complex social whole, whether that whole is labelled system, society, polity, government, or state. I can hardly think of any democratic theorist who is not ultimately concerned with the "big picture." Even a minimalist voting-oriented account of democracy such as Schumpeter's is to some extent systemic, because it proposes a way of connecting parts (citizens, elites) through the mechanism of voting in order to constitute a legitimate whole. As Przeworski puts it, for Schumpeter a "democracy is just a system in which rulers are selected by competitive elections" (Przeworski 1999: 12). Democratic theory broadly conceives democracy as a more or less complex whole. My aim below is to retrace *how* that whole is conceived. On the occasion of the systemic turn in deliberative democracy, this whole was labelled *system*, and it is likely that a large part of the contributions in democratic theory favor this label. Thus, the label of system is taken here as the most relevant *entry point* to discuss the different ways of conceiving democracy as a complex whole.[5]

There would not be much sense in attempting an exhaustive genealogy of the idea of system in democratic theory. Where would one start? In ancient Greece, at the Enlightenment, with Easton's political

---

[5] The kindred concept of "network" could represent an alternative entry point. Some authors discuss related issues with a focus on "networks." Within the deliberative systems literature, Knops (2016) proposes to refocus the debate over deliberative *networks*. This move would prevent a dilution of deliberation's critical bite, which he believes the systemic approach does. If network is taken as expressing a complex *whole* made of different *parts*, I have no objection to taking it as an alternative entry point to that of system. However, I don't think it expresses exactly the same meaning: Could we equate a political system and a political network? The former conveys a sense of comprehensiveness, emergent structures, organized complexity, and multiple overlapping levels. The latter rather conveys a sense of nodes of interaction between multiple kinds of *actors* on some complex issues (see the definition of democratic governance networks by Sorensen & Torfig 2007: 9). It expresses something much smaller than the systems; networks can be important components *of* a system. A system encompasses other elements than just actors or networks of actors: institutions, symbols, principles, rules, mechanisms. Consequently, I don't think that both entry points lead to the same challenge for democratic theory. My only claim is that a systemic perspective is preferable to challenge what democratic *systems* are. Moreover, except maybe Castells (1996), I am not aware of a theory of networks that is as developed as theories of systems are. These remarks, however, are not intended to disregard the potential utility of the empirical method of social network analysis to grasp core issues of democratic systems.

system (1953), Dahl's polyarchy (1989), or with Habermas's deliberative democracy (1996)? My aim is not to retrace the historical emergence and progressive reshaping of the idea of democracy as a system. Rather, my goal is to clarify how democratic theorists are *currently* using the idea of system when theorizing about democracy. Arguably, the emphasis on system was partly set aside in democratic theory from the nineties to recently, with a broad focus on particular democratic institutions and innovative devices. This has particularly been the case in the deliberative model of democracy, a possible reason why the systemic turn, or more accurately *return*, started from this model too. More recently, the systemic approach has also been applied to democracy *per se* (Warren 2017; Jäske & Setälä 2020; Dean et al. 2019; Saward 2021). It now enjoys an important, if not predominant, place in democratic theory.

However, within the current debate on democratic systems, different understandings of *how* democracy is a system coexist, or compete without direct confrontation. This debate could be enriched by an articulated position on what exactly makes democracy a system. Consequently, I critically present below the progressive reemergence of the systemic emphasis in democratic theory these past two decades, with a natural emphasis on deliberative democracy. It is important to insist that I do *not* start this reconstruction with Habermas, for two reasons. First, because I see him as having developed, largely on systems theory's grounds (Talcott Parsons in particular), a grand theory of society in which deliberative democracy is only one (nonetheless salient) feature. Second, because the reemergence of the systemic emphasis in democratic theory does not really have explicit recourse to Habermas's conception of systems and society. For these reasons, Habermas's theory will be discussed in the following chapters on the more abstract grounds of systems theory.

From its diverse origins (see Floridia 2018) to Habermas and its consolidation as a paradigm in the nineties, deliberative democracy has come a long way, growing in importance and diversity (see Dryzek et al. 2019). Narratives of deliberative democracy's evolution, especially in terms of "turns" (Dryzek 2010; Owen & Smith 2015) or "generations" (Elstub & McLaverty 2014) are widely present in the literature. With a focus on the systemic turn in deliberative democracy, I present the progressive reemergence of systems in democratic theory.

Deliberative systems' first intuitions: distribution and sequencing

The point of departure is arbitrary, but perhaps there are no correct starting points, only useful ones. My starting point is an oft-quoted first mention of "deliberative systems" with Mansbridge's (1999) call for considering "everyday talk" as a core component of a deliberative system. Concerned with the narrowness of the venues of deliberation, she argues that deliberation can occur much more broadly than previously conceived, insofar as we accept that different standards of deliberation should apply to different venues. This claim is highly contested within the field of deliberative democracy. The opposition between a *unitary* model and the *disaggregation* and *distribution* of deliberative standards is "the major dividing line within deliberative democracy today" (Chambers 2017). Each view can generate a different picture of the deliberative system: the unitary model imposes the mandatory *addition* of specific moments of what Chambers labels "the full-menu of deliberative conditions" (ibid.: 167); the disaggregated model allows the spreading of these deliberative conditions and the *summative* emergence of "deliberativeness" through the complex interplay of its parts (Parkinson 2016; 2018). Advocating the possibility of disaggregation, Mansbridge proposes a scaling-up of the deliberative concern from its components to the system itself:

> The criterion for good deliberation should be not that every interaction in the system exhibit mutual respect, consistency, acknowledgement, open-mindedness and moral economy, but that the system reflects those goods. (1999: 224)

By doing so, Mansbridge appears to contrast two level of analysis: parts and whole, characterized here respectively by *interaction* and *system*. However, Mansbridge does not really discuss what a system is for her, besides suggesting that "the different parts of the deliberative system *mutually influence one another* in ways that are not easy to parse out" (ibid.: 213, emphasis mine). While this is not explicit, these parts seem to include both practices and institutions in Mansbridge's deliberative system. Regarding the mutual influence between these parts, she does not develop further. Interestingly, in a reedition of this chapter, Mansbridge specifies in a footnote that:

> By using the word "system" I do not want to imply that the parts of the whole have a mechanical or perfectly predictable relation to one another, although both of these attributes are connotations of the words "system" and "systematic" in ordinary speech. Rather, I want to imply an interrelation among the parts, such that a change in one tends to affect another. (2019: 114)

Mansbridge's caution is illustrative of an underlying issue posed by understanding democracy as a system: it pushes her to take position on what a system is or is not, and to specify that her conceptualization diverges from preexisting systems theory. Mansbridge seems here to distance herself from a "mechanistic" conception of systems. This is important because much of the reluctance from democratic theorists to confront systems theory comes from the mechanistic image that it reflects. It leads to a perception of systems as *machines*, with a predictable and reliable functioning, where the same inputs always produce the same outputs. This legitimate reluctance will be discussed, and partially tempered, through a critical reengagement with systems theory in Chapters 3 and 4. In order not to appear mechanistic in describing connections between the parts, Mansbridge favors the vagueness of a *tendency* of parts to impact each other, instead of a strict interdependence between the parts. The interactions or connections between parts, and their level of interdependence, are a central feature of systemness. The metaphors of transmission (Dryzek 2009) and coupling (Mansbridge et al. 2012; Hendriks 2016) portray different images of how these interactions must be conceived. Since systems are largely characterized by the connections between their parts, the features of these connections thus become a central issue in the discussion. Therefore, in the next chapter I will provide a detailed discussion on the important question of connectivity within democratic systems.

Working from Mansbridge's distributed approach, Parkinson (2003) develops the core idea of deliberative systems. He takes Mansbridge's proposal as conducive to solving the "scale problem" of deliberative democracy: simply put, the more people participate, the less their interaction can be deliberative; therefore, deliberative democracy can hardly be both democratic and deliberative *at the same time* (see Fearon 1998; Walzer 1999). Time is indeed central here, as Parkinson contends that "legitimacy is created in the openness of the linkages between moments, rather than relying on ideal legitimacy of each moment taken separately" (Parkinson 2003: 193). He then suggests that these moments constitute a chronological sequence of the four following stages: *define, discuss, decide, implement* (Parkinson 2006). In the same vein, but outside/beyond the model of deliberative democracy, Saward (2003) proposes a sequencing of devices "enacting democratic principles." The structure of his sequence follows four similar stages of a collective decision-making process: *agenda-setting, debate and discussion, the moment of decision itself, and the moment of implementation.* This idea of sequencing has been also reemployed within the model of deliberative democracy by Goodin (2005). Like Parkinson, Goodin is concerned with the feasibility constraints bearing upon deliberative democracy. He then defends what can be summarized as "different steps, different deliberative expectations." More precisely, he proposes a *distribution* of deliberative virtues across stages of decision making, such that each stage keeps a certain deliberative quality while not being fully deliberative. Goodin's assumption is that ideal deliberation cannot practically happen *all along the way*, and therefore the deliberative labor has to be divided; if each stage fulfills its own relevant deliberative expectations, the overall system is deliberative *enough*:

> I offer a model of "distributed" (or "delegated") deliberation – with different agents playing different deliberative roles – as an alternative to the "unitary actor" model of deliberation. It might be "good enough", deliberatively, for the component deliberative virtues to be on display sequentially, over the course of this staged deliberation involving various component parts, rather than continuously and simultaneously present as they would be in the case of a unitary deliberating actor. (2005: 182)

Concretely, deliberative virtues (in italics) are distributed along the decision-making sequence in the following way: *authentic claim-making* in the caucus room, *justification and respect* in the parliamentary debate, *participation and orientation to the common good* during the election campaign, and *consensus-seeking* during the post-election arguing and bargaining. This precise sequence is mostly illustrative, and Goodin acknowledges that the phases/steps of the political process he relied upon could be drawn otherwise.

However, this sequence is also illustrative of an important underlying issue posed by the definition of different steps. When labelling these steps, one can be more or less abstract. In that regard, there is an obvious contrast between Goodin's steps and those of Parkinson and Saward. Goodin's steps (caucus room, parliamentary debate, election campaign, post-election arguing and bargaining) are very *specific* and clearly tied to the institutions of representative democracies. In some cases, these steps appear even to be specific to precise *venues* (caucus room, parliament, etc.) and therefore to specific *actors*, political parties, and parliament representatives, respectively. Consequently, the framing of Goodin's steps implies that the virtues displayed along this sequence *cannot* be enacted through different venues or institutions, or by different actors. In contrast, Parkinson's and Saward's steps are drawn much more *generically*, by displaying a quite traditional sequence of decision-making. This greater abstraction has the advantage of allowing the possibility for multiple and diverse actors, practices, and institutions to enact democratic values at each of the steps. The striking contrast in terminology between these accounts reveals a major and deeper issue: the one of *context-sensitivity* within the conceptualization of the elements of democratic systems.

Conceptualization of the system's elements and context-sensitivity

The issue of context-sensitivity is easily framed: Can democratic arrangements be sensitive to contexts? I can hardly imagine someone answering a straight "no" to this question, although some accounts of democratic theory have generated a quite rigid and universal picture of how democracy should be arranged (e.g., Schumpeter; Dahl). In contrast to these accounts, Saward is openly context-sensitive in assuming that:

> Democracy will be done differently – with emphasis on different principles, enacted through distinctive combinations of devices, sequenced differently – in different times and places. Democracy is not one-size-fits-all. (2003: 169)

However, assuming the possibility of different arrangement across contexts does not say much about the appropriate *extent* of this context-sensitivity. Arguably, it would be unlikely that *anything goes*. As Parkinson (2012: 152) insists when acknowledging the possibility of many different arrangements for deliberative systems, "'many different' is not the same as saying 'infinite.'" The appropriate level of context-sensitivity obviously lies somewhere between "anything goes" and "one-size-fits-all." Empirical work, by highlighting feasibility constraints and cross-contextual regularities, is key to providing a good approximation of the relevant extent of context-sensitivity for democratic systems. The point here is not to discuss, in light of the numerous empirical cues on the matter, where an appropriate middle-ground could be found. My point is to insist on the fact that the theoretical *definition* of the elements of a system (here, decision-making steps) already embeds and reproduces some presuppositions on the extent of context-sensitivity.

The more specific and concrete these steps are, the less they are applicable to different systems. Indeed, if one considers (as Goodin does) these steps to be enacted by traditional institutions of representative democracies (such as an elected legislature or party competition), one cannot see how different institutions or practices could do the same job in other contexts. Therefore, one would wrongly conclude that the system in question is poorly deliberative (or democratic), precisely because it lacks *these* specific institutions. On the contrary, if one draws steps in a more abstract and generic vein, as Parkinson and Saward both do, one could then see other (and perhaps unexpected) institutions and practices doing the job at these steps or in these venues. It could turn out that for some generic steps only some specific institutions could do the job, and perhaps these institutions are precisely those of contemporary representative democracies. However, this is a general empirical conclusion still to be reached, not a relevant theoretical starting point.

In addition, the issue of context-sensitivity is also present beyond the sole definition of these steps. It reappears in the *attribution* of specific normative criteria to these steps. In Goodin's illustration, each step is supposed to enact a *specific* normative criterion. For instance, the step of the parliamentary debate is expected to perform *justification and respect*, instead of *consensus-seeking*. Indeed, Goodin considers that "the deliberative virtues [must come] in the right combinations and the right order" (2005: 193). Presumably, and Goodin anticipates this, the rightness of the combination may vary across contexts, and must be responsive to "different ways of arranging our political affairs" (ibid.). But still, even considering the features of a specific context, one can wonder what actually makes a combination more or less "right."

By asking this question, we must remain open to the possibility that some specific institutions or practices, or even some combinations of institutions and practices, are the *only* possibilities for doing a specific part of the overall normative job. As we see now, this issue of context-sensitivity of the system's features (i.e., steps here, but spaces or arenas below) is important and can profoundly impact the scope of applicability of a theoretical framework of democratic systems. When drawing these features, it is important to consider to what extent they can presuppose the possibility of particular arrangements and therefore steer the attention towards those, while simultaneously concealing other possibilities.

Sketching deliberative systems: the descriptive and normative layers

There is a second important issue lurking within Goodin's illustration of a distributed model of deliberation, which is also present in most of the accounts of deliberative and democratic systems. The model advances *two different layers*: steps and virtues. Other accounts also feature this duality, with different labels such as *components* and *deliberative capacities* (Dryzek 2009) or *arenas* and deliberative *functions* (Mansbridge et al. 2012). There are both commonalities and differences in the *content* of these two layers across the existing accounts. I will discuss and contrast their specific content in the next section. For now, precisely because these accounts share a *distinction* between these two layers, I want to focus on this distinction.

This dual structure appears at first sight to portray a distinction between *descriptive* elements (steps, components, arenas) on the one side, and *normative* criteria on the other side (virtues, capacities, functions).[6] As I see it, the reason for drawing a demarcation between these two dimensions along the descriptive/normative divide comes from the attempt to reconcile the normative and critical bite of the deliberative democratic ideal with the feasibility constraints of real-world politics. Moreover, some of the motivation of the systemic turn is precisely to *describe* how deliberative or democratic systems are shaped and function in the real-world (Parkinson: 2018). In addition, it is also

---

[6] Dean et al. (2019: 52) similarly distinguish *normative* building blocks (norms, functions) from *operative* ones (practices, actors, arenas, interactions, and levels) along an ought/is distinction.

certainly related to some of the possible *empirical* applications of these theoretical accounts. Indeed, the descriptive layer would arguably allow us to *map* deliberative or democratic systems, and the normative layer would provide a flexible basis for the normative *assessment* of what is mapped. Assessing must not be solely understood as measuring, but also and mostly *diagnosing* current problems in order to propose some specific solutions.[7] Schematically, the descriptive layer would say, "these elements are what the system is made of." And by saying so, it would insist on the two levels of analysis: parts and whole. Therefore, the descriptive layer would be composed of analytical tools and *selection* criteria enabling *identification* of the parts that compose the whole. The normative layer would consist of normative criteria and would say, "these criteria are what can make the whole more democratic (or deliberative)." In consequence, that would lead to a questioning of *how* to apply these normative criteria to the described political reality.

If this interpretation of the rationale for this distinction makes sense, an important question arises here: What is to be mapped? I can see three possible answers to this question. First, the descriptive layer is supposed to map a *political* system. By saying this, I mean *any* type of political system, regardless of its *a priori* democratic and/or deliberative merits. Importantly, we can consider a political system as not necessarily state-centered, but potentially also issue-centered. The purpose of the descriptive layer would thus be to identify these moments (steps, stages) or places (arenas, sites, spheres) within existing political systems. And from there, it would be possible to assess the democratic and/or deliberative merits of the whole system. Second, what is mapped are instead *democratic* systems, as they are in a particular context. This means that the descriptive layer would instead depict a system that is already, to some extent, democratic. This appears to be the case, for instance, in Mansbridge et al. (2012: 7–8) when they state the need to focus on "systems that are broadly defined by the norms, practices, and institutions of democracy," that is, on systems that are "at least loosely democratic." Nevertheless, as we will see below, the

---

[7]   Mansbridge et al. (2012: 4) are clear on this point by stating that "a systemic approach allows us to see more clearly where a system might be improved, and recommend institutions or other innovations that could supplement the system in area of weaknesses." Moreover, the medical analogy portrayed by the term "diagnose" resonates well with Mansbridge et al.'s use of systemic "pathologies."

depiction of their descriptive layer does not fully mirror this statement. On the contrary, their definition comprising four constitutive arenas is much closer to a description of a *political* system than a *democratic* one.

In any case, if the descriptive layer aims to depict a democratic system, this descriptive layer starts to contain a normative dimension, in the sense that "a democratic polity is an empirical premise" (Erman 2016: 266). In that scenario, one would "only" be able to assess, for instance, the "deliberative qualities *of* a democratic system" (ibid., original emphasis) or the extent of democraticness of such a democratic system. The third possible answer is to consider that the descriptive layer depicts a *deliberative* system, or a *"potentially* deliberative" system as Dryzek puts it (2016: 211, my emphasis). This seems to be the case for Neblo's (2015) description of a deliberative system as composed of a dozen distinct sites of deliberation. As he contends, his description is based on a reconstruction of "implicit normative standards already at work in modern democracy" (ibid.: 17). By doing so, he explicitly observes and reconstructs the reality of modern political systems *through a deliberative lens*. Plus, he contends that his model of a deliberative system could instead be labelled "political system" (ibid.). Therefore, his description itself already contains strong presuppositions on how a political/democratic system *should* be organized in order to be minimally or potentially deliberative, leaving little room for systems that do not feature this architecture. Thus, with recourse to the normative layer, one could "only" assess the *extent* to which a (potentially) deliberative system can be made *more* deliberative.

The literature of the systemic turn is slightly ambivalent on which of these three routes is privileged. Perhaps this is partly due to the double ambition of the systemic turn: to describe how deliberative systems are in reality, while arguing on how they should be. However, I agree with Erman (2016) that the first route (the one that attempts to map, assess, and/or diagnose *political* systems) is in all likelihood the one privileged by democratic theorists endorsing the systemic turn; the point is indeed to assess the democratic and/or deliberative merits of *political* systems. In any case, this route is presumably worthwhile, and this is the one I follow here. If this route is relevant, I suggest that the descriptive layer must facilitate the mapping of *political* systems of any type. Accordingly, the descriptive layer should remain descriptive, precisely in order to encompass all the possible forms of what has to be assessed in democratic or deliberative terms. Once the descriptive layer explicitly or implicitly contains some normative presuppositions or expectations, it is inevitably more demanding regarding the mapping of the system under scrutiny. Thus, it risks excluding some elements that do not *a priori* meet these expectations. We clearly see how the issue of context-sensitivity highlighted above reemerges here, since in order to be encompassing of political diversity, the descriptive layer needs to be context-sensitive.

Another issue regarding the context-sensitivity of the existing descriptive layers is that they depict very *static* entities. As Bächtiger & Parkinson (2019: 87) note in discussing Neblo's model (2015), his multiple sites of deliberation have fixed relationships with one another, and there is a clear attribution of deliberative expectations for each of them. The definition of specific sites and actors, the rigid display of stable relationships between them, and their attribution of particular normative contributions prevent the mutations and diversity in this picture from being envisioned, or as Bächtiger & Parkinson call it, the *dynamism* of systems. The descriptive layer must be context-sensitive enough to capture the dynamic reconfiguration of these sites and their normative contribution.

To summarize, the purpose of this distinction between two conceptual layers is not justified: I am not aware so far of a discussion or justification of this theoretical distinction in the existing accounts. I assume that it encapsulates a descriptive/normative divide in order to map and assess existing political systems. Following that hypothesis, I argue below that the main accounts cross that line in the definition of the elements on each side of the distinction and that we can notice inconsistencies with layers that contain both descriptive and normative elements.

Two models of deliberative democratic systems

In order to show these inconsistencies, and at the same time to highlight the diversity of the accounts, I present below their specific content. I focus here on the two main sources of the systemic turn in deliberative democracy (Dryzek 2009; Mansbridge et al. 2012). Figure 1 depicts and contrasts their descriptive and normative layers, which are discussed in detail below.

	Descriptive layer	Normative layer
Dryzek (2009; 2010)	• Private sphere • Public space • Empowered space • Transmission • Accountability • Meta-deliberation • Decisiveness	• Inclusion • Authentic deliberation • Consequentiality
Mansbridge et al. (2012)	• Informal talk related to decisions on issues of common concern that are not intended for binding decisions by the state • Informal talk related to binding decisions by the state • Activities directly related to preparing for binding decisions by the state • Binding decisions of the state (both in law itself and its implementation)	• Ethical • Epistemic • Democratic

FIGURE 1 Descriptive and normative layers in Dryzek (2009; 2010) and Mansbridge et al. (2012)

Dryzek's deliberative capacities model

Starting with John Dryzek's account, it is important to highlight his explicit position regarding context-sensitivity. According to him, the sketching of deliberative systems should not be "tied to the institutional specifics of developed liberal democratic states" (Dryzek 2010: 8). Instead, he contends that deliberative systems can feature a variety of different institutional architectures. For Dryzek, not every deliberative system needs to contain the traditional institutions of contemporary democratic systems, even the most basic ones, such as a constitutional separation of powers, a legislature, political parties, or competitive elections. Indeed, "a deliberative system and its component elements do not require any specific institutions" (ibid.: 13). Therefore, Dryzek conceives the component parts of deliberative systems in quite a generic manner, in order for these to be applicable to a large variety of contexts.

For Dryzek, all deliberative systems are composed of the seven following component parts, which constitute the *descriptive* layer. First, there is the *private sphere*, "where people converse within households, with friends or in a workplace" (Dryzek & Stevenson 2014: 27). Second, comes the *public space*, which is characterized by more open and accessible communication than in the private sphere. Third, the *empowered space* is the location of institutions producing collective decisions. The fourth component is the *transmission* of influence from the public space to the empowered space. The fifth component is the *accountability* mechanisms from the empowered space to the public space, ensuring "that the claims and actions of empowered actors are subject to scrutiny and challenge in the public space" (Dryzek & Stevenson 2013: 3). The sixth component is *meta-deliberation*, that is, "the capacity of a deliberative system to examine itself and if necessary transform itself" (ibid.). The seventh and last component is *decisiveness*, defined as "the degree to which the previous six elements acting together actually determine collective outcomes" (ibid.). The descriptive layer composed of these seven elements relies on a *spatial* metaphor ("spaces"), in contrast with the *temporal* metaphors ("steps," "moments," "stages") discussed above.

Dryzek's *normative* layer is composed of three criteria: authentic deliberation, inclusiveness, and consequentiality. Deliberation is authentic if it is able to induce "reflection noncoercively, connect claims to more general principles, and exhibit reciprocity" (Dryzek 2009: 1382). Inclusiveness refers to the inclusion of the "range of interests and discourses present in a political setting" (ibid.). Consequentiality means that the deliberative processes have an impact, direct or indirect, on collective decisions and social outcomes (ibid.). In order to be deliberative, systems must for Dryzek "feature authentic deliberation in elements 2–6, will be inclusive in elements 2, 3 and 6, and will also be decisive when it comes to collective outcomes"[8] (2010:14). Despite these relatively demanding standards, Dryzek suggests the possibility of compensatory and undermining relations between components. These are Dryzek's normative criteria and the way they should be applied.

My aim below is to pinpoint the fact that Dryzek's conceptualization entangles the descriptive and normative dimensions, and is conceptually inconsistent regarding some elements. At the outset, we can notice that Dryzek's seven components are of a very different nature. First, there are three *spaces* (private, public, empowered). As the basic

---

[8] NB: Dryzek added the first component of "private sphere" in publications posterior to that quoted sentence. Therefore, I have changed the numbers accordingly to keep the meaning unchanged.

structure of the system, these spaces are characterized by different features. The private sphere and the public space are defined by the specific type of *communication* they feature. The empowered space is characterized by its capacity to produce binding collective decisions and implement them. Second, the component of transmission serves as a *connector* between the public and the empowered space. While Dryzek admits that "transmission in reality is not necessarily intrinsically deliberative and can also involve demands and threats" (Dryzek & Stevenson 2014: 28), it obviously refers specifically to the transmission of *communications*. This focus on communication flows is not self-evident, because one could see other practices such as voting as a transmission mechanism. Regarding the component of accountability, one might expect it to be the reverse connector, from the empowered space to the public space. However, for Dryzek, accountability is instead a *normative duty* of responsiveness for the empowered space to the public space's transmissions. It is surprising that a normative duty (moreover specific to the empowered space) is considered as a descriptive component in itself, rather than a normative criterion (as authentic deliberation, inclusion, and consequentiality are for Dryzek).

Regarding the sixth component, meta-deliberation is the practice of deliberation on a particular topic: the functioning of the system itself. However, it can be also interpreted as a particular *normative expectation* of how a deliberative system should work. For this reason, it is striking that it appears in the descriptive layer as a component to be assessed *by* the normative criteria. Moreover, "authentic deliberation" as a normative criterion could probably conceptually cover meta-deliberation, since some reflexivity over the way discussions are held is arguably an important condition for any deliberation. Decisiveness as the last component is here a feature of the whole deliberative system, reflecting its capacity to determine collective decisions. Yet, it is also meant to apply to *each* of the other components (e.g., the decisiveness of the public space). As such, this component is conceptually redundant with the normative criterion of "consequentiality," whose specific purpose is to assess this decisiveness. Moreover, to some extent, both consequentiality and decisiveness are conceptually entangled with the component of "empowered space," since what characterizes this space is precisely that it produces *binding* collective decisions, that is, *ultimate decisiveness*. Furthermore, one can also wonder if consequentiality (or decisiveness) is an appropriate normative criterion to be applied to the system's *parts*. Indeed, such a system might sometimes demand that some events, venues, and moments should *not* be consequential (Parkinson 2018: 437). Finally, the emphasis on decisiveness and consequentiality in Dryzek's account suggests that, for him, the deliberative system and its elements are supposed to be consequential *on* the democratic system. By doing so, it portrays the deliberative and the democratic systems as two different entities, which is far from being obvious.

To summarize Dryzek's account, the various natures of the elements of his descriptive layer is obvious. He puts spaces, connectors, normative duties, and impact requirements in the same conceptual basket. Plus, there is an apparent conceptual overlapping between some of his normative criteria and some of his descriptive components. Furthermore, he demands from each component the *same* normative contribution, thus avoiding any division of labor. Importantly, the normative criterion of "authentic deliberation" keeps deliberation *united*; it is not disaggregated as in Goodin's account, for instance. Hence, we can wonder if and to what extent Dryzek endorses the *distributed* model of deliberation or sticks to the unitary model. Finally, several of his components presuppose some deliberative features, such as a public space, transmission of communication, and meta-deliberation. In sum, it seems that Dryzek's descriptive layer enables a democratic system that is *already* deliberative to some extent to be mapped. This is not to say that this conceptual strategy is not relevant *per se*, only that it has a restricted scope of applicability.

Mansbridge et al.'s "manifesto" for the systemic approach

The other major version of deliberative systems is offered by Jane Mansbridge, John Parkinson, and several of the most prominent deliberative democratic theorists. It presents itself as an "over-arching approach to deliberation" (Mansbridge et al. 2012: 4) and would later be labeled as "the manifesto" for the systemic turn (Owen & Smith 2015).

While Dryzek simply stated the component parts of the deliberative system, Mansbridge et al. explain further what the system is "made of." For them, a deliberative system is composed of discussions that involve matters of common concern and have a practical orientation. These discussions occur within four different *arenas*, which can reasonably be considered the descriptive parts of the system: "The binding decisions of the state (both in the law itself and its implementation); activities directly related to preparing for those binding decisions; informal talk related to those binding decisions; and arenas of formal or informal talk related to decisions on issues of common concern that are not intended for binding decisions by the state" (ibid.: 9).

Contrary to Dryzek's account, the component parts of Mansbridge and her colleagues's approach are of the same conceptual nature. Indeed, each of them represents an *activity* related to collective decision-making. These activities being quite generic, Mansbridge et al.'s descriptive layer enables a wide variety of deliberative systems to be encompassed. Indeed, although the authors focus on the nation-state as the relevant unit for deliberative systems, they acknowledge that deliberative systems could also exist within the boundaries of "non-governmental institutions, including governance networks and the informal friendship networks that link individuals and groups discursively on matters of common concern" (ibid.). Furthermore, according to them, deliberative systems are not necessarily institutionally circumscribed but can also be issue-based. Therefore, there are many different types of deliberative systems (in plural form) that coexist and overlap. In addition, Mansbridge et al. provide a long list of "nodes" in the deliberative system (in singular form), such as partisan forums, blogs, or universities. But then, we can wonder if these nodes are themselves deliberative systems, or subsystems of an encompassing deliberative system. If they are several *distinct* deliberative systems or subsystems, two important questions arise: What constitutes the respective *boundaries* of these systems or subsystems and what are the *relationships* between these systems or subsystems. I will discuss these two central issues in the second chapter.

Regarding the *normative* layer, Mansbridge et al. employ functionalist semantics, stating that the system requires a "*functional* division of labour" (ibid.: 4, emphasis mine). The performance of some "functions" is necessary to promote the goals of the system. The functions here are not specific tasks, but normative criteria that promote the "legitimacy of democratic decision-making" (ibid.: 12). First, the *democratic* function enforces inclusive political processes of decision-making. It avoids exclusions "without strong justification that could reasonably be accepted by all citizens, including the excluded" (ibid.: 12). Second, the *ethical* function aims "to promote mutual respect among citizens"; ensuring that they are treated as autonomous agents rather than passive subjects and remain "open to being moved by the words of another" (ibid.: 11). Finally, the *epistemic* function aims to "produce preferences, opinions and decisions that are appropriately informed by facts and logic and are the outcomes of substantive and meaningful consideration of relevant reasons" (ibid.).

Since these three functions can come into conflict in one location, they are distributed and located in different parts of the system. For instance, some parts promote the ethical function while others the epistemic. A specific function *itself* can be distributed across "various subsystems" and therefore does not need to be "fulfilled optimally in one location" (ibid.: 12). Interestingly, Mansbridge et al. assert that their systemic approach "does not require that every component have a function" (ibid.). I think that what they mean here is not that some elements don't matter at all, rather that not everything in the system matters *in terms of the three deliberative functions*. Some elements do not perform these functions. But if they still matter, with regard to what? As we will see in the second chapter, this assumption opens the road for the introduction of a distinct set of functions or normative criteria, *democratic* ones.

Focusing for the moment on the *deliberative* functions presented above, recall the importance of the difference between the two levels of analysis: parts and whole. Mansbridge et al. clearly state that "the system should be judged as a whole in addition to the parts being judged independently" (ibid.: 5). In their account, it appears that the same normative criteria apply to both levels of analysis. However, the authors of the manifesto mostly describe how the parts can perform these normative criteria. In particular, they brilliantly make a case for the following counterintuitive assumption: non-deliberative elements (or even anti-deliberative ones) can nevertheless perform deliberative functions and therefore positively contribute to the system. For instance, expert bodies can be connected with citizens in order to increase the epistemic quality by relying on "citizens' expertise" about some issues, promote the ethical function by increasing the respect between experts and citizens, and enhance the democratic function by including citizens' perspectives. Another compelling example regards protest and pressure; the authors argue that while violating multiple deliberative standards, protest can nevertheless be beneficial to the deliberative system by acting as "a remedial force introduced to correct or publicize a failure or weakness in fulfilling any or all of its key functions" (ibid.: 18). Protest can, for instance, clearly expose a striking lack of inclusion of people or perspectives in the decisional process, thus enhancing the democratic function. Yet, as they insist, this beneficial effect of protest might be at the expense of civility and respect. Therefore, *trade-offs* between the deliberative functions are often unavoidable. This necessity of trade-offs echoes Thompson's assumption that the distribution of deliberation within the system requires us "to decide under what conditions which value should have priority, and which combination of the values is optimal" (2008: 513). This opens the complex question of how to decide which value should trump another in case of normative trade-offs.

For now, it is important to restate the major point made by the manifesto: a part of the system that performs poorly in terms of one deliberative function (e.g., the ethical function in the case of a protest) may have a positive contribution at the system level in terms of *another* deliberative function (e.g., the democratic function). It is less clear in the manifesto whether the performance of the *same* deliberative function can have both negative effects at the part level and positive effects at the system level, or vice versa. Dryzek (2017: 620) considers that some inclusions (e.g., the inclusion of white supremacists in some political venues) could in the end produce exclusionary outcomes at the systemic level. And conversely, some exclusions (e.g., *non-mixité* or *mixité choisie*) can facilitate the construction of an articulated perspective representing a marginalized group, a perspective that could then be included in the public debate. As we see now, each part of the system can simultaneously perform diverse and multiple contributions regarding the three deliberative functions, contributing positively and/or negatively at both the part and system levels.

If non-deliberative elements can have positive deliberative consequences at the system level, the opposite is also true according to the manifesto: genuine deliberative elements can contribute *negatively* to the deliberative quality of the system as a whole. For instance, a perfectly deliberative mini-public can *displace* existing advocacy groups, such as political parties or social movement representatives. Apparently, displacement occurs when two elements fulfil the same function. In their example, the function in question is the epistemic one: a mini-public creating "citizen experts and trusted proxies [...] disadvantaging political parties and advocacy that had previously invested considerable political and social capital in creating deliberative trust" (ibid.: 17). Displacement is thus a *negative* relationship between the parts of the system. However, Mansbridge and colleagues recognize that, in some cases, displacements are "exactly what the system as a whole needs" (ibid.), while in other cases, displacements risk undermining some of the deliberative functions of the whole system. A more *positive* relationship between the parts of the system is *complementarity*. It occurs when "two venues, both with deliberative deficiencies, can each make up for the deficiencies of the other" (ibid.: 3). It means that where a part of the system is weak regarding a deliberative function (e.g., ethical), this weakness can be compensated for in another location. Both displacement and complementarity are complex relationships between the system's parts, but some work is still required to clarify how they operate and especially how we can assess them.

Contrasting the models

In this section I summarize the main features of the manifesto's account of deliberative systems by contrasting them with Dryzek's account. Regarding the descriptive layer, both accounts put decision-making at their core and divide the system's parts according to the kind of contribution made to collective decision-making. In both accounts, parts are mostly characterized by *communication* (talk, discussions), with a similar distinction between communication occurring in the public sphere and those directly connected to decision-making. This common feature resonates with Habermas's distinction between informal and formal public sphere (1996). This distinction broadens the scope of deliberative systems beyond institutionalized practices, including a vast range of societal practices or communications. Besides these similarities, their respective descriptive layers vary greatly. For instance, Dryzek advances *transmission* as a component in itself, to be assessed by the same normative criteria as the public and empowered spaces. Plus, Dryzek includes in the descriptive layer a few additional normative expectations such as accountability, meta-deliberation, and decisiveness. In doing so, he entangles the descriptive and the normative layers. In contrast, the manifesto is much more consistent in keeping the two layers clearly distinct. Moreover, the manifesto's descriptive layer is more context-sensitive by being less demanding in terms of deliberative preconditions. As such, it enables a broader range of political systems to be mapped and their deliberative democratic quality to be assessed.

Regarding the normative layer, the main commonality is the (unsurprising) presence of the criterion of inclusion (*democratic function* for Mansbridge et al.). Apart from some definitional differences, inclusiveness and the democratic function express the same normative expectation. Besides that, however, their normative layers are very different. The main difference is that Dryzek's keeps deliberation united, with the criterion of "authentic deliberation," while the manifesto disaggregates deliberation into two normative criteria: the ethical and the epistemic functions. Hence, by keeping deliberation united, Dryzek's account is more demanding in terms of deliberative quality; it avoids the possibility of complementarity and trade-off relationships according to the respective strengths and weaknesses of the system's parts in terms of deliberative standards. Another contrast between Dryzek and the manifesto regards the criterion of "consequentiality" and the component of "decisiveness." Both are present in Dryzek's account, but not at all in the manifesto. Yet, one can nevertheless perceive this idea of consequentiality/decisiveness in the manifesto's components: the four "arenas" appear to vary regarding their level of consequentiality or decisiveness on decision-making. Indeed, informal talk is obviously less consequential/decisive than activities to prepare binding decisions, which are less consequential than binding decisions themselves. While for Dryzek, the deliberative elements must be consequential, in the manifesto the more or less consequential elements must foster one or several of the three deliberative functions. To put it differently, in Dryzek's account, consequentiality is a *normative* criterion: deliberative elements must be consequential on decision-making. In contrast, in the manifesto, consequentiality appears to be an implicit *descriptive* feature: parts of the system are more or less consequential.

In light of this difference, I do not intend to take a definitive position on consequentiality and decisiveness in this chapter. Nevertheless, I do want to question the relevance of these concepts in the discussion and suggest another way to tackle their concerns. To start with, I doubt the relevance of the use of consequentiality as a normative criterion applied *to the parts* of the system. Instead, as Parkinson (2018: 437) contends, some parts of the system should *not* be consequential. For example, if a deliberative process monitored by political authorities is instrumentalized to legitimize a pre-given policy option, it shouldn't be consequential as a more virtuous deliberative process.

Accordingly, consequentiality cannot be an expectation for *every* element of the system.

Moreover, if consequentiality and decisiveness are defined, as Dryzek has it, as direct or indirect impacts on binding decisions, I wonder whether they capture something more than the bottom line of the systemic approach; all elements have different types and levels of impact on each other and on the whole system, but they all contribute to it, and that whole cannot be reduced to the allegedly more "impactful" (that is, consequential or decisive) elements among them. I suggest that the concern with consequentiality and decisiveness comes from the fact that the elements of a *political/democratic* system are intrinsically impact-oriented or consequence-oriented. I agree with Chambers (2012), the elements of such a system are "decision-oriented," as the system as a whole is too. And this is precisely what we are talking about in the end: an intrinsically decisive/consequential *political* system that can be more or less democratic and/or deliberative.[9]

I suggest that the extensive focus on consequentiality and decisiveness is after all related to the central concern about the *connections* between parts of the system. In my opinion, Dryzek introduces consequentiality/decisiveness because he fears the possibility of a highly deliberative system *disconnected* from decisional instances. A similar fear is present in the manifesto with the idea that parts of the system risk being *decoupled* (Mansbridge et al. 2012: 23). Moreover, the manifesto also warns that parts can be too *tightly coupled*, that is, too consequential or interdependent on one another to allow for mutual compensation or correction. For them, "the ideal of a deliberative system is a *loosely coupled* group of institutions and practices that together perform the three functions" (ibid.: 22). Loose coupling is then the appropriate level of connection between components, being somehow a middle-ground between dependence and independence. Alongside decoupling and tight-coupling, three other "pathologies" prevent political systems from being (more) deliberative. First, *institutional domination* means the control by some members of the political apparatus of some parts of the system, such as civil society organizations.

---

[9] The opposite relationship, a deliberative system that should be consequential *on the* political/democratic system, seems implicitly endorsed in Dryzek's account (2009; 2010). Here it is likely that Dryzek shares Habermas's (1996) requirement that the informal public sphere effectively influences the formal political system. "Influence" for Habermas has the specific meaning of consequentiality in this context.

Second, *social domination* is the control by a group of people (an economic elite or a particular religious or ethnic group) of several parts and organizations of the system, such as the media. Third, entrenched partisanship expresses an extreme polarization of social groups preventing the impact of the claims from one group on another. Interestingly, all these five pathologies have at their core the question of the connections between the different parts of a system. Some connections are desirable while others are not; some elements must be "consequential" on others, while others should not. I then suggest that the question of consequentiality and decisiveness is actually better understood as the central issue of connectivity, which I treat in detail in Chapter 2.

A final major difference is that the manifesto describes and illustrates in greater detail than Dryzek's account the core tenet of the systemic approach: the different levels of analysis of parts and whole. Each part performs several contributions in terms of the three deliberative functions, at both the part and system level simultaneously. A part that is poorly inclusive in itself can strengthen inclusion at the system level, and conversely. The manifesto is clear on the fact that assessments of deliberative quality should refer to *both* the parts taken independently and the whole system. The normative criteria to do so appear to be the same at both levels of analysis. While it nicely illustrates how these criteria are applied to the *parts*, it remains unclear how these should be applied to the *whole*. As Dryzek (2017: 621) contends, "what is still missing is some metric to assess the performance of the system as a whole." Both accounts fail to provide such a metric. Moreover, some further clarity is needed on how to assess the trade-offs between the normative criteria and on which basis to determine if a displacement is either positive or negative. The systemic approach requires further work to develop its assessment potential.

Conclusion

The systemic approach to deliberative democracy (re-)opens the black box of politics as a complex whole and faces the complexity of its functioning. In doing so, it mobilizes an array of conceptual tools (most of them imported from or inspired by systems theory) to *describe* this functioning, in order to *assess* it with normative criteria deriving from the deliberative ideal. Ultimately, both Dryzek's account and the manifesto have displayed the main features of the systemic approach and soundly illustrated its relevance. Moreover, they share some important similarities in their conceptualization. Of primary importance, they both develop a conceptual toolkit of deliberative/democratic systems composed of two layers, each with a clear focus on the descriptive or normative dimensions. Their content diverges for both layers, leading to different pictures of deliberative democratic systems. However, the respective content of these layers is mostly stated, rather than explained and justified. This raises the general question of *how do they arrive at that precise content?* Furthermore, the diverging content of these alternative accounts of deliberative democratic systems varies according to implicit assumptions or explicit answers given to the six questions listed below, that I contend are central for the construction of a systemic approach to (deliberative) democracy:

Regarding the descriptive layer:

1. *If deliberative/democratic systems are composed of parts, what are these parts "made of"?*

    It is important to determine what "material" we are working with when investigating deliberative and/or democratic systems. Are the parts of the system made of institutions, rules, actions, practices, communications, actors, or norms? We need a clear understanding of what is the basic unit composing systems (such as cells in organic systems) in order to be able to distinguish types of this unit (e.g., democratic and non-democratic institutions, institutionalized and non-institutionalized practices) and to envision clusters of this unit (e.g., parts of the system such as the public space). Furthermore, since the ultimate goal of developing a framework for democratic systems is to contribute to its potential empirical applications (assess, compare, design, diagnose), it is essential to have a clear idea of what material will be targeted in those empirical tasks.

2. *On which grounds can we distinguish the system's parts?*

    As democratic/deliberative systems are complex entities with a margin of contextual variations, we need a strategy of analytical representation. On which grounds do we make distinctions within a system to represent its internal complexity? Is the system divided into different spaces, actors, functions, or moments? A clear answer to this question is crucial for the *mapping* of real-world political systems in order to assess their deliberative and/or democratic quality.

3. *If the system's parts are connected in complex ways, how can we conceptualize these connections?*
Systems are characterized largely by their connectivity: without complex and selective connections between elements, there are no systems. But how exactly can we understand and conceptualize connections? Are connections better understood as *transmissions*, as in Dryzek's model, or as *couplings* as in the manifesto? In addition, the deliberative and/or democratic quality of a political system depends to some extent on the appropriateness of its connections. Consequently, it is crucial to discuss how we can assess existing systemic connections.

4. *What are the boundaries from and connections with other systems?*
To map is to distinguish: identifying existing democratic/deliberative systems requires us to establish their boundaries with the multiple other social systems they are connected to and overlap with. This enables us to interrogate the ongoing transformation of the democratic systems in reaction to complex environments. In order to analyze existing boundaries and connections, we need conceptual clarity on what distinguishes democratic systems from other social systems.

Regarding the normative layer:

5. *What kind of criteria should the normative layer be comprised of?*
The normative criteria characterizing deliberative/democratic systems vary largely according to the accounts. Before taking a position on *which* criteria are more relevant, it is essential to discuss *what* normative criteria are and what role they have within the theoretical architecture of deliberative/democratic systems.

6. *How does the normative layer apply to the parts, connections, and/or the system as a whole?*
The normative layer serves to lead assessments of deliberative/democratic systems. However, the application of normative criteria to political realities is not self-evident. It is not obvious whether these criteria apply to parts of the system, connections between them, and/or with the system as whole. Moreover, normative

trade-offs between criteria, and complementary and displacement relationships between parts of the system are also features of the systemic approach to (deliberative) democracy that require further theorizing.

On the occasion of the systemic turn, several further accounts of (deliberative) democratic systems suggested diverse answers to these six questions, which have substantially grown in complexity, but also in diversity. Two transversal issues profoundly impact these new conceptualizations. One is the focus on deliberative democratic systems or democratic systems *tout court*. The other field of variation is the extent of context-sensitivity that the different models allow, both in the definition of their component and in their attribution to some specific normative expectation. In the next chapter, I discuss the most seminal accounts of the literature along these six questions that will serve to structure the exploration of the systemic dimension. By investigating the systemic approach beyond its metaphorical use, I open the conceptual black box of deliberative/democratic systems.

Opening the black box of democratic

2 | systems

Democracy can take not just many different forms, but in principle an unlimited number of overlapping forms, driven in complex ways by different combinations of principles and institutions. (Saward 2021: 21)

In this chapter, I investigate the complex functioning of whole (deliberative) democratic systems. After Dryzek's account (2009; 2010) and the manifesto (Mansbridge et al. 2012), several important contributions have tackled this task, with an increasing level of theoretical complexity. Indeed, the relevant features of a democratic system have been multiplied and diversified. For instance, Dean et al. (2019) suggest seven "conceptual building blocks" for the development of a systemic theory of democracy: functions, norms, practices, actors, arenas, levels, and interactions. Regarding the descriptive dimension, and focusing on the *deliberative* system, Neblo (2015) details more than a dozen deliberative sites, diverse enough to include deliberation within, campaigns and elections, and the judiciary. Regarding the normative dimension of the deliberative system, Bächtiger & Parkinson (2019) distinguish five *deliberative* goals and three *democratic* ones, contending that the two can sometimes conflict. With an emphasis on the design of democratic systems, Saward (2021) divides the normative layer into a few *required* principles and more than forty *ordering* principles. These examples clearly illustrate the increase in theoretical complexity and diversity of the accounts of deliberative/democratic systems. Relying on a close reading of the most relevant literature, this chapter discusses in detail a variety of answers to the six questions identified in Chapter 1 as crucial for the construction of a systemic theory of democracy.

The descriptive layer

As described in Chapter 1, the descriptive layer consists of the elements that constitute a deliberative and/or democratic system. It is a tool of analytical representation. Its purpose is to *map* how systems are structured, that is, to identify the differences that shape them. As a descriptive tool, it does not (or is not supposed to) contain normative criteria, which belong to the normative layer whose purpose is to *assess* what is described. This does not mean that what is mapped does not contain normative elements at all. It means that analytically speaking, the descriptive layer's purpose is to orient the observation towards constitutive features of systems *regardless of their normative quality*. If it is conceptualized as such, the descriptive layer would be context-sensitive enough to map any type of political system and would do so without conveying normative presuppositions on what the system under analysis *should* look like. In what follows, I present the main answers from the literature to the structuring questions identified in Chapter 1.

If deliberative/democratic systems are composed of parts, what are these parts "made of"?

Democratic systems are composed of multiple elements, that is self-evident. The various conceptualizations of building blocks have resulted in lists of items composing them. Yet, it is far from clear what democratic systems are essentially "made of"; what is their raw material? Just as organisms are composed of cells in complex relations, what are the elements within a *democratic* system? The systemic turn is largely reacting to an excessive focus on *institutions* as the material of (deliberative) democratic systems. This focus was not only problematic because it mostly targeted institutions in isolation rather than in connection, but also because it disregarded something else. This overlooked element is generally considered to be *practices* occurring in the society, such as social movements or mediated public debate (see

Felicetti 2021). The deliberative system came to be defined as a "loosely coupled group of institutions *and practices*" (Mansbridge et al. 2012: 22, my emphasis). As a result, the system goes beyond an ensemble of political institutions and includes "deep-rooted, real-world practices" (Bächtiger & Parkinson 2019: 39). Practices came to be the new focus, and a few important contributions shed light on what is meant by them and why they matter for a deliberative/democratic system.

Warren's problem-based approach to democratic theory displays seven generic and common political practices as "ideal-typical social actions that are commonly organized or enabled by institutions that serve democratic functions" (2017: 43). These practices are recognizing, representing, deliberating, resisting, voting, joining, and exiting (ibid.). *Practices* as social actions are thus the ontological element of social systems; *these* seven practices are the specific materials of political systems. *Institutions* are a special kind of practice: "Rule-based, incentivized, and sociologically stable combinations of social actions that assign roles to individuals" (ibid.). For Warren, to interpret institutions as being primarily made of practices insists on their "agent-focused" nature (ibid.). Moreover, to portray institutions as a combination of generic practices which are *political* but non-inherently *democratic* enables us to question to what extent these practices are actually democratic while performing democratic functions.

Saward (2021) considers Warren's seven generic practices as too narrow a set. He contends that Warren's "generic" framing occults the variability and versatility of the contextual realization of these practices. Yet, Saward similarly insists on institutions as constituted and daily reproduced by multiple practices, hence "highlighting unambiguously the grounding of 'structure' in 'agency' (practice)" (ibid.: 69). Moreover, his framework for democratic design also praises getting "back to the 'elements themselves' of democracy – its practices and principles" (ibid.: 54). For Warren, the "dual core" of democracy is represented by *functions and practices*, and for Saward, *principles and practices*. According to the latter, a democratic *design* consists basically of "practices that enact principles" (ibid.: 67). I think he would contend the same about a democratic *system*. Although conceptually, practices and principles can be distinguished, they are actually inseparable. Saward explains:

> Practices depend on principles, and vice versa, for their effective presence in political life and political structures; practices are invariably

practices of principles, and principles do not have form or texture without enactment in practices. (ibid.: 68)

Both parts of Saward's claim are strong. First, *all* political practices enact principles, meaning that they "embody or are constructed around principles" (ibid.: 83). Second, principles exist only[10] through practices "generating their presence in context" (ibid.: 84). Furthermore, this depiction explicitly puts individual and collective agency at its heart, with people as "carriers (creators, sustainers, modifiers)" of both practices and principles (ibid.: 70). The contextual and agential aspects of practical enactment imply that *interpretations* of principles are enacted with a particular meaning by practices in different contexts. From this understanding of the raw material of democratic systems, Saward suggests a "practices matrix," distinguishing different types of practices and discussing which matter more for democratic *design* (governing institutionalized practices), while other types remain important to some extent. We will come back to this important issue in Chapter 6. For now, it is enough to understand Saward's suggestion of the practices-principles couple as the basic material of democratic systems.

Another enlightening contribution on the elements of democratic systems comes from the deliberative model. This contribution emerges from an ambiguous context of how deliberative and democratic dimensions are articulated from proponents of deliberative democracy. As Warren and Saward do for democratic systems, the deliberative system model of Bächtiger & Parkinson (2019) puts practices at the core. As a reminder, a deliberative system is not only made of institutions and practices *of deliberation,* but also of *other things.* Deliberation is a "distinctive communicative practice" (ibid.: 21/24), conceptually distinct from bargaining and storytelling, for instance. The practice of deliberation is thus "just one mode of communication that is valuable in a democracy" (ibid.: 25). The authors imply that besides practices of deliberation, other *communicative* practices intervene within a democratic system. The conceptual core of these communicative practices,

---

[10] Saward argues that principles get their meaning *only* through practical enactment, insisting that "they do not have an original, foundational, or purely abstract meaning apart from such enactment" (ibid. 84). I think he is right on the fact that principles originate from practices, but as we will see in the next chapter, principles can *also* exist by occurring within communication or by being the object of communication. Consequently, they can exist *independently* of their practical enactment.

deliberation among them, is what Bächtiger & Parkinson call "memes." They define *memes* as "units of meaning that may be focused on a word or group of words but are also likely to include physical symbols, even actions or action sequences" (ibid. 97). Memes can include collective narratives, normative statements, ontological claims, proposals for action, and factual assertions. The authors suggest that memes are "transmitted" across the system. As such, memes represent the material that circulates within a deliberative system, and it seems, within a democratic one too. Practices remain central here, because "memes become institutionalized in practices and routines which then continue over time" (John 2003 in Bächtiger & Parkinson 2019: 115). Memes form, reproduce, and transform practices. The authors insist on memes being the "real 'stuff' of politics: units of meaning that have both linguistic and everyday practice elements, clustered together, wielded by agents, and structured by power" (ibid.: 116). Importantly, and we will discuss this in the section on connections, this memetic account allows us to conceptualize the transformation of memes within the process of their transmission.

Parkinson (2019) expands and improves this discussion on memes. He repositions the issue of communication within the social and cultural processes of *meaning-making*. People create and transform meaning together; it is through the communicative processes of meaning-making that people "makesense of ideas, problems, conditions, situations" (2019: 7). Importantly, people do so by using memes/scripts/symbols that are meaningful to them; they create new meaning by remodeling pre-existing meaning. They employ "pre-scripted, pre-loaded tools in a more-or-less shared toolkit." This stance echoes Habermas's idea of the lifeworld as a "reservoir for taken-for-granteds" (Habermas 1987: 124). Moreover, countless contextual features embed and *communicate* specific meanings: the disposition of a venue, the clothing of the participants, the timing of their activities, etc. The main implication for deliberation is that "communicative power is not merely a matter of outward form but of the myriad, below-the-radar ways in which humans signal and reproduce status, inclusion and exclusion, and domination in ways that vary with context" (Parkinson 2019: 7). In particular, all these *meaningful* contextual features participate in the construction and reproduction of a "community of practice" or "normative space." Therefore, Parkinson's conception of democratic communication as meaning-making implies consideration of "a much wider range of practices that establish a community of practice and a normative space for that community to operate in" (ibid.: 2). According to Parkinson, a democratic system would then be composed of a multiplicity of communicative processes and practices of meaning-making.

To summarize this section, I do not take a definitive position on this ontological question. I instead notice commonalities and differences regarding what deliberative/democratic systems are made of. The centrality of *practices* is obvious, yet with variables emphasis on the principles they necessarily enact (Saward) or the meaning that shape them and which they carry (Parkinson). The different emphases steer the focus in diverging directions, and the persistent deliberative/democratic divide is certainly due in part to these ontological differences, and conversely. In addition, it is important to distinguish the question of what these systems are made of, from the question of what *matters* in these systems. Here too, there are differences between Saward's main focus on institutionalized practices and Parkinson's consideration of multiple communicative practices of meaning-making.

Finally, a careful reader may note that I omitted to discuss concepts such as *spaces* and *moments*, and that there exist other proposed building blocks such as *actors, norms, functions, interactions*. To this remark, I would answer the following. First, *norms* and *functions* are indubitably related to practices, but this complex relation deserves a discussion on its own in the next section on the normative layer. Second, there are multiple *interactions* or connections between practices, and this is precisely what a system is about. But this too needs to be tackled on its own in the section on connections. Third, *spaces, moments,* and *actors*[11] are all concepts that are directly related to the basic material (for instance, a moment is always a moment *of* practices; an actor is so when performing a practice; a space is a place *of* practices). In the next section, I thus discuss on which grounds we can distinguish practices and represent clusters of practices such as spaces or sequences.

---

[11]   One can wonder why the material of democratic systems is not after all *individuals* or *people*, especially since all the discussed accounts explicitly defend the importance of agency. Before developing in detail the question of people's agency within social systems in Chapter 3, a brief answer will be that, individually and collectively, people do many things that have not much to do with democracy. They go to the doctor when they are sick, they go to restaurants and on vacation. Democracy as a system is made of practices *relevant* to democracy and does not encompass everything that is happening in a society. People as such are not part of democratic systems, only some of their actions are. This ontological question is wholly independent from the normative question of individuals' *inclusion* in democracy-relevant practices.

On which grounds can we distinguish the parts of the system?

Opening the black box of complex systems means observing what is going on *within*. It entails distinguishing parts of the whole.[12] We now have cues on what the system is basically made of, but that does not tell us how it is *internally structured*. An observer of the human body may know that its object of scrutiny is made of cells, but that does not explain how it is structured. The functioning of a system certainly depends on connections between its elements, but it also depends on the structuration of these elements along distinct ensembles. Back to the organic analogy, one can observe the different *organs* as structures or parts made of cells, but one can also focus on the *subsystems* (nervous, digestive, etc.) that operate within the human body, subsystems that are also part of the same whole (human body) and made of the same stuff (cells). Both organs and subsystems are types of distinctions representing the complexity of the human body. The point is that the distinction of the parts of a system has first and foremost an *analytical* purpose; it allows a schematic representation of the whole system, a *simplification* of its complex structure.

The accounts of deliberative democratic systems discussed in Chapter 1 distinguish parts or components quite abstractly (e.g., spheres, moments). One important reason for being so abstract is to avoid presenting a (deliberative) democratic system as a rigid ensemble of traditional institutions, as Goodin (2005) does to some extent. To be more generic enables us to distance ourselves from the presuppositions regarding which institution or practice can or must operate in these spheres or moments. As an alternative to rigid institutional pictures, two alternative representations of (deliberative) democratic systems have been advanced: a *spatial* representation and a *temporal* representation. While the first intuitions (Parkinson; Saward; Goodin) of the systemic turn focused on the *temporal* representation, the *spatial* representation is favored by both Dryzek's approach and the manifesto. The former puts an emphasis on *spaces*, while the latter on *arenas*, but the

---

[12] It is important not to conflate the analytical *distinction* of parts, with the normative *distribution* of features (e.g., deliberative qualities) to these parts, and the *attribution* of roles, function, or venues to these parts.

spatial focus is similar.[13] There is not much discussion on the choice of this representation strategy, only broad statements that "those are the components of the system." To my knowledge, only Parkinson (2018) and Bächtiger & Parkinson (2019) comment on these alternative representations,[14] which they take as representational "metaphors."

Parkinson considers the spatial metaphor as being too *static* to illustrate a dynamic reality. Indeed, it often portrays the deliberative system as a *stable* set of locations or sites, both formal and informal, with *fixed* relationships between them. Their classic shape revolves around Dryzek's distinction between the public and empowered spaces (which is quite close to Habermas's two track strategy), with (often institutionalized) ties of transmission and accountability between them.[15] I think that, for Parkinson, the static problem with spatial metaphors is threefold. One part of the problem is that these metaphors occult the evolving nature of both the boundaries and the relationships between these spaces. The second part is their strict attribution of roles to actors in these spaces, and the attribution of specific functions or norms to perform. Finally, Parkinson highlights that spatial representations "fail to capture dynamics, they tend not to be very good for representing things like critical junctures in a process: moments of collective decision, or an agenda-setting moment" (2018: 439). Indeed, the empowered space somehow becomes a black box of decision-making, without much insight on the processual dimension of such decision-making.

For these reasons, Parkinson favors the temporal metaphor, mostly known as the *sequential* account, which clearly represents "the dynamics of issues, actors, and venues over time" (Bächtiger & Parkinson 2019: 88). Basically, it distinguishes parts of the system as *moments* of a sequence of decision-making. Generally, these moments include agenda-setting,

---

[13]   Dean et al. rightly note that "the deliberative focus has obscured other potential bases for differentiating between arenas [...] [for instance] the traditional functional differentiation between executive, legislature and judiciary" (2019: 49).

[14]   Hendriks et al. 2020 also comment on these alternative representations, but they do so under the prism of *connectivity*. I therefore discuss their conception in the next section dedicated to systemic connections.

[15]   In particular, as Parkinson notes, this theoretical sketch often leads to the analysis of *networks* of actors, representing clusters and nodes of actors and the relationships between them (see Cinalli and O'Flynn 2014). For Parkinson, the network representation is good at "modeling patterns of communicative inclusion and exclusion, including the theoretically important concept of deliberative enclaves" (2018: 439).

preferences formation,[16] decision, and implementation. According to Bächtiger & Parkinson, one of the advantages of the sequential models is their emphasis on decision *processes*: "They thus raise questions about what needs to have happened prior to the decision point in order to legitimate the decision; and [...] what happens afterwards" (ibid.). However, one weakness they acknowledge is that in practice, the journey of decision-making does not always follow this schematic path. It may be for that reason that the temporal metaphor provides more room for *agency* and *power* than the spatial one: actors do "play" strategically with time and steps of decision-making, and that is an important part of politics. Nevertheless, while politics does not always follow an idealized sequence of decision-making, it often does so (and perhaps *should* do so), opening the possibility for *normative* proposals of a "right" sequence. An abstract and generic sequence serves to determine "what counts as the right practice at the right moment" (Bächtiger & Parkinson 2019: 119). For Bächtiger & Parkinson, the right sequence for deliberative systems is listening, structuration, and deciding. Alternatively, Ercan, Hendriks, & Dryzek (2019) suggest that listening and reflection should mostly occur *after* justification and expression. This illustrates disagreements about the "right sequence."

Saward (2021) also clearly sticks to the temporal representation. The ultimate function of democratic systems is to reach binding collective decisions, and they do so through procedures as "sequences of practices intended to enact principles" (ibid.: 100). Saward refines the idea of sequence in distinguishing horizontal sequences from vertical ones. *Layering* (vertical sequencing) refers to the division of labor between levels of governance (ibid.: 104). By doing so, Saward complexifies the temporal representation by reinjecting spatial elements (hierarchical relationships between territorial/administrative units). Interestingly, the spatial representations discussed above (e.g., Dryzek's spaces), although supposedly applicable to any level of governance, always displayed the deliberative systems *horizontally*: one governance level *at a time* (often with the nation-state level as an implicit reference). In contrast, Saward insists on the possible *interaction* between these levels of

---

[16]   The framing of this step is particularly tricky. Both Parkinson (2003) and Saward (2003) labelled this step "discussion," and we can clearly see how it leads almost automatically to a vision of deliberation as necessary to operate this step. Warren (2017) makes a similar claim in attributing to deliberation a particular importance in the performance of the function of "collective agenda and will formation."

governance: there are cases where "vertical and horizontal sequences intersect" (ibid.). Importantly, Saward does not suggest a "right" sequence, he simply emphasizes *sequencing* and *layering* as important "structuring factors" for the design of democratic systems (ibid.: 107). As Saward is openly context-sensitive, he argues that "a 'system' needs not to take a set form of interests, actors, or spaces" (ibid.: 111). I think that he would contend the same for the moments or "phases" of a system, for which he would favor *sequencing* over "right sequences." Although I share the importance of being context-sensitive in our description and (re-)design of systems, I fear that Saward's (intended) abstractedness leaves us without many reference points to *map* existing systems. I instead suggest that we need a common analytical anchor enabling contextual variations of system representation. Below, I suggest such an analytical anchor.

To conclude this section, it is clear that a system is structured into different elements, and that any representation of a system is first and foremost a representation of internal *differences*. I won't take a position on whether these differences should be taken as moments or spaces, for two reasons. First, all schematic representations of a system face the challenge of representing *both* stability and dynamism. The spatial model focuses more on structures, the temporal model focuses more on processes. But it is likely that they are both *partial* representations of the same things *from a different perspective*. Second and more importantly, there are fewer differences than meets the eye between these two models. Indeed, within each model, the difference between steps or between spaces revolves on *what is supposed to happen* in each of these steps or spaces. Take the examples of the step of agenda-setting and the public space characterized by wild debate on matters of common concern: both represent more or less the same thing, *a particular task or activity*. This task is performed by the system's material, whether practices or communicative units of meaning-making. My point is that the sequential and spatial models both silently take the production and implementation of collectively binding decisions as *the* broad function of (deliberative) democratic systems; and their distinction of moments or of spaces are actually distinctions of *smaller tasks* necessary to perform this broader function. In a nutshell, both spatial and temporal metaphors are *functional* representations of systems.[17] They focus on what is to be done. In that sense, they are different pictures of the metaphor of functional *division of labor*. Accordingly, the analytical anchor enabling contextual variations in the representation of systems would be *functions*. I develop this crucial point in Chapter 6.

If the parts of the system are connected in complex ways, how can we conceptualize these connections?

If we can distinguish different parts of a system, these parts must somehow be connected, otherwise they are not part of the same system. As Dryzek puts it, "there cannot be a system without connectivity" (2016: 213). For Ercan, Hendriks, and Boswell (2018: 7), "a deliberative systems' understanding of deliberative democracy is all about connections" and connectivity "is central to the functioning and legitimacy of any deliberative system." Connections are pivotal in the two foundational accounts, under the label of "transmission" for Dryzek and "coupling" for Mansbridge et al. Therefore, connections have been (in contrast with other features of systemness) largely debated in the systemic turn.[18] Connections in a deliberative/democratic system are illustrated by two metaphors: transmission and coupling.

To start with, the metaphor of transmission advanced by Dryzek (2009; 2010) illustrates the transfer of *influence* from the public space to the empowered space. Dryzek does not greatly develop the concept, despite suggesting that this process can occur through different means (e.g., political campaigns, social movements) and that influence may take "the form of advocacy, or criticism, or questioning, or support, or some combination of all four" (2010: 11). Building on Dryzek's work, Boswell, Ercan, and Hendriks (2016) investigate theoretically and

---

[17]   Interestingly, Warren's (2017) "normative functions" are empowered inclusion, collective agenda and will formation, and collective decision-making. We see clearly that (with the exception of empowered inclusion) what is supposed to happen (functions) in a democratic system is also at the core of his account.

[18]   Several contributions focus on *particular* connections (or lack thereof), notably on how to connect mini-publics to deliberative systems (Felicetti et al. 2016; Curato & Böker 2016) or representative systems (Gastil et al. 2015; Setälä 2017). Actually, these contributions mostly highlight the specific contributions (in deliberative terms) of mini-publics to deliberative or representative systems. However, they do not really specify *what connections are*. Furthermore, they remain ambiguous on whether mini-publics are a special type of connector between component parts, or if mini-publics themselves need to be connected, somehow, to other parts of the system.

empirically the concept of transmission. Theoretically, they suggest that what is transmitted are *ideas, claims,* and *evidence* so that "they can be challenged and 'laundered' through the system" (ibid.: 264). Empirically, they analyze three types of transmission mechanisms:[19] existing institutions (e.g., government inquiries), democratic innovations (e.g., mini-publics), and discourses (e.g., narratives).

Regarding *institutional transmission*, the authors observe that institutional ties do not guarantee transmission, which also depends on the "discursive opportunity structures" of the broader society. Regarding *democratic innovation*, a mini-public has been specially designed to transmit ideas from the public to the empowered space of a parliamentary committee. Interestingly, this mini-public has been established as an institutional mechanism for the transmission of ideas and claims, but it also transmits "democratic norms" to the parliamentary committee. In their third case study, narratives are seen as a *discursive transmitter* of claims and ideas, through the consecutive diffusion of mass media, then experts and stakeholders, to the empowered space. Important distortions of the narratives are observed, which lead the authors to highlight that transmission sometimes involves *transformation*. Finally, as a more general conclusion, the authors suggest that transmission depends on both existing structures and individual agency.

The alternative metaphor of "coupling" has been introduced by the manifesto and further theorized by Hendriks (2016). She argues that "the coupling metaphor evokes images about relationships – for example, linkage, interaction, interdependence and networking" (2016: 46). The metaphor of coupling leads us towards a more relational and less unidirectional picture of connections than the metaphor of transmission. The parts of a system are coupled through "processes of convergence, mutual influence and mutual adjustment" (Mansbridge et al. 2012: 23). As Hendriks highlights, coupling has so far been mostly discussed in terms of the *strength* of connections, with the suggestion that *loose* coupling is an ideal level, and tight coupling and decoupling are systemic "pathologies." In contrast, Hendriks argues that "the desirable strength of coupling between sites and activities depends on what is being connected, and where" (2016: 57). Indeed, in some cases decoupling and tight coupling might well be desirable. For

---

[19] The authors also advance other transmission mechanisms such as voting, social media, political parties, and social movements. Mendonça (2016) suggests other mechanisms such as bureaucrats and activists as "inducers of connectivity," which can generate opaqueness and disconnection instead.

instance, decoupling might be crucial in the case of enclave deliberations of marginalized minorities.

A second added value of coupling is, according to Hendriks, that it steers attention towards what occurs *between* parts of the system. For instance, a mini-public could serve as a connector by being set between the public and the empowered space to connect them. Here, the focus is very much on coup*ling* as an intentional action, a focus naturally leading to the idea of *designed* coupling. Indeed, Hendriks wonders whether coupling will always "emerge organically" from the system, or if it might be sometimes institutionally activated. She observes that coupling can be both self-generated by actors or institutions and intentionally "designed" to formally connect different parts. If the self-generation of coupling emphasizes individual and collective agency, it may sometimes undermine the system's quality, by leading, for instance, to coupling pathologies such as tight coupling, social domination, and economic domination (see Mansbridge et al., coupling pathologies in Chapter 1). Therefore, Hendriks contends that *designed coupling* is necessary to create appropriate connections that do not emerge spontaneously. Moreover, designed coupling has the advantage of providing procedural guarantees and facilitating the mutual influence and adjustment of the coupled parts.

In a vein close to the "coupling" picture, Neblo and White (2018) develop further this conception of connections in a deliberative system. They suggest that each connected space must feature to some extent four conditions. When all four are adequately met, they allow "the system to function successfully" (ibid.: 447). First of all, deliberative sites must be aware of each other. Regarding this condition of *awareness*, the authors contend that total knowledge of the other elements of the system would be an ideal situation. However, we can object that such a demanding awareness might instead overburden the capacity of a single site. The authors do recognize that this ideal is unlikely to be reached in practice, and they therefore suggest that if several sites perform the same function (i.e., redundancy), at least one of them will probably be aware of what occurs in another site. In addition, they rightly argue that not all sites need to be directly connected to each other, but only that there aren't gaps in the "communicative chains." Neblo & White also highlight the close relation between awareness and publicity. However, since not all sites may benefit from being public, awareness sometimes requires other forms than publicity.

The second condition is *translatability*. The idea is that "inputs" must be understood, and "outputs" must be understandable. Sometimes that requires translation, or modification of the form of the communicated content. There is an inevitable tension in keeping the meaning unchanged while transforming its form. The third condition is *receptivity*, which goes beyond awareness through a genuine consideration of what comes from other sites. Neblo & White insist that receptivity "falls between the poles of excessive insularity and excessive openness" (ibid.: 450). In order to navigate between these two poles, sites must develop discernment about what to consider or not. The fourth and last condition is *flexibility*, which means the capacity to respond "creatively" to other sites; a condition falling between the poles of "total rigidity" and "total amorphousness" (ibid.). The authors illustrate the relevance of these four conditions of connectivity by applying them to what they take as the main sites of deliberation (media, citizens, parties, etc.). In doing so, they sketch a rigid picture of how these sites *should* be connected and interact with each other. I will discuss in Chapter 6 how these conditions can serve to assess and diagnose existing systemic connections in a more context-sensitive manner.

The issue of connections in deliberative systems is also the focus of Hendriks, Ercan, and Boswell's book *Mending Democracy: Democratic Repair in Disconnected Times* (2020). They see *disconnection* as the main source of the current democratic malaise and call for a "connective turn" in deliberative democracy as a way to address this issue. The authors identify three major *disconnects*: between citizens and elected representatives, between citizens themselves (e.g., polarization), and between citizens and administrative policymaking processes.[20] Moreover, Hendriks et al. raise several criticisms towards the existing accounts of connectivity in deliberative systems. Regarding the transmission metaphor, besides opposing the reductive binary of transmitted/non-transmitted, they also contend that it portrays the possibility of a "communicative miracle" that a homogeneous public opinion might emerge and be transmitted, a miracle they consider as unlikely given the fragmentation of the public sphere (ibid.: 25).

Hendriks et al. raise another important issue regarding systemic connectivity: the risk for distortion and disruption at each point

---

[20] Interestingly, by identifying these problematic disconnects, the authors implicitly suggest that these connections are *necessary* in a deliberative democratic system. It also raises an important question: beyond the common-sense appeal for the necessity of these connections, how do they diagnose these disconnects?

(whether site or step) of the system.[21] Indeed, connections between parts of a system are not static but dynamic; connection as a constant process is far from being "seamless" and without potential contestation from multiple actors. It also involves disconnection, reconnection, misconnection, etc. Therefore, attempts to provide "ideal configurations" of connections are somehow misplaced. In reaction to these shortcomings, Hendriks et al. calls for an opening up of the black box of connectivity in deliberative systems. They propose a "bottom-up" conception of connectivity that refocuses the debate on how citizens perceive and create connections, opposing the "architect's-eye view" on those connections. As the authors put it in a previous draft, such an approach "re-directs our analytic attention away from optimizing participatory institutions and towards examining real-world practices of connection and disconnection in democratic politics" (Ercan et al. 2018: 12). Indeed, their bottom-up approach analyzes *actual* connections in existing deliberative systems, allowing us to better grasp the wide and constantly renewed possibilities of democratic connections, as well as the agency of actors in (re-)shaping these connections.

The lesson from Hendriks et al. (2020) is clear: connectivity is a matter of agency, and not only do "macro-connections" matter, but also, and perhaps more often, "micro-connections" between agents (sometimes surprising and "performative" connections too). Thus, they call for the debate to be refocused on actual small-scale daily efforts to repair disconnections, *mending* as they label it. In addition, we have to redirect our efforts towards the analysis of *actual* connections and disconnections, instead of *ideal* ones. Finally, as an important insight, the authors demonstrate that connective practices are "relational, creative, adaptive, co-constituted, and iterative" (ibid.: 17). Nevertheless, these important lessons do not constitute an *alternative* view of connectivity, nor do they reject the importance of examining and theorizing macro-connections with what they call "abstract institutional architecture" (Ercan et al. 2018: 15). If we dismiss broad structural connections from the picture, I doubt that our analysis can still be labelled *systemic*.

Before concluding this section on connectivity, I briefly come back to Bächtiger & Parkinson (2019), as they highlight a further important

---

[21] They target this critique at the sequential model of deliberative system, but I think this is misplaced since it is not *per se* a model of connection but of internal differences (see the previous section). Instead, I suggest that the critique applies to both conception of connectivity (the transmission and coupling models).

issue. They discuss the two metaphors (transmission and coupling), and they criticize the metaphor of transmission[22] because it portrays connections as "input/output" mechanisms, where what is transmitted is received as such by the addressee. Parkinson contends that connections within a deliberative system are much more complex and must combine "two conflicting deliberative requirements: the expectation that a system faithfully transmits ideas, yet also transforms them" (Parkinson 2018: 441–442). Their point is mostly a *normative* one: people must be able to recognize the impact of *their* contributions to the system, yet each contribution must be malleable enough to be challenged and evolve through the system. Taking memes as what is basically transmitted, Bächtiger & Parkinson suggest a way to resolve the transmission/transformation dilemma. According to them, "memes [...] are carried, shared, and transformed by agents, often with strategic goals in mind, connected with practices in institutions" (ibid.: 118). Thus, this transformation process leads to the structuration of this myriad of memes into a few policy options and reasons supporting them. Their solution is that before this structuration process a *visible listening* process takes place in which the authors of memes are listened to carefully and are asked: "Here is what we think you are saying – did we get it right?" (ibid.: 101). By doing so, a deliberative system can faithfully and visibly connect memes to decisions, thus balancing transmission and transformation requirements.

To summarize this survey on systemic connectivity, I suggest a distinction of the main questions tackled by the literature. First, there is the question: *What are systemic connections, theoretically?* Here, we have contrasted two metaphors that both emphasize an important dimension of connectivity. The metaphor of transmission highlights that something circulates across the system, sometimes in an unexpected manner. Whether this something is ideas, norms, preferences, policy-proposals, or memes (or perhaps all of these) remains an open question. But as Bächtiger & Parkinson argue (2019: 122–126), sometimes it is important that something be transferred *as such* from one place to another, and that this transfer be clearly noticeable. Yet, this does not erase the inevitably of *some* transformation in the process, transformation that may have both negative (e.g., loss of the proposal's original meaning) and

---

[22] In an unpublished draft, Parkinson (2019) suggests that the use of *transmission* to characterize the connections of a deliberative system is in part due to an erroneous understanding of communication as a transmission of ideas through language.

positive aspects (e.g., filtering of "bad" proposals). Moreover, transformation is sometimes *needed*, as some ideas may not be imported as such in decisional venues. Transmission also denotes an intention, the clear objective of transferring something, hence emphasizing the agency of people intending to transmit something. In contrast, the metaphor of coupling insists on the stability of some connections, on their structural aspect. When elements are institutionally coupled, it is more predictable to what extent "inputs" will be transformed or not (even if translation is often a condition of understandability). Moreover, coupling focuses on mutual relationships between connected elements and on *internal* features of those relationships, as in Neblo & White's conditions of connectivity. To summarize, transmission and coupling are both relevant metaphors for the connectivity of (deliberative) democratic systems but with different emphases.

The second crucial question about connections is: *Which connections actually matter in a democratic system*. In that regard, Hendriks et al. (2020) clearly warned us not to focus exclusively on macro-connections, but also on the myriad of micro, shifting, and creative ties between the people that operate within deliberative systems. It is certainly an important warning, but it should not divert us from questioning macro-connections as well. Indeed, broad systemic "pathologies" (Mansbridge et al. 2012) and major "disconnects" (Hendriks et al. 2020) are the main problems faced by democratic systems today. Yes, micro-connections might crucially help mend these disconnects, but institutional "repair" of macro-connections is also inevitable. Thus, it is important to consider both, and the way they are interrelated, when analyzing connections in real-world deliberative/democratic systems.

The third and main issue of connectivity asks: *Which connections are desirable or not, and how to identify these*. Mansbridge et al. suggested systemic pathologies along the lines of more or less appropriate couplings. In the same vein, Hendriks et al. diagnosed a few disconnections as the main sources of current democratic deficits. From the reverse perspective, Neblo & White rigidly draw the connections that should exist, for instance, between the media and the public. All these suggestions of good or bad connections point towards a major issue: the normative quality of the system. And the deliberative and/or democratic quality is not, arguably, only a matter of what is connected to what, but mostly of what democratic principles and norms do these connections perform or enable, an issue tackled in the second part of this chapter.

What are the boundaries between, and connections with, other systems?

So far, the discussion over connectivity has tackled the issue of connections *within* deliberative/democratic systems. Indeed, the debate was on the connections between the different parts of the system. As discussed above, to assume that parts are more or less connected presupposes that they are differentiated. *Internal* connections depend on internal boundaries. However, systems do not exist in isolation from an external reality. Therefore, a deliberative/democratic system is demarcated from an outside, and inevitably has some connections with it. As Papadopoulos (2012) forcefully reminds us, deliberative systems are embedded into a broader context of policy-making, which is itself evolving. Dryzek too (2017) questions the relation of the deliberative system with something outside. According to him, deliberative systems should be conceptualized as embedded into a *polity*, rather than more globally into the whole *society* "because [society] has dimensions that are not necessarily political" (ibid.: 623). As the polity is embedded in the society, so too would the deliberative/democratic system, at least indirectly. Whether directly or indirectly, a deliberative /democratic system is both differentiated and connected with other elements of the society as a whole.

The issue of *external* boundaries and connections matters for two interrelated reasons. First, it matters for the theoretical construction of what democratic systems are. Indeed, to define is largely to differentiate from; it is crucial to have a good idea of what democratic systems are *not* in order to identify them. Moreover, as Papadopoulos argues, deliberative/democratic systems are nowadays deeply impacted by a few major transformations. He provides compelling examples: "New public management and its derivatives; the trend towards cooperative governance mechanisms; agencification, the rise of independent regulatory agencies; judicialization, the increasing role of courts as policy actors; the internationalization of policy-making" (2012: 129). According to him, all these examples illustrate various mutations that are (to different degrees) alien to the goals of deliberative/democratic systems. But we can wonder, are these changes occurring *outside* deliberative/democratic systems? Or are they in fact mutations *of* the deliberative/democratic systems? And if so, to what extent are they triggered by internal dynamics (ideally, democratic deliberation) or imposed by external powers such as the globalized political economy? Some conceptual clarification regarding external boundaries is necessary here to investigate *sociologically* the rapid ongoing transformations of democratic systems, and to further discuss *normatively* how to deal with these mutations and how to steer them (ideally, democratically) to fulfill democratic goals.

Second, external boundaries and connections matter regarding the empirical *mapping* of existing deliberative/democratic systems. To map is to draw boundaries/differences, both external (excluding elements from the picture) and internal (distinguishing the elements on the picture). If one wants to analyze a *specific* deliberative/democratic system, one needs to map its boundaries. This mapping allows its connections, or lack thereof, with other systems such as the global economy or the mass media to be investigated. To be sure, there are inevitably some overlapping of systems in real-world settings. Mapping is always a conceptual *simplification* of real-world complexity, often exaggerating differences to bring analytical contrast. Therefore, Dryzek (2016) is certainly right to insist that *interpretive judgements* are inevitable when mapping the boundaries of real-world systems. However, interpretations must rely on sound conceptual distinctions, which so far are largely absent from the debate or are presented as self-evident.

Up to this point, the question of external boundaries has been tackled in the literature through one question: Which elements are in and which ones are out? This question has been dealt with at the "micro" level by "providing an admission test for particular components of a system" as Dryzek (2016: 211) puts it. Smith (2016) discusses two different ways of answering this question. The first is to adopt Mansbridge et al.'s definition of the boundaries of the deliberative democratic system, that is, to include all activities oriented towards decision-making. The second is "a more functionalist perspective, through suggesting that the boundaries of a deliberative system should be drawn around action that contributes to realizing its deliberative capacity" (ibid.). In my opinion, the two ways are exactly the same: *contribution* is their core feature, and only their respective orientations vary (decision-making for the first, deliberative capacity for the second). Smith believes that this approach would lead to a consideration that "everything" contributes somehow to the system. Well, I disagree. My purchase of bread this morning at the bakery obviously does not contribute to the democratic system (but it does to the economic system). Warren (2017) endorses the "contribution" approach to the question of the system boundaries. According to him, boundaries are indeed defined by the functions themselves. Consequently, only the "features of political systems relevant to democratic problems" (ibid.: 41) are part of the democratic system, that is, the practices performing one of his three democratic functions.

Internal and external boundaries matter, both conceptually and empirically. There is no way of investigating systems without relying on internal and external distinctions. These are necessary to envision *connections*, both existing and more or less desirable ones. The necessity of interpretation in doing so? Of course, citizens themselves have their own interpretation of existing boundaries, for instance, of the boundary between politics and administration or between the economic and political systems. Furthermore, these boundaries (and others) are likely to vary across contexts. However, we need to rely on a clear and sound set of conceptual distinctions of boundaries to analyze how existing systems are actually positioned regarding these conceptual references. In Chapter 6, I suggest a way to map internal and external boundaries using "political functions" instead of "democratic functions."

Summary

In the first part of this chapter, I have argued that deliberative/democratic systems can be broadly described along the lines of four central questions. I have displayed and critically discussed the existing answers from the literature to each of these questions. These answers, diverging to a variable extent, form what I have called the *descriptive layer*. Two transversal issues bring content variations: the emphasis on the deliberative or democratic dimension and the importance given to context-sensitivity. A sound conception of the descriptive layer is crucial for the assessment of deliberative/democratic systems. It allows us to *map* the system to be assessed. However, the conceptual effort regarding the descriptive layer is still in its infancy. Major conceptual differences remain, and a lack of confrontation maintains them. The discussed contributions provide grounds for the development in further chapters of a descriptive layer suitable for normative assessments of democratic systems. Besides the descriptive layer, the *normative layer* is pivotal for such an aim, as it provides the normative orientation of the assessment.

The normative layer

The normative layer consists of the features that make a system *deliberative* or *democratic*. It contains the normative resources to *assess* the normative quality of what the descriptive layer allows us to *identify*. It may appear that the display of the normative layer is after all only a normative question, and all that suffices is to state its criteria according to one's own normative affinities. Yet, the normative layer also faces *conceptual* issues in a systemic perspective. I now discuss two questions that need to be answered in order to develop an appropriate normative layer of democratic systems, analytically suitable for the aim of assessing the democratic quality of political systems.

What kind of criteria should the normative layer be composed of?

A striking feature of the literature on deliberative/democratic systems is the wide use of the term *function* to fill the normative layer. In the manifesto (Mansbridge et al. 2012), three deliberative functions are the normative goals of the deliberative system: epistemic, ethical, and democratic functions are expected to be performed across the system. For Bächtiger & Beste (2017), the deliberative functions are instead epistemic advancement, mutual understanding, accommodating diversity, and individual transformation. There are variations across these lists of functions, as well as commonalities. I do not aim to discuss the details of these functions for now, nor take position on the appropriate normative criteria to assess democratic systems. I instead want to focus on the use of *function* as a label for the normative criteria of deliberative/democratic systems. The concept of "function" has a heavy baggage in social sciences history. To use it in a normative sense naturally invites a barrage of criticism: conservatism (Curato et al. 2019), objectivism, and loss of normativity (Asenbaum 2018; 2022), and so on. All of these critiques are to some extent relevant, and I tackle these in Chapter 3. For now, it is more important to discuss *how* functions are employed to represent normative criteria in the systemic approach, and what does this framing imply. I thereby discuss three major conceptions of the normative layer that use *function* differently.

A. Warren's "normative" functions

To my knowledge, only Warren (2017) explicitly discusses his use of this concept. The author defends this functionalist semantic by distinguishing his approach from structural functionalism. According to him, this latter approach "objectifies social systems" by specifying the "objective functions necessary for the system to reproduce itself" (ibid.: 42), without taking individual and collective agency into account, and leading to ideological conservatism. The alternative, he contends, would be to "conceptualize the notion of a 'function' more normatively, and the idea of a 'system' more contingently" (ibid.). Warren insists that functions are not "objective" but "*normative* because identifying a *democratic* function is the same as claiming that a system *should* function in ways that support democratic ideals" (ibid.). Warren's functions highlight *what needs to be done* minimally in a democratic system.[23] As he frames it:

> What problems does a political system need to solve if it is to function democratically? If a political system empowers inclusion, forms collective agendas and wills, and organizes collective decision capacity, it will count as "democratic". (ibid.: 39)

Those are the normative criteria that differentiate a democratic political system from a non-democratic one. Put in a less dichotomizing mode, these normative criteria would "push political systems in democratic directions" along a continuum (ibid.: 41). Fine, but that does not really explain why Warren uses the label of "functions" for the normative criteria of democracy. The author is less explicit on that, but I think that his functionalist semantic comes from a *teleological* idea of task-performance, related to the metaphor of division of labor and deeply present in the systemic turn. Indeed, what Warren calls functions are the "normatively desirable *consequences or outcomes* of practices within their encompassing context" (ibid., emphasis mine). Moreover, for him the generic practices in question are not *inherently* democratic, and their effects are contingent on their environment

---

[23] I am not sure that Warren avoids "objectifying" functions by flagging them as normative. He insists that these three functions are normatively *necessary* and sufficient to democracy: "All the other goods associated with democracy [...] are conceptually and practically implied in these three agent-focused functions, but can also be justified independently of democracy" (ibid.: 43). Warren's democratic functions are still presented as *objective*, as they cannot be other "normative functions" relative to democratic systems.

(i.e., the system to which they contribute). Therefore, democratic normativity resides in the contextual/systemic *performance* of these functions through some political practices, that is, the extent to which these practices support or undermine some of these three democratic functions.

To perform is the key verb in this discussion: practices *perform* functions. The practice of representing, for instance, effectively performs the function of empowered inclusion, as do the practices of voting and recognizing. Importantly, *different* practices can perform the *same* functions. Therefore, the purpose of the practices/functions dyad is precisely to combine the *rigid distinctiveness* of democracy (functions) with the *flexible realization* of this distinctiveness (practices). The difference between practices and functions can thus be interpreted through a means/ends perspective (Dean et al. 2019); practices are democratic *means* and functions are democratic *ends* (see Neblo 2015 for a similar perspective on deliberative means/ends). Accordingly, democratic means vary, democratic ends do not. Universal normative core on the one hand, and contextual performance on the other.

Function denotes rigidity, objectivity, and teleology. To use it "normatively" is not trivial. Asenbaum (2018) perceives in this functionalist framing a loss of normative groundings for democratic theory. Dean et al. (2019) question instead whether Warren's functions are actually *normative*. I share this concern, and I think it deserves some attention. As Warren argues, a function is normative because saying that the system should perform it is a normative statement. Therefore, saying that a democratic system should perform the function of *collective decision-making* can be taken as a normative statement. The same goes for the function of *collective agenda and will formation*. However, are these functions really related to a *norm*, a *value*, a moral or political *principle*? Consider another of Warren's functions: *empowered inclusion*. Here, the normative character is salient: the conceptual connection of inclusion with the principle of equality is straightforward. But for the functions of collective will formation and collective decision-making, such a connection with a normative principle is less evident. To some extent, Dean et al. (2019: 45) are right to state that "norms have been eclipsed in democratic systems accounts by the focus on functions."[24]

---

[24]   This is mostly true for Warren (2017) and much less for Bächtiger & Parkinson (2019) since they emphasize more clearly the deliberative norms that uphold their deliberative functions/goals.

As the authors suggest, the conceptual relationship between the suggested functions and their underlying norms needs to be clarified further in accounts of democratic systems.

Nevertheless, the problem appears bigger to me. The counterintuitive framing of normative criteria as *functions* invites great confusion into the context of the systemic approach. The proposed sets of functions evidently vary, and they are contested. For instance, some consider that Warren's list of functions is not exhaustive, adding as necessary democratic functions such as "constraining sovereignty" and "responsive outcomes" (Dean & Geissel 2018) or "agenda-setting" and "accountability" (Jäske & Setälä 2019). These two examples clearly highlight the diversity of proposed candidates for democratic functions. Just compare agenda-setting and accountability: the first is clearly a *step* of decision-making, while the second is clearly a normative principle of democratic governance. Could they really fit under the same conceptual banner and do the same analytical job? Another move of Jäske & Setälä illustrates the conceptual tension between functions and norms. Besides adding two functions, the authors take out Warren's function of empowered inclusion and make it a normative criterion that applies to *all* the democratic functions. Consequently, if agenda-setting or accountability are taken as functions needed to fulfill the principle of inclusion, that conceptual relation is very different from Warren's.

The lesson from such major conceptual differences is threefold. First, the conceptual relation between functions and norms is far from self-evident and is poorly theorized in the systemic approach to democracy (see also Dean et al. 2019). Second, several kinds of functions have been proposed, and they vary regarding their normative load. Third, and more importantly, some of the proposed functions (agenda-setting, collective will formation, collective-decision-making) are very similar to the elements filling some accounts of the *descriptive* layer. Take, for instance, the sequential representation of Saward (2003): agenda-setting, debate and discussion, the moment of decision itself, and the moment of implementation. Consider also the spatial representation of the manifesto: arenas of activities from informal talk to binding decisions. Indeed, these elements (collective decision-making etc.) are in some accounts *normative criteria* (Warren) and in others *descriptive features* (Mansbridge et al. 2012; Dryzek 2009; Saward 2003; Parkinson 2003). Therefore, and this is crucial, such functions (e.g., agenda-setting, decision-making; etc.) are employed both as selection criteria of *what to look at* in a system and as normative criteria of *what this should look like*. What "functions" are and what their role is in a democratic systems framework remains for now an open question, that I treat in Chapter 6 when suggesting my own normative layer. My hint here is that since "functions" are a central analytical category in the analysis of systems, this question is pivotal and largely neglected so far.

B. Saward's required and ordering principles

Saward (2021) also adopts a teleological understanding of normativity, but without couching it in a functionalist semantic. He proposes the dual core of practices *enacting* principles. Practices are generally oriented towards a purpose: "Like all forms of practice, democratic practice [...] conveys a lived directionality and telos of the practice" (Nicolini 2009 in Saward 2021: 66). Saward's *enactment of principles by practices* and Warren's *performance of functions by practices* are broadly similar (besides terminological differences). There are nonetheless important divergences between the two authors regarding their respective normative layer.

First, Saward calls us "to consider a more extensive menu of principles and practices" (ibid.: 25), thereby echoing the previous adding of functions to Warren's minimal list. Second, Saward's political principles avoid Warren's ambiguities regarding their normative character. Indeed, Saward clearly defines a political principle as "a value or a good" (ibid.: 81). Third, and more importantly, Saward divides the normative layer into two dimensions: *required* principles (e.g., equality, freedom) and *ordering* principles (e.g., deliberation, representation, transparency). Required principles are necessary for the realization of the democratic minimum[25] in any context: they must be enacted by some practices (arguably, in different forms and by different practices in different contexts). Ordering principles, however, are *not* necessary, but they have an essential role in most democratic contexts. Saward uses these ordering principles to orient his *design* work: they "may be

---

[25] To be precise, Saward packs six requirements or circumstances into his democratic minimum: equality, freedom, community, governance, resources, constitution. The six can be both requirements *or* circumstances, depending on whether we want to see what democracy *requires* or whether we want to *identify* democracy in a given context. I agree partly, but I suggest we unpack these two dimensions (requirements and circumstances) precisely in order to assess the latter with the former.

invoked as informing, animating, or defining democratic designs or plans" (ibid.: 82). Ordering principles are also at work in actual political configurations and are often called upon to be enacted as such by political actors. Therefore, they are also relevant analytical concepts for the study of existing democratic *systems* and must be articulated somehow to the normative layer.

The distinction between required and ordering principles emerges, I think, from Saward's concern for context-sensitivity. It allows democracy's distinctiveness in its fulfillment of the democratic minimum to be retained, as well as the variability of this fulfillment through various principles emphasized in different contexts. For instance, some contexts may give more importance to the ordering principle of social justice and others to self-government, but both are enactments of the required principles of equality and freedom. This gives Saward's framework a greater context-sensitivity than Warren's. Indeed, the latter only allows contextual variation of democratic *means* (practices), while the former enables, to some extent, the variability of democratic *ends* (ordering principles). Moreover, "a required principle may also be enacted through practice as an ordering principle" (ibid.), for instance, the ordering principle of decentralization along federal lines might enact some understanding of the required principle of equality. I guess that *all* ordering principles are conceptually related to the required principles; they are all concrete enactments of these abstract required principles. Ordering principles can be *interpreted* differently as well, think of deliberation, for instance. They endorse a "specific meaning or importance through practical enactment" (ibid.: 84). Importantly, the meaning of required and ordering principles depends on their actual performance and does not rely on a "reference to some philosophical outside" (ibid.: 85), and therefore remains always subject to (reasonable and limited) interpretation.

Saward's *two level* normative layer is appealing because it combines both the commonality and flexibility that characterizes the democratic system. However, the functionalist semantic reemerges in his theoretical apparatus and conceptually clashes with his ordering principles. Indeed, when defining procedures, Saward speaks of sequences of practices as "configured to serve a range of functions" (ibid.: 91). His examples of functions are multiple and diverse: drawing on expertise, debating principles, shifting opinions, enabling participation, agenda-setting, final decision, facilitation, deliberation, representation, implementation, contestation, election, and many others. All these functions are *phases* of the "ultimate function" of making collective decisions. They all tend towards this global aim. Analytically speaking, to divide the phases of decision-making into multiple functions would serve to drive "attention away from specific practices or devices in order to gain a broader picture of the *purpose* of the proposed or extant sequences" (ibid.: 105, emphasis mine). It questions what specific practices or sequences of practices are *supposed to achieve*. Saward displays a long indicative list of practices, detailing the key functions they can generally achieve. For instance, the governing institutionalized practice of "executive departments or agencies" has as key functions: policy development, policy advice, research, implementation, security, management, and others. Schematically, this list indicates what practices *can do* and what they are often *good at* in terms of functions.

Functions are *goals* that practices can achieve with more or less success. But so are ordering principles. Thus, I wonder what is the conceptual articulation of these two different kinds of goals, *functions* and *ordering principles*. Do ordering principles qualify the performance of functions? For instance, executive departments (practice) can fulfill the function of say, implementation. But a range of ordering principles can *qualify* the way they do so, for instance, with transparency or citizen engagement. If that is indeed the conceptual relationship between functions and ordering principles, the important lesson would be that principles are always principles *in* functions, they always refer to functions; they qualify the actual performance of a function by a practice. Therefore, functions would be pivotal between practices and principles: both would be oriented by particular functions.

C. Bächtiger and Parkinson's deliberative and democratic functions

Bächtiger & Parkinson (2019) rely explicitly on Warren's approach regarding the normative functions of a democratic system, but with a greater emphasis on its *deliberative* quality. Their "unpacking" of deliberation insists on the contingency of its fulfillment, largely depending on its few potential deliberative *goals* (or functions): epistemic, ethical, emancipatory, transformative, clarifying, and legitimacy-oriented. The form of deliberation, that is, the specific *practices* that may qualify as deliberation, vary depending on their specific function. Practices are oriented by a specific function, and in order to count as *deliberative* they must somehow perform the two deliberative principles: reason-giving and listening. A few remarks are important here.

First, deliberative *functions* are distinct from deliberative *principles*. Here, principles are what defines the normative core of deliberation as a practice that "shape-shifts" according to various functions. Second, the difference between deliberative *practices* and deliberative *functions* allows the authors to conceive the possibility that non-deliberative practices can nevertheless perform deliberative functions. The authors provide the example of a dance performance that is not in itself *deliberative* because it has nothing to do with reason-giving, but nevertheless contributes to the ethical function by representing, for instance, respect for others. Third, the functions only *orient* the practices, they do not totally determine them because actors use deliberation (and all other practices) *performatively*. According to the authors, the performative feature of deliberation avoids "functionalist fallacies, where goals and contexts predetermine the deliberative or communicative cluster that is enacted" (ibid.: 154).

The deliberative quality (or "deliberativeness"), as defined by the authors, is a salient feature of deliberative *democracies*. But many other things matter, such as "inclusivity, problem-definition and information-production processes" and especially "political equality and collective popular control" (ibid.: 6). Therefore, Bächtiger & Parkinson articulate the *deliberative* functions with three basic *democratic* functions: inclusivity, representation, and collective decision-making and decisiveness. The authors, as deliberative democratic theorists, insist on the "unique contribution of deliberative goals to realizing basic democratic functions" (ibid.: 18). These three democratic functions are thus conceptualized through a deliberative lens but can conceptually stand independently of deliberation. The distinction between deliberative and democratic functions is "necessary to carefully theorize and empirically study the conditions under which deliberation supports democratic governance and when it trades off with important democratic goods" (ibid.: 20). The authors provide an example of such trade-offs: epistemic advancement might conflict with inclusivity, by necessitating "certain modes of abstract reasoning" which can have exclusionary effects (ibid.: 37). But if epistemic advancement's importance can challenge inclusivity, why is it not *itself* a democratic function that indeed could trade-off with other democratic functions? It is not because deliberation can perform epistemic advancement, perhaps better than any other practice, that epistemic advancement becomes specifically a *deliberative* function instead of a democratic one.

The conceptual distinction between *deliberative* and *democratic* functions appears to me both unnecessary and a source of conceptual confusion. Bächtiger & Parkinson argue that "without it, there is no way to make sense of 'non-democratic' or 'authoritarian' deliberation; or conversely to think about what a non-deliberative (i.e., purely liberal and aggregative) democracy looks like" (ibid.: 106). Although I agree that deliberation is not necessarily democratic, the systemic approach precisely states that deliberation does not have to *be* democratic (e.g., fully inclusive, representative, accountable, public, epistemic, etc.); it only has to *contribute* to a democratic system. Regarding the converse example of a non-deliberative democracy, the authors' acknowledgment that democracy *can be* non-deliberative paves the way for the claim that democracy *should be* deliberative. The qualificative "deliberative" matters for Bächtiger & Parkinson's aim of conceptualizing *deliberative* democratic systems as the best type of democracy, thus providing the tools to map such systems and assess their *deliberative democraticness*. Nevertheless, it matters little[26] for my present aim whether and to what extent a particular democratic system is deliberative or not. Instead what matters is, on the one hand, how the practice of deliberation under its multiple forms can contribute to democratic systems, and, on the other hand, if, how, and to what extent "deliberativeness" *per se* (reason-giving, listening) or "deliberative functions" (e.g., epistemic advancement, legitimacy, etc.) are themselves essential *democratic* functions or principles of a *democratic* system. For these two aims, I doubt that the distinction between deliberative and democratic functions is relevant and helpful.

To summarize this section, a few lessons are important regarding the kind of criteria that should compose the normative layer of democratic systems. First, a teleological understanding of normativity appears to be common to all three accounts: What matters is the normative performance/enactment/contribution of parts to the broader whole of democracy. Second, there is clearly a conceptual entanglement of functions and principles. The importance of distinguishing

---

[26] Although labelling might have its own performative benefits in practice. To declare (in a constitution, for instance) that the state is ruled by a regime of *deliberative democracy* might contribute to (yet arguably not suffice for) its practical enactment.

both will be treated in Chapter 6. Third, the normative core of democratic systems resides in an articulation of the *practices/principles/functions* triad, an articulation conceptualized differently in the three accounts. In particular, this conceptual articulation varies regarding the level of context-sensitivity and the emphasis on deliberation or democracy. In that regard, the distinction of two normative levels (such as Saward's required and ordering principles) substantially increases the context-sensitivity of his framework. Fourth, the emphasis on the deliberative or democratic dimension entails different pictures of the normative layer. Far from being a simple question of normative affinities, the place of deliberativeness within a framework of democratic systems is a crucial issue that needs to be explicitly tackled as such. An appropriate content of the normative layer and the conceptualization of the practices/principles/functions triad is developed in Chapter 6. Finally, I suggest that conceptual work on the normative layer largely depends on its intended analytical use. Consequently, I conceptualize a normative layer specific to my aim of building a *diagnostic tool* of democratic systems, on the helpful grounds of the three accounts discussed above.

How does the normative layer apply to the parts, connections, and/or system as a whole?

As previously noted, the systemic approach insists on the distinction between parts and whole. The manifesto made a clear point in stating that "the system should be judged as a whole in addition to the parts being judged independently" (Mansbridge et al. 2012: 5). This implies that the whole must feature a normative quality that not all its parts need to feature. This leads to the analytical *disaggregation*[27] of the whole normative ideal, say the deliberative or democratic quality. For instance, the whole must be deliberative, but its parts must only feature *a share* of this packed normative ideal, for example, the epistemic function for Mansbridge et al. (2012). The performance of the epistemic function by a part, even if that part poorly performs other functions, contributes to the deliberative quality of the whole system. According to this logic, the normative *criteria* apply to the parts, while the

---

[27] Disaggregation also appears to be the norm in comparative studies and measurements of democracy (see Coppedge et al. 2011).

normative *ideal* qualifies the whole. This is the idea of the "distribution"[28] of analytically disaggregated normative elements, where "deliberative ideals [are] distributed *both spatially and temporally*" (Bächtiger & Parkinson 2019: 40, original emphasis).

This distributive approach to deliberation allows for what Parkinson labels a *summative* view of deliberative quality. He contrasts that view with what he calls an *additive* perspective, where the deliberative quality of a system depends on the *addition* within that system of "institutions that generate strictly defined deliberation at critical points of the system" (Bächtiger & Parkinson 2019: 104). On the contrary, in a *summative* approach, deliberativeness is a quality "produced by the scale and the complexity of a given system" (ibid.: 8), through the complex interactions of its component parts, producing "a whole which is more than the sum of its parts" (ibid.: 110). To illustrate this point, Parkinson uses enlightening metaphors:

> Just as life emerges from the complex interplay of non-living units, or as a song is made up of elements which are not themselves "song", so deliberative democracy is a complex and dynamic pattern of human practices which are not themselves deliberative democracy. (Parkinson 2018: 432)

In a summative perspective, the system acquires its normative quality (here, deliberativeness) at the systemic level. In other words, the deliberative quality of the system emerges from multiple elements that do not share such a quality. Of course, each component part embodies in itself some features of this normative quality, hence its distribution along them. But is also in the *interaction* between these parts that this quality emerges. As Bächtiger & Parkinson put it: "[The] *interplay* of sites, agents, discourses, and other macro forces [...] produces an overall deliberative quality" (2019: 136, emphasis mine). Therefore, we can consider the extent to which the *connections* between the parts should themselves count towards the normative quality at the systemic level, and thus be assessed on their own. And if so, should this assessment be done with the same criteria as those applied to the parts?

---

[28] Some sets of normative criteria include deliberative quality as a specific criterion (e.g., Dryzek 2009). By doing so, they keep the normative whole of "deliberativeness" packed, hence its various normative dimensions are not distributed.

These two approaches to systems normativity (additive and summative) clearly reveal different ways of assessing the normative quality of a deliberative/democratic system.[29] This leaves us with major interrogations. Should the normative criteria apply to parts, connections, and/or the systemic level? For instance, one could wonder to what extent *a part* (say the public space) is inclusive, *a connection* (say the media) is inclusive, and the system as a *whole* is inclusive. Or should some normative criteria apply exclusively to some dimensions? One could argue that since the "systemic test should take priority" (Dryzek 2010: 82), the normative criteria must be applied at this level only. I think this is Neblo's perspective, since he contends that we would make "a category mistake by applying standard deliberative criteria like equality or reasonableness directly to every site in the political system" (2015: 9). I agree that the ultimate question is to what extent the system is deliberative or democratic, opening the room for components that do *not* perfectly feature such qualities. But can we get an appropriate answer if we turn that question into a checklist of normative criteria to be applied at the system level (by asking, for instance, if the system is inclusive, reasoning, listening, etc.)? Broad judgements on the quality of the system are conclusions of normative assessments. Yet don't they emerge from normative evaluations of what *the parts* perform in themselves and in interaction? Of course, the parts' normative quality is not what ultimately matters, but to what extent is it *analytically necessary* to reach ultimate conclusions about the normative quality of complex systems? Moreover, how do we combine the "additive" normative quality of parts (of, say, an inclusive and transparent electoral process) with the "summative" normative quality of the whole (an inclusive and transparent democratic system). Put differently in Bächtiger & Parkinson (2019: 35), how do we articulate "features of particular venues" with "system-level judgements"?

To conclude this section, the main lesson is that there is nothing self-evident in applying normative criteria to a *system*. Beyond disaggregating and distributing normative criteria, focusing on the system level, and allowing the *summative emergence* of normative quality, we

---

[29] Of course, between these two poles (additive and summative), hybrid approaches may exist. Bächtiger & Parkinson (2019: 139) suggest, for instance, a sophisticated additive approach in which the normative quality is disaggregated, and all the normative criteria must be present and distributed spatially and temporally in the system, but in which the weaknesses of one criterion in one location can be compensated for in other locations.

do not have clear guidelines on how to conduct a normative assessment of whole systems. The few questions highlighted above must be answered in order to do so. Moreover, another major issue remains: How to normatively assess the relations between the normative criteria, such as potential *trade-offs* between them or *balancing/complementary relationships* between parts of the systems? For instance, there might be cases where the criterion of inclusion might be trumped by the criterion of, say, epistemic quality. How can we normatively assess when one should normatively trump the other? And how can this trade-off be *compensated* for in another venue where inclusion would trump epistemic quality? Answers to these questions are essential for the assessment of the deliberative/democratic quality of whole systems. I take position on these issues in Chapter 6.

Summary

In the second part of this chapter, I have investigated how to conceptualize a *normative layer* suitable for the assessment of (deliberative) democratic systems. The main accounts of the literature have been discussed, with different contents filling their normative layer, and diverse conceptual strategies to do so. I have identified two major issues in that regard. One issue is the conceptual entanglement of the normative criteria with the *functions* of the system, along a teleological understanding of normativity. Another issue regards the complex application of the normative layer to the elements (parts, connections, systemic-level) of the descriptive layer, with the possibility of potential normative trade-offs. Again, two transversal features profoundly impact the conceptual work: the emphasis on the deliberative or democratic dimension and the variable importance given to context-sensitivity. The general lesson emerging from this discussion is that much work remains to be done to *conceptualize* and *apply* the normative to the descriptive layer in order to assess (deliberative) democratic systems.

Conclusion

In this chapter, I have tackled the increasing diversity and complexity of the seminal literature on deliberative and democratic systems. I have attempted to systematize this conceptual work in discussing six main questions whose answers largely determine existing conceptions of such systems. By contrasting different answers to these questions, I have put into emphasis their main commonalities and differences. The general outcome of this discussion is the following: several central questions require further careful consideration and sound answers in order to develop a systemic theory of democracy.

To conclude the first part of this book (Chapters 1 and 2), the following remarks are important. If the idea of *system* is not only taken as an illuminating metaphor but rather as the conceptual essence of an innovative approach to democracy, I hope to have shown that much work remains to be done to envision what democratic systems could be. These two chapters were an attempt to reread the progressive emergence of the systemic approach to democracy through a particular lens: the systemic dimension of (deliberative) democracy. This particular rereading has brought to light, or so I hope, the important diversity of conceptions of deliberative/democratic systems in this literature, a diversity that is not only caused by different normative affinities but also by diverging conceptions of the systemic dimension. At the same time, commonalities exist along differences, but remain occulted by a lack of explicit discussion. In addition, only a few aspects have been discussed in the major accounts, and a consistent articulation is still missing. Consequently, the challenge now is to propose a sound theoretical framework of democratic systems. This is precisely the challenge of this book.

In order to do that, the next step will be a critical reengagement with *systems theory*. As discussed in the introduction, systems theory is taken here as a challenging perspective on democratic systems. The aim of the next two chapters is to grasp how systems theory conceptualizes the complexity of systems (*social* systems in Chapter 3, *political* systems in Chapter 4). Since systems theory developed a comprehensive articulation of systemic features, it provides some crucial insights for our theorization of *democratic* systems. On these grounds, in the rest of the book (Chapters 5 to 7) I connect the general features of systems with the specificities of *deliberative/democratic* systems. Some tenets of systems theory will be adapted to our particular object of study: democratic systems. Yet, I contend that we must substantially confront systems theory rather than regarding it with suspicion and unfamiliarity, while borrowing abundantly from its conceptual toolkit.

Systems theory:
3 a critical reappraisal

A meaningful critique of what exists is possible only as an immanent critique of systems [...]. Critique is possible only as the analysis of systems, as the re-exposing of problems that are solved by means of familiar norms, roles, institutions, processes, and symbols, and as the search, for other, functionally equivalent possibilities. (Luhmann 1982a: 120)

In Chapters 1 and 2, the literature on the systemic turn in democratic theory has been thoroughly examined. I focused on "systemness": the features that makes democracy a *system*. Through this close reading of the relevant literature, a range of central issues have emerged: the idea of a functional division of labor; the distinction of several parts of an encompassing whole; the interdependency, connections, and relations between these parts; and the boundaries of the system. These systemic features are central to the systemic approach to democratic theory. Yet so far, this literature hasn't expended much effort on conceptualizing these, nor to articulating them within a coherent theoretical framework. Somehow, democratic theorists endorsing the systemic turn have acted as if *the idea* of a system was clear enough to build a normative theory upon or lead empirical research. Due to this lack of development and confrontation regarding systemness, the systemic turn in democratic theory has so far failed to provide a sound account of *democratic systems*.

As highlighted in the introduction, democratic theorists did not engage with systems theory for several reasons, ranging from its alleged conventional death as a social theory to its reifying and conservative implications, insisting notably on its neglect of individual and collective agency. Yet at the same time, democratic theorists advanced and justified the systemic approach to democracy through several concepts of systems theory. The label of "systems" itself qualifies this distinct approach to democracy, but democratic theorists also made sense of it with the help of other systemic concepts such as emergence, coupling (tight, loose, decoupling), division of labor, differentiation, integration, etc. Democratic scholars also abundantly reemployed the concept of "function," often equating it with the idea of normative criteria. This particular use generated the oxymoron of "normative functions" (Warren 2017: 43), illustrative of the difficulty of bringing together the normative/critical aspirations of democratic theory with the alleged mechanistic functionalism of systems theory.

The tension between rigid functionalism and critical aims was precisely the grounds for a long controversy between two major figures of social theory of the twentieth century: one the one side, one prominent founder of deliberative democracy, Jürgen Habermas, and on the other side, the most influential contributor to modern systems theory, Niklas Luhmann. For Habermas, in line with the Marxist roots of the Frankfurt school, systems theory is a kind of "social technology," ruling out the critical potential of social theory, treating practical questions as technical ones without subjecting them to public discussion, and thus serving the dominant interests rather than exposing them to rational criticism (Kervégan 2003: 137). Moreover, for Habermas, "the systemic approach applied to societies implies the rejection of the distinction between *is* and *ought*," and therefore the possibility of normativity itself (ibid., my translation).

Therefore, the current systemic turn in democratic theory is a revival of the relation and tension of these two streams of ideas, that after having been discussed together, evolved on their own diverging paths.[30] Admittedly, the minimization of subject agency, the absence

---

[30] It must be noted that Habermas in *The Theory of Communicative Action* (in particular volume 2) abundantly employs (Parsonian) social systems theory to develop his own social theory. The distinction of systems and lifeworld, and the subsequent thesis of their uncoupling and of the colonization of the latter by the former, cannot be detached from social systems theory (see Baxter 2011: 45).

of the normal dimension, the lack of critical potential, and the resulting conservative tendency are *still* nowadays the main criticisms raised by democratic theorists against systems theory. It was exactly for these reasons that systems theory was attacked by social scientists in general, and partly abandoned in the seventies and early eighties. The theoretical foundations of systems theory were and are still perceived as not conducive to "a sufficiently radical critique of modern society" (Luhmann 2012: 5). As Luhmann himself states: "The system was understood, not without reason, as something rather technical, as an instrument of planning and modelling social institutions, an ancillary instrument for planners whose intentions were nothing other than repeating, improving, and rationalizing the ruling conditions" (ibid.: 6). Although several theoretical weaknesses of systems theory were pointed out (including by systems theorists themselves), Luhmann makes a point in highlighting that the main source of its rejection relied mostly on *ideological* grounds, precisely because systems theory was seen as inherently conservative (ibid.: 5).

The question arising now is *not* whether the conventional death of systems theory in social sciences is justified, nor what explains democratic theorists current reluctance to reengage with systems theory. The question is whether by rejecting systems theory, democratic scholars are "throwing the baby out with the bathwater." Since the systemic approach to democracy uses many concepts and ideas articulated during the historical development of systems theory, one can legitimately assume that systems theory could to some extent be helpful for democratic theory's current attempts to conceive democracy as a system. Perhaps the entire potential of systems theory has already been exploited by democratic scholars. Thus, it might prove useless to reread systems theory with the explicit aim of enlightening the current debate on democratic theory. However, as suggested in the introduction, the systemic approach to democracy so far relies mostly on a *metaphorical* use of the features of systemness. This metaphorical use was crucial to make the point of the systemic turn, yet it also obscured a large part of the theoretical complexity implied by understanding democracy as a system.

This chapter's starting assumption is that by opening the black box of enlightening metaphors, such as system and function, this theoretical complexity can be apprehended and potentially overcome. Therefore, I consider it necessary to critically reengage with systems theory.

I insist on the *critical* aim of such a rereading of systems theory. The aim is not to adopt an account of systems theory, nor to build an alternative full-fledged systemic theory. The starting assumption is *not* that systems theory (or specific accounts) is "right" and provides us with the key for building a systemic theory of democracy. The point is rather to take systems theory as a constructive antagonist, as a serious challenger for democratic theory. By confronting systems theory and democratic theory, one might perceive some major theoretical issues in a new light, with different challenges and possible solutions.

Arguably, for decades systems theory developed complex and comprehensive articulations of systemness features, later borrowed by democratic theorists and highlighted in Chapters 1 and 2. From these theoretical grounds, we can grasp insights on how to rearticulate these features for our specific purpose. Of course, not every concept "extracted" from systems theory matters for *democratic* systems, and even for *political* ones. Yet it would be a mistake to start directly from existing theories of *political* systems such as David Easton's account (1953). Indeed, an important tenet of systems theory is that "the structures and processes of a system are only possible in relation to an environment, and they can only be understood if considered in this relationship" (Luhmann 1982a: 257). Therefore, to grasp the specificities of the *political* system, we should start with its environment; that is, society as a whole and its other social subsystems. However, *social* systems are also a particular type of system; governed by specific mechanisms but always in accordance with *general patterns* of systems. Accordingly, we must start this discussion with the general essence of systems, the ontology and epistemology of systems theory, followed by the features of *social* systems, and only then the specificities of *political* systems. The next chapter tackles the issues of the *political* system's particularities, as a subsystem of society. Chapter 5 discusses what can make such a political system a *democratic* one. This discussion benefits from insights from systems theory regarding what normativity could be within a social system. This final move paves the way for a discussion on what can "push political systems in democratic directions" (Warren 2017: 41).

Before doing so, a methodological caution is important. Systems theory covers a wide range of the history of social sciences. Most of the founding fathers of sociology were all systems theorists to some extent, notably Durkheim with his "division of labor," but also Marx,

Weber, and Simmel. Besides its long intellectual career, systems theory remains *intrinsically* complex, as it "simulates complexity in order to explain complexity" (Knodt 1995: xix). Furthermore, as Luhmann attacks Parsons' theory with a criticism that certainly also applies to his own, systems theorists were "overly concerned with [their own theoretical] architecture" (Luhmann 1982a: x), developing extremely complex conceptual tools to make sense of it. This internal complexity was even explicitly conscious for Luhmann, who wrote that his "course of argumentation was neither linear nor circular but labyrinthine" (1982a: 270) and that his "theory's design resembles a labyrinth more than a freeway off into the sunset" (1995: lii). In addition, despite its apparent universal pretentions, Luhmann stresses the "unavoidable contingency of systems theory" (Gilgen 2012: xvi) and his intention of "producing contingent (non-necessary) truths" (Luhmann 1982a: 270). Finally, systems theory is characterized by its continuous attempt to bridge divides, between, for instance, theories of action and theories of structure, and by its reluctance to resort to dichotomies such as stability and change, structure and process, consensus and conflict, by insisting instead that one always *presupposes* the other (ibid.: 261). Systems theory's endeavor was indeed an effort to produce a theoretical synthesis, a transdisciplinary and combinatory grand theory of society.

Acknowledging these characteristics of systems theory, this chapter *cannot* be an exhaustive review of systems theory. Contrary to Chapter 1, close reading is here unthinkable. Obviously, not every concept discussed in this chapter will necessarily be employed in the following chapters. Yet, it is important to display most of systems theory's core in order to select from its useful concepts. This reengagement with this theoretical stream is authentically "profane" and highly interpretative. It mostly focuses on Luhmann's systems' theory.

At the outset, I must tackle a straightforward interrogation: *Why Luhmann?* First, because his theoretical account of systems is uncontroversially the most developed and consistent so far. Consequently, one could answer "who else?" to this question, provocatively for sure, but probably rightly so too. One cannot seriously discuss systems theory without dedicating an important section to Luhmann's theory[31] Fur-

---

[31] In the International Encyclopedia of Political Science (Badie et al. 2011), the entry *Systems Theory* (Stichweh 2011b) states: "The two most influential suggestions [of systems theory] were the comprehensive sociological versions of systems theory which were proposed by Talcott Parsons since the 1950s and by Niklas Luhmann since the 1970s."

thermore, systems theory is by essence an interdisciplinary endeavor, and Luhmann pushed interdisciplinarity very far. Indeed, Luhmann's range of theorization is extremely comprehensive: it starts from the highest level of abstraction (with the system/environment difference as the universal explanatory category) to a thick theoretical description of each major social system (politics, religion, art, economy, law, love, family, mass media, education, etc.).

Second, Luhmann built his theory on the grounds of Parsonian structural functionalism and made a considerable effort to diverge from it. A focus on Luhmann's theory thus enables the two major accounts of systems theory to be discussed: Parsons and Luhmann. In addition, Luhmann's theory integrates answers and solutions both to problems of structural functionalism and to critiques from critical theory, raised notably by Jürgen Habermas. From the Luhmannian paradigm, we can thus confront the theory of democratic systems with a systemic perspective that has bypassed most of structural functionalism's shortcomings and which has already been criticized by a parent of contemporary democratic theory (Frankfurt school of critical theory, notably the Habermassian stream). Finally, Luhmann's systems theory is abstract and generic enough to provide some flexibility for its specific application to political and democratic systems. Consequently, it can serve as an appropriate ground to confront democratic theory and systems theory in order to build a theory of *democratic systems*. Moreover, even if systems theory can "only" play the role of a constructive antagonist for democratic theory, this starting point would arguably remain a good one. To be sure, starting from Luhmann's perspective does not imply complete endorsement. This reappraisal will necessarily be selective. His theory is taken here as a challenging inspiration, rather than a standard to adhere to. In line with his epistemology, this chapter will be a critical reappraisal of systems theory *from* the scientific system to which I belong, namely democratic theory, from its own perspective and for its own particular needs.

The chapter is structured as follows. In the first part, I present systems theory as an overarching metatheory. To do so, I start by discussing the ontological and epistemological assumptions of systems theory, with a focus on its anti-reductionist and constructivist features. Then, I display the features of the concept of system at the abstract level of general systems theory, highlighting the transition from the input/output model and the parts-whole tradition to the paradigm of systems-as-difference and autopoietic systems. I conclude this chapter's first part in tempering the main criticisms raised against systems theory: inherent conservatism, predictability, and complete interdependence. In the second part, I switch the focus towards *social* systems. I start by showing how social systems are characterized by *communication* instead of *action*. I then display the three types of social systems composing the whole society, which are differentiated systems of communication. Thereafter, I present the specificities of *functional differentiation* as the type of communicative differentiation characterizing modern society. In particular, I detail the features of functions, codes, and programs as the main elements of functionally differentiated systems. Finally, I show that since a system's programs are not bound to its identity, these can be transformed on purpose by the system itself through self-reflexive processes. Accordingly, I argue that attempts at normative steering should be conceived as the search for normatively superior functionally equivalent programs.

Systems theory

The idea of *system* is very ancient; its origins are pre-Socratic (Pickel 2011). The basic systemic intuition was already put forward by Aristotle, with his famous statement that "the whole is more than the sum of its parts" (see von Bertalanffy 1972: 407). From its Greek roots to the twentieth century, the idea of systems has been firmly present in the works of several prominent thinkers such as Leibniz, Marx, and Darwin (ibid.: 408–409). The label of "systems theory" encompasses a variety of streams, each giving different meanings to the idea of system. Indeed, systems theory belongs to such diverse disciplines as living systems theory, mathematical systems theory, cybernetics, and, of course, social systems theory (Adams et al. 2013). Nonetheless, these streams of systems theory broadly share a specific core ontology: "Everything in the universe is, was, or will be a system or a component of one" (Bunge 2004: 191). This strong claim entails at least the more modest assumptions that "there are systems" (Luhmann 1995: 12) and that "systems are real entities" (Pickel 2011: 247).

"Observing the observer": a glance at the epistemology of systems

At the ontological level, the systemic approach is first and foremost an anti-reductionist perspective. Reductionism is the ontological assumption that wholes are *aggregates* of smaller parts. Anti-reductionism or holism opposes this assumption by putting forward the phenomenon of *emergence*. As in Aristotle's claim that *the whole is more than the sum of its parts*, emergence expresses the idea that wholes have properties that their parts do not have, properties that *emerge* at a certain level of complexity of the articulation of the whole's parts. These diverging ontological premises have two important epistemological implications.

Firstly, reductionists hold that "a satisfactory explanation of a compound reality may be obtained by analyzing, by decomposing it into its components or elements" (Agazzi 1978: 350). In addition, the specification of smaller components is not sufficient for reductionists, since "*the relations between the individual parts* also have to be specified" (Beckenkamp 2006: 6, original emphasis). In this hierarchical understanding of systems, lower levels explain upper levels (Spencer-Smith 1995: 114). Yet, there is a bottom level: "The central claim of reductionism is that these different ways of seeing things are *reducible* to one distinguished way of seeing them" (Beckenkamp 2006: 7, emphasis mine). For instance, this bottom level is cells in biology and atoms in physics. In social sciences, reductionist explanations generally rely on *individual* (inter-)actions and intentions, and thus are closely related to methodological individualism.

Conversely, anti-reductionists or holists oppose this approach on two grounds. First, they contend that "the explananda are irreducible, that even though they may depend on the things to which reductionists appeal – thought on brain cell activity, for example – they have *emergent properties* or powers which cannot be reduced to those of their constituents without residue" (Sayer 2010: 5, original emphasis). Indeed, holists hold that the explanation of some phenomena such as communication or consciousness cannot be reduced to the smallest units composing them, but instead must be understood at *their own level* (Sayer 2005). This holist assumption has been overextended further by some (e.g., Bunge 2001) in suggesting that lower levels would be determined by upper levels, or "structures." This is, however, a misleading distortion of the differences between reductionism and holism to a basic dichotomy between upward and downward causation. Since systems are emergent phenomena, or rather since *every* emergent phenomenon can be conceived as a system, systems theory has been often perceived as holist in this pejorative "structuralist" way. Although systems theory is organically related to the idea of emergence (and therefore to holism), its proposition should not be conflated with downward causation. Indeed, this would be plain wrong, since systems theory is intrinsically against *one-way* or *linear* causality (von Bertanfally 1972: 37). This rejection of one-way causality goes for *both* ways, bottom-up, of course, but also top-down: "The investigation of organized wholes of many variables requires new categories of interaction, transaction, organization, teleology, and so forth" (ibid.). Systems theory, in line with its cybernetic parent, relies strongly on *circular* causality (see Dent & Umpleby 1998), better known as the *feedback* mechanism. As will become clear in this chapter, systems have a *recursive* mode of functioning.

The second epistemological implication regards the role of the *observer* in the construction of scientific knowledge: "Systems epistemology is critical of the empiricist view that perception is a reflection of 'real things' and knowledge an approximation to truth or reality" (Pickel 2011: 242). As such, the epistemology of systems theory leans clearly towards constructivism. The emergences of systems theory (especially its cybernetic branch) and constructivism are even deeply intertwined (Hertig & Stein 2007). Basically, constructivism opposes the idea that there is an objective truth out there to be discovered, grasped, and formalized *as it really is*. Constructivists hold that "it is the observer who 'constructs' his own reality by observing it and thus any statement of the observer about his observation is only his *interpretation* of the observation itself" (ibid.: 2, emphasis mine). This assumption can be confusing since I said earlier that systems theorists generally hold that there are *real* systems. To be sure, "constructivism does not reject the existence of a real world, but only rejects the possibility that the person experiencing the world can obtain a true representation of it" (Rasmussen 1998: 560). Therefore, this position challenges the subject/object dichotomy central to the positivist epistemology. As Luhmann puts it, "the observer does not exist somewhere high above reality [...] nor is he a subject outside the world of objects, [...] he is in the middle of it all" (Luhmann 2012: 101). Indeed, the demarcation between the subject and the object is blurred precisely because, instead of being "objective," this distinction is done *by the subject herself.*

Of course, the scientist as an observer can draw this boundary herself, constructing her object of investigation. This approach was held by the first wave of systems theorists, including Parsons and Easton, coined as "first order" cyberneticians by von Foerster, for their focus on the object, that is, on *observed systems.* Nevertheless, the observer not only constructs the object of investigation, he or she is "part of and interacts with the world he or she is observing" (von Foerster in Rasmussen 1998: 562). Consequently, "second order" cyberneticians focus instead on *observing systems,* including in their analysis "the ways [the] observer's consciousness affects the objects being observed" (Rasmussen 1998: 562). To reach a genuine understanding of their observed system, this approach puts a greater attention on how this system is *observing* itself and its environment.

This shift in focus towards the observer's influence on the observation and the abandonment of the subject/object dichotomy are accompanied by the introduction of the central concept of *self-reference,* closely related to the idea of *autopoiesis.* In a nutshell, the biologists Maturana & Varela invented the term "autopoiesis" to characterize biological systems' "self-reproduction of life by those elements that have in turn been produced in and by the living system" (Luhmann 2012: 43). Two related features are important here: the centrality of the "self" and the obvious circularity (or recursivity) *from* the self *to* the self. Autopoiesis, as the idea that a system creates its own operations only from its own previous operations, is conceptually dependent upon *operational closure*: the systems' operations are only possible inside a system, they are "closed" within its boundaries and cannot intervene in its environment, and conversely. Therefore, the system's operations, being exclusively its own, are what *distinguish it from its environment,* and each operation recursively reproduces this distinction. Precisely, it is the operation of *observation,* or rather *self*-observation, that produces this distinction.[32] Again, the circularity or recursivity is central since the "observation is produced by a system that in turn is produced by the observation" (ibid.: 102). Consequently, "the distinction between

---

[32]   For Luhmann, to observe means to draw *distinctions*, since "nothing can be observed without distinction" (2012: 103).

system and environment depends on the system's own observation, which distinguishes self- and hetero-reference" (Gilgen 2012: xv). Put otherwise, the difference between a system and its environment *is* the difference between self- and hetero-reference (Rasmussen 1998: 564).

As we see now, Luhmann replaces the subject/object dichotomy with the system/environment distinction. Moreover, since observations are operations, observers operate themselves. As Luhmann explains: "On the one hand, the observer observes operations; on the other hand, he is himself an operation" (2012: 102). Consequently, the observer *is* always a system, a self-reflective system that observes itself, and from there, not itself too. In case of self-observation, the observer is "either the system itself, or a reflective part or specifically developed moment of reflection inside the system" (ibid.: 108). For instance, regarding the legal system, the *doctrine* is the legal system observing and describing itself (Kervégan 2003: 150). Each system has its own "rationality" (Rabault 1999: 464), and we must add, *bounded* rationality[33] because of the system's operational closure and self-referential observation. A system understands the world only through the perception that it has of itself (ibid. 452). Furthermore, for Luhmann "rationality refers only to the system, not the world" (2012: 136). An important epistemological implication is that a theory must, when describing a system, consider how *this system describes itself.* Thus, the resulting methodological directive is to *observe the observer.* Second-order observation is indeed the observation of a system's operations of self-observation, hence Luhmann's *operative constructivism.*

A second epistemological implication regards the status of knowledge, and precisely of scientific knowledge. Because of the systems' operational closure, each system constructs its own reality and its own knowledge of its reality. Knowledge is *immanent,* bounded by the autopoietic operations of systems; its content is "integrated to the context of its own development" (Rabault 1999: 464). A functionally differentiated society hence implies the coexistence of a plurality of self-descriptions and thus somehow features an "exacerbation of relativity" (ibid.: 457). Scientific knowledge is not an exception in that regard: the scientific system is no longer "beyond all systems" (Luhmann 2012: 39), it is a self-referential system observing *its* knowledge. Scientific

---

[33] Luhmann relies here on the seminal work of Herbert A. Simon (1982).

truth is thus curtailed to be a "partial semantic" (Rabault 2015: 214).[34] However, Luhmann attributes to science a special capacity of knowledge production: "The scientific system can analyze other systems from perspectives that are not accessible to them, [that is] discover and thematize latent structures and functions" (Luhmann 1995: 14). This assumption relies upon the belief that, although complexity cannot be observed as such but only *reduced* through observations, "science can survey, comprehend and control more complexity than any other subsystem of society" (Luhmann 1982a: 362). Systems *theory*, as a *reduction* of real-world complexity, is a sound illustration of that optimistic belief.

Accordingly, we can clearly notice that systems theory is more than a theory *about systems* as a specific object. Systems theory is a "super-theory" (Rabault 1999: 452) or "meta-theory" (Hertig & Stein 2007: 15) aiming to be universally applicable. Any investigation, any field of study from physics to politics, could borrow the lens of systems theory to attempt to grasp *some* of the complexity of the real world. Moreover, systems theory has the amazing particularity of applying its explanatory scheme to itself, "[subsuming] itself to a systemic perspective" (Adams et al. 2013: 5). The reason being that "systems research is itself a system; it cannot formulate its basic concepts so that it would not itself come under that concept" (Luhmann 1995: 482). In that sense, systems theory is "autological"; it (re-)produces its own ontological and epistemological grounds. Systems theory is a conceptual system to observe actual systems.

To summarize this section, systems theory rejects the epistemological stance of reductionism, holding instead that most phenomena (systems in particular) are *emergent*. At the same time, it also rejects the holistic view that those emergent phenomena causally determine the smaller units they encompass. Instead, it endorses a complex conception of circular or recursive causation. In addition, the Luhmannian vein of systems theory is a constructivist paradigm, where reality cannot be grasped as such by external observers. It abandons the subject/object dichotomy and replaces it with the focus on self-reference and self-observation. As such, it shifts the focus of scientific inquiry from *observed* systems to *self-observing* systems. Consequently,

---

[34] The same goes *within* the scientific system, as each of its subsystems (disciplines) distinguishes itself from all the others.

Luhmann's operative constructivism invites scientists to observe how systems observe themselves.

Despite its great sophistication and encompassing ambition, systems theory does not have predictive power (Luhmann 2012: 37), and its explanatory power is quite limited (Hertig & Stein 2007: 12). Systems theory for Luhmann is instead a "heuristic tool to approach problems in a different and thus more creative and innovative way" (ibid.). In Luhmann's words, the real achievement of systems theory is in providing "the possibility of inserting probes into the established conceptual language and to see whether it still works or has to be changed" (Luhmann 2012: 139). In accordance with this particular epistemology, systems theory is taken here as a "probe" into the solid conceptual foundations of democratic theory. Before applying systems theory to democratic theory, or reading and reconstructing the latter with the former's lens, it is first necessary to lay down the complex conceptual scheme of what systems are. In order to do so, the basic features and evolutions of *general systems theory* have to be presented. In a second phase, the discussion of the specificities of *social* systems provides the conceptual tools to question in the next chapter what a *political* system is.

What are systems? An outlook on general systems theory

Systems are *complex* entities. Actually, systems are even characterized by complexity, or more precisely by a certain kind: *organized* complexity. This oxymoron is the starting point of systems theory: "How is organized complexity possible?" (Knodt 1995: xvii).[35] To answer this question, we first must consider the notion of *complexity*. For Luhmann, complexity means "the totality of possible events" (Luhmann 1982a: 147). The concept of complexity articulates two fundamental notions of systems theory: *elements (or components)* and *relations* (Luhmann 2012: 124). Elements are the units of the system that cannot be reduced further. Yet, elements are not "ontically pre-given, [...] [an] element is constituted as a unity only by the system that enlists it as an element to use in relations" (Luhmann 1995: 22). They always stand in relation to other elements, otherwise they are not part of a

---

[35] This basic question has often led to related ones such as how organizations can be *stable* or in *equilibrium*.

system. As von Bertalanffy (1972: 411) describes it, *organized* complexity is "the interrelations between many but not infinitely many components." This situation comes from the fact that a multiplication of a system's elements implies a greater increase in the *possibilities* of relations for each single element. The "quality" of each element depends on the extent of its "connectivity requirements" (Luhmann 2012: 124): an element can hardly be connected to every other element beyond a certain threshold (depending, of course, on the system under consideration). Therefore, "from a certain size upwards, each element can no longer be connected with every other, and relations can now be created only *selectively*" (ibid., emphasis mine). The necessity to be selective implies a *reduction of complexity* leading to a structured or organized complexity.

Selectivity determines which events occur in a system. The fact that systems have to be selective in their internal and external relations is the reason why there can be such a diversity of systems made of the same units (e.g., atoms or organic cells). Consequently, reduction of complexity is both what systems *do* and what systems *are*: "Without it, there would be nothing, no world consisting of discrete entities, but only undifferentiated chaos" (Knodt 1995: xvii). While organized complexity is central to systems theory, its conception has profoundly evolved. Therefore, we can grasp some major mutations in the conception of systems by tracking the evolution of the way organized complexity is conceived.

A. Parts, wholes, and input-output relations

Before the autopoietic turn advocated by Luhmann, systems were primarily conceived as "open systems"; open because systems exchange something with their environment. This exchange between a system and its environment was understood in terms of input/output relations: inputs being what the system *gets* from the environment, outputs being what the system *exports* back to it. For instance, in the field of politics, Easton's conception of the political system (1953) followed perfectly the input/output model. For him, inputs are demands and supports for actions, while politics is a *transformative* mechanism (i.e., a system) producing outputs as the "authoritative allocations of values" (ibid.: 319). This basic understanding of the input/output relation is mechanistic: systems are machines transforming various inputs into various outputs *in a predictable way*; the same inputs always produce the same outputs. Moreover, this model often contends that the system is autonomous from its environment, meaning that it can choose among environmental factors "on what it has to rely on as its input, and what it passes on to its environment as its outputs" (Luhmann 2012: 30). Therefore, systems were broadly conceived as stable and reliable, as machines would be. The *mechanistic* connotation of systems theory largely comes from that conception.

However, systems theorists faced empirical cues that this model was often misleading. Indeed, different inputs can produce similar outputs, and the same inputs can produce different outputs (Luhmann 2012: 31). Therefore, the regularity of a transformative mechanism, by which they identified a system, was not always so reliable. Moreover, the input/output model of systems left unanswered the question of what is actually going on *within* a system. Due to these shortcomings, the idea of input/output itself has been widely abandoned by Luhmann and other systems theorists. As we will see in detail below in the discussion of *autopoietic* systems, "there is no inputs of elements into the system and no outputs of elements from the system" (Luhmann 2012 in Echeverria 2020: 100). Instead, the environment creates *perturbations* or *irritations* for a system, that will select among those it considers as relevant or not. These perturbations are not inputs, first because the environment does not necessarily direct them towards the system, second because it is the system that selects which ones are to be treated, and third because the reaction to these perturbations "is entirely dependent on the specific structures and characteristics of this system" (Echeverria 2020: 103). The same goes for outputs, as the system "producing" them cannot decide on behalf of another system whether these "outputs" will be considered by this other system, and how they will be treated if considered as relevant. Consequently, the input/output model was supplanted by a model of autopoietic systems where systems are more autonomous from one another, and where interactions between them are seen as processes of indirect and mutual influence.

When opening the black box of what is going on *within* systems, one is quickly tempted to distinguish *parts* of an encompassing whole. This is quite intuitive, and precursors of systems thinking such as Aristotle thought in these terms. Systems were then understood as composed of parts in standing and stable relationships. Therefore, the focus was mostly on subsystem-to-subsystem relationships, as parts of a more encompassing system. The problem is that there are different levels of "subsystems," in the sense that subsystems themselves potentially have subsystems. In consequence, "the parts themselves [have] to be differentiated into higher and lower elements with different affinities to the whole" (Luhmann 1982a: 235n7). Moreover, this understanding presupposes a *unity* of systems as encompassing wholes and a *unity* of parts as the units composing them. However, for Luhmann, "[a system] is not made up of small units that constitute larger units, it is rather based on differences that constitute more differences" (Moeller 2006: 40). Indeed, Luhmann sees a paradox in considering the unity of something that is made of continuously changing parts hence is always changing itself (Luhmann 1982a: 37). He contends that difference (or distinction), rather than unity, constitutes the essence of a system. And the relevant distinction for a system is always from *its own* environment (see above the discussion on *self*-reference). For Luhmann, what matters is not merely "the internal ordering of the parts of a whole, but instead the systems' negotiations with its environment" (ibid.). Therefore, Luhmann replaces the ontological distinction between parts and whole with the difference between system and environment.

This shift does not totally suppress the idea of the unity of a system, or its identity as a specific system. The challenge now becomes to conceive the *unity of a difference*. Luhmann's theory then states that the system's unity is the replication of its difference with its environment. Indeed, for Luhmann "the system is the unity of the system/environment difference" (Brunczel 2010: 42). In that sense, "the unity of the system and the distinction between system and environment coincide" (Gilgen 2012: xi). Since subsystems replicate the distinction between the system and its environment, this occurs also *within* the system, as Luhmann explains:

> System differentiation does not mean that the whole is divided into parts and, seen on this level, then consists only of the parts and the "relation" between the parts. It is rather that every subsystem reconstructs the comprehensive system to which it belongs and which it contributes to forming through its own (subsystem-specific) difference between system and environment. Through system differentiation, the system multiplies itself, so to speak, within itself through ever-new distinctions between systems and environment in the system. The

differentiation process can set in spontaneously; it is a result of evolution, which can use opportunities to launch structural changes. It requires no coordination by the overall system such as the schema of the whole and its parts had suggested. (Luhmann 2013 in Echeverria 2020: 103)

This focus on the system/environment difference has also the major implication of "de-ontologizing" or "de-essentializing" systems. Systems are how they are not in virtue of an objective essence, but as a result of a continuous *process of differentiation* (Dubé 2017: 387). They could be otherwise: in their core identity, and in their structures and operations of replication of this identity. Consequently, the idea of *contingency* is central to the approach of *systems-as-difference*. In sum, as an alternative to both the input/output model and the parts/whole tradition, Luhmann advances the idea of systems as difference, better known as autopoietic or self-referential systems.

B. Systems and environment: autopoiesis, operational closure, and structural coupling

As discussed above, autopoietic systems are operationally closed within their own boundaries from their environment. Their specificity lies in their ability to produce and maintain these boundaries, through the circular or recursive operation of self-reference. This means that "systems refer to themselves (be this to elements of the same system, to operations of the same system, or to the unity of the same system) in constituting their elements and their elemental operations" (Luhmann 1995: 9). In other words, systems recreate themselves, that is, their distinction from their environment, by a constant reproduction of this distinction. Yet systems need an environment in which to exist, that is, from which to *be differentiated*; thus "boundary maintenance is system maintenance" (Luhmann 1995: 17). In consequence, only autopoietic or self-referential *operations* belong to the system: everything else is part of the system's environment.

There are a few important remarks regarding the system's environment. First, there is no such thing as *the* environment, something common to all systems (except the whole universe). There are system environments: each system has its *own* environment. Plus, unlike systems, environments do not have boundaries: they are instead characterized by "open horizons" (ibid.). Second, other systems might be part of a system's environment. For instance, in the environment of political systems, there are other social systems such as the legal and economic systems. But environments are not systems in themselves; thus "the environment has no self-reflection or capacity to act" (ibid.). Consequently, they do not produce inputs *for* the system. Rather, they create "perturbations" for the system that it will or will not deal with internally. Third, systems cannot consider every possible perturbation, they must *select* some. In this context, "the environment becomes relevant as a circumstance which impacts on any selection event in the system" (Stichweh 2011a: 294). It is by observing its environment, and selecting perturbations and reactions to these perturbations, that the system becomes differentiated from its environment, that is, "itself." It can then refer to itself, and from there, not itself: the reference to the environment (hetero-reference) is only possible from self-reference.

This abstract insight into the boundaries between a system and its environment triggers the question of the *interactions* between these two. The general idea is that the basic operations or major transformations of autopoietic systems are produced *internally*, rather than being caused by inputs from their environment. In other words, through a constant recursive operation, "everything that is used as a unit by the system is produced by the system itself" (Luhmann 1990: 3 in Hertig & Stein 2007: 10). It means more concretely that "everything which functions as a unity in a system – element, operation, structure, boundary – is due to the production processes of the system itself" (Stichweh 2011a: 300). Therefore, nothing can be imported from outside regarding the basic functioning of systems. This does not mean that autopoietic systems are closed, that is, hermetic to environmental stimuli. Autopoietic systems are thus only *operationally* closed, hence meaning that "their capacity to respond to such external stimuli is restricted by their system-specific codes" (Knodt 1994: 82). Indeed, operational closure guarantees the system's observation and interaction with the environment *from its own perspective* and *through its own operations*. Therefore, it is precisely because a system is operationally closed that it can refer to itself as a system distinct from its environment, and therefore "conceive" that it has an environment which is outside itself.

An *operation* is "an occurrence on the level of elements, which are indispensable for the preservation and change of the system" (Luhmann 1995: 49). Operations are events with momentary existence: the sequential succession of operations provide some temporal continuity to a system. That is why operations rely on previous operations; thus, operations can only exist if they connect to each other. *Structures* are "the set of constraints governing the system's internal processes" (Poli 2010: 14). Structures limit and orient "the connectibility of operations" (Brunczel 2010: 50), or more accurately, "structures are *expectations* in relation to the connectivity of operations" (Luhmann 2012: 72, emphasis mine).

Structures and operations are deeply interlinked and have a "circular relationship" (ibid.). A structure is built only through operations and exists as long as operations use and reproduce this structure. A structure is not fixed but is instead "an emergent order that is dynamic and continuously changing" (Knodt 1995: xxviii). Operations are constrained by the structures, which limit the possibilities of operations and operation connectibility. In consequence, a system cannot be open towards its environment at the level of its operations, because these can only occur within it. However, a system can "connect" with its environment when its structures "are formed in contact with the structures of another system" (Stichweh 2011a: 300). This allows two systems to be connected, "coupled" at the level of their structures, which orient operations between them. The structural couplings of systems are "relatively stable links of irritation that force other systems to resonate with them" (Moeller 2006: 39). Being structurally coupled, each system "[interprets] the outputs of the other in its own terms on a continuous basis" (King & Thornhill 2003: 33). To illustrate, the legal and political systems are each operationally closed, yet structurally coupled together: the process of *legislation* is a structural connection between them, where each understands and integrates the other's perturbations through its own operations and from its own perspective.

Structural coupling is thus the only way systems can be connected to other systems in their environment: "The causalities that occur between system and environment are located *exclusively* in the domain of structural coupling" (Luhmann 2012: 85, emphasis mine). Structural coupling is a way to process complexity. Environments are always more complex than systems, as the latter are reductions of complexity. Take, for instance, the brain as a system. Through the eyes and ears, the brain is *structurally coupled* with its environment, full of "noise" and "forms" as perturbations. Indeed, the eyes and ears can and must reduce the complexity of what occurs in the environment, in order for the brain to make it intelligible for itself. Listening and seeing are selective mechanisms, reductions of external complexity, allowing the brain to build internal complexity, for instance, complex ideas or feelings. Consequently, "the reduction of complexity is the condition of the increase in complexity" (Luhmann 2012: 86). Structural coupling is thus a basic process of the functioning of systems: the development of systems' internal structures and the connectibility of operations depends on it.

Structural coupling is potentially unlimited, but it faces a major limitation: it must be compatible with autopoiesis. In other words, structures can vary greatly, as long as they do not interfere with the operational self-reproduction of the system (that is, to maintain itself as a differentiated system). What is reproduced through autopoiesis is the *capacity to self-reproduce* and not specific content (since this evolves continuously). A system can transform or abandon structures and create new ones, as long as these structures are at least *functionally* equivalent to the previous structures, hence maintaining the autopoiesis of the system. I discuss in the second part of this chapter what the *function* is for a system. For now, it is important to stress that structures and their countless possible different shapes are constrained by the *function* of the system. The function is the unmodifiable feature of a system, as it is its *raison d'*être, it portrays its identity as a system distinct from its environment.

When they are structurally coupled with systems in their environment, systems remain *relatively autonomous*. This means that a system has "the ability to settle upon selective criteria for transactions with the environment and to change them if need be" (Luhmann 1982a: 142). On the one hand, systems are completely dependent on the environment, in the sense that there must be some compatibility with it in order to be structurally coupled with it. Accordingly, the structures of a system must be compatible with its environment. On the other hand, systems are fully autonomous in the operational realm, only structural coupling must be compatible with autopoiesis. Why is this idea of relative autonomy important? First, because it implies that if two systems are structurally coupled, they are to some extent co-dependent: they rely on each other's complexity to develop internal complexity. More concretely, it implies that no system dominates another, "no system can exert influence without itself being influenced" (Moeller 2006: 39). If systems can influence each other, they remain strictly separate in operational terms: they cannot *overlap*. Nevertheless, two systems might *interpenetrate* each other at some points. The interpenetration of two systems implies that an "active operation of a system depends on complex achievements and conditions that must be guaranteed in the environment" (Luhmann 1982a: 196), that is, in another system. In short, interpenetration requires a system to condition some of its operations on the operation of another system.

Second, relative autonomy also applies to the structural couplings *within* systems.[36] It could be considered that systems are characterized by a complete interdependence of their internal elements, in the sense that everything is connected with everything else. Consequently, one could conclude that a change in one element will thus mechanically produce changes in all the other elements. However, complete interdependence is not an ideal of connectivity, nor a likely empirical condition of a system. As we said earlier, complexity requires selectivity: the systems' elements are not *all* connected to one another. Accordingly, the connection of some elements does not necessarily mean causal determinacy. Instead of complete interdependence, the idea of "loose coupling" has been proposed, generally framed in opposition to the concept of "tight coupling," which is seen both as a non-desirable and unlikely state for systems.

Coupling means that elements are structurally connected and therefore have "some degree of determinacy" on one another (Orton & Weick 1990: 204). The *loose* intensity of coupling suggests that these elements remain "subject to spontaneous changes and preserve some degree of independence and indeterminacy" (ibid.). Inversely, when elements are *tightly* coupled, a perturbation at the level of one element is very likely to deeply impact all the elements to which it is tightly coupled, and therefore it could also impact the entire system. For instance, state planned economies are a good example of tight coupling between the political and economic systems. In social

---

[36] If one has carefully followed the presentation of the theory, one would have noticed that there is actually no difference between the relations of a system and its environment, and the relations between parts of a system, since each part is a (sub)system itself within an environment

systems, "if social processes are tightly coupled, conflicts spread" (Luhmann 2012: 252). A single perturbation then triggers an immediate and significant change in the system. Instead, *loose coupling* maintains the responsiveness between elements, but this responsiveness is counterbalanced by distinctiveness (Orton & Weick 1990: 204). Elements still influence one another, but this influence is sudden (rather than continuous), negligible (rather than significant), indirect (rather than direct), occasional (rather than constant), and eventual (rather than immediate) (ibid.). Thus, loose coupling somehow depicts the paradox of a system as something that is simultaneously *stable* and *flexible*. In loosely coupled social systems, conflicts can be contained or isolated and therefore do not spread as they would in tightly coupled ones. The system deals "locally" with the perturbations coming from the environment or other (sub-)systems. Since only specific elements or networks of elements are affected by these single perturbations, they do not produce substantial transformations for the whole system. For instance, in most modern societies, political and religious systems are generally loosely coupled: a doctrinal change is unlikely to trigger a change in government. For Luhmann, loose coupling is the condition for the relative stability of constantly evolving social systems:

> The thesis that stability, contrary to what the old of systems theory had assumed, is based precisely on the interruption of connections, on loose coupling, and on the non-proliferation of effects, is in turn compatible with the thesis of the omnipresence of conflicts and possibilities for conflict, and of society's dependence on the most diverse possibilities of holding such conflicts in check. (Luhmann 2012: 252)

Loose coupling is thus conceived by Luhmann as the appropriate intensity for the connections of the systems' elements, in comparison to tight coupling. More than tight coupling, loose coupling between and within systems simultaneously favors both operational closure and structural openness. Loose coupling is thus considered as the standard coupling intensity of systems that are both stable and dynamic.

Summary

To summarize the first part of this chapter, the epistemological status of systems theory and its diverse ways of conceptualizing systems have been surveyed. As a metatheory, systems theory proposes a framework to perceive *any* empirical phenomenon as evolving through a system-environment relationship. It starts from a genuine acceptance of the world's complexity, assuming it can only be grasped through a theoretical reduction of this complexity. Its resulting conceptual apparatus hence remains relatively complex and abstract. Moreover, systems theory opposes conventional views of the scientific community, such as linear causality to which it favors circular causality, or the positivist/empiricist misleading faith in the objectivity of the external observer. To this latter view, systems theory relies on the constructivist perspective to advocate second-order observation as a methodological guideline, precisely because each system self-produces its own bounded rationality. With an epistemological perspective congruent with its conceptualization of systems as its object, or vice-versa, systems theory is well armed to serve as a "critical probe" within *any system*, whether empirical or theoretical/conceptual.

In order to apply it to the realm of political systems and to the normative apparatus of democratic theory, the idea of system required some additional substance. This brief survey of general systems theory shows that system as a concept is far from being self-evident, nor conventionally settled as attested by its historical evolutions. Instead, it is straightforward that if *system* is a central operative concept, its intrinsic complexity and its implications cannot be grasped through a group of definitions. Even the above pages of articulated summary are probably too reductive to be an exhaustive and reliable depiction of the subtleties of systems theory in general, and of the Luhmannian approach in particular. However, I hope it has at least achieved two broad goals.

The first is to prove the usefulness of a critical reappraisal of systems theory for democratic theory, but also more broadly for political science and social sciences in general. In particular, I consider as crucial insights the abandonment of both the input/transformation/output model, and the parts-whole paradigm. The reason is that these are still largely, in democratic theory, the frame for the depiction of systems (see Chapters 1 and 2). In this field, the shift towards autopoietic systems (and the Luhmannian paradigm in general) has not been considered yet. Hence, the autopoietic perspective might prove enlightening for our discussion on the political system. It does not mean that this perspective must necessarily be endorsed, but only that by considering it can we challenge our current understanding of political systems. This is a task I tackle in Chapter 4.

The second aim is to put aside a number of criticisms that somehow prevent democratic theorists from tackling systems theory in depth. It does not mean that these are necessarily irrelevant critiques, only that if they are taken for granted, they prevent meticulous examinations to temper them. I am thinking here notably of the critique of the inherent conservatism of systems theory. For Luhmann's systems theory, systems are ever-changing entities. Their continuous transformation is inevitable; the point of systems theory is to suggest that this change is a particular process, a *structured* or *orderly* process. It is true that systems tend to preserve their own identity by reiterations of their distinction from their environment. As such, it is correct to consider that they lean towards self-reproduction, which we could incorrectly equate to self-*conservation*. Indeed, since environments are constantly evolving, so too are the self-referential operations of a specific system, and therefore this goes too for their boundaries and their internal complexity. If systems "aim" to reproduce themselves, they inevitably change in doing so. Furthermore, autopoietic systems are changing in *unpredictable* ways: they are not machines that can be manipulated from the outside. Systems instead have at their disposal several alternative answers to external perturbations: "It is precisely upon this elasticity that [a system's] stability rests" (Luhmann 1982a: 38). Another commonplace notion destabilized in this survey is the idea of *complete interdependence*, and its more striking implication: a slight change at the level of one element will impact the entire system. Instead, structural coupling as the connective mechanism, and loose coupling as the connective intensity required to allow internal stability and flexibility, provide a richer and more complex depiction of the relations between and within systems, one which properly depicts a system as a *relatively autonomous organized complexity*.

Now that we know more about systems in general, we can turn our attention towards a special type of systems: *social* systems, which are characterized by some specific features. In addition, I introduce a few central concepts not discussed in this presentation of systems theory, such as *functions* and *codes*. The presentation of the features of social systems will provide the material we will use in the following chapters to tackle a theoretical reconstruction of what a *political* system is (Chapter 4), and what a *democratic* one could be (Chapter 5).

Society and social systems

Society is a system. That is the basic assumption systems theorists endorse when studying society. However, this assumption faces some particular obstacles because society is a very particular system. To start with, society is not a clearly delimited object of study as would be a machine or an organism, for example. Plus, its internal functioning is harder to understand. This pushed Parsons to suggest that his theory of social systems is only a *second-best* theory, trying to determine what are the *minimal* conditions of existence (and persistence) of a society. Parsons thus drew an ad hoc list of minimal conditions of existence (or functions), based on the assumption that some domains were *necessarily* parts of any society, such as the economy and politics. Parsons' theory was then structural-functional: it starts "with given social structures which are subsequently analyzed in their functionality" (Stichweh 2011a: 293). Luhmann proceeds the other way around: from social problems as *functions*, he questions and compares the capacity of existing yet contingent social structures to solve these problems (ibid.). Moreover, he contends that if we consider as non-contingent the current existing domains in our society, we cannot critically assess *this* particular shape of society and potentially seek other societal realities (Luhmann 1982a: 59). For these reasons, against Parsonian structural functionalism, Luhmann rejects the rigidity of "necessary functions" and instead places *contingency* at the heart of his theory of society: contingency of the features of society and of social theories themselves.

Another analytical issue is that society has no clear-cut criteria of persistence: contrary to living organisms, it is not clear when a society ceases to be, or when it is so deeply transformed that another society replaces it. For Luhmann, a social system can be deeply transformed without becoming another system, that is, without changing its core identity. From this assumption, Luhmann shifts the problem of functionalism from *maintenance/persistence* to *transformation*. A final problem is that society was defined, or rather societies were compared, by reference to some salient features: for instance, capitalist societies or liberal societies. This frame gives primacy to one of the functional domains of a society (respectively, the economic and political realms in these examples). For Luhmann, it is misleading to characterize societies by their (allegedly) most salient feature. On the contrary, society as a generic concept must encompass all possible forms of differentiated society and all possible differentiated subsystems (Luhmann 1982a: xii). Accordingly, the conceptualization of society must put at its heart the *process of systems differentiation*. In order to present this particular perspective on society, I start with a discussion on what society is "made of."

What is society made of? From action to communication

To start with, in opposition to most sociological approaches, systems theory considers that society is *not* composed of an aggregation of individuals. This crucial point will be discussed later in relation to the issue of agency, but for now it is important to stress that *individuals* are outside society, and even outside *any* social system. Why is this so? Parsons famously considered that "the actor is subordinated to the action" (Luhmann 2012: 9), and not the reverse. This means that the actor is only one precondition among others (e.g., the context of action) for the realization of action; actors are only one moment of action. Actually, an action as a single act is an *emergent* property of systems of action. Indeed, interactions between individual actors create systems coordinating actions; and action-systems are relational schemes structuring interactions (Parsons 1951). Agreeing partly with Parsons' assumption, Luhmann nevertheless considers that "action" is not a good candidate to constitute the elementary unit of a theory of social systems. Indeed, he stresses that action is actually not so *relational* after all, in the sense that actions are not limited to social contexts; an action can be a "solitary operation" (Gilgen 2012: xi). Plus, action alone cannot "generate its own continuance" (ibid.), and therefore it cannot function and reproduce itself as a system. Instead of action, Luhmann favors communication as the "stuff" social systems are made of.

Communication is the central concept of Luhmann's theory of social systems. To understand it, I must first discuss a related concept: *meaning*. Contrary to systems such as organisms and machines, psychic and social systems are characterized by their use of meaning (instead of matter and energy, for instance) in their interactions with their environments. The complexity of the respective environments of psychic and social systems is a complexity made of meaning, that is, of *possibilities* of specific meanings. Meaning has "an actual/potential form" (Arnoldi 2001: 7); a specific meaning is "the conjunction of a horizon of possibilities with selection or choice" (Luhmann 1982a: 345). An actual meaning is meaningful because of the simultaneous existence of potential meanings, that could have been selected but were not. Therefore, it is through the *medium*[37] of meaning that psychic and social systems process and reduce complexity, by making selections of specific meanings.

While in psychic systems this process of meaning-selection takes the form of consciousness, in social systems it takes the form of communication. Social systems are processes of communication: "They include all events that for them have quality of communication" (Luhmann

---

[37] The concept of *medium* is pivotal in Luhmann's theory, and intervenes at different layers of abstraction, including at the specific level of *social* systems. I present in this footnote the generic conceptualization of medium. A medium is "an area of loose couplings of abundant elements, such as particles in the air or physical carriers of light" (Luhmann 2012: 164). Light is a medium that can take many different forms (e.g., a rainbow or a shadow); language is a medium that can take many different forms through countless possible articulations of words in sentences; sentences are then specific forms of the medium of language. A medium is then "the relatively elastic realm of possibilities from which form selects a certain and no other possibility" (Luhmann 1987: 107). Forms are the temporary transitions from the loose coupling of countless possible elements (medium) to the tight coupling of some of these elements (specific forms). A medium is invisible, while forms are visible: a medium is only perceptible through the forms it takes and is always reproduced by creating forms. Medium and forms are "linked together as two sides of one distinction" (Guy 2019: 138): one cannot exist without the other. A medium can take a vast number of forms; and "if restrictions occur it is because products of form mutually disturb each other" (Luhmann 1987: 103). For instance, a government (form B) supplants another (form A), but both are forms of the medium of power. As illustrations of the encompassing character of the concept of medium, the following elements are media: light, language, meaning, communication, money, power, law, truth, etc.

1990: 5). They are an uninterrupted chain of connected communicative events. It must be specified that communication can take a wide variety of forms, such as language, gestures, sound, images, power, money, etc. As we will see in detail below, society encompasses all the specific communications produced by specific social systems, from face-to-face interactions to whole systems such as the political system.

The concept of communication is not understood by Luhmann as a *transmission* of preformed information between a sender and a receiver through a specific channel, it is rather a process of *coordination* between two or more psychic systems, where none of them is in complete control of the process (Guy 2019). Since the selection of an action by a psychic system is to some extent a *precondition* for the selection of an action by another psychic system, these two systems must *coordinate* their actions. Communication systems (and therefore social ones) exist only insofar as there is a need for coordination. It is important to understand that communication is *necessary* to create and stabilize (continuously evolving) structures of expectations that orient actions, and thus allow *coordination*. Importantly, communication facilitates coordination, by absorbing *some* of its uncertainty; it does so by "stabilizing expectations, not by stabilizing behavior" (Luhmann 1995 in Guy 2019: 147). As such, social structures are *expectational* structures.

Communication can be defined as "a synthesis of three selections: information (a selection from a repertoire of referential possibilities), utterance (a selection from a repertoire of intentional acts), and understanding (the observation of the distinction between utterance and information)" (Knodt 1995: xxvii). Therefore, communication is achieved when these three selections are realized, that is, when *understanding* (including *mis*understanding) is reached between the persons in communication. However, communicators A and B, for instance, are "black boxes for each other" (Arnoldi 2001: 5): both have different expectations about the other that are unknown to the other, thus they cannot predict each other's reactions. In addition, both expect that the other expects something about him/her. As a consequence, when in interaction, A and B are necessarily in a situation of *double contingency*. This situation means that *both* of them "make their behavior contingent on the behavior of the other" (Knodt 1995: xxviii). For Parsons, contingency was understood as "depending on," but for Luhmann, contingency expresses the idea that current things could have been otherwise.

Thus, Luhmann reframes double contingency as a situation where "both know that both know that one could also act differently" (Vanderstraeten 2002: 77). For Parsons, double contingency was a *paralyzing* situation solved by the orientation of both behaviors towards supposedly preexisting normative consensuses. For Luhmann, double contingency is instead "positive" in *initiating* communication (as a contingency-reducing process through the three selections mentioned above). This process of communication "inevitably constitutes a social system as a network of meaningful reciprocal selections – which reproduces the very problem of double contingency" (ibid.: 88). Therefore, communication *temporarily* solves the problem of double contingency, since this situation is inevitably recreated by communication. To temporarily solve the problem of double contingency means "forming complementary expectations and enacting suitable actions and action sequences" (Luhmann 2012: 236), that is, *coordination*.

However, there is, of course, a "negation potential" inherent in communication; that is, the possibility to deceive the other's expectations. Indeed, "every proposition, every demand opens up many possibilities for negation: not this but that, not this way, not now, and so forth" (Luhmann 1995: 154). But negation always comes *after* understanding. Therefore, it is important to note that the acceptance or rejection of a specific communicated meaning is outside the act of communication itself. Actually, "one must distinguish the addressee's understanding of the selection of meaning that has taken place from acceptance or rejection of that selection as a premise of the addressee's own behavior" (Luhmann 1995: 147). Indeed, a communicative event *creates* a situation for acceptance or rejection of this meaning, as a precondition for subsequent actions or communications. For this reason, communication opens the possibility for further communication; it therefore recreates itself, and in this sense, communication is an *autopoietic* system.

As such, a communication system reproduces itself continuously and recursively: "Each new operation of communication builds on the preceding operations by referring back to them, either to expand on them or, on the contrary, to correct, contradict or reject them" (Guy 2019: 149). The communication system is then referring to itself through each of its operations, forming a self-reproducing chain of events. This process implies the continuous construction, transformation, and replacement of structures conditioning the shape of possible further communications. Of course, communication requires the contribution of psychic systems (that is, "individuals") to continue its course. However, the people standing in communication do not *directly* communicate, a system of communication stands between them, so to speak. For Luhmann, "only communications can communicate" (Luhmann 1992: 251). Individuals can only coordinate each other *through* a communication system: "[Communicators] can only influence the communication by impulses, stimuli and irritations they are addressing to the communication system" (Hertig & Stein 2007: 11). In consequence, as it was the case with Parsons' actors, "persons as concrete psycho-organic units" are not part of a system of communication, they remain in its *environment* (Luhmann 1982a: 247). They can only *perturb* communication, that is, social systems. Concretely, in the interaction between two persons, each of them can only *influence* the communication, not determine it. As we saw above, a system will deal internally with these perturbations through its own operations, some of which can lead to transformations of the structures of the system in question. Communication, it shall now be understood, is a process of constant transformation of structures of expectations that orient and coordinate actions: communication "attributes, assigns and constructs actions but it is not action itself" (Luhmann 2012: 223).

Social systems: interactions, organizations, and societies

All social systems are made of communication. When there is communication, some social systems necessarily emerge, and there cannot be communication outside of social systems. Social systems exist when communication between persons can be distinguished from an environment. For example, a group of friends at a bar table have a conversation that is differentiated from all the other conversations simultaneously occurring at the bar. Through this conversation, topics and ideas can be connected and expanded further by every participant: this group of friends form a very basic autopoietic social system (i.e., an interaction system, see below). It is important to specify that there are three different types of social systems (interactions, organizations, societies) that vary precisely according to their modes of differentiation from their environment (that is, communication processes of self-reference and boundary-formation).

First, there are *interactions*, such as a family dinner, a queue at the theater, or a taxi ride. Social systems as interactions require personal presence,[38] the mutual perception of this presence, and the "perception of the mutual perception" of this presence (Luhmann 1982a: 71). In addition, only one person can speak at a time, and several topics cannot be dealt with simultaneously but only sequentially. Therefore, such systems cannot be very complex (comparatively with the two other types of social systems: organizations and societies), whether internally or in their relations with their environment (largely constituted by other social systems). The function of interaction systems is to solve the problem of double contingency, that is, to allow coordination. Importantly, *trust* helps to reduce and overcome double contingency, and thus the reproduction of interaction systems. Indeed, it allows information to be accepted, without needing verification for the entirety of the communicated information. Trust also increases the attribution of positive utterances to the other interlocutor, and as such, facilitates coordination between communicating individuals.

Second, there are *organizations*, such as, for instance, a school, company, or political party. Contrary to interactions, organizations systems "link membership to specific conditions, that is, which make entrance and exit dependent upon such conditions" (ibid.: 75). Conditions of membership are therefore impersonal. Being a member conditions a large part of the individual behavior: the organization has more or less formal *rules* conditioning membership. The organization does not require personal motivation or moral adherence for each action required: "Motives are *generalized* through membership" (ibid.: original emphasis), thus stabilizing expected behaviors. Organizations systems are the only kind of social system "capable of producing the motivational generalization and the behavioral specification required in several of modern society's most important functional domains" (ibid.: 76). Indeed, organizations are systems able to stabilize relations between members and the encompassing system, and therefore to perform the function of this system in a very efficient manner. For Luhmann, *states* are an example of organizations performing some functions of the political system (see below and Chapter 4), and citizenship is generally the criterion of membership to this organization. To be sure, the state as a broad organization is internally differentiated into multiple smaller organizations and interaction systems.

---

[38] While all these examples are of *physical* presence in the same location, phone calls or online meetings are evidently included in this category.

Third and finally, there are societies. A society includes all the communications considered as such by some social systems: "[Society] is the encompassing social system which includes all communications, reproduces all communications and constitutes meaningful horizons for further communications" (Luhmann 1982 in King & Thornhill 2003: 7). For Luhmann, we should no longer really speak of *societies* in the plural: the only existing societal system is "world society." This is the case because nowadays each communication could potentially be connected to every other communication, with the marginal exception of few isolated tribes in the Amazon or some remote islands. As already mentioned, society is not composed of the sum of individual actions. Since it is instead composed of communication, society can be defined as "the comprehensive system of all reciprocally accessible communicative action" (Luhmann 1982a: 73). Communication must be accessible and understandable in order to be meaningful and to coordinate behaviors. Therefore, the boundaries of society are those of "possible meaningful communication" (ibid.). Perturbations from the environment become meaningful for society precisely when society communicates about them. In addition, the whole society is always *presupposed* in any communication of every other social system, including each interaction and each organization system. Society is indeed the "ordered and prepatterned environment" (ibid.: 87) of any other social systems, whether the taxi ride or the state's institutions.

To be sure, the existence of a world society does not imply homogeneity or unity. The modern world society is *functionally differentiated* in several (sub-)societal systems, which are themselves *internally* differentiated in organization and interaction systems. The political system[39] is, for instance, a social system that is a subsystem of society as a whole. Society as the environment of social systems of lower levels reduces the complexity of its own environment, allowing these subsystems to process their own selective operations, and to do so with a relative autonomy regarding the encompassing system (society). More generally, broader systems allow and constrain the possibility for

---

[39] To be clear at the outset, even if this will be discussed (and criticized) in the next chapter, Luhmann considers that the functionally differentiated political system is *internally* differentiated, under the form of *segmentation*. He explains: "As a general rule we can say that territorial borders no longer limit entire societies, but only political systems (with all that belongs to them: in particular jurisdiction). Territorial borders have the task of differentiating the world society into segmentary political functional systems: that is in equal states" (Luhmann 1982b: 240).

smaller systems to distinguish from their environment, and therefore to exist and operate as unified systems. Luhmann provides the example of a faculty meeting at the university. As an interaction system, the faculty meeting is limited by both organization and societal systems, for instance, by organizational roles and resources, and by the societal (un-)desirability of some scientific and educational goals. However, these limitations precisely allow "specific expectations about behavior or results to have a chance to emerge and survive" in the faculty meeting (ibid.: 86). The reduction of complexity effected by societal and organization systems thus allows the development of some internal complexity within the faculty meeting.

It is important to clarify further the articulation of these three types of systems. They are not *necessarily* mutually exclusive. In this example, the interaction system (the faculty meeting) belongs to an organization (the university); in the case of the taxi ride, the interaction between the driver and the customer does not belong to any organization, but it certainly belongs to society, and in particular to the economic subsystem. Indeed, every interaction and organization system inevitably belong to society as a whole, but not always to each of its societal subsystems. While it belongs to society as a whole, the communications of an interaction system (taxi ride) or an organization (university) are not necessarily *relevant* for a societal system (such as the political system). We will see in Chapter 4 how, through a "code," a societal system can recognize a communication as relevant or meaningful for itself in order to deal with it. Moreover, the more these three types of systems are differentiated from one another, the more complex is broader society. For Luhmann, the increased differentiation of the three types of systems provides the possibility for functional specification. In order to preserve itself, society mostly needs to ensure "the compatibility of the disparate functions and structures of all its subsidiary units or parts" (ibid.: 79).

In addition, the differentiation of these three types of systems increases the likelihood of *conflict* in the society, while reducing its pervasiveness. Conflict occurs when the "negation potential" inherent in communication is employed during an interaction, implying the rejection of expected behavior. The more a society is complex, the more interests and perspectives are diverse, increasing the opportunities for negation. For this reason, negations (and thus subsequent conflicts) arise very often, but they are generally circumscribed to the social system in which they arise and need to be resolved only in "critical cases." Somehow, complex societies have a high "tolerance" for conflict (ibid.: 83). Concretely, conflicts at the level of interaction systems hardly reach societal level, or do so only through "a more or less artificial (that is, political) aggregation of interests" (ibid.: 84). In order to avoid the spread of conflicts, societal functions tend not to be performed by any single and unified organization. Obviously no organization simultaneously endorses all societal functions, and no organization handles the full burden of a specific societal function. Take, for instance, the political function: it is distributed among several organizations – government and bureaucracies – but also political parties and interest groups, and the broad public, of course. Therefore, in addition to society, its subsystems themselves are *internally differentiated*.

System differentiation: segmentation, stratification, and functional differentiation

The differentiation between *types* of systems increases the complexity of the encompassing society. At the same time, this growth of complexity offers new opportunities for reduction of complexity, that is, the creation of new systems or transformation of existing ones. *Internal differentiation* is defined as the "replication, within a system, of the difference between a system and its environment" (ibid.: 230). As a result, there are two different kinds of environments within differentiated systems: an *external environment*, which is the same for every subsystem in the encompassing system; and an *internal environment*, which is specific to each subsystem. As an illustration, a political party as an organization system shares with other political parties the external environment constituted by the other organizations of the political system and by what is outside it.[40] Yet at the same time, other political parties are parts of the *own* internal environment of this specific party. Similarly, the political system treats the other subsystems of society (e.g., the economic system) as the internal environment of society, while what is outside society is its external environment. As Luhmann puts it, "it is through the construction of diverse internal versions of

---

[40]   Although a political party as an organization system belongs largely to the political system because most of its communications are political, it must be specified that it can also be structurally coupled with the legal and economic systems, for instance, when it uses legal and economic communications.

the entire system (produced by disjoining subsystems and internal environments) that facts, events, and problems obtain a multiplicity of meanings in different perspectives" (ibid.: 231). It is important to note that the purpose of this process of differentiation is to broaden the opportunities for selecting meaning and increase the possibilities for variations and choices in response to perturbations from the environments. Social systems do so in terms of *communication,* in order to provide to other communicative systems the opportunity to use their communications: "They give meaning to events which otherwise would be meaningless for society" (King & Thornhill 2003: 9). Differentiated systems do not, through communication, primarily organize social action, but meaning. In the end, society is nothing else but *organized meaning.*

According to Luhmann, there are three forms of societal differentiation, each implying a different degree of complexity. It is important to specify that these three forms are not mutually exclusive: they often coexist and even compete with each other. First, there is *segmentation,* that is, the differentiation of society into subsystems of *equal* societal importance. For instance, families are segments of a tribal society; the adding or removal of a specific family does not significantly affect the structure of society (Stichweh 2011a: 304). Second, there is *stratification,* which is the differentiation of society into *unequal* subsystems. It features a more or less strict and sealed hierarchy of different social groups (e.g., castes); these differentiated groups as subsystems self-identify in this hierarchical perspective, and their existence is largely ruled by their belonging to their respective strata. Third, there is *functional differentiation,* which "organizes communication processes around special functions to be fulfilled at the level of society" (Luhmann 1982a: 236).

Functional differentiation displaces these functions from society to the level of subsystems. By relocating a function to a lower level, a function is integrated in a new difference between system and environment, allowing the emergence of new problems and solutions that cannot exist at the level of society (ibid.). It shall not be understood here that the society confers *preexisting* functions to lower levels. The function, and therefore its related subsystem, is a *specialization* developed by society in order to deal with a specific problem it has itself created, in reaction to repeated environmental perturbations (Dubé 2017: 386). As such, this specialized subsystem selects some specific communications, treats and organizes them, providing to other sub-systems the possibility of relying upon them for their own operations. Thus, functional subsystems are "functionally specialized communications" (Luhmann 1982a: 236). Each of these societal subsystems are "domains of communication that have structured their recursive meaning-processing to such a degree that they have become codified" (Arnoldi 2001: 6). As a consequence, the boundaries of each of these systems are constituted by their different modes of processing meaning through communication (ibid.).

In performing their function, social systems do so for *themselves*; not for the environment, for society as a whole, for other systems, or for individuals (Dubé 2017: 386). As autopoietic systems, they need to operate continuously in order to self-reproduce; and all these operations are oriented by their function. Since a subsystem is specialized around a function, no other subsystem can relieve it or substitute it. Indeed, the political system can influence to some extent the scientific system by funding research, but it cannot itself produce truths. Similarly, the economic system can influence the political system, through lobbying and corruption, of course, but it cannot itself exercise power for implementing collective decisions.

Functionally differentiated subsystems are also characterized by *inclusivity* regarding individuals. Indeed, in functional subsystems "the access to functions has to be equal, that is, independent of any relations to other functions" (Luhmann 1982a: 236). Thus, exclusions can only be justified by reference to the function of the subsystem, which is indifferent to characteristics relative to the function of other subsystems. For instance, the economic system only excludes based on the payment/non-payment code; it does not matter whether the payment is made by a scientist, a priest, or a politician. Similarly, the scientific system considers theories based on their relation to "truth"; it does not matter whether the scholar is rich or poor. In that sense, a functionally differentiated society does not have a "unitary principle of inclusion or exclusion" (Echeverria 2020: 105) operating in every subsystem.

In the case of functional differentiation, all of the societal special functions are *necessary* for society: they are problems faced by society as a system. All of them have to be fulfilled. Consequently, there is no functional *primacy* among them, which does not mean functional *exclusivity*. Indeed, several subsystems might also partially deal with this problem, but only one of them makes this problem its specialty.

For instance, the function of the legal system is to "stabilize normative expectations" (ibid.). However, the religious system also performs this function through its formulation of moral precepts, such as "you shall not kill." But the specific function of the religious system is instead to "make definite the indefinite, to reconcile the immanent and the transcendent" (Luhmann 2013). This example also provides a good illustration of the process of differentiation, as for a long period of history, these two functions (and therefore these two systems) were merged. Again, the differentiation between the religious and the legal system is a mere contingency. In our (Western) modern society, the political, economic, scientific, legal, religious, educational, and family systems are functionally differentiated. They are relatively autonomous and therefore "mutually furnish environments for one another" (Luhmann 1982a: xx). The functional differentiation of these systems is contingent and variable. Consequently, the identification of social systems must rely on empirical (second-order) observation of society, rather than on an "axiomatic position" as it was for Parsons' minimal conditions of existence (Rempel 2001 in Dubé 2017: 388n33).

It is important to stress the difference between the function of a system from a theoretical point of view, and the function as the system in question perceives it itself. Indeed, *function* and *self-description* of a system are different perspectives on the same object, namely the core identity of a specific system. For instance, the political system might self-describe its function as "providing a democratically accountable (legitimate) government" (King & Thornhill 2003: 10), which serves to orient its operations towards what it perceives as *legitimate*. Yet this self-description by the political system of its own function is a highly contingent interpretation of a more stable and constitutive feature of this system, which is the special function of "formulation and execution of binding decisions" (Luhmann 1982a: 239). The function is not an *evaluation* of the system's identity or a direction for its self-description, it is the *limitation* of the system's identity: the unity of its difference. A function can indeed be defined as "the unity of the difference between a problem and various equivalent solutions" (Knudsen 2010: 126). In other words, the function serves to circumscribe the specific problem of a system that has the purpose of tackling it by selecting between possible solutions.

Again, it is all about the reduction of complexity: a system reduces a specific part of a larger complexity, offering to other systems a reduced complexity they can employ for their own purposes (Garcia Amado 1989: 19). This reduction of complexity through the selection of a possible solution is a *contingent* answer to the functional problem of the system. Luhmann precisely conceives contingency as "functionally equivalent ways of dealing with a complex environment" (Holmes & Larmore 1982: xxvii). To each functional problem, there is a range of functionally equivalent solutions at the system's "disposal." But these solutions are not predetermined. Therefore, an observer of the system or the system itself can use the method of *functional analysis*[41] to "open a limited field of comparisons" (Knudsen 2010: 3) between functionally equivalent solutions, and between existing and potential solutions. Functional analysis is also helpful to uncover which problem a particular solution actually solves.[42] This is how functions are analytically distinguished in the first place. However, this method does not include generic and comparative metacriteria to choose between possible solutions; it only spurs the comparison of limited sets of alternative solutions.

By reintroducing contingency of both problems and solutions, functional analysis is a way "to break through the illusion of normality [...] by explaining the normal as improbable" (Luhmann 1995: 114), and therefore *potentially different*. As such, it "enables scientific research to surprise itself" (Knudsen 2010: 134), by both expanding and limiting the range of alternative solutions for each problem. Accordingly, functional analysis in a Luhmannian vein is very different from its conception by the "maintenance functionalism" of Parsons and Merton notably, where the purpose of functional analysis is to detect "necessary" functions for the *maintenance* of a particular system. For Luhmann, functional analysis tackles instead the issue of the continuous *transformation* of a system in its relations with its environments, by organizing "a context of comparison and substitution [...] of equivalent services" (Wagner 2012: 38).

---

[41] Here, Luhmann considers that "the function is not a causal cause, but a regulative formula of meaning that organizes an arena for comparisons of equivalent solutions" (Luhmann 1991 in Knudsen 2010: 3).

[42] Here it should again be recalled that a specific problem (or function) is also contingent as resulting from a particular process of a system's differentiation.

System codes and programs

Within a functionally differentiated subsystem, functions are like a "mailing address in communicative relations; [...] [a function] directs and justifies communication" (Luhmann 1982a: 239). A specific communication is not necessarily relevant for every subsystem; most communications occurring in a society are indeed irrelevant for most subsystems. It is then necessary for a subsystem to differentiate events and communications emerging from its environment as relevant or not.

This is where the concept of "code" is used as a *filter* of events and communications relevant for a specific system. From the perspective of a particular system, not every environmental perturbation is relevant; some are only disturbance or "noise" (Luhmann 1995: 142), while others are relevant communications. The code allows the system to distinguish which ones must be considered or excluded. For instance, to fulfill its function of stabilizing normative expectations, the legal system applies the legal/illegal code: every event or communication that mobilizes this code is part of the legal system. If an event or communication mobilizes another code such as true/untrue, it is part of another system (here, the scientific one). The code serves as a filter for a potential communication to enter a system, where it will then connect to other communications and participate in the self-reproduction of the system (Dubé 2017: 390). The code is also necessary for the system's operational closure: it is how the system "recognizes [some] operations as its own and rejects all others" (Luhmann 1993 in King & Thornhill 2003: 24). As a broad filter of relevant communications, the code complements the function in the distinction of a system from its environment and other systems.

If it did not share the same code, a communication could not connect with other communications: the code guarantees their compatibility of meaning. To be sure, the code has only a *selective* purpose; it does not itself *treat* the coded communication. To return to the example of the legal system, the legal/illegal code says nothing about *how* the system will decide whether an event is legal or illegal, only that an event has been thematized as potentially legal or illegal. Therefore, "a code establishes and stabilizes a system-specific perspective on the environment and thereby permits abstraction" (Luhmann 1982a: 172), and thus it facilitates inclusion/exclusion. Consequently, as for the function, the code of a system is not alterable because it is both the expression and the "guardian" of the system's identity. In the same vein, a code is always binary and cannot become trinary, for instance, otherwise the system would face some communicational dead-ends and dilemmas of connectivity blocking its operational capacity (Dubé 2017: 394).

After the code's filtering, the purpose of *programs* is to attribute to an event or a communication one of the two sides of the code. In other words, programs *apply* the code, they provide *content* to the code. As we said, codes cannot be modified, but programs can: "[They] provide a flexibility, a plasticity which allows them to be moulded into whatever shape is necessary to apply the [...] code to whatever has been pre-formulated (through the system's coding) as an issue for itself" (King & Thornhill 2003: 26). For instance, health issues are not relevant *per se* to the legal system. But some of them can be thematized as legal/illegal, and therefore the legal system will tackle them through medical law as a specific program. Programs are decisional premises or criteria: they "define criteria for correct decision-making" (Seidl & Becker 2010: 28) in dealing with environmental perturbations. There are two different types of programs. *Conditional programs* are standard decisional processes triggered by specific conditions, limiting the scope of relevant decisions in relation to a particular input (Dubé 2017: 396). They generally take an "if/then" form. For instance, self-defense to an act of aggression is legal *if* it is proportionate. Teleological or *goal programs* are decisional processes oriented towards a specific objective. For instance, in an organization system such as a private company, increasing its market share could be a goal program. Of course, goal programs and conditional programs are often intertwined (Luhmann 1982a: 111), since some goals are conditioned and some conditions themselves fulfill specific goals.

Contrary to functions and codes, programs are *not* necessary to differentiate the system from its environment. More accurately, since each program already *presupposes* the code, it also inevitably reproduces the distinction between the system and its environment. Since they are not directly the "gatekeepers" of the system's identity, programs can be transformed, abandoned, and displaced by other programs. This is where the concept of *functional equivalence* reenters the discussion. The transformation of the programs is always oriented by the function of the system; it is in that sense that Luhmann speaks of functional equivalence. Moreover, if different programs are *equivalent* regarding their functional contribution, could they be of lower or greater value *regarding other references*? In other words, would it be possible to normatively assess the comparative merits of functional equivalents, that is, to detect *normatively* superior functional equivalent programs? To answer these questions, we have to interrogate the status of normativity in Luhmann's systems theory.

System normativity and individual agency

Tracking Luhmann's approach to "normativity" is a precarious task, because his position is unsurprisingly complex and provocative. My aim is not to provide a complete restitution of his perspective on normativity. What I seek in this chapter's critical reappraisal of systems theory is solely a sound conception of *systems* that could enrich a normative discussion on democratic systems. However, since the friction between systems theory and democratic theory is notably related to the issue of normativity, it is important to sketch how Luhmann's systems theory is positioned regarding normativity.

To start with, Luhmann was deeply skeptical about normativist accounts of society, for several reasons. The most obvious was the contention with Parsons about what allows the integration of society and the relative stability of social order. Parsons thought that "a society is always already integrated either morally or by means of values or normative symbols before anyone can act in it" (Luhmann 2012: 9)., Luhmann, however, considers modern society too complex and functionally differentiated to rely on common moral beliefs to guarantee its unity. Moreover, he observes the integration of modern society and its "orderly change" despite (or even thanks to) the absence of deep moral consensuses" (Holmes & Larmore 1982: xvii, original emphasis). Precisely, the (amoral) process of functional differentiation itself maintains the integration of society in dissolving (or we might say decoupling) social conflict among its constitutive systems. Of course, functional differentiation has suppressed much of the social bonds (and probably a certain kind of solidarity too) that guaranteed the inclusion of individuals in a limited social group within past societies characterized by segmentation or stratification (Valentinov 2019: 109). But this is precisely what allowed the conditions of inclusion of individuals within autonomous functional systems to be "blind" to individual characteristics, notably regarding the morality of these individuals or their belonging to a social group. For Luhmann, only the reference to the function of a system can justify inequalities and limitations of freedom in that system, individual morality cannot (Luhmann 2008). Therefore, moral consensus is no longer the cement of society: its members do not have to agree on what is "good" to participate in its function systems.

Individuals nevertheless endorse "much more abstract series of dichotomies and disjunctions, such as good/bad, right/wrong, legal/illegal and just/unjust" (Holmes & Larmore 1982: xviii). Based on the general acceptance of the classification of actions (or more precisely, communications) in terms of these dichotomies (i.e., systems' *codes*), *expectations* can be structured and actions coordinated through communication systems. Structures of expectations reduce the complexity and contingency of society, and thus of processes of communication. They emerge from the redundancy of some communications that stabilizes expectations, hence creating these structures of expectations that allow for their own reproduction. Yet expectations are often not satisfied.

There are two types of responses to unfulfilled expectations, a *cognitive* and a *normative* one. The difference between these two is related to the distinction between learning and not learning (Rottleuthner 1989). When expectations are not met on a repeated basis, a *cognitive* response implies that systems adapt their expectational structures, or in Luhmann's terms, they *learn*. Conversely, a *normative* response is the maintenance of expectations "despite disappointments" (ibid.). Norms[43] are therefore "counterfactually stabilized behavioral expectations" (Luhmann 1972 in Rottleuthner 1989: 783). Structures of expectations are system-specific; norms serve to articulate and stabilize some of these expectations as important for the functioning of the system. As such, norms are social *facts* emerging from social systems: they are "gradually evolving and incrementally formative of society's capacities for adapting to and generating complexity" (Thornhill 2008a: 48). Norms thus allow communication to be more stable, plausible, and necessary (ibid.: 49). Social systems "normatively [instrumentalize] structures to secure complementarity of expectations" (Luhmann: 1976 in King &

---

43 *Legal* norms are normative expectations generalized on three dimensions: *temporal*, stabilized over time; *substantive*, "expectations refer to persons, roles, programs or values"; and *institutional*, expectations are expected also by a third-party (Rottleuthner 1989: 783).

Thornhill 2003: 32) in order to facilitate the continuation of communication and the fulfillment of their function.

A second reason for Luhmann's skepticism about normativity derives directly from the concept of autopoiesis. If social systems are autopoietic, their operational closure entails a rationality bounded within systemic frontiers. Accordingly, the idea of an encompassing rationality is misleading. Indeed, society cannot be observed from the perspective of the entire society, but only from the partial perspective of its subsystems (political, scientific, economic, etc.). If we accept Luhmann's contestable assumption that the political system is not the decisional "head" of society, these subsystems cannot be coordinated from something "above." Actually, even if we assume that the political system is "above" society, it would still operate from its own limited perspective and could never endorse the self-steering of society in its entirety. Hence Luhmann's "'governance pessimism' according to which any form of rational steering of society is largely futile" (Valentinov 2019: 106).

Society cannot be transformed by society, nor is a concerted coordination between its subsystems truly possible for overcoming major problems affecting society as a whole, such as global warming or a pandemic. Of course, each subsystem can be steered, or rather *steer itself*, according to some normative orientation. But Luhmann's pessimism tempers even this hope, by considering that attempts to change the functioning of a system will inevitably "produce new and surprising problems, which will stimulate the growth of new systems, which will again interrupt interdependencies, create new problems, and require new systems" (Luhmann 1990 in Valentinov et al. 2016: 600). Consequently, the normativist should from the outset abandon the idea that some norms have the capacity to solve once and for all the problems faced by a functionally differentiated society, since it is in its very nature to create new problems continuously, that is, new systems, requiring new norms to steer their own functioning.

A third reason regards Luhmann's rejection of *moral* principles as normative orientation for social systems. One might suggest binding the functioning of systems to some moral standards; for instance, supplementing the code of the political system (holding office/not holding office) with certain moral standards; that is, to determine who can *morally* hold an office or not. However, Luhmann has a particular conception of morality: it "indicates the conditions under which persons can praise or blame one another and themselves" (Luhmann 1995: 82). Morality refers to communication, that is, it "designates the conditions under which esteem and disesteem can be communicated" (Luhmann 1996: 29). Morality is relative to certain *individual* qualities: whether someone is a good person or not. Like other types of communication, moral communications are distinguished according to a binary code: good and bad. And like the codes of the functional subsystems, this rigid code itself does not indicate what is *actually* good or bad.

This is the role of programs as decisional criteria to specify the conditions under which a specific behavior is good or bad. Unsurprisingly, these conditions are contingent, and "there are no eternal or logical or natural basis for these conditions, no principles, transcendental judgement or values that are valid *per se*" (Luhmann 1996: 29). However, according to Luhmann, there is a general empirical condition for the emergence of any criterion/program of morality: the *interdiction of self-exemption*. Concretely, someone advancing a moral claim regarding someone else's actions tacitly implies that this claim is also valid for himself. As such, moral communication is always "structured symmetrically" (Dallmann 1998: 90). This means a *reciprocity* of content of the moral communication, "for if we allow for self-exemption, communication would not generate morality but power" (ibid.). But besides this empirical condition, the programs of moral communication are contingent and evolving. In addition, Luhmann rejects *values* as appropriate moral programs. According to him, the taken-for-grantedness of values make them "silent persuaders," yet they "decide nothing, because decisions are necessary only in case of value conflict" (Luhmann 1996: 31–32). The indisputability and stability of values is precisely due to their ambivalence and their vagueness, but this prevents them from being reliable sources of decision; that is, a program or a norm.

The fact that morality refers to individuals and not to systems makes it largely inadequate to tackle the problems of a functionally differentiated society (Valentinov 2019: 107). Moral communications can even create problems and conflicts by misleadingly "ascribing individual responsibility for systemic problems" (ibid.). Because of their person-centeredness, moral communications do not develop a function system separate from the others; yet moral communications can pervade any social system (Valentinov et al. 2016). Indeed, moral communications are always produced and reproduced within subsystems, but they tend to be relegated by functional subsystems to their environment because the code of morality is not congruent with the codes of these subsystems[44] (Dallmann 1998: 89). Consequently, the temptation to transpose the moral code (good/bad) onto the codes of other subsystems, such as the payment/non-payment code for the economic system, is hazardous, since that would imply that the payer of a transaction is morally good while the non-payer is morally bad. To fulfill their function autonomously and integrate all the communications relevant for themselves, function systems must operate "completely free of any moral connotations" (Valentinov 2016: 603).[45]

It appears therefore that the normativity relative to social systems cannot be drawn from a general reservoir of morality external yet common to all subsystems of society. Any attempt at normative steering is restricted within a particular system's boundaries. Thus, systems develop their own "system-specific ethic" (Dallman 1998: 94). As a reminder, Luhmann locates the possibility of change in the system's *programs*, the only feature of a system that can be changed while keeping the system's identity, contrary to the function and the code. Again, the "contingency and revisability of given social practices" (Holmes & Larmore 1982: xxviii) operate at the level of programs. What is more, the inescapability of program transformation and the subsequent development of "procedures to carrying out change" (ibid.) characterize for Luhmann *modern society*. Contrary to premodern societies, modern society generally favors a cognitive reaction to disappointed expectations, therefore it *learns* more. According to Luhmann, "the very identity of a modern social system tends to consist in such procedures, rather than in particular elements it holds immune from change" (ibid.). For instance, the political system is now characterized by the "institutionalization of precariousness," rather than by "incorrigible ascriptions" such as dynastic lineage or divine law (ibid.). The same goes for the legal system: even if its function is to stabilize

---

[44] In *Between Facts and Norms*, Habermas makes a similar claim in restricting moral communication to the lifeworld (1996: 81).

[45] This does not mean that morality is not important from a societal perspective. Although supplanted in modern society by system-specific media of communication such as money and power, moral communication maintains the role of an "alarm" in society and its subsystems about "urgent societal problems that cannot obviously be solved by means of symbolically generalized communication media and in the corresponding functional systems" (Luhmann 2009 in Valentinov 2016: 603). Moral communications are thus useful to "generalize conflicts" when they must scale-up to be appropriately solved (Luhmann 2012: 250).

normative expectations, it is now characterized by the *legitimation by procedure* of the continuous change of these expectations rather than by some intangible natural law.

Once again, the feature of *contingency* in functionally differentiated social systems is deeply consequential. It has the major implication of leading systems, by making their own contingency explicit and by designing procedures to tackle it, to become more and more *self-reflexive* (ibid.). As we know now, systems have relations with their environment and with other systems, but they also have relations towards *themselves*. That is what Luhmann calls "self-thematization," that is, the process by which a system becomes "a topic within itself as *a system in an environment*" and therefore becomes "contingent for itself" (Luhmann 1982a: 328, original emphasis). As a consequence, the system opens a horizon of other possibilities for itself, upon which "it may be consciously varied and strategically adapted to meet changing conditions in its environment" (ibid.). For instance, the political system's self-thematization triggers the self-reflexive process of subjecting the political power to political power through elections and lobbying (Holmes & Larmore 1982a: xxviii). Moreover, a system's self-thematization enables it to distinguish what it considers as contingent or not. Luhmann sees in this process of self-thematization the "form of rationality corresponding to social evolution" (Luhmann 1982a: 346).

Opposing the Enlightenment's core postulates, Luhmann contends that social change does not primarily ensue from *people*'s rationality, but from the processes of rationalization of *systems* (King & Thornhill 2003: 132). Luhmann's charge against rationality is fundamental to understand his skepticism regarding normative accounts of society, as it "shifts the explanation of society away from its normative focus on human endowments" (ibid.:133). The author seriously doubts the (*still* metaphysical) assumption that the human use of reason, assumed to be common and uniform to every individual, can produce essential truths and ground immutable universal principles for ruling social reality. He instead sees rationality as unfolding primarily at a *systemic* level. For him, rationality is "the operative self-organization of a system in its autonomous contingency and complexity" (ibid.: 134). Rationality is thus the effective functioning of a social system. Social transformation actually emerges from the multiple (and often conflicting) attempts of rationalization of social systems. The point is that there is no overarching and immutable rationality, allegedly possessed by all individuals, that can transcend the particularities of social systems and drive all of society towards a coordinated progression, such as the realization of the "true nature" of humans as rational beings. On the contrary, each social system develops its own rationality through its own ongoing process of self-reproduction. As a consequence, systems "cannot be held to account by standards of rationality they have not themselves generated" (ibid.: 132). A system's rationality is bound within its own operational boundaries; it is somehow *recursively immanent*.

It is precisely on the ground of *rationality* that Luhmann and Habermas's close views on modern society mostly diverge, leading to different views regarding normativity. Habermas's distinction between systems and lifeworld opposes Luhmann's perspective on the bounded rationality of systems, and therefore reintroduces normativity into the debate. According to Habermas, modern society is not only composed of differentiated functional systems generally governed by technical and instrumental rationality, but also encompassed by a *lifeworld*, that is, a "reservoir of taken-for-granteds" (Habermas 1987: 124) or an "underlying consensus" (Luhmann 2012), self-reproduced by a practical and communicative rationality. In the lifeworld, Habermas reinjects normativity: first by assuming that individuals perceive each other as reasonable agents holding justifications for their behaviors and claims; second, in contending that this posture entails their willingness to orient themselves towards an ideal-speech situation where they would expose these justifications to others' criticism and where some sort of consensus is the ultimate goal. These two assumptions are both descriptive-explanatory and normative-critical, since Habermas sees them as empirical preconditions for the reproduction of a lifeworld *and* as normative orientations for any intersubjective interactions.

For Luhmann, the idea of a lifeworld itself is misleading and is directly discarded by the concept of functional differentiation. Even admitting that such consensuses can be achieved, they will still be "subject to observation and contradiction" by other systems (Knodt 1994: 99). More importantly, Luhmann rejects Habermas's introduction of normativity within *communication* itself. By distinguishing instrumental and communicative rationality, Habermas conceives communication as "an agreement concerning the *validity* of an utterance" (Habermas 1987: 120, emphasis mine). This goes much too far for Luhmann, because the act of communication stops with *understanding*. The function of communication is not to produce acceptance, to persuade someone else. For Luhmann, communication instead produces understanding as a bifurcation, with the possibility of "[accepting] or [rejecting] what has been understood as the premise for further communication" (Luhmann 2012: 223). Schematically, "yes" and "no" are always options *after* understanding, and he concludes that "it would be terrible if communication itself was already weighted against the no's" (ibid.: 224). As such, Luhmann claims that communication is not *oriented* towards agreement or acceptance between participants, but towards understanding. Yet, this position appears at odds with his own insistence that communication serves social *coordination* specifically. With this critique, Luhmann attempts to reject Habermas's normativism on the sociological ground of communication, rather than solely on the ground of idealism and impossibility.

Where, then, do these considerations regarding normativity in systems theory leave us? Certainly, without much stable ground to build upon. Moral consensuses and morality itself are unfit to serve as normative orientations to a functionally differentiated society. Norms are contingent and constantly evolving structures of expectations instrumentalized by systems to fulfill their function. Rationality is bounded within systemic boundaries, operating according to contingent programs. Communication is unfit to contain itself the seeds of normativity as Habermas had hoped. Yet the self-reflexivity characterizing functionally differentiated systems allows the internal development of *procedures* of self-steering; that is, of *programs* conditioning the possibility of systemic transformation. The following quote clearly summarizes the tight opportunity for normativity that Luhmannian systems theory provides us with:

> A meaningful critique of what exists is possible only as an immanent critique of systems [...]. Critique is possible only as the analysis of systems, as the re-exposing of problems that are solved by means of familiar norms, roles, institutions, processes, and symbols, and as the search, for other, functionally equivalent possibilities. (Luhmann 1982a: 120)

That conclusion on the possibility and shape of normativity within social systems is certainly disappointing: it strips normativity from all transcendental dimensions, without providing any alternative grounds. Since the critique of systems is necessarily *immanent*, we remain without normative references *external* to the contingency of systems. Therefore, we cannot rely on clear and stable normative criteria to compare and select functional equivalents. We are bound to draw blurred contours of what kind of normativity could be *compatible* with systems theory. To be sure, any form of moral realism is obviously incompatible with it. Sharing some ontological features with systems theory, moral constructivism is *a priori* compatible with it. If this is correct, systems theory is broadly compatible with the (pure) proceduralist approach to democracy that I endorse in this book. I come back at length to this important question in Chapter 5.

Before concluding this part, I must say a few words regarding the issue of individual *agency* within social systems. As the lack of individual and collective agency was the main critique raised against systems theory, it is necessary to mitigate it in light of the above description of systems theory. In one reading, Luhmann's account appears to erase people's agency within these all-powerful and dominating social systems. Indeed, he relegates individuals to the environment of systems, denying them the centrality they have in most sociological theories. Furthermore, he opposes the Enlightenment's metaphysical construction of the human being and its illusion that "the entire evolving complexity of the social world [is] revolving around the fixed intellectual faculties of individual persons" (King & Thornhill 2003: 136). In the *social* reality, individuals are instead "constructions of the system that is communicating about them" (Baralou et al. 2012: 296). Individuals are topics of communication for social systems: they are framed by social systems as "reasonable men" or "rational beings" as in the discourse of the Enlightenment (ibid.). What Luhmann rejects here is the grounding of sociological theories on *generalizations* about the individuals' understanding and observation of the social world, independent from the systems of communication through which they occur. Moreover, the framing of individuals by social systems conveys presuppositions on what individuals "truly" are or expectations regarding what they should be. For instance, in a society characterized by stratification, individuals are first of all identified by social systems according to their belonging to a social group, with all the expectations that this belonging entails. The implication for Luhmann is that the issue of agency must be primarily *sociological*, not *normative*. Of course, agency is normatively important, or framed differently, individual freedom or autonomy are normatively essential. But the normative importance of agency has nothing to do with its sociological reality within a particular society: agency *within existing social structures* should be the main analytical focus for the critical observation of social systems.

In a functionally differentiated society, specific individuals are in general functionally "replaceable" within social systems, their role could *a priori* be fulfilled by other individuals as functional equivalents. Moreover, individuals cannot operate in *only* one of the subsystems of a highly functionally differentiated society: they are always participating in multiple systems. At the same time, each subsystem and society as a whole display to a large extent "abstraction from and indifference to multiple aspects of the lives of concrete individuals" (Holmes & Larmore 1982: xx). This is why Luhmann provocatively contends, inverting Aristotle's famous quote, that *the whole is less than the sum of its parts*. The indifference of the system to most individual specificities is the grounds for the *inclusivity* characterizing functionally differentiated subsystems, and also constitutes the possibility for the autonomous development of individual specificities. Indeed, a social system only "cares" about individuals and their specificities to the extent of their functional contribution though communication to that system. For instance, individuals are only of interest to the political system when they express political communications: their meetings with the doctor, choice of studies, or sport activities are politically irrelevant. Therefore, Luhmann's relegation of individuals to the system's environment could ironically be taken as the mere condition of a genuine individual agency. It is precisely because individuals themselves are not *parts* of a system,[46] but only *occasional perturbations* when they act, that individuals can act *as individuals* in relative autonomy from the systems through which they act. This systemic indifference to the whole singularity of individuals grounds their agency; "for a person the autonomy from the structures of social systems is a kind of freedom" (Stichweh 2011a: 295).

However, in another reading, Luhmann's account advocates a solid place for individual agency within social systems. As a reminder,

[46] Individuals are not parts of social systems, they are instead structurally coupled with social systems through communication, such that "persons cannot emerge and continue to exist without social systems, nor can social systems without persons" (Luhmann 1995: 59). As operationally closed systems themselves, individuals are as highly indifferent to much of their environment, including many social systems. Of course, the kind of individual agency actually varies depending on the type of differentiation characterizing society. In a functionally differentiated society, agency is greater than in stratified or segmented societies.

every social system, organization, institution, or interaction, is made of communication between people. Concrete individuals of flesh and blood are the only (with the exception of artificial intelligence) *vectors of communicative acts*. In the intrinsic "negation potential" that individuals have within any communication lies their *agency within systems of communications*. As a reminder, communication allows coordination between individuals, by stabilizing *expectations* not *behaviors*. Freedom of choice (acceptance or rejection) always remains, yet it is constrained by a "prepatterning of behavior" (Luhmann 1982a: 124) on which mutual expectations rest. This is Luhmann's conception of individual agency within communicative structures of expectations. The agency of individuals is thus both narrowed to their marginal contribution to specific communications, but simultaneously omnipresent in every social system since they are made of communications. The rejection potential from individuals in any communication, as it creates new meanings, is *the* mechanism of transformation of social systems and society itself. It will depend on the connectibility of communications to other communications, to which other people can marginally contribute too, to be reproduced enough to emerge and create new systems or transform structures of existing systems. To summarize, all social systems are constituted and transformed by people's communication, not by people themselves. This conceptual subtlety enables us to analyze agency within existing social systems, to question how this agency is constrained or facilitated by a system's structures, and how agency can bring change within and through these structures.

Summary

To conclude this part of the chapter, I will summarize (and simplify) the important points that have been put forward. I have discussed the specificities of social systems in general, in order to build in the next chapter a sound conception of *political* systems. This analysis took place within the Luhmannian paradigm of *systems-as-difference*. At its heart lies a process of system *differentiation*. This process differentiates *communications* as the "stuff" of social systems. Differentiated communications stabilize and structure expectations and thus allow actions to be coordinated. Communication is an autopoietic system: communicative acts open the possibility for further communicative acts. Therefore, systems of differentiated communication are what Luhmann considers as "social systems." He distinguishes three types of interrelated social systems: interactions, organizations, and societal systems. The complexity of the society depends on the extent of differentiation of these three types of systems. Moreover, he distinguishes three types of societal differentiation: segmentation, stratification, and functional differentiation. The latter type is characteristic of modern society. Functional differentiation displaces emerging societal problems (functions) to lower levels, specializing subsystems over one of these societal functions. Accordingly, legal, political, and economic systems are specialized communication systems. All are equally necessary for society, so there is no functional primacy among them. The function constitutive of a system's identity is the simultaneous limitation of a problem and of possible solutions. Therefore, functionally equivalent solutions can be compared and selected by the system.

On the normative front, Luhmann's highly contingent perspective on normativity leads to some normative indeterminacy. Although Luhmann rejects all forms of "relativism, or the basic arbitrariness of anything goes" (Luhmann 2008: 27), he does not provide normative grounds either. However, he does offer some contours for normativity. Norms are independent from the function of the system; they are not determinants of the system's core identity. They are not immutable but subject to potential transformations. As programs themselves, norms are generated by the system to orient the selection and operation of other programs. Their purpose is to structure mutual expectations within the system and thus stabilize its functioning. With this understanding of norms, the question becomes how they matter within functional analysis, that is, the comparison of the respective merits of functional equivalent programs. Put differently, how is it possible to assess the system's programs not only in terms of the function they perform more or less efficiently, but also regarding the *normative* merits of these programs. By not grounding any normative anchor *external* to the contingency of systems, Luhmann does not provide guidelines and standards to assess the normative merits of a social system's features.

Conclusion

In the first two chapters, I interrogated *what makes democracy a system*. I detailed the main answers to this question and argued that, so far, democracy's understanding as a system is far from being exhaustive and systematic. In this third chapter, I attempted to reread systems theory with a critical lens in order to enrich and challenge the understanding of systemness currently at play in democratic theory. Of course, this reappraisal of systems theory is not exhaustive and remains interpretive of an immense body of work. However, in line with systems theory, this chapter is a necessary meaning reduction (i.e., selection), and thus *simplification*, of a much broader and complex theoretical apparatus. As reductive as it may be, I consider it sufficient to depict the major contours of systems theory *for democratic theorists*.

Unequivocally, I focused on Luhmann's theory of systems. This choice is admittedly controversial, as would be any choice of perspective. The fact that this discussion is restricted to one single author may appear "too narrow" to some readers (even if I doubt that the same perception would have arisen if the author in question was more famous or conventionally validated within the scientific community, such as Jürgen Habermas, Michel Foucault, or John Rawls). Although Luhmann's contribution to social theory is enormous and notorious enough to be the focus of books (not only chapters), I defend this alleged narrowness differently. An alternative to focusing on Luhmann would have been to intentionally ignore his prominence, depicting systems theory through the multiple and fragmented contributions of much less famous and compelling scholars. The resulting picture of systems theory would have been at best incomplete and inconsistent, at worst an erratic patchwork. Another option would have been to focus less on Luhmann and allow more space for his critics. The outcome of such a strategy could have been a more moderate and balanced depiction of what systems are. However, considering the complexity and completeness of Luhmann's theory, such a critical examination would have required a book in itself. Furthermore, since his theory is a huge conceptual system, even a slight transformation of its core concepts (e.g., structural coupling, autopoiesis, operations, functions, etc.) would have implied a potential breach to its overall coherence, a breach that I doubt I would have been able to solve. The strategy of focusing on Luhmann's theory has the merit of maintaining its internal consistency and offering us *a* full-fledged systems theory, maybe not a perfect one, but arguably (one of) the best available so far. What Luhmann proposes, and what I am convinced should be accepted, is a conceptual language to understand and explain social realities as systems. As I am interested in developing a *systemic* theory of democracy, this is precisely what I need here.

Using Luhmann's language does not mean accepting all of its implications. I admit that, at this level of abstraction, I don't have fundamental words to add to Luhmann's language of systems, nor essential meanings to contest. The general theory of systems is thus taken *as such* as a perspective to interrogate issues specific to democracy (e.g., connectivity in democratic systems). It does not make this perspective a standard to defend *against* accounts of deliberative/democratic systems: the aim of this book is not to take Luhmann's systems theory and contradict the theories of deliberative/democratic systems. That wouldn't make sense anyway, as these two debates unfold at different levels of abstraction. Rather, the aim is to use the former to enrich the latter.

Luhmann's theory is a *heuristic tool*, a complex language about systems that questions the relevance of the current language and conceptual apparatus of deliberative/democratic systems' theories. The goal is to go *beyond* what we have so far in this literature, to complexify it, develop its subtleties and conceptual distinctions, in order to strengthen it and enhance its potential uses. To a large extent, the helping hand of Luhmann's theory will mostly substantiate and clarify central concepts of the deliberative/democratic systems' literature that remain poorly conceptualized, such as *system* itself, *function, coupling*, and *boundaries*. By its internal consistency, the theory also offers suggestions for some conceptual articulations between these concepts. As such, the intervention of Luhmann's theory in the debate will be primarily a complement. But to a lesser extent, his theory will also challenge some of the core assumptions of the debate, such as the conceptual equivalence of *functions* and *norms*. To challenge does not mean to stand in sharp opposition, but to question evidence and transcend it if need be. The point is that in this book, Luhmann's theory is not a standard to stick with; it is a challenging perspective to think through, deviate from, and build something else upon.

However, some democratic theorists may still conclude at the end of this chapter, that, as they previously thought, systems theory is a thing of the past, a conservative, reifying, and uncritical agenda. If that is the case, the question is whether they really can ignore it, while cherry-picking its core concepts, without conceptualizing and articulating these in a consistent framework. Probably, democratic theorists could develop the systemic approach to (deliberative) democracy without the help of systems theory. But by doing so, they would ignore a very insightful and challenging perspective that is well armed to develop the *systemic* side of the democratic systems equation. Conversely, one could also conclude at the end of this chapter that democratic theory could indeed benefit from something from systems theory in order to develop a *systemic* perspective on democracy. From what exactly it would benefit remains to be discovered in the following chapters, notably in Chapter 6 where I sketch a core framework for democratic systems, fueled by both systems theory and democratic theory. From this reappraisal, which theoretical elements exactly can be used as such, imported with adaptations, or instead ignored, will, of course, be contested. Some democratic theorists might see other insights from systems theory. However, it appears important to me that a debate be opened; that a confrontation take place between systems theory and democratic theory.

Although imperfect, the foundations of systems theory laid in this chapter are probably sufficient to attempt the construction of a *systemic theory of democracy*. This has to start with a theoretical reconstruction of what a *political* system is. To that end, I endorse the "by default position" of being consistent with the Luhmannian paradigm. I place myself within his conceptual system, and explicitly depart from it when necessary. The architecture and basic functioning of a political system will be discussed in Chapter 4. On this basis, in Chapter 5 I will tackle the issue of what can make such a system a *democratic* one. Or put differently, how to conceive the normativity of a political system, wondering where normative potentials reside and could be steered, compared, replaced, and transformed *by the political system*. By doing so, I will place the normative debate on democracy on the firm sociological grounds provided by systems theory. In brief, I will discuss how the political system can reflexively select normatively superior functional equivalent programs to govern itself towards democratic horizons.

The sociological boundaries of political systems

4

Rising demands on the political system and on the capacity of its political and administrative decision-making processes require that the political system be differentiated from the rest of society, that its roles and decision-programs be separated from those of other social domains (e.g., the economy, religion, culture, the family) and their moral codes. (Luhmann 1982a: 113)

In the three previous chapters, the idea of "system" has been traced, firstly within democratic theory and secondly within systems theory. This focus provided us with the conceptual tools necessary to eventually develop a *systemic* theory of democracy. Taking the idea of *system* as a central operative concept for democratic theory rather than solely as an enlightening metaphor, I critically reconstructed and reappraised systems theory. I did so by focusing on Niklas Luhmann's approach, considering it as an insightful perspective to develop a systemic theory of democracy. To endorse the Luhmannian perspective does not mean to approve it entirely: below, I explicitly disagree on some points. Nevertheless, his complete theory of systems serves as a clear and consistent baseline from which we can depart and justify our deviations. Such a comprehensive toolkit is crucial given the complexity of the object.

In this chapter, I develop the conceptual toolkit portrayed in Chapter 3, with considerations specific to political systems. I argue in particular that although Luhmann's paradigm offers a solid sociological conception of political systems, it nonetheless lacks normative resources to steer those towards democratic shapes. I take Luhmann's conception of political systems as the more consistent and enlightening *systemic* theory of the political. I argue that it provides strong *sociological* grounds on which a *normative* theory of democratic systems could rely. However, Luhmann's political perspective comes with some major theoretical challenges. I therefore discuss his theory through a focus on four main challenges. First, I discuss the *contingency* of the modern political system, with an accent on its function and code(s). Second, I tackle the question of the relations of that system with its *environment*, and particularly with its two main neighbors: the legal and economic systems. Third, I present the shape of the *internal differentiation* of the political system, and the interactions between its subsystems. Fourth and finally, I present Luhmann's particular conception of *legitimacy* and highlight its lack of normative bite.

Besides these theoretical challenges, Luhmann's political perspective is also challenging for *political theory*. I must insist on this point at the outset in order to alert the reader on the particularity of his conception. Luhmann's theory has not been wholly considered by most political theorists: a vast majority of scholars, especially from the Anglo-Saxon tradition, have hardly even heard about him. Among those who have, a majority considers Luhmann's theory as irrelevant for political theory (Thornhill 2006: 34). Apart from the apparent absence of normativity in Luhmann's framework, its global rejection by political theorists has to do with the "sociological transformation of political theory" that Luhmann aims to trigger by "[undermining] the constitutive assumptions and concepts of political theory" (ibid.). Besides the rejection of the centrality and predominance of politics within society, Luhmann's theory also opposes the grounding of political theory in substantive principles and values (often external to politics), which allows political theory's assertions to be deduced from these substantive premises through a process of logical and rational argumentation (ibid.: 36). On the contrary, Luhmann sees the foundational principles and values of political theory, and the attempt at a rationalization[47] of politics as well, as "*autocommunicative* forms of

---

[47] Luhmann rejects a universal conception of rationality that bypasses differences between social systems (see Chapter 3).

the political system" (ibid., emphasis mine). Put otherwise, political theory would be "an abstract form through which the political system observes itself" (Albert 2016: 11). As such, political theory largely contributes to the self-reflection or self-thematization of the political system, and therefore to the boundary formation and maintenance of the political system, that is, the (re-)production of the *unity of its difference*. Through political theory, the political system would "accept and explain the paradoxicality of its formation, and so to refer to itself, paradoxically, as a consistent unity of meaning" (Thornhill 2006: 36). In consequence, political theory mirrors the *contingency* of the political system, and Luhmann's perspective invites political theorists to "reflect on the context of its particularism" rather than relying on universalist and foundationalist assumptions (Albert 2016: 14); hence Luhmann's advocacy for a *sociological* transformation of political theory.

I take seriously Luhmann's charge on political theory, especially since context-sensitivity is a central concern for conceptions of democratic systems (see Chapter 1). Concretely, this charge entails that a theory of democracy must start by displaying a *sociological* conception of political systems, and then draw upon it. Indeed, the manner in which we conceive of political systems largely conditions the extent and forms of opportunities for the democraticness of such systems. It is hence crucial to specify how we conceptually arrive at the features that we take as potentially more or less democratic (what I have called the *descriptive layer*). The reappraisal of systems theory in Chapter 3 displayed a theory of communication and a consecutive theory of society and social systems. These general sociological grounds both determine the possibility of societal transformations and limit the extent of opportunities for the normative steering of these changes. By restricting the potential of steering and the scope of individual agency, systems theory appears at odds with most contemporary streams of normative political theory. For systems theory, democracy is not only, and even primarily, a normative ideal promoted by agents. It is also, and perhaps mainly, a self-description of the political system in a particular societal position. A central aim of this book is to develop a normative theory of democratic systems from the challenging sociological grounds of systems theory. In order to do so, it is necessary to depict how Luhmann's systems theory conceives *political* systems in general, and from there, to identify some normative tipping points towards democratic systems. Thereafter, I lay the sociological grounds of political systems by discussing four challenges for democratic theory.

The first challenge is the pervasiveness of *contingency* within the paradigm of systems-as-difference. This implies the contingency of the shape of social systems emerging from processes of system differentiation. As I insisted in Chapter 3, the idea of contingency pervades systems theory, from the specific forms of society's differentiation to the specific programs of each social system. Of course, the distinction of a *political* system from other social systems, although contingent itself, shall not reasonably be questioned for our analysis of modern societies. Nonetheless, an acknowledgement of the contingent character of the political system would at least remind democratic theorists of the inevitable fluctuation of its external boundaries and internal features, and to integrate this crucial feature into their theorizing. Luhmann's hyper-contingent perspective is a challenge for the definition of generic components of democratic systems (see Chapter 1). It pushes for a very abstract and general framing of the conceptual distinctions necessary to map democratic systems, that is, the elements of the *descriptive layer*.

The second challenge is the inescapable position of a system within an *environment*. The political system is no exception in that regard, whatever we take as constituting *its* environment. If we agree on this matter, any theory of democratic systems must elaborate conceptual articulations of how democratic systems *distinguish from* and *interact with* their environment. A related challenge is the non-primacy of the political system over other societal systems such as the legal or economic systems. This assumption is very challenging for current political science and political theory, because it pushes theorists to stop perceiving politics as *the* driving force of society, to conceive it as "above" society or as the "center" of society (Albert 2016: 3). For Luhmann, the vast majority of communications constituting society occur instead "in an attitude of relative indifference towards power, politics and legitimacy" (Thornhill 2006: 35). By relocating politics in a horizontal position regarding other societal systems, Luhmann's theory repositions the study of politics within a broader investigation of society as a whole. This entails an understanding of modern political systems according to their structural couplings with legal and economic systems notably, and the restriction of *power* as the specific communicative medium of politics.

The third challenge comes from the complex *internal differentiation* of political systems. The endorsement of systems-as-difference and autopoietic systems implies the rejection of the simplistic input/output model. The majority of existing conceptions of political systems belong to the latter; they are de facto discarded by my endorsement of Luhmann's perspective. Notably, Easton's theory of political systems (1953) is not discussed here. Indeed, the autopoietic perspective implies that political systems (as well as all other social systems) are operationally closed: they do not *shape* their environment with outputs as in Easton's model. Political systems perturb other social systems, which deal internally with these perturbations in an unpredictable way. Conversely, external perturbations also affect the internal functioning of the system. In consequence, the internal configuration of the political system, that is, the division of labor between its "parts" *as systems themselves*, is continuously changing. The challenge is then to open the black box of the internal functioning of political systems to distinguish its subsystems, how they are structurally coupled together, and to what extent this contingent articulation of modern political systems is related to their democratic character. Again, this requires an attentive eye on the extent of context-sensitivity in our description of internal features: we avoid attributing specific institutions to political systems, as these could turn substitutable by equivalent institutions in other political contexts.

Fourth and finally, Luhmann has a challenging understanding of *political legitimacy*. Denying its grounding in standards external to the political system, he reduces political legitimacy to the *self*-restraint of the political system within its functional boundaries and its ability to maintain these boundaries regarding other social systems. In addition, Luhmann perceives legitimacy as "the self-reference in which the political system accepts its own contingency" (ibid.: 38). Accordingly, the political system is always *self*-legitimized; it cannot be legitimized by another social system. In particular, the political system of modern society self-describes as "democratic" in order to uphold its legitimacy. Moreover, Luhmann contends that the greater legitimacy attributed to democratic systems relies on the *functional adequacy* of "democracy" with its modern environment. Thereby, he reduces democracy as a particular *adaptation* of the political system to some contingent features of modern society. This purely sociological and anti-normative source of political legitimacy is presented by Luhmann as an alternative to normativist accounts. The challenge it poses is threefold: Does this depiction of political legitimacy have any relevance and value? If yes: Does it represent a viable alternative to normativist versions? And if not: Does it still highlight important features of legitimacy that could be combined with a clear normative perspective?

The implications of Luhmann's systems theory poses some puzzling challenges for democratic theorizing. Nevertheless, if democratic theorists seek to conceive a *systemic* theory of democracy, they will benefit from confronting these challenges. In doing so, my strategy is to start from a *systemic* view of politics, that is, a detailed conception of political systems in their environment, in order to envision the distinctiveness of democracy as one potential (and desirable) form political systems can take. Put differently, the sociological boundaries of political systems are drawn in this chapter, in order to identify, in the next chapter, normative tipping points towards democracy. In what follows, I depict the sociological boundaries of political systems in discussing successively each of these four challenges.

The contingent function and codes of political systems

What is the political system? That is this chapter's first interrogation. In Luhmann's systems theory, the political system is a subsystem of a functionally differentiated society. Alongside the economic, legal, religious, familial, scientific, educational, and media systems, the political system is specialized on a specific function that is necessary for modern society. This function can be framed differently, but it converges towards the same meaning: *the production and implementation of collectively binding decisions.*

According to systems theory, the function of the political system is contingent; it represents a *specific* problem only in a functionally differentiated society. In other types of societies, although the need for collectively binding decisions exists, of course, it is not a problem sharply differentiated from other problems, such as the question of transcendental truths. Therefore, in such a society, the political system and the religious system would not be *functionally* differentiated. Nowadays, some states such as Iran or Saudi Arabia are still in a transition towards a functional differentiation of these two social systems. The extent and shape of differentiation of the political system from other systems differs from place to place and constantly varies. Nevertheless, there is little doubt that today most political systems are (to a variable extent) functionally differentiated from other systems. And there is little question that the demarcating line is the function of the political system of *producing collectively binding decisions* (Parsons 1969; Luhmann 1982a). Importantly, this function is actually compatible with a broad array of forms of government or types of regimes: it certainly applies to democracies, but also autocracies, monarchies, aristocracies, and so on.

The important question is what this function means exactly. It is useful to start from what this function does *not* mean. Indeed, the function of producing collectively binding decisions for society might easily lead us to think that the political system is the steering center of society. After all, the political system is precisely specialized to that end and has developed a "high degree of organization of collective capabilities to act in the context of [this] function" (Luhmann 1997: 47). But this does not imply that the political system can steer *society* itself. As with any other function system, the political system can only steer *itself*, through self-observation. Of course, it can also attempt to steer the environment, but it will always be *its* environment, as it perceives it. Indeed, the political system cannot "transcend itself and act on higher orders," representing and steering society *as a whole* (ibid.). The self-steering of the political system undoubtedly has effects on the other functional systems, but these effects are produced by the self-steering programs of these other systems, in reaction to the political system's perturbations. The political system cannot *control* the self-steering of other systems, but only attempt to *influence* it. For instance, the political system cannot steer the economy or even economic sectors, because this ultimately requires money and thus the economy itself. Nonetheless, the political system can influence the programs of self-steering of the economy, for instance, by prohibiting or taxing a product. Therefore, the function of producing collectively binding decisions does not imply that the political system can steer and shape the *whole society* according solely to its will.

In a functionally differentiated society, most of the issues faced by society are tackled and solved by one or another of its function systems. The scientific system does not need decisions from the political system to discuss the merits of different theories. The daily economical transactions of individuals, or the daily care practices of doctors and nurses, do not involve political decisions: they are operated according to the structural constraints of the economic and health systems respectively. And when these systems face an issue, such as an excess/lack of commodities in storage, or a new type of infection, they generally solve it themselves. However, *some* issues cannot (from the perspective of the political system) be solved within the boundaries of a particular function system, and thus they require collectively binding decisions from the political system. Typically, this is the case for issues that concern more than one system, such as the health consequences of water pollution from a factory. In this case, the economic and health systems have different perceptions and interests over the same situation, which can bring about *conflict*. The function of the political system is to import this conflict from its environment inside the system, in order to transform "cases of outright opposition to being cases of regulated, articulate struggles to influence the decision-making centers" (Luhmann 1982a: 149). This enables external conflicts to be represented as contradictions internal to the political system. Somehow, the political system "amplifies" existing conflicts, generalizing particular issues into new political *themes* (Ferrarese 2004: 105).

Another typical situation triggering the need for the political system is a "crisis produced within one system which threatens to damage other systems" (King & Thornhill 2003: 71). One can take here as a good example the financial crisis of 2008, where states massively funded the financial system in order to avoid a major and global crisis of the entire economic system. In such a case, the political system aims to contain the issues within a system's boundaries. A final example of the necessity of political power is a tight coupling of two systems that blocks the "normal" communications of these systems, such as "widespread judicial corruption," undermining the legal system, and therefore indirectly the political system (Thornhill 2008b: 511). In this kind of case, the role of the political system would be to "re-differentiate" the tightly coupled economic and legal systems (ibid.: 512).

The need for collectively binding decisions is not restricted to situations of conflict or crisis. Although the function of the political system is ultimately to *settle* issues, it first *thematizes* issues that arise within or between other systems. The question now becomes: What makes an issue relevant for the political system? One could find an answer in posing the question slightly differently: What makes an issue *political*? Luhmann would certainly contend here that no issue is *intrinsically* political. Instead, some issues are *politicized* while others are not (Ferrarese 2004: 102). A politicized issue is one that is thematized as *requiring* a binding decision. Bindingness is not understood here as solely relative to formal (or legal) validity. Instead, what makes a decision *binding* is that it substantially impacts the structures of expectations of those affected by the decisions, becoming the most likely premise for their future behavior (Luhmann 1982a: 145). The need for a binding decision is precisely the need for a (re-)structuration of mutual expectations. The *collective* dimension of bindingness is that these decisions are binding even for those who favored an alternative decision. One particularity of the modern political system is that the bindingness of its decisions tends to transcend the boundaries of its own system, being generalized through the medium of law.

Without the limitation of an essence of "the political," issues that require collectively binding decisions can and *must* remain of very different kinds. Thus, the political system holds a "structural abstraction" regarding the type of issues that may require binding decisions, in order to ensure openness "towards the fluctuation of problems in society" (Luhmann 1982a: 146). In order to be encompassing with regard to the types of issues that could be politicized, Luhmann considers that the political system includes all the issues that must be resolved by the application of *power*. As political decisions are collectively binding and restructure expectations, power always "latently contains the threat and potential for the coercive securing of compliance" (King & Thornhill 2003: 104). Power is the communicative medium of the political system, and in the next chapter I dedicate an entire section to this pivotal concept. For now, it is important to note that "most issues occurring in society require neither power nor collectively binding decisions" (ibid.: 70), and that the political system can (and should) "only" deal with issues that *must* be regulated by power. Politicized issues are then those thematized as requiring the application of power to (re-)structure expectations. This presupposes that the political system *filters* issues that must or must not be tackled through the medium of power.

Recall that, in order not to be overburdened with external complexity, systems must be selective in considering environmental perturbations. Political systems filter communication related to power through a *code*. The concept of code has an analytical purpose, it allows a variety of different phenomena relative to the political to be encompassed and identified without "concepts like 'essence', 'value' or 'goal'" (Luhmann 1982a: 176). Instead, it focuses on the *forms* of communication specific to the political system, allowing to distinguish these from other forms of communication. A code serves as an encompassing filter because it reduces "the surfeit of meaning in such a way as to make additional criteria for decision-making necessary and possible" (ibid.: 171). A code is a *difference*, instead of an *essence*. As discussed in Chapter 3, every communication bears a negation potential: the general code of communication is therefore yes/no, or acceptance/rejection. Indeed, a code is a selective tool that has embedded in it the possibility to "assign a specific counterpart to every single item"; a code includes in any communication the opportunity of "choosing otherwise" (ibid.: 169). The form of the code, the binary scheme that it represents, structures the possibility of choice, and thus of variation, within a social system. Function systems develop specific codes relative to their medium, that is, *power* in the political system.

What is the *political* code? The code is quite stable, but it can vary depending on the broad form of differentiation of the political system from the rest of society. For this reason, Luhmann insists that "[this question] should not be posed ahistorically for all times and all societies" (ibid.: 173). For a political code, ancient and premodern political systems generally only had the distinction between *government* and *governed* (King & Thornhil 2003: 117). This basic code distinguished *persons*: those in government that apply power, and those not in government as governed and subject to power. With this code, the issues relevant to the political system were the issues relevant according to the persons in government. In these stratified societies, "the coding of power referred strictly to the holding of office and to the personal competition for high-ranking offices" (ibid. 72). The activity of the political system focused mainly on the *personal* competition for political roles. Power was then enforced to those subjected to its exercise under the form of *prerogatives*. In these systems, often within stratified societies, prerogatives were generally held and kept by the dominant strata: ancient and premodern states are political systems that "balance the claims and prerogatives of the dominant societal groups" (Stichweh 2021: 31).

With the growing differentiation of the political system from other social systems (notably the religious, legal, and economic systems), its inclusivity increased as well (ibid.). The differentiation between

persons and their political *role*[48] deepened: the fulfillment of political roles depends much less nowadays on the performance of other
social roles, such as being a good Christian or an honorable warrior,
or the belonging to a particular group, such as nobility or an economic class (Luhmann 1982a: 140). In modern societies, roles are generally held and vary independently of each other: they rely on rules of
attribution/membership and standards of quality that are *system-specific* (ibid.: 141). Roles are not given once and for all at birth, tied by
the mere belonging to a specific group. They vary during a lifetime
and across systems. In this context, "decisions about the inclusion and
exclusion of persons in social systems have their basis in the ongoing
communicative operations that constitute social systems" (Stichweh
2021: 16). Accordingly, modern political systems are mainly connected to other systems through *communications* instead of depending on
external roles or traditional strata (Luhmann 1982a: 175).

Besides the greater inclusivity of *persons*, modern political systems
are also more inclusive of *issues* that can be thematized as political or
not. The specification of a range of political functions or prerogatives
(e.g., in French *"fonctions régaliennes"*) is replaced by an indeterminacy
and fluctuation of the realm of the political, with a potential inclusivity of *any* emerging issue. In this context, modern political systems "do
not generate absolute criteria for regulating which communications
can be categorized as political, and which not" (King & Thornhill 2003:
85), making this categorization a more contingent and *political* process.
However, for Luhmann, the broadening of the issue of inclusivity also
increases the risk of the political system becoming *too inclusive*, with
the dangerous aim of solving all *societal* issues. This "undifferentiated
inclusivity" (ibid.: 87) can provoke a dedifferentiation from other systems, notably the economic.

The political system's greater inclusivity hence progressively led
to the development of a new distinction within the government side

[48] Roles are "set of expectations addressed to someone," and decisions about inclusions
and exclusions of persons in a social system rely primarily on the fulfillment of a role in
terms of obligations and rights (Stichweh 2021: 17). Roles stabilize the decisions regarding the inclusion or exclusion of individuals. There are broadly two types of inclusion
roles. The first (i.e., *performances roles*) is selective, since it is restricted to those who
contribute to constitutive performances of the system's function (ibid.: 18). It refers to
professionals/performers (e.g., doctors, politicians). The second (i.e., *observers' roles*) is
non-selective, and includes potentially every individual through system's relevant communications (e.g., a patient, when communicating potential illness). This inclusion role
refers to clients, the public, or observers (ibid.: 17–19).

of the political code: that between *government* and *opposition*. It does not replace the government/governed code but is a second coding that stabilizes an emerging internal differentiation within the political system. Government and opposition are here understood broadly as a distinction between types of communications: those related to the *current* exercise of power and those related to *potential/alternative* use of power. This code ensures the structural presence in the political system of the possibility to choose otherwise; it structures and normalizes the contingency of that system, flagging the fact that things can always be done differently. Somehow, the government/opposition code "institutionalizes the 'no' in politics" (Ferrarese 2004: 105, my translation). Therefore, such a political system *constantly* includes antagonistic and often conflicting alternatives for the application of power (King & Thornhill 2003: 118). The opposition can thus describe itself in contrast to the government, and vice versa. Disagreement and conflict are made permanent; the political system is thus always open to potential change. The system becomes oriented, not towards final consensuses, but towards new and better disagreements.

In addition, the resulting multiplicity of perspectives, and their subsequent confrontation, provides the political system with a greater variety of possible reactions to environmental perturbations. This internal diversity allows the political system "to describe, test for itself, and then (where necessary) modify the options and alternatives which it presents to the public and through which it includes the public in its communications" (ibid.). For Luhmann, writing in the eighties, political parties are the central actors in this process of differentiation and confrontation of political communications. In addition, he particularly has in mind a bi-partisan division as the embodiment of the government/opposition code. Furthermore, he is keen to supplement this code with the conservative/progressive and left/right dichotomies. But this depiction is only relevant for one (arguably large) part of the political systems of his time. The government/opposition code is a much broader feature of the modern political system. As such, it encompasses many other manifestations, especially today with other kinds of oppositional actors such as social movements.

To summarize this section, the political system is a subsystem of society which is centered on the problem of building and implementing collectively binding decisions. It has power as a medium to do so. However, it cannot control society as a whole, only attempt to influence other subsystems. The modern political system is structurally open to a vast array of issues: no issue is intrinsically political. Yet it filters relevant communications through a code. This code guarantees the compatibility of meaning of communications (i.e., *political* ones). It marks the broad internal distinctions of the political system today, that is, the distinction between government (i.e., actual exercise of power) and opposition (i.e., potential exercise of power). The internal differentiation and structures of the political system are profoundly impacted by this basic divide. Indeed, the political system is structured by programs (e.g., elections) that have as a broad purpose to attribute communications towards one or the other side of this code. Before discussing the internal functioning of the political system, it is important to describe the environment in which it is embedded, since the former largely depends on the latter.

The environment of political systems

The political system differentiates from an environment. Its progressive constitution and transformation depend on differentiation processes. In particular, this functional differentiation enables "the concentration and generalization of resources of power" (Baraldi 2021: 172). In focusing on power, the political system distinguishes itself from "other regions of complexity" and meaning (King & Thornhill 2003: 91). The modern political system has neighboring function systems such as notably the economic and legal systems, but also mass media, religion, education, science, and so on. These systems are *relatively autonomous* from each other; they accept that some communications are irrelevant for themselves but relevant for some neighbors. Their respective autonomy relies on their mutual operational self-limitation. However, these systems are also to a large extent *structurally coupled,* in the sense that some of their mutual perturbations are stabilized, structured, and sometimes institutionalized.

The autonomy of the political system from its environment rests on three conditions (Luhmann 1982a: 143). First, the system needs time to react to environmental perturbations; it requires time to select and apply its own programs of decision-making. Of course, the political system often needs to react quickly, such as in the case of an environmental catastrophe or a terrorist threat, but such reactions always depend on its own timing, which is hardly coordinated with the timetables of its environment (ibid.). Second, the political system is autonomous insofar it is "more or less generally accepted in its social environment" (ibid.). This does not mean that its specific decisions are generally accepted but only that there is a "wholesale acceptance" of its specific function of making collectively binding decisions. Third, the political system must not face a major competitor in its environment, as the Church was for a long period of history.[49] When these three basic preconditions are met, the political system can efficiently *specialize* in its function of producing collectively binding decisions and operate in relative autonomy.

Although relatively autonomous from other systems, the political system is also structurally coupled with some neighboring systems. In particular, the shape of the modern political system depends on both its relative autonomy from the *legal system*, and its structural coupling with it. With the progressive abandonment of divine and natural law as sources of legal validity, the legal system experienced the positivization of law. The validity of law no longer relies on stable and allegedly objective standards (e.g., metaphysical/religious truths) nor on personal prerogatives, it now relies on *decisions* (ibid.: 94). Choice is then institutionalized, and law is made *contingent* and rests upon a "principle of variation: it is the very alterability of law that is the foundation for its stability and its validity" (ibid.).

Decisions are central in this scheme: decisions about specific actions, but also about premises for further decisions. The positivization of law thus leads to the "normative regulation of the formation of norms" (ibid.: 95.) mostly under the form of *procedures*. For Luhmann, a procedure is "a short-term subsystem which reduces complexity and legitimates decisions" (ibid.: 158). In the absence of stabilized sources of validity, procedures ensure some operational and normative stability under the condition of contingency. But even these procedures remain open to transformations. Since the legal system is characterized by the principle of variability, it is the specific role of the political system to ensure the stability of the social order secured by law (ibid.: 96). In this context, stability depends on constant decisions from the political system, with decision-making becoming the continual task of this functionally specialized system. In order to fulfill such a task, "decision-making procedures get divided into a number of decisions,

---

[49] We can today wonder to what extent Big Tech is a serious challenge to state-centered political systems or even to functional differentiation itself.

some of which provide premises for the others" (ibid.: 94). The legal system is then constantly fueled by political decisions. Modern society is thus largely characterized by this structural coupling between the differentiated political and legal systems.

The modern political system produces binding decisions that only law can ultimately implement. Indeed, the political system cannot *directly* act with its power: "It requires a general medium for communicating the options which power contains" (King & Thornhill 2003: 112). This medium is precisely *law*: it provides a "manageable general form" to political decisions that could hardly be applicable if they were to be enforced under the form of direct coercion or personal prerogatives (ibid.). Communicated under the form of law, power can secure generalized compliance and therefore disseminate more deeply and stabilize within society. The ability of law to enforce decisions relies on its "conditional reference" to the medium of power that is principally produced in the political system (ibid.: 107). For Luhmann, residual manifestations of power occurring in other social systems always latently refer to *political* power. Moreover, the conversion of the medium of power into law "unburdens" the political system from the concrete implementation of decisions (ibid.: 112). Political decisions, when communicated as law, are to some extent de-problematized, and thus depoliticized. The political system can thus focus on producing other decisions. The counterpart of the structural coupling between power and law is that the former must be restricted by the latter. Power no longer stands above the law: "Owing to its transformation into law, power must also accept its restriction by the code of law" (ibid.: 109). The operations of the political system (its "procedures") are themselves tied to legality. Consequently, the shape of the legal system (as an important part of the environment of the political system) profoundly impacts the internal shape and functioning of the political system, and vice versa. For Luhmann, the positivization of law and the subsequent communication of power *by law* and *as law*, is a necessary precondition for a *democratic* political system.

Another important neighbor of the political system deserves particular attention: the economic system. There is a tendency in social sciences (notably utilitarian and Marxist approaches) to "conceive of society itself in economic categories" (Luhmann 1982a: 191). Society is often reduced to its economic system, as illustrated, for instance, by the label of *capitalist society*. But just as the political system is not the center of modern society (or worse, its essence), nor is the economic system: it is only one function system among others, though arguably a very important one. By distinguishing society as a whole from the economy as one of its subsystems, the relation between these two can be problematized, and different articulations envisioned (ibid.: 222). In particular, this distinction allows us to conceptualize the functional differentiation of the economic from the political system (and inversely) as a key feature of modern society.

The specific problem of the economy is *scarcity* (Luhmann 1982a: 194). This does not mean that the function of the economic system is to *erase* scarcity. Instead, scarcity is the problem of reference that allows the economic system to "define temporal, material and social problems of distribution" (ibid.: 195). The economic function is to develop ways to deal with scarcity, thereby "temporally guaranteeing the satisfaction of needs" (ibid.: 197). This function (as others) is necessary for society and the other function systems. Scarcity refers initially to the scarcity of goods but is now generalized and institutionalized under the scarcity of the medium of *money*. Symbolically generalized mediums of communication (simplified thereafter as *mediums*), such as money, power, and law, serve to stabilize expectations. By doing so, they make communication more likely and social coordination easier. Money makes comparisons between goods effortless, and it requires an abstraction towards other features of the transaction, such as the personal characteristics of the actors involved. Through the mechanism of the market, money "neutralizes the relevance of the other roles of the participants, and it removes the mutually binding moral controls that evaluate persons and thus moral engagement as well" (ibid.: 199). This is the core of the functional differentiation of the economy from other systems. It allows the economic system to develop some system-specific premises for decision-making (i.e., programs): "Actions that otherwise would have had to rely on wide-ranging considerations about all of society can thus be specialized for purely economic functions" (ibid.: 201). With the global institutionalization of money as independent from power (and morality), an economic "rationality" can develop, and specific expectations can be stabilized. System-specific norms can emerge, such as productivity, growth, or profitability.

In such a context, the economic and political systems differentiate and become relatively autonomous from one another. For Luhmann, this differentiation is "the most precarious yet also the most important case of systemic differentiation, the realization of which is pivotal to societal plurality" (King & Thornhill 2003: 99). It is precarious because the economic system remains structurally coupled with the political system: some issues occurring in the former can be transferred to the latter, or rather some issues are endorsed by the latter as politically relevant. Since its function is to decide over certain societal problems, the political system must tackle *some* economic issues. The risk, for Luhmann, is that the political system undermines economic autonomy by undertaking *most* economic issues.

Luhmann has an ambiguous view on the scope of politics. On the one hand, the political system holds a structural abstraction about what might be politicized: its scope is encompassing and virtually open-ended. On the other hand, only the issues that *require* power and binding decisions are potentially relevant to politics. As such, Luhmann endorses a restrictive view of politics, "which is reluctant to politicize social problems which could not be effectively solved by binding decisions" (ibid.: 85). This ambiguity of Luhmann's theory is salient in the case of the structural coupling between the economy and politics. It leads him to defend a normative position (concealed behind sociological considerations) which is anti-interventionist and against sustained political attempts to regulate the economy.

To support this position, Luhmann contends first that the political system is not *able* to solve economic problems, and second that by attempting to solve issues that it cannot effectively solve, the political system will inevitably undermine its own legitimacy. The reason for this alleged incapacity is that issues of scarcity cannot be communicated through the medium of power, but only through the medium of money: "The application of power to the economy (as redistribution, regulation of production or welfare provision) always tends to obscure the scarcity of goods, and to blur the basic reference under which economic communications occur" (ibid.: 102). Such political interventions are likely to cause further problems, risks, and instability, which will demand new political interventions and mobilize important resources to do so. Nevertheless, the assumption of the political inability to deal with economic problems (and the counterproductivity thereof) is far from self-evident. Luhmann's general perspective on the steering of systems (see Part 1) contends that the political system cannot *control* the economic system as such, *not* that any attempt to influence it is condemned to fail or even create worse problems.

The second claim supporting Luhmann's political non-interventionism in the economic realm is more interesting. He contends that the political system, by attempting to regulate the economy, will necessarily "[tie] its own legitimacy to its success in administering the economy" (ibid.: 99). That is likely to be the case indeed, at least partly. However, this is problematic only if this attempt is *a priori* condemned to inevitable failure. If not, the political system should intervene and regulate *some* economic issues. There are several issues relative to all social systems (including the economic system) that cannot be solved by the system in question, and thus *require* political binding decisions. For instance, when the economic system tends to bypass its own boundaries, pervading other systems such as the health or scientific systems, the political system has as a function to prevent this "dedifferentiation." It is precisely the function of the political system to apply power to solve some problems occurring in other function systems. If most economic issues are not relevant to the political system, some inevitably are. Accordingly, its legitimacy is also tied to its ability to *select* the relevant economic issues to tackle. Unfortunately, Luhmann's own ideological posture on this matter excessively restricts the political system's latitude to *decide* for which economic issues it must make decisions, or not. Moreover, his anti-interventionist position is to some extent at odds with his own theoretical apparatus. Despite arguing at length for the contingency and variability of the boundaries of all social systems, he freezes the respective boundaries of political and economic systems. Plus, by emphasizing the need for the *relative autonomy* between these two systems, Luhmann tends to forget that this does not prevent certain *structural couplings* between them. Hence, Luhmann's skepticism over any political interventionism blurs the fact that some economic issues *must* be tackled politically, bracketing the fact that it is precisely the function of political processes to filter which ones to consider or not.

The functional differentiation of the political system from its environment allows the development of its own autonomy and simultaneously the autonomy of other systems such as the legal and economic, and the stabilization of structural couplings with them. Both the extent of autonomy and couplings (relatively tight or loose) are constantly evolving, and these have important repercussions on the shape and internal functioning of the political system. The above sketching of its relationship with the legal and economic systems are broad-brush, but they nonetheless describe the shape of its actual environment.

To conclude this section, it is important to note that for Luhmann, the current boundaries of the political system from its environment are mirrored in the *constitution*.[50] For him, the constitution does not represent "a universalizing project for a good society" (ibid.: 115), grounded on external rights. Nor is the constitution a device imposed on the political system from outside in order to limit its power by guaranteeing these rights. Instead, the constitution is the "self-limitation" of the political system: it is a document (or one of several) that portrays its differentiation from other systems, basic rights being the landmarks of its frontiers. The constitution broadly describes the issues that the political system can or must tackle, or not. For instance, the guarantee of religious freedom expresses some separation of politics and religion, and it insists on the fact that questions of transcendental truths are not relevant for the political system. Similarly, the legal guarantee of individual and collective property depicts a basic differentiation of the political and economic system. Finally, the constitution as a *legal* document declares the self-limitation of power by law, and its expression as law. In sum, the constitution itself mirrors the contingent self-restraint of the political system and its subsequent limited responsibility in dealing with some societal problems, and it sketches the structural couplings it has with its neighboring systems.

The internal differentiation of political systems

As a "self-description of the political system" (ibid.: 114), or more precisely, of its distinctiveness from its environment, the purpose of the constitution is also to describe and stabilize the *internal* differentiation of the political system. Indeed, the political system is divided into several subsystems. As a reminder, in order to deal with environmental complexity, systems develop their own internal complexity, that is, selective relationships between their elements. In order to adapt to the continuous transformation of society and "to hold ready collectively binding decision-making capacities" (Ahlers 2021: 39), political systems constantly foster their *internal* differentiation. The development of internal complexity of the political system requires internal

---

[50] This also includes uncodified constitutions such as in the United Kingdom or Canada. However, countries like Saudi Arabia using Islamic law as an equivalent to a political constitution cannot be said to have a *political* constitution, precisely because they do not have a differentiated *political* system (from religion in this case).

differentiation into relatively autonomous and structurally coupled subsystems.

In line with his strong emphasis on contingency, Luhmann claims that it would be "deeply mistaken to assume that the political system incorporates an anthropologically or sociologically specific set of activities, which can be invariably described as *political*" (King & Thornhill: 90). However, *modern* political systems (whether democratic or authoritarian) tend to share some broad common features of internal differentiation: they "adhere to a basic global set of subsystems and institutions, a specific semantics, a repertoire of procedures and symbols, and formal inclusion roles" (Ahlers 2021: 41). The display of this commonality is crucial for establishing the distinctive features of *democratic* political systems. Following Ahlers' (2021) detailed description of the internal differentiation of political systems, I treat separately the *vertical* and *horizontal* dimensions of this differentiation. The vertical dimension refers to levels of collectively binding decision-making, that is, levels of governance. The horizontal dimension relates to internal divisions into subsystems, institutions, organizations, and inclusion roles.

Regarding the *vertical* dimension, the political system as a functional subsystem of "world society," is first of all internally differentiated under the form of segmentation. This is the separation into equal segments, whose current form is *sovereign states*. To illustrate this idea, contrast it with the economic system. In the twenty-first century, the economic system is largely globalized. Therefore, as a functional system, it is not internally segmented on the territorial basis of sovereign states. In contrast, the political system as a whole, the *international* system as International Relational (IR) scholars call it, is differentiated into (formally) equal segments. Territorial and administrative borders do not separate whole societies, they just demarcate political systems (or rather segments of the broad political system), and the legal system that comes with it. In a general context of functional differentiation, the territoriality of political systems is only of residual importance; it is "the great survivor of segmentary differentiation" (Buzan & Albert 2010: 329). Of course, this assumption is reductive. Applying the concept of differentiation to IR theory, Buzan & Albert (2010) suggest that the current international system instead combines *segmentation* (sovereign equality), *stratification* (hegemonic tendency, core-periphery relations) and *functional differentiation* (deterritorialization, transnational actors). Nonetheless, the massive state-led reactions to the COVID-19 pandemic certainly reinforces Luhmann's assumption that the political system is still strongly internally segmented. This form of differentiation still prevails today regarding the political system: the sovereign state remains the primary center of political power (Ahlers 2021: 52). Membership of a state, such as citizenship, is still a major condition for access to most political "outputs" and for formal inclusion in the whole political system.

Each segment of the political system (i.e., a sovereign state) also features a vertical *internal* differentiation (ibid.: 58). Functionally differentiated political systems establish, or rather stabilize and formalize,[51] internal subdivisions. Indeed, the process of centralization of authority that led to most European modern states has reshaped the relationship with preexisting subunits, such as cities or dukedoms. While these relationships were generally "volatile, malleable and often personalized" (ibid.: 55), they became more structured and legally codified, in order to avoid conflict and maintain the stability of the state. Within these states, levels of governance and relationships of governance are now stabilized. Each level is segmentarily differentiated: each segment is a distinctive part of the encompassing level. Ahlers points out that "almost all countries now display subdivisions around a 3-plus level structure (national – regional – communal/grassroots)" (ibid.: 59). This structure appears quite stable; even after regime change or revolution: "There is a lot of re-scaling but usually no re-shuffling" (ibid.).

The organization of the relationships between these levels varies greatly, along an axis from unitary to federal states (compare, for instance, the centralization of France with Swiss federalism).[52] The tendency these past decades appears to be globally in favor of decentralization (ibid.: 61). Following this trend, some state subunits are developing their capacities for collective decision-making (expertise, resources, etc.) to the extent that some issues appear primarily relevant

---

[51] As Ahlers (2021: 58) notes, in most European states, and in contrast with post-colonial states, most of the actual subdivisions preexisted the constitution of the modern states.

[52] The type of relationship between governance levels within a state, along an axis from unitary to federal states, might be more or less conducive to a democratic regime. While it appears in the first instance that federalism, with its emphasis on pluralism and local self-rule, would support a democratic regime, it is not always the case (see Lane & Ersson 2005): some federal states can be authoritarian and some democratic states can be unitary, and vice versa. As Lane & Ersson's empirical findings suggest, federalism is not significantly positive for democracy.

at their level of governance (ibid.: 63). New forms of governance are also emerging: *cross-country* regional governance, *supra-national* governance, *multilevel* governance,[53] and, of course, *global* governance on issues such as the environment. The more they are differentiated and autonomous from other levels of governance, the more these levels of governance become political systems themselves, or rather segments of the whole political system that are functionally specialized on some issues. As such, they may develop *specific* inclusion roles, political processes and institutionalized procedures, and normative expectations (ibid.: 69).

Regarding the internal *horizontal* differentiation of political systems, remember that their function is to make collectively binding decisions. In order to fulfill this function, their capacities to do so must constantly be "updated" to face new issues that require political decisions. Their internal horizontal differentiation thus varies, yet some features are quite stable and present in the vast majority of contemporary political systems, regardless of whether they are democratic or not. A methodological caution is warranted here. The point of the following description is to highlight the basic internal differentiation of *modern* political systems, that is, functionally differentiated ones. However, some degree of distinctiveness and autonomy of the political system from other functional systems (notably the legal and economic systems) is already a necessary *precondition* for a democratic system. Therefore, the following depiction of internal horizontal differentiation refers to political systems that could be conceived as minimally democratic, although they are instead "only" modern, that is, functionally differentiated from other systems. The caution is then the following: it is not yet the moment to draw a normative boundary between political and democratic systems. For now, it is instead important to detail the sociological grounds on which this boundary could be drawn.

To start with, the modern political system is centered around the state, but it is not restricted to it. Instead, the political system encompasses many other communicative systems (organizations such as political parties or lobbies, interactions such as protests). For Luhmann, the state is "a formula of unity for the self-description of the

---

53 The emergence of multilevel governance might destabilize this *vertical* (that is hierarchical) understanding of differentiation. Perhaps this is precisely a step towards an internal *functional* differentiation of the political system.

political system" (Luhmann 1990 in King & Thornhill 2003: 77). The state is the simplification endorsed by the political system to demarcate itself from its environment; "it enables political communications to simplify themselves and give a solid point of reference for the social motivations, for the interactions among people and organizations, on which these communications rely" (King & Thornhill 2003: 77). In a political system, communications of power flow across multiple venues and actors, some of which are outside the formal boundaries of the state. For Luhmann, the state therefore does not equate to the whole political system. While most political communications are oriented and directed towards the state, some politicized issues are in the end not taken as being in need of collectively binding decisions by the state and are left undecided (which is in itself a political decision).

Modern political systems are internally divided into three distinct subsystems: *politics, the administration,* and *the public.* This basic differentiation allows them to differentiate relevant communications, hence better processes increasing external complexity. *Politics* is specialized in the "establishment of decision-premises for future decisions" (Luhmann 1966 in King & Thornhill 2003: 79). More concretely, politics generally *defines the issues that require binding decisions, produces broad guidelines to take these decisions, and selects some of the individuals in charge of deciding.* In addition, the subsystem of politics also has an important "symbolic" legitimizing task (Thornhill 2008: 501): it produces legitimacy by "giving form and unity to the entire political system" (King & Thornhill 2003: 80). While politics has the task of producing symbolic legitimacy, this resource is used by the *administration* in order to fulfill its own specific task of "elaboration and issuing of binding decisions, in accordance with politically prescribed criteria of correctness" (Luhmann 1970 in King & Thornhill 2003: 79). Without a distinct administration,[54] the political system would only rely on politics for issuing all binding decisions, which would overburden it. Indeed, in the absence of an administration to process a significant part of complexity, modern political systems would place all their functional burden on some people and/or organizations, increasing the "risk of self-delegitimization" (ibid.: 80). The existence of an autonomous administration can

---

[54] For Luhmann, the administration includes "parliaments, sub-executives, councils, regional committees, discussion-groups, quangos, tribunals and so on" (King & Thornhill 2003: 79). However, I think that tribunals belong to the legal system; Luhmann appears inconsistent on this point.

foster the development of an internal complexity that better mirrors external complexity, simultaneously relieving a part of the responsibility burden of politics. Therefore, as they are complex systems on their own and relatively autonomous from one another, politics and administration can develop "autonomous criteria of rationality and efficiency" (ibid.: 84) in operating according to the imperatives of their own specific function.

Moreover, the administration can develop the organizational capacity to transform political decisions (that is, the medium of *power*) into generalized and legally binding forms (the medium of *law*). The administration "imposes legally appropriate forms on the political contents which it processes" (ibid.: 87). Accordingly, the administration has the functions of *legislation* and *implementation,* and as such represents an intermediary step between political decisions and the codification of power as law by the legal system. Here, one can clearly see that this basic internal differentiation of the political system is a restatement (however, it is more of a sociological depiction than a normative claim) of the importance of the *separation of powers*. The relative autonomy of politics and administration allows their mutual observation ("checks"), and their co-existence as distinct systems of communication makes them structural counterweights, avoiding the concentration of power in one or the other ("balance"). For Luhmann, this "separation of powers" primarily provides the political system with the capacity for *self-observation* (ibid.), that is, reflexivity and self-thematization allowing the political system to conceive its own contingency and legitimacy (or lack thereof).

In the modernization trajectory of political systems, their internal differentiation is deepened by a third component: the *public*.[55] To be sure, in all kinds of society, there is always a public of social events. But in a functionally differentiated society, the public of specifically *political* events acquires another meaning and function. During the functional differentiation of modern society, individuals progressively switched from being *subjects* of power to *addressees* of positive law. This has two implications. Firstly, the public is a specific part of the political system through its direct contact with power. With the emergence of a distinct administration, this contact is mediated and generalized

---

[55] Here it might be useful to remind readers that the public primarily endorses an *observer* type of inclusion role (non-selective), while politics and administration are composed of *performance* inclusion roles (selective).

through law instead. The asymmetry and arbitrariness of this contact is then reduced, and the public shifts from "subjects" to "users" or even "clients" (Ahlers 2021: 77). In addition, increasingly complex subsystems of politics and administration enable the development of "new avenues of communication between the political system and its public" (King & Thornhill 2003: 80). In particular, the more the administration is complex, the more it has "contact" with the public, thus providing multiple occasions of recursive feedback or even new routes of politicization through "the inclusion of administrative clients in specific processes, for instance, via practices of public deliberation" (Ahlers 2021: 77).

Secondly, and at the same time, the public is also the mass of individuals (plus the interaction and organization systems they can form) endorsing first and foremost the role of *observers* of the political system (more precisely, of politics and administration). Although the public can participate (to a variable extent) in politics and contribute to decision-making, its initial function is *observation* (Ferrarese 2004; Le Bouter 2015). By being outside both the subsystems of politics and administration, the public can observe them from a different angle. As autopoietic systems, politics and administration operate according to their own observations and bounded rationalities. Therefore, they observe society, its subsystems, and the issues that arises within them through their own lenses, with their inherent biases. Contrary to politics and administration, the public is a subsystem constituted by a non-selective inclusion role: virtually, *everyone* can observe social events. Furthermore, the public observes society without system-specific imperatives, in a much more "chaotic" way. The public thus forms an internal environment within the political system: this internal disjunction produces an intermediary reduction of complexity between the "real" environment (i.e., society) and the political system. This enables the political system to orient itself according to the thematizations arising from the public's observations.

The purpose of the public is not only and primarily to observe society on behalf of the political system. Indeed, politics and administration also observe society, and their bounded rationality entails an allegation to observe it "better." Where the public is essential for them, and for the whole political system, is that it also represents a meaning reduction/simplification of the whole society observing the political system. As such, the public fulfills its main task: it allows the political system to *observe itself* through its own observation of the public. More concretely, the political system (politics and administration in particular) observes itself by looking at how society perceives it through the public. The public then ensures in the political system the presence of a "self-produced uncertainty" (Luhmann 1997 in Ferrarese 2004, my translation) because it perceives politics and administration through the lens of contingency, hence of potential legitimacy/illegitimacy. As a consequence, the political system must consider the fact that it is observed and orient its operations accordingly (Le Bouter 2015: 160). As such, the public virtually impacts *all* political operations and allows the self-orientation of the whole political system (Ferrarese 2004: 103). Besides the consequentiality of its mere presence, the public has a more or less broad set of formal and/or practical opportunities to influence politics and administration. In democratic systems, this set generally includes forming and expressing "public opinion," electing performers of politics, campaigning and demonstrating, complaining to the administration, civil disobedience, etc. In any functionally differentiated political system, the public has for functions *observation* and *orientation*. The range of levers at the public's disposal to perform these functions, whether institutionalized or not, varies according to the political system in question.

In sum, modern political systems internally articulate three subsystems: politics, administration, and the public. Being functionally differentiated, there is no primacy of one of these subsystems over the two others. As such, Luhmann's depiction of the political system replaces a top-down perspective with a cyclic and recursive model of mutual influence between three complementary components (Ferrarese 2004: 103). In this model, influence goes both ways under the specific form of power. On the one hand, the public influences politics through observation and both institutionalized and non-institutionalized practices of expression of its observation; politics set premises of decisions to the administration; which makes and apply concrete decisions under the general form of law to the public; which reacts to these decisions by expressing its observations to administration and politics (ibid.). On the other hand, the administration often proposes to politics its own decision premises; politics offer to the public (through parties but also the mass media) a reduced range of policy-options (hence testing their relevance and support), and by doing so it delivers an image of itself that impacts the public's observation; and the public applies pressure on the administration through interest groups or individual complaints, for instance (ibid.). For Luhmann, the complex internal differentiation (both vertical and horizontal) of the political systems in autonomous but structurally coupled subsystems of communication makes modern politics more flexible, able to deal with increasing external complexity, and thus more able to uphold their legitimacy.

The legitimacy of political systems

The question of legitimacy brings Luhmann's political sociology to highly controversial standpoints. In line with his anti-normativism (see Chapter 3), he rejects all external grounds of legitimacy, such as natural rights or rationally deduced norms. Nor does legitimacy rest on an "invariable process" of decision-making (King & Thornhill 2003: 90).[56] Moreover, legitimacy is not a resource produced "by any localized or personalized point of communication in the political system" (ibid.: 73), it is rather an emergent property produced by the entire political system. For Luhmann, political systems can be legitimate in many different, unpredictable, and even contradictory ways. Accordingly, he refuses the possibility that legitimacy can be "condensed into normative postulates" (Thornhill 2008: 501). Instead, he endorses a purely *descriptive* account of legitimacy. Following the centrality of contingency in his systems theory, and in order to highlight the unsettled character of legitimacy, Luhmann takes it as the *formula of contingency*[57] of the modern political system.

In pre-modern societies, the specific question of legitimacy was not posed as such. First, because political systems were poorly demarcated from other social systems. Second, because their authority often rested on divine law or other stabilized sources of validity such as dynastic

---

[56] More critically for democracy, Luhmann considers that to tie the legitimation process to public participation is dangerous because the development of participatory processes will certainly lead to the overburdening of the administration (King & Thornhill 2003: 73).

[57] A formula of contingency is what makes the improbability of events *compatible* with the existing system, and this improbability "acceptable" for this system (Ferrarese 2015: 91). For instance, "God" is the contingency formula of the religious system, because any event is and must be explained in relation to God. The same goes for the legal system, whose contingency formula is *justice*. A contingency formula is then an uncontestable *form* (rather than a specific norm) within a system, and the system constantly seeks to position itself regarding to it. Luhmann employs this concept to depict the "ephemeral and intricately fabricated nature of legitimacy" (King & Thornhill 2003: 75).

lineage (King & Thornhill 2003: 73). In such contexts, the continuation of society's operations did not specifically depend on legitimacy. In functionally differentiated political systems, the reference to legitimacy allows the *compatibility* of communications with and within the political system. The reference to the contingency formula of legitimacy enables political systems to "explain themselves to themselves in internally consistent terms" (ibid.). The goal is for the system to make its operations more predictable, coherent, and thus more "likely to be met with compliance" (ibid.: 74). For this reason, a political system is always *self*-legitimized, through and by its operations as contingently valid. Legitimation is a *recursive* process: a political system is legitimate if it "accepts or even institute its own process of legitimation" (Bourricaud 1961 in Luhmann 1982a: 382n38). Legitimacy is then not only a descriptive concept that observers use to assess the political system, it is a form for the *self-description* of the political system.

As the function of the political system is to issue binding *decisions*, it is mostly through these that it is demarcated from its environment. Indeed, decisions are the momentary events of distinction from other systems and of recognition by them of its distinctive political function, and thus the possibility for the political system to refer to itself as legitimate (Thornhill 2010). For Luhmann, the legitimacy of a political system depends on its "ability to secure recognition of decisions" (ibid.: 504), whatever their content is. To be specific, because they are recognized as legitimate decisions, they can be generalized and stabilized as positive laws. The recognition (or acceptance) of decisions as legitimate relies on the public's observations. The difficulty for the political system is that it must "combine and equalize incompatible motives [for the acceptance] of the most different forces, so that an almost unmotivated and matter-of-fact acceptance of decisions can arise" (Luhmann 1982a: 146). This is precisely the role of *power*. As a symbolically generalized medium of communication, power motivates the acceptance of binding decisions. This is where the importance of *legitimation* enters Luhmann's political sociology. Operations of the political system, decisions in particular, but more generally any display of power, requires a process of legitimation in order to be recognized by the public (and then by the entire political system) as legitimate.

There are two different internal grounds/references of legitimation employed by the political system to legitimate its power and subsequent decisions. The first is the *self-limitation* of the political system within its functional boundaries. Since modern society is function-ally differentiated, Luhmann fears the risks of *dedifferentiation*.[58] For Luhmann, the political system cannot solve *all* societal issues; its mis-leading attempts to do so, for instance, the illusionary aim to fully control the economic system, lead to a probable delegitimation. Fur-thermore, the relative autonomy of the political system also depends on the respect of other social systems' autonomy, which would be threatened by "excessive politicization" (Kim 2015: 367). As a conse-quence, the political system must refrain from "excessive inclusivity" of its communications (King & Thornhill 2003: 81). However, one major characteristic of modern political systems is precisely their increasing inclusivity regarding both political issues and political roles. In this context, there cannot be definitive criteria of inclusion for political communications.

However, inclusivity cannot become undifferentiated either, oth-erwise the principle of inclusivity itself would be undermined by becoming indefinite; all societal communications could then become political. As a result, the other social systems would potentially become "annexed to the political systems" (ibid.: 83), thus undermin-ing their autonomy. The point is not that the political system must necessarily be blind to some societal communications, but only that it must relieve its operational burden for efficiently performing its spe-cific function. In addition, the political system must observe commu-nications from other social systems with a perspective *distinct* from those systems' observations, in order to determine whether they must be politicized or not. For these reasons, the political system must not dedifferentiate: it must maintain itself as a distinct unity of meaning. In other words, the realm of power must be limited, and first of all for functional reasons.

The external and internal differentiation of the political system is thus for Luhmann its main source of legitimacy. Interestingly, one can see here a shift from Luhmann's *description* of modern political sys-tems as functionally differentiated, to a normative *injunction* to main-tain this state of affairs (Kim 2015: 367). Functional differentiation is the sociological condition of modern society, and Luhmann considers it as highly conducive to a functional and legitimate political system.

---

[58] Besides the risk of *external* dedifferentiation, this threat also exists for the *internal* differ-entiation between the political subsystems.

As such, a modern political system must be differentiated from other social systems, but also internally differentiated both vertically and horizontally. Accordingly, Luhmann considers that the question of political legitimacy should be refocused around "whether and under what conditions a differentiated political system, specified on the production of binding decisions, can be stabilized in its societal environment" (Luhmann 1970 in Thornhill 2006: 38). Nevertheless, as Kim (2015: 371) argues, Luhmann's defense of differentiation as the condition of political legitimacy is quite trivial: it only states a very basic "condition for possibility for vibrant politics."

But Luhmann's seemingly normative injunction for differentiation can be interpreted in another way. It does not simply mean that the political system must be differentiated, even less that it has to maintain its *current* form of differentiation. Quite the contrary, the maintenance of the legitimacy of a political system requires its *flexible* differentiation, that is, the constant fluctuation of its boundaries in an adaptive effort to its environmental perturbations; it necessitates the "installation of possibilities for learning" (Luhmann 1985 in King & Thornhill 2003: 75). More concretely, this implies that the realm of political decisions *must* constantly fluctuate. In this context, the primary question of legitimacy is thus whether an issue thematized as political demands collectively binding decisions. Indeed, as Luhmann (1982a: 149) puts it: "There is so much expected of [political systems] that even making no decision is imputed to them as a decision." Consequently, the legitimacy of the political system rests primarily on its adequacy of making a decision on a politicized issue or not, rather than solely on the specific content of this decision.

This is only the halfway point on the path towards the legitimacy of the political system: it has also to obtain acceptance for the specific *content* of its decisions. This is where the second ground for legitimation intervenes: the instrumental use of *values* or *norms*. While the legitimacy of modern political systems rests upon their capacity to learn and adapt to evolving circumstances, it also demands plausible and consistent decisions. Put otherwise, the political system must constantly adapt, and simultaneously provide "the impression of continuity" (Luhmann 2000 in King & Thornhill 2003: 93). Actually, the legitimacy of the political system depends on the balancing of these two opposite objectives: its *flexibility* towards environmental transformations through cognitive responses (see Chapter 3) and its *stability*, that is, the coherence and predictability of its operations through normative responses. The use of values (for instance, freedom, equality, or accountability), as broad and abstract sources of (contingent) validity, serves this latter purpose. Indeed, values constitute points of reference (i.e., stabilized expectations) that orient decisions: "[They] form a convenient matrix in which the political system can make its internal operations externally persuasive" (ibid.).

The instrumental use of values provides a source of legitimation for decisions and thus motivate their acceptance by the public. Whether they are system-specific (such as lack of corruption or responsiveness) or more widely held across society (like freedom and equality), Luhmann contends that "values can no longer be systematized by means of rigidly ordered priorities [,] they have to continually win validity and urgency from one situation to another" (Luhmann 1982a: 159). Hence, he considers that values are *instrumentalized* to secure legitimacy. Indeed, the mobilization of some values instead of others is a strategic choice in favor of the functioning of the system. In that sense, the use of values for legitimation is always functionally oriented. Moreover, values represent crucial tools of *self-reference.* As abstract structures for system orientation, they allow a flexible self-description of the political system in order to legitimate its decisions. Accordingly, the value of *democracy* as the main self-description of modern political systems represents "a unifying form to the self-reproducing contingent reality of the political system" (King & Thornhill 2003: 94).

However, Luhmann also hints that a political system is more likely to be legitimate (that is self-legitimated) if it *is actually* more "democratic." As a reminder, the political system's legitimacy firstly depends on its *differentiation* from the rest of the society. The political system should not "de-differentiate" from other systems, nor put itself *above* other social systems in order to attempt to coordinate them (ibid.: 40). Its legitimacy also rests on its *internal* differentiation: a separation of powers, of course (between politics, the administration, and the public), but also the co-existence of several political parties and a structural presence of both government and opposition. These features serve *the functioning of the political system.* For instance, multiple parties can drive multiple perspectives from an increasingly complex environment, and structurally coupled subsystems such as politics and administration can check and adjust one another. Furthermore, this internal complexity is *necessary* because society – as the environment of the political system – is increasingly complex, that is, differentiated and decentered. As a consequence of this external complexity, meaning is pluralized and contingently produced by countless autonomous systems; an increased number of communications must then be included in each system (King & Thornhill 2003). It implies that plurality, autonomy, and inclusion are general features of the modern society that the political system must deal with, by increasing its own internal plurality, autonomy, and inclusivity. Consequently, for Luhmann, the "democratic" character of the modern political system derives primarily not from normative considerations and agential steering, but from its own mirroring of salient societal features. In sum, the greater legitimacy attributed to democratic systems relies on the functional adequacy of "democracy" as a particular adaptation of the political system to some contingent features of modern society.

Among those features is *inclusivity*, often taken as the central normative feature of a *democratic* system. As discussed in Chapter 3, a particularity of a functionally differentiated society is that it is inclusive.[59] Individuals are included or excluded in social systems only in reference to the function of these systems: individual specificities do not matter. In addition, modern society is characterized by the importance given to individuality as a paradoxical balancing between equality and singularity, with individuality now constituting a broad principle that is displayed differently across its subsystems (Stichweh 2021: 23). In the political system, the fulfillment of individuality switches the framing of individuals from dependent subjects to autonomous citizens (ibid.). As a citizen, every individual is first and foremost a beneficiary of generalized political decisions. That makes her simultaneously an observer of political events, who can communicate her observation or be observed by other observers (ibid.: 24). In modern political systems, the inclusion role of observers ("the public") is thus non-selective,[60] and this is certainly the most basic feature of democracy: everybody must be able to observe the political system. It is instead regarding the inclusion in *performance*

---

[59] According to Stichweh (2021), "inclusion revolutions" leading to the prominence of this societal feature mostly started in pre-modern Europe with the religious universalism of Christianity, and more marginally in the education (through religious and public education) and economic systems (through monetization).

[60] Nevertheless, the *expression* of observations remains selective. Indeed, voting rights, for instance, are often restricted to formal citizens, adults and mentally healthy individuals. This is also the case for democratic innovations, such as deliberative mini-publics, which generally include some restrictions in their initial sample for random selection.

roles that modern political systems vary the most regarding their democratic character. For instance, authoritarian or populist political systems often *formally* provide the opportunity for anyone to be included in most performance roles, but *in practice* they largely restrict their access and even displace individualized performance by mass mobilization (ibid.: 26). Conversely, a "system of militia" like the Swiss one reduces to some extent the selectivity of performance roles in order for non-professionals to be able to perform most political roles (ibid.).

The development of internal differentiation in political systems has led to the emergence of *new* political roles. Indeed, the question of inclusion now concerns roles such as party members and administration staff, but also the formal and practical possibility for the public to participate in mechanisms to express its observations, both institutionalized (elections, referendums, public consultations) or non-institutionalized (social movements). By their mere existence, these additional systems demand inclusion roles, and therefore inclusion/exclusion criteria. Actually, *all* social systems demand inclusion roles: the question/problem of inclusion/exclusion is always present in a social system (from societal systems to organizations and simple interactions). The point is that, before being a *societal value* with particular relevance and instrumental potential in the political system, inclusion is a *functional problem* for all social systems: who can participate or not in the communication.

Therefore, inclusion (and exclusion) depends firstly on functional necessities. For instance, the non-selective inclusion of observers is functionally necessary for the political system in order to have access to a non-partial observation of society and to rely on it to steer itself accordingly. Another example, the exclusion of some individuals from some groups of discussions of marginalized people (in French "*mixité choisie*" or "*non-mixité*") is functionally necessary for the creation and maintenance of a differentiated communication system ("discursive enclave"). The fact that inclusivity is one of the major features of modernity makes it the dominant norm of democracies, which is employed to justify a large number of political operations. Inclusion in itself is indeed an important norm to value and attempt to enhance, but it is first of all a basic boundary problem that does not contain internal criteria to be settled. It is a norm that is enacted differently (that is with different criteria) across the multiple systems constituting democracy. Democracy as a normative ideal evidently pushes towards maximal inclusion. However, other important features of a democratic system, notably its internal differentiation or the autonomy of its subsystems, prevent it from being *totally* inclusive by getting rid of any selective criteria for each inclusion role in each of its multiple systems. Functionally speaking, not every system composing a political system can and *should* be maximally inclusive. The multitude of systems composing the political system do and must have different criteria for inclusion (e.g., inclusion in the government and in the administration are based on different criteria and are often explicitly mutually exclusive). Inclusivity must thus be differentiated in order for democracy to remain an internally (vertically and horizontally) differentiated system.

To summarize this section, Luhmann conceives legitimacy as something elusive in constant need of renewal, not as something stabilized by external standards. Legitimacy is produced by the system itself, as a whole instead of some particular points within it, by its capacity to gain public acceptance for its decisions. Public acceptance relies on two grounds of legitimation: the evolving self-limitation of the political system within its functional boundaries (whether an issue requires collectively binding decisions or not); and the instrumental use of values to uphold its specific decisions. Democracy is thus for Luhmann the self-description of the modern political system as legitimate. Importantly, the particular form of *democracy* is not primarily due to the fulfillment of societal values, but to an adaptative response of the political system to the increase in the complexity of its environment. Importantly, the features of inclusivity, pluralism, and autonomy, before turning eventually into regulative norms, are characteristics of the modern society that the political system mirrors in order to cope with the complexity they impose. Consequently, legitimacy has an important *functional aspect*, which represents "the ability of a political system to adapt to its functional objectives, to provide political performances that are accurately adjusted to the specific structure of a given society, and generally to use power in a manner that effectively stabilizes the social environments in which it is located" (Thornhill 2011: 139). Functional necessity is for Luhmann the source of most basic features of democratic systems, such as the transformation of power in positive law through decisions, the self-limitation of the political system in the form of a constitution, its external differentiation with the economic and legal systems, its internal differentiation (both vertical and horizontal), and the differentiated inclusivity of its composing systems.

Conclusion

To conclude this chapter, Luhmann's political account proposes a systemic description of the emergence and shape of the modern political system. His historical and sociological perspective enables us to think of a political system without the foundationalist reliance on any essentializing concept of *the political*, but instead to conceive it as a contingent social reality facing ongoing transformations. It forces us to observe the modern political system in its broad societal context and historical contingency. By depicting a political system without any definitional limitation of its essence, Luhmann leaves us *on purpose* without any precise idea of the issues that a political system must deal with. He brilliantly puts the burden of answering this question on the political system itself. I suggest that we can accept that the extent of the realm of the political indeed fluctuates and, more importantly, is always a *political* question. In this understanding, there cannot be definitive criteria of inclusion for political issues nor for political roles: political systems themselves institutionalize criteria and procedures of selection for relevant issues and roles.

Nevertheless, Luhmann provides a basic way to distinguish elements that are relevant for the political system or not, under the form of communications. The government/opposition code is used by the system to filter relevant communications, and as such it provides a significant (yet very abstract) analytical tool to identify political communications. Indeed, political communications are those related with the *current* exercise of power *and* those related with *potential/alternative* use of power. As such, Luhmann has quite an expansive conception of the political system. Although the code is an abstract analytical tool, it allows us to envision the boundaries of the political system without appealing to allegedly intrinsic political issues or themes, nor to restrict it to normalized institutions, organizations, and actors. Since the code qualifies communications, it poses a simple question: is a particular communication relevant in terms of the political code?[61] This might not be a very precise indication, but structural abstraction appears to be the cost of the de-essentialization of the political.

---

[61] To be sure, a communication can be relevant for several social systems at the same time. During the Covid pandemic the refusal to wear a sanitary mask in public venues or be vaccinated, was a communication meaningful for at least the political, legal, and health systems simultaneously.

Besides this limited hint, Luhmann offers greater clarity on the immediate environment of the political system: the legal and economic systems notably. The above depiction is a simplification of their marks of differentiation and the shape of their couplings. However, it is probably good enough for understanding the broad functioning of the political system, in order to envision its opportunities for democratization. It highlights that several preconditions of a democratic system rely on the relationship between the political and its two closest neighbors. In particular, Luhmann's description of the structural coupling of the media of power and law is a plausible way of grounding in a systemic vein one of the main preconditions for a democratic system: a mechanism of self-limitation for power.

Similarly, Luhmann's functional portrayal of the internal differentiation of political systems proposes a common frame of reference for their *mapping*. This frame of reference is not specific to democratic systems but is relevant for any other type of political system. Indeed, his depiction suggests a kind of systemic "isomorphism" (Ahlers 2021), with broad similarities of vertical and horizontal internal differentiations across existing modern political systems. He frames these differentiations as functional imperatives in a complex modern society, making each level of governance and horizontal subsystems increasingly autonomous systems on their own, developing their own rationality. Their autonomy and the structural couplings between them provide some preconditions of a democratic system, under the form of a sociological understanding of decentralization and of the separation of powers. Furthermore, Luhmann's non-hierarchic, triadic, and recursive model enables us to conceive the mutual influence between these subsystems. And importantly, the internal differentiation of the political system, notably with the structural presence of a "public," enables its self-observation as a functional root to its self-legitimation.

Finally, Luhmann's conception of legitimacy opens up a slight normative horizon. As a formula of contingency, legitimacy is a mode of self-description, in constant need of renewal and public's recognition. Processes of self-legitimation mobilize the flexible differentiation of the political system from its environment and guarantee its self-limitation to the politically relevant issues. For him, a large part of the process of legitimation is about the appropriateness of deciding or not upon a politicized issue. The legitimacy of the content of decisions is merely dependent on the instrumental mobilization of contingent values and norms, as abstract structural references that orient decisions. In this understanding, democracy is the main reference for the self-description of the political system as legitimate.

If Luhmann is right, the transformative journey of society led to the form of the modern political system described here above. By no means is this particular shape about to be crystalized into a definitive form. But it would constitute, *for now*, the contingent circumstances in which democratic theorists must question democracy. Luhmann's depiction of modern political systems, although he portrays these as contingent, may sound like a universalist picture of what political systems intrinsically are. Indeed, he explicitly states that these have a specific function, are differentiated from other social systems, and are internally shaped following a distinction of politics, administration, and the public. One might then ask whether some political systems can be completely distinct than this rigid picture, in different times and places. On the temporal front, the answer would be "probably, but not *for now*." This portrayal of the political system is purposively bound to the context of modernity, and in that it is *contingent*. For most of human history, societies were characterized by a segmentary differentiation and then by stratification these few past millennia. In these societies, the need for collectively binding decisions was, of course, a reality, but it wasn't a necessity functionally differentiated from other issues, such as the questions of "the will of God" or the legal validity of dynastic lineages. The point is that only when collective decisions become a *specific* problem can we start speaking of a political *system* and investigate its democraticness. Before that, the sociological object of analysis is different, for instance, a stratified society dominated by a religious caste. But in present times, functionally differentiated political systems share these broad features, and we have to consider how to strengthen *their* democraticness.

On the spatial front, is Luhmann's picture of the political system bound to Western liberal states? Yes and no. Yes, because *modernity* was the Western self-description of its own contingent circumstances; these circumstances were those of the Western world, globalized by its predominance (for better and for worse). It is ultimately a Western reading of what the political system is, but from an observation of what this system *actually* is in the Western world, and now beyond. Therefore, simultaneously, this portrayal of the modern political system is *not* limited to the Western world. Take China as an example. Its society features these broad characteristics, but with major differences: the differentiation of the political and the economic system is less pronounced than in most Western states, as is clearly its lack of internal differentiation between politics and administration. Take Iran as another example: it also features *some* functional differentiation characteristic to modernity, but its political system is poorly demarcated from its religious system. Both China and Iran are to some extent *modern* states, but differently to most Western states.

The main point of portraying political systems along important differences as Luhmann does is not to take these differences as rigid and defining the essence of political systems. Quite the opposite, it enables the *variable shapes and degrees* of these differences to be seen; for instance, the distinct levels and types of differentiation between the economic and political systems in Germany and China. Modernity itself is a matter of degree. Hence, Luhmann's conception of the political is not a *universalist* picture of what the political system *has to be* in order to be a political system. Far from it, the core of this conception is the specification of analytical distinctions, emerging from the *contingent* circumstances of modernity, to depict how a particular political system *actually is*, in its own singularity within these contingent circumstances. Perhaps these analytical distinctions are not appropriate, are sociologically wrong, or are too biased by their Western origin. Maybe they are no longer relevant in the twenty-first century. But as wrong as these may be, they nevertheless enable the description of the particularities of *any* political system, without conveying normative expectations regarding what political systems should look like.

In consequence, Luhmann provides us some *sociological* boundaries for the political system, both external and internal. As abstract as they may be, these analytical distinctions are nonetheless reference points to analyze different elements of the whole political system, whether horizontal segments such as states or local collectivities, or particular subsystems like the administration. Their abstractedness is what enables us to perceive a diversity of political systems. Put otherwise, they provide common analytical references that remains context-sensitive to particular trajectories of the modernization of politics. As such, Luhmann's political sociology delivers us a *descriptive layer*, freed from institutional presuppositions and normative expectations, and flexible enough to be applicable to a large array of political realities.

However, Luhmann's "reluctant normativism" (Kim 2015: 365)

provides only a minimal ground for the critique of existing political systems. It restricts the critical potential of political theory to the adequacy of a political system's internal shape and current state of differentiation from its environment. Arguably, Luhmann's theory successfully displays the major *preconditions* for democratic systems under the prism of systems' differentiation.[62] However, if this is taken as our sole normative orientation, our diagnostic task remains quite limited. The Luhmannian pessimism might be right, in that at the end of the day "we can only support, channel, and sometimes deviate flows of differentiation and the growing complexity of systemic articulations" (Vincent 1999: 363, my translation). The problem is that Luhmann does not provide us with the normative tools to determine what the appropriate shape of differentiation would be *for a particular political system at a particular moment*, nor a clear normative orientation towards which we could attempt to steer or deviate flows of differentiation *according to contextual necessities*. I suspect, however, that this omission is intended. Perhaps, and that would make Luhmann very consistent with his theoretical apparatus, we may have to extract some normative compasses from our own contingent reality.

---

[62] Note how Luhmann's critical lens under the prism of differentiation is quite similar to Habermas's thesis on the uncoupling of lifeworld and systems, and of the colonization of the former by the latter. Interestingly, this echoes even more loudly Mansbridge et al.'s (2012) systemic "pathologies" (decoupling, tight coupling, social domination etc.).

From power to justification: the normativity of democratic systems

5

> The only form of critique that merits the name is one oriented to rational standards because it confronts the test of discursive justification. That it is always "immanent" in the sense that it takes the status quo as its starting point is trivial; what is not obvious, however, is the demand that it should orient itself to "settled," "pregiven," "accepted," or "inherent" norms. (Forst 2017: 5)

In Chapter 4, I presented Luhmann's political conception, providing strong sociological grounds to conceptualize democracy in a *systemic* perspective. Moreover, it represents a theoretical depiction of political systems explicitly and intentionally exempt of normative load. As such, it constitutes an adequate operative basis for mapping political systems (what I called the *descriptive layer* in Chapters 1 and 2). However, the counterpart to this normative indeterminacy is that it does not contain any orientation to form the *normative layer*. In order to assess democratic systems, a clear normative orientation is needed. In consequence, our path towards *democratic* systems leaves Luhmann here, and must find other resources to ground the normative dimension. To develop a normative horizon that is broadly compatible with his sociological grounds, I start *from within* the endorsed conception of political systems. Put differently, I *deviate* from some of Luhmann's positions, but I do not wipe them all out. I operate this deviation from his understanding of the constitutive element of political systems: *power*. In bypassing the limitations and flaws of Luhmann's understanding of power, I find some normative and critical grounds that remain compatible with his overall systemic approach.

As the constitutive element of political systems, the concept of *power* is an appropriate terrain in which to seek normative pivots towards the normativity of democratic systems. I first discuss Luhmann's conception of power, highlighting its ambiguity on whether power is the political medium or a more general phenomenon, as well as its limitation in tying power to the threat of negative sanctions. Then, I present Habermas's theory of communicative action, focusing on the distinction between systems and lifeworld, and the different forms of power (steering and communicative, respectively) that he ties to each of these spheres. Habermas's claims that in some contexts of social coordination power requires a rational (and not only empirical) motivation and that communicative power must legitimate steering power are taken seriously as a potential source of normativity for political systems. However, I contend that the dichotomization of steering and communicative forms of power on the one hand, and of systems and lifeworld on the other hand, are theoretically unsustainable. I instead follow Rainer Forst in the rejection of systems as "norm-free" social structures that need to rely on the *external* normative resource of communicative rationality. In contrast, he makes normativity emerge *from power*: "Power is the art of binding others through reasons; it is at the core of normativity (2017: 64). I discuss his reconceptualization of power as a noumenal phenomenon occurring along a continuum of types of reasons/justifications. I endorse Forst's grounding of the metanormative criterion of the *right to justification*, allowing morally valid justifications to be distinguished. This normative anchor is an appropriate basis on which to develop a theory of democratic systems that is both sociologically grounded and normatively compelling, or so I argue.

Power and normativity: from Luhmann and Habermas to Forst

Political systems are characterized by *power* (see Chapter 4). The focus on this distinctive feature aims to connect the sociological insights of Luhmann's systems theory with the normative issue of the legitimacy of political systems in general, and their democratic quality in particular. Depending on how power as a specific social phenomenon is conceived, diverse normative positions regarding its legitimacy can emerge.[63] Its centrality in political systems prevents the concept of *power* from being taken as a self-evident and implicit notion (as the concept of *system* is dealt with to some extent within democratic theory). For this reason, I contend that an appropriate "grounding" of democracy's normative substance requires a clear specification of its underlying theory of power. My strategy is to seek, within the sociological reality of power characterizing political systems, the most basic, abstract, and allegedly universal normative pivots towards democratic systems. In short, this chapter proposes a form of democratic normativity that emerges from a particular (yet explicit) conception of power. This section describes Luhmann's conception of power, then Habermas's, and finally Forst's, where I find the best conceptual connection between power and normativity.

Niklas Luhmann

Luhmann opposes causal understandings of power. In particular, he denies that the power-holder's behavior *causes* the power-subject's behavior. In addition, he rejects power as a *resource* that can be possessed and exchanged in a zero-sum game (Borch 2001: 157). Instead, power is intrinsically *relational* for Luhmann; it represents "a mechanism for regulating contingent selections" (ibid.: 159) in situations of double contingency (see Chapter 3). Recall that, for Luhmann, communication itself is not oriented towards *acceptance*, but *understanding*.

---

[63]   In normative political philosophy, the focus is often more on the concept of *authority* than *power*. Some readers of this tradition might be puzzled by my emphasis on power instead. There is a rationale for it, besides consistency with the semantics displayed by the discussed authors, including Forst, who belongs to this normative tradition. On my understanding, power conceptually subsumes authority, as the latter is a specific type of the former. Authority is a positional notion that conveys a sense of entitlement to some individuals or groups. Authority is power granted to and/or held by some people or institutions. Authority is always a form of power, as it influences courses of action. But it is *authorized* power, so to speak, in virtue of some normative considerations (e.g., consent, democratic decisions, moral standards). Hence, the issue of authority is intrinsically related to the question of political *legitimacy*. Sociologically speaking, political systems are made of power, not authority: political systems do not *functionally* require authority for their operations, but power. Authority is a *normative* expectation for political systems. Focusing on power, instead of authority, prevents us from rushing directly into the normative debate regarding the more appropriate sources, forms and holders of legitimate power. A discussion on power as a sociological phenomenon provides a better ground for identifying the most specific distinctive feature(s) of *legitimate* power.

Communication is a complex and time-consuming process, and its success is never guaranteed. That is why symbolically generalized media of communication (thereafter simply *media*[64]) developed to facilitate this process. A medium reduces the double contingency in making expectations complementary, and therefore understanding and potential acceptance much more likely. Media, such as power, money, or law, are then "functionally equivalent means of coping with increasing societal complexity" (ibid.: 156). Hence, power shares the same function as money or law: it has a *motivation*[65] function for the acceptance of communication and social coordination (Ferrarese 2004: 102). Media are useful precisely because they make acceptance and coordination their main expectations. Media "free [individuals] from the efforts to negotiate basics all the time" (Baum in Habermas 1987: 262): they facilitate acceptance hence favoring the continuation/reproduction of communication and "[overcoming] the risk of action sequences falling apart" (Habermas 1987: 262).

The growth in complexity of modern society amplifies the "linguistic freedom to introduce deviation and variations" (Luhmann 1982a: 266). Therefore, power as a medium of communication is necessary to increase the likelihood of acceptance of meaning selections, and particularly of decisions in the political system. As Luhmann puts it, the concept of medium expresses "the non-random character of variations in social relations" (Luhmann 1986 in Chernilo 2002: 43). Although the medium of power limits the possibilities of variation, it nonetheless always requires the freedom to deviate.[66] Power is useful to *orient* communications towards acceptance, but acceptance cannot be coerced (i.e., physically forced). Power and physical coercion are "antithetic" (Guzzini 2001: 8). Power stops when coercion as mere force starts, because coercion entails the refusal of any contingency, while the relational exercise of power is an attempt to reduce contingency.

[64] Not be confused with *diffusion media*, such as writing, printing, and telecommunications, having for function and effect to "uncouple communication from co-presence contexts" (Chernilo 2002: 437). Not to be conflated either with *mass media*, which is a specific social system in modern societies and whose specific function is the diffusion of societally relevant information.

[65] For Luhmann, power itself *is* the motivation, and it does not require preexistent and external sources of motivation such as morality (Baraldi et al. 2021: 175).

[66] This strongly echoes Foucault's assumption that "power is exercised only over free subjects, and only insofar as they are free" (Foucault 2002 in Forst 2015a: 122). Free subjects would mean for Luhmann that the participants in communication are free to accept or reject the understood meaning.

Formally speaking, power "transmit[s] preselected and reduced possibilities for action from one person to another" (Luhmann 1982: 334). Luhmann approaches here Michel Foucault's understanding of power, whose exercise implies "to structure the possible field of action of others" (Foucault 1982 in Borch 2001: 158).

Although it does not require coercion, and is actually opposed to it, power nonetheless relies on the *possibility of negative sanction*, a possibility known and undesired by *all* participants in the interaction. Neither the powerful nor the subject of power want the application of a negative sanction, because it is unpleasant or even costly for both. Yet both know that a negative sanction is *possible*. For Luhmann, this "threat" (more or less latent) is constitutive of power:[67] it represents an alternative to expected behaviors that both the powerful and the power-subject prefer to avoid.[68] The intrinsic asymmetry between the powerful and the power-subject comes from their *different appraisal* of the possibility of the sanction. There is power when the latter wants to avoid the sanction more than the former. Plus, the same sanction might not be appraised equally by two power-subjects, one being readier to face it than the other. In that case, the same power actually varies in its extent according to its addressees. This implies that the exercise of power inevitably takes shape in a context of double contingency where the relation of power is never *preexistent*. Therefore, power for Luhmann does not solely facilitate communication and social coordination, power "is itself in fact socially constructed through communication" (Guzzini 2001: 9).

Luhmann's conceptualization of power appears to encompass two different concepts of power. On the one hand, there is power *as a relational attribute* to bypass the problem of double contingency within interactions. On the other hand, there is power *as a medium* specific to the political system. While Luhmann argues at length that power is a

---

[67] To be sure, negative sanction is not restricted to the use of physical means. Luhmann gives as another example the "withdrawal of a relationship" (1982: 151).

[68] One question arising here is whether the generation of power always requires the threat of *negative sanctions*. For instance, Habermas's communicative power does not rely on negative sanctions, but on *rational* motivations. Foucault's "subjectivation" is another example of power without the threat of negative sanctions. Another limiting case is the concept of "nudge," which intrinsically rejects negative sanctions, yet whose function is to orient selections (that is, "choices") by altering the architecture of the choice (Thaler & Sunstein 2008), and as such is arguably a form of power. Forst (2015a) also proposes a model of noumenal power in which threats of sanction *and* rational arguments are both types of reasons/justifications operating in relations of power.

medium only related to the political system, he also suggests that power, contrary to the media of money and law, for instance, is a broader and less circumscribed phenomenon. As Guzzini highlights, Luhmann sometimes grants power a wider societal relevance in considering that:

> Wherever humans communicate with each other, there is the probability that they orientate themselves by taking the possibility of a mutual harming into account, thereby having influence on each other. Power is a life-world based universal of social existence. (Luhmann 1975 translated by Guzzini 2001: 15)

If power is not only the political medium, but also a relational attribute present in any interaction, a distinction becomes necessary within the concept of power. A possible distinction, non-explicitly made by Luhmann but arguably consistent with his theory, is between power as *a general phenomenon* potentially present in any communication system and political power as the *specific medium* of the political system. Luhmann explains that power is a medium because even though power ultimately relies on physical force, it is "not identical with its basic process, instead the medium arises by surpassing it in performance, by generalization" (Luhmann 1982a: 211). The threat of sanctioning non-compliance loses some of its concreteness and becomes *latent*. However, the capacity to secure compliance remains, and as Max Weber famously argued, is supposed to be monopolized by the state. Accordingly, Luhmann's limitation of power within the political system's boundaries can be understood as a precondition for its *legitimacy*.

Functionally speaking, power as a medium is a "good thing": it enables the political system to fulfill its function of issuing collectively binding decisions within a very complex environment. For Luhmann, the medium of power is *necessary* within an increasingly complex functionally differentiated society to ensure the social coordination related to the political system, that is, the production and implementation of *binding* collective decisions. If power is functionally necessary, the important question is what makes it *normatively acceptable*. A question for which Luhmann does not have much to say besides, to exaggerate slightly, "it depends on the system itself" (see Chapter 4).

Jürgen Habermas

In contrast, Habermas has more to say regarding the normative dimension of power. Both Luhmann and Habermas explicitly start and deviate from Parsons' systems theory, and especially from its conception of media. As a result, Habermas's conception of power is to some extent similar to Luhmann's. The medium of power also has for Habermas the function of easing social coordination, in a context of double contingency, by a *replacement* of actual communication (Chernilo 2002: 441). Habermas and Luhmann appear to converge as well on the idea that "power acquires its empirical motivation force externally, through the physical force acting as its security base" (ibid.). But Habermas introduces here a crucial distinction. While accepting that power as a medium provides an *empirical* motivation to individuals' acceptance, Habermas insists that some contexts of coordination require a *rational* motivation for acceptance:

> In the areas of life that primarily fulfill functions of cultural reproduction, social integration, and socialization, mutual understanding cannot be replaced by media as the mechanism for coordinating action – that is, *it cannot be technicized* – though it can be expanded by technologies of communication and organizationally mediated – that is, it can be *rationalized*. (Habermas 1987: 267, original emphasis)

The distinction between empirical and rational motivation for social coordination follows and sustains Habermas's distinction between systems and lifeworld. On one side, Habermas ties to the *systems* the steering media (money, power) replacing mutual understanding by providing an *empirical* motivation for acceptance. Power as a medium "uncouples the coordination of action from consensus formation in language" (ibid.: 263); it thus replaces rational motivation by empirical motivation, hence its ultimate backing by the possibility of negative sanction. To ease the operations of the political system, the steering medium of power operates according to an instrumental rationality, functionally oriented by the imperatives of the political system. On the other side, Habermas attaches to the *lifeworld* the communicative media (influence, value-commitments) that condense the mutual understanding achieved in the lifeworld and thus carry a *rational* motivation for social coordination (ibid.: 181). Communicative media emerge in the undistorted discursive realm of the lifeworld, from the *actual* mutual understanding of the individuals interacting within it, and according to its own functional imperative: the symbolic reproduction of the lifeworld. These are condensations of instantiations of communicative rationality, from which *communicative power*[69] emerges.

Communicative power is distinct from the steering medium of power because it does not need to be backed by empirical motivations in order to facilitate social coordination. Instead, the motivation for social coordination emerges through communicative *rationality*, "a different kind of compelling force which motivates rationally through propositions that can be argumentatively sustained" (Chernilo 2002: 441). As Habermas contends: "A communicative power of this kind can develop only in undeformed public spheres; it can issue only from structures of undamaged intersubjectivity found in nondistorted communication" (Habermas 1996 in Flynn 2004: 435). Communicative power is then the "normative resource" emerging from the lifeworld that carries rational motivation for social coordination (Flynn 2004: 433).

From this conceptual distinction, Habermas advances one of his main claims: there is a problematic *uncoupling* between the systems (economic and administrative) and the lifeworld, meaning that the former is progressively indifferent to the communicative norms constitutive of the latter. The steering media's emergence disconnected most social coordination from lifeworld contexts, and thus from mutual understanding and rational motivation. In short, there is an uncoupling of the steering media and the communicative media. In response, Habermas pushes the normative claim that "systemic mechanisms need to be anchored in the lifeworld: they have to be institutionalized" (Habermas 1987: 154). Power as a steering medium must be institutionally[70] tied to the communicatively generated power (Flynn 2004: 435).

Power as a steering medium, which Habermas often calls *administrative power*, relieves some of the communicative burden and thus eases social coordination; it "largely spare[s] us the costs of dissensus" (Habermas 1987: 263). As such, it is functionally useful and even

---

[69]   There is an ambiguity on the nature of communicative power in Habermas's account regarding its precise location of emergence: exclusively from the lifeworld, from the functional systems as well, or from the interplay between the two (see Flynn 2004).

[70]   That is "secured by positive law" (Baxter 2011: 34).

necessary for the systemic reproduction and integration of the political system (notably for the production and implementation of political decisions). However, the steering medium of power, contrary to money, requires *legitimation*. In a power-relation, there is an intrinsic asymmetry or "disadvantage to one of the parties" (ibid.: 271). For him, this asymmetry can be compensated only with "reference to collectively desired goals" (ibid.). Consequently, power is "made dependent on processes of consensus formation in language" (ibid.: 272) and "its exercise remains connected to the recognition of normative validity claims" (Baxter 2011: 42). In short, the *legitimacy* of administrative power depends on the communicative power generated in the lifeworld.

Habermas contends, with the uncoupling thesis, that steering and communicative media are increasingly disconnected. Administrative power bypasses actual processes of communicative action, such that "the lifeworld is no longer needed for the coordination of social action" (ibid.: 183). Worse, administrative power tends to "colonize" the lifeworld, which is the realm of communicative power, preventing its generation and connection to the former. Finally, Habermas argues that in the systemic realm in general, steering media like administrative power are "consolidated and objectified into *norm-free* structures" (ibid.: 154, emphasis mine). The medium of administrative power emerges and develops within the political *system* and operates following its functional necessities, with imperatives of instrumental reason and strategic action, and "behind the backs" of concrete actors. Therefore, administrative power is not tied to the norms (discourse ethics) that Habermas conceives as inherent to the communicative activity of the lifeworld. As a steering medium, administrative power is "delinguistified" (ibid.).

Interestingly, the uncoupling of systems and lifeworld, and the colonization of the latter by the former, can both be read in a systemic (even Luhmannian) vein. Habermas is saying schematically that systems and lifeworld as differentiated "wholes" (not to say systems) must be coupled, but not too tightly (rather loosely), otherwise the former will colonize the latter, leading to a problematic *dedifferentiation*. As Baxter provocatively suggests, "the critical model Habermas develops in *Theory of Communicative Action* is more functionalist than straightforwardly normative" (2011: 10). Habermas's distinction of lifeworld and systems primarily highlights the opposition (and to some extent incompatibility) of their respective functional imperatives and rationalities. The main problem he identifies is that the economic and administrative systems prevent the symbolic reproduction of the life-world. As such, his critical thesis is "normatively minimalist" but rather systemic (ibid.: 25).

More critically, Habermas's tendency to dichotomize concepts (such as systems and lifeworld, steering and communicative media, administrative and communicative power, instrumental and communicative rationality) leads him to advance a very controversial claim: that systems are "norm-free structures" (see Baxter 1987 and Baxter 2011). This assumption is quite unlikely. Even for Luhmann (who is not the greatest advocate of normativity), norms are instrumentalized by systems for their reproduction since they are very effective ways of stabilizing expectations and ensuring the continuation of communication. Forst himself (Habermas's own student and current leading figure of the Frankfurt school) opposes Habermas on this point:

A "second nature" of acting (or "functioning") within certain structures presupposes acceptance of the rules of these structures, as well as of certain justifications offered for them, such as ideas about property, cooperation, or efficiency, but also notions of fairness, desert, and the like (and again, it must be added that such acceptance need not be based on critical reflection but can also be of an ideological nature). Thus, such structures are not "norm-free" rather, the norms and justifications they rest on allow for certain forms of strategic action that disregard traditional and ethical norms, potentially "colonizing" the lifeworld (in line with Habermas's analysis). (Forst 2015a: 119)

Forst is right here to contest the "norm-free" character of systems and highlight instead that they can rely on norms (efficiency, property, etc.) more conducive to strategic action than others.[71] Habermas himself corrected this point in *Between Facts and Norms*. There, his conception of the political system is no longer "norm-free": he opens the possibility for communicative action and its attached norms to operate *within* the core of political systems, such as within legislature activity (Baxter 2011: 171). Regarding the concept of power, he drops the sharp distinction between administrative power and communicative power, and adopts instead a "continuum between purely 'de facto' power and 'power

---

[71] Forst explicitly differentiates his theory from Habermas's on that issue *in particular*: "A key difference from Habermas, however, is that [Forst's theory] also specifically captures 'systemic' contexts of the economy and the state in their quality as contexts of justification and explores the narratives and justifications on which they and their power effects are based" (Forst 2017: 13).

transformed into normative authority'" (ibid.: 15). This reconceptualization of power as a matter of degrees rather than of categorical differences, is a more plausible theoretical position towards the normativity of political systems. Forst pursues and succeeds on this theoretical path by grounding normativity within his concept of *noumenal power*.

With the Luhmannian and Habermassian conceptions, power stands in tension between several distinctions. Is power the political medium or/and a more general phenomenon? Does it need to be backed by an empirical motivation such as the possibility of a negative sanction or/and can it be rationally motivated? Does it replace communication and mutual understanding or/and can it condense and enforce them? And, crucially, is the exercise of power free of norms or can it be normatively oriented?

Rainer Forst

Forst's concept of *noumenal*[72] power (2015a) answers these questions in an original way. His starting definition is similar to Luhmann's and Habermas's emphasis on the *motivation* function of power. He defines power as "the capacity of A to motivate B to think or do something that B would otherwise not have thought or done" (ibid.: 115). For this, B must have a minimal freedom to deviate: "At least one alternative way of acting" (ibid.). Instead of distinguishing between empirical and rational motivations, Forst's substantial move is to subsume the former under the latter. An empirical motivation such as the threat of a negative sanction – in his illustration, pointing a gun at someone – is to *give her a reason*. This reason has to be accepted as "good enough" to act accordingly (that is to produce empirical effects). The point is that the threat of a gun first and foremost has an effect within the "space of reasons" or the "realm of justifications" (as Forst tends to equate these terms[73]). Therefore, for the gun to have a motivation function,

---

[72] His framing of power as *noumenal* does not do much conceptual work. He discards the inevitable Kantian connotation of "things in themselves" and refers instead to noumenal as "in thought" (Forst 2018: 297). The insistence on *noumenal* (and on the *cognitive* dimension) is mainly useful to semantically homogenize all the manifestations of power as occurring within the space of *reasons* or *justifications*.

[73] A careful reader might notice here that Forst is equating three concepts: *motivations, reasons*, and *justifications*. Although this is a source of potential confusion, especially when combined with the two-fold (descriptive and normative) use of reasons and justifications, this is not a substantial obstacle for Forst's conception.

something must occur in this noumenal space of reasons/justifications (hence Forst's insistence on the *cognitive* dimension of his approach). Basically, the phenomenon of power always implies a *change* in the space of reasons/justifications. Forst also stresses that reasons (such as being physically threatened by a tank) can be appraised differently, hence the different reactions to the same reason (while most people would run away in front of the powerful reason of a threatening weapon, some would still stand in front of it).

Power can operate through many different reasons: good and bad reasons can motivate people to act in certain ways. Forst's concept of power is therefore "normatively neutral" (ibid.: 111): it does not contain in itself the criteria to distinguish between good or bad reasons/justifications. Thus, power can rely on "bad" reasons such as a physical threat or on "good" ones such as a relevant argument. Accordingly, power *can* but is not *required* to have an asymmetrical form, if, for instance, deliberative reason-giving is to be included as a form of power. Forst's *descriptive*[74] use of reasons and justifications aims to encompass "reasons" of any type, without any recourse to specific conceptions of rationality, nor any grounds of justifiability. Particularly, he wants to avoid any conflation with "the felicitous forms of power Habermas called 'communicative'" (Forst 2018: 295).

While Forst's depiction focuses mainly on interpersonal ("*inter-agential*") relations between some A and B agents, his concept of noumenal power also applies to collective agents, social structures, and more globally to social orders. Social structures can have a life on their own, and they enable and constrain the action of agents (ibid.: 300/304). As he stresses: "In modern society social structures are highly differentiated and complex" (Forst 2015a: 119). However, they are not, *pace* Habermas, *norm-free*. Indeed, he insists that "every social order, and every social subsystem in particular, is based on a certain understanding of its purpose, aims, and rules – in short it is a normative order as *an order of justification*"[75] (ibid., original emphasis).

---

[74] Forst distinguishes *descriptive* and *normative* uses of the notion of justification. The former relates to "the justifications that exist in the social and political world or the justifications that gain social acceptance, whether they are acceptable or not in a normative sense" and the latter to "'good' and valid justification, assuming that we know what the standards of validity are" (2018: 295).

[75] Forst's understanding of "orders of justifications" relies on the sociology of criticism of Boltanski and Thévenot (1991) (see Forst 2017: 14–15).

Forst's assumption is that social structures, orders, and systems[76] are grounded upon *narratives of justifications*: social orders are inevitably *orders of justifications*. Narratives of justifications "work in forming, stabilizing or destabilizing a normative order" (Forst 2018: 295). They constitute the basis of acceptance of these orders/structures/systems. And importantly, these structures *reproduce* these justifications. Hence, social structures and the justifications that uphold them "limit what can be imagined as possible" and thus have power over actual people[77] (Forst 2015: 120). Social structures "structure action"; they *enable* and *constrain* the ability of actual persons to exercise power over others, yet they do not exercise power themselves (Forst 2018: 300). Again, the noumenal power of these structures can be based on good or bad reasons: structural power can represent forms of domination or oppression but also legal limitations of some forms of power or even legitimate institutions of democratic governance. The point is that there is a "normativity of the power structures that surround us that fix and 'normalize' identities and that determine what can be said and what not" (Forst 2014: 192). A structure of power is always a *normative* order: it embeds a "normalizing normativity of the established, often unexamined justifications, some of which may be so reified that they are insulated against further problematization" (Forst 2017: 23). This *descriptive* understanding of normativity, about the existing norms at play in a social order, must be distinguished from a *critical* understanding of normativity that aims to problematize this existent normativity. The added value of Forst's theory is precisely to lay the critical grounds of "a theory of validity that always transcends existing justifications" (ibid.: 67). Put differently, he proposes a critical normativity to problematize the existing normativity of particular power structures.

To summarize this section, I departed from Luhmann's normative dead-ends by presenting the Habermassian and Forstian alternatives regarding the question of power. By exploring their similarities, I envisioned grounds for a theoretical junction between Luhmann's sound description of political systems and Habermas/Forst's critical and normative resources regarding their democratic character. On the

---

[76] One would certainly notice that in Forst's language, at least for the purpose of this discussion, *orders* and *systems* are practically interchangeable.

[77] To be precise, Forst distinguishes *power* and *influence*, the latter being applicable for cases "where power is not intentionally exercised by persons over others" (Forst 2015a: 120), such as in the case of the power of structures.

sociological terrain, the three conceptions of power are not that different. They all conceive power as a relational/interactional matter, whose function is motivating others rather than coercing them, hence power always requires freedom. Surprisingly, both Luhmann and Forst consider that "power always unfolds in the space of communication" (ibid.: 63), communication both through interagential relations and as broader social structures/orders/systems. The three authors contend that the power emerging from these structures/systems is necessary for society in general and social coordination in particular; what matters is its legitimation/justification.

Forst's particular descriptive account of power paves a valuable path towards developing a critical normativity. His main interest is not ultimately in the *power of justifications*, but rather in the *justification(s) of power*. Despite his depiction of power as normatively neutral, Forst's conceptualization retains a central normative ambition. Indeed, he connects noumenal power to his famous normative concept of *the right to justification*. As he states, however, "a descriptive theory cannot ground a normative one" (Forst 2018: 299). But it appears that Forst proceeds the other way around: he develops a descriptive theory that fits its normative one. Nonetheless, I suggest below that the connection between his plausible description of power and his normative model of justification is well justified. If I cannot display here the details of this theoretical junction, I describe it shortly to use his theory of justification as a normative compass for democratic systems.

From practices of justification to democratic legitimacy

Forst's connection between the noumenal phenomenon of power and normativity is grounded on the fact that both rely on the practice of *justification*. Justification is both a "basic social and dynamic practice" (Forst 2007: 302) that occurs in relations of power, and a "normative practice with built-in principles of discursive conduct and criteria for arriving at good justifications" (Forst 2018: 318). I reconstruct below how Forst connects the social and normative dimensions of the practice of justification to ground his right to justification.

Forst starts from the anthropological assumption of the human as a "justifying being [...] who uses and 'needs' justifications" (Forst 2011a: 966). Sociologically speaking, justifications are crucial to "orient oneself autonomously in social space" (ibid.). From that sociological understanding, we need "grounds" for a normative critique of existing relations of power/justification. Although he self-qualifies as a Kantian constructivist, there is no point here in entering metaethical debates about normative grounding, as Forst himself does not really mind whether his constructivist grounding is taken as "foundationalist" or "non-foundationalist" (Forst 2014: 182). Instead, he claims to restrain himself to the *reconstruction* of the practices of justification that necessarily occur in social contexts. Two practices of justification are pivotal here.

The first is *critique*, which is in essence the questioning or rejection of existing justifications, whether crystalized as social structures or punctually emerging within interagential power relations. Critique targets and challenges existing justifications. For Forst, the practice of critique embeds a "normative power" (ibid.: 189); through the critique of existing justifications or the proposal of better ones, the basic claim to justification is inevitably raised. There is thus an inherent *normativity* in the practice of critique that demands justifications (ibid.: 193). Forst rejects a hyper-contingent, immanent, and groundless understanding of critique, some kind of genealogical critique as redescription (that he attributes in particular to James Tully, see Forst 2011b). For him, the critique raised by citizens over existing justifications "is not just that these were contingent or historically arbitrary, but that they were *wrong* in the light of principles and norms that from the participants' perspective are as *true*, as *foundational* as they can be, and worth fighting for" (ibid.: 120, original emphasis). Therefore, the critique of contingent configurations cannot rely exclusively on "contingent resources," but also requires a more stable ground, one that is implied by the practice of critique itself: *the right to justification*. Furthermore, this basic normative ground requires critique to remain reflexive, in that it demands that the contingent norms orientating critique must be justified too and cannot be reified (Forst 2014: 191).

The second practice of justification is *morality*. Forst reconstructs "the logic or normative grammar [...] [of the practical context of morality] and extrapolate[s] and abstract[s] the kind of recognition that is specific to this context" (ibid.: 190). The moral context is "a special area of justification" (ibid.: 173), yet one "that critically cuts through the others" (ibid.: 191) (for instance, through the political context) insofar as moral validity claims are raised. He relies here strongly on Kant's coupling of morality to practical reason. Since individuals have the capacity to provide reasons/justifications for their actions, they have in moral contexts a *"duty* of justification to provide morally justifiable – reciprocally and generally non-rejectable – reasons for actions that concern others in a morally relevant way" (ibid.: 173, my emphasis). The corollary to this duty is the *right* to justification. Forst does not only postulate this duty/right, he establishes two *criteria* of moral justification.

The validity of moral claims depends on their *reciprocal* and *general* form. Concretely, moral claims intrinsically support norms or ways of action that are allegedly *reciprocally* and *generally* valid and binding. From this assumption, Forst proceeds recursively in considering that if reciprocity[78] and generality are the *validity* criteria of all norms, they must also be the *normative* criteria for the justification "of all actions or norms that affect [people] in morally relevant ways" (Forst 2011a: 966). For him, what matters is not only the *acceptance* of justifications, even if consensual, because justifications can be of more or less justifiable from a moral point of view. What matters is the moral justifiability of justifications. That is why reciprocity and generality are for Forst "criteria of the justifiable or unjustifiable rejectability of claims" (2014: 196). Reciprocity and generality are Forst's normative criteria of *moral* justification. As Forst puts it:

> In justifying or challenging a moral norm (or a mode of action), no one can make specific claims that she or he denies to others (reciprocity of contents); moreover no one can simply assume that others share his or her perspective, evaluations, convictions, interests, or needs (reciprocity of reasons), such that one would claim, for instance, to speak in the "real" interest of others or in the name of an absolutely indubitable truth beyond the reach of justification. And, finally, it follows that no affected person may be prevented from raising objections and that the reasons that are supposed to legitimize a norm must be such that they can be shared by all persons (generality). (Forst 2011a: 969)

The normative criteria of reciprocity and generality apply to the justification of relations of power, social structures, and the norms

---

[78] I strongly agree that *reciprocity* is an inescapable form of validity of any moral claim. I see here a striking parallel with Luhmann's understanding of moral communication as limited by the general condition of *the interdiction of self-exemption*. For him, someone advancing a moral claim regarding someone else's actions tacitly implies that this claim is also valid for herself (see Chapter 3).

upholding them. They actually provide a normative and moral anchor to the critique of existing relations of justifications. Forst endorses here what he calls a "justificatory monism and diagnostic-evaluative pluralism" (Forst 2007: 294), making the right to justification the most basic right "on which all other basic rights are founded" (Forst 2011a: 968). That implies that other evaluative norms must be at least justified by reciprocally and generally non-rejectable claims. These more contingent norms can then uphold different normative orders as orders of reciprocal and general justification. Within normative orders, a "basic structure of justification" must be set in place to secure the right to justification: without such a structure, this basic right is violated (Forst 2014: 197). All those subjected to a normative order (in the sense of *binding*) must be free to participate in this structure of justification, as "equal normative authorities" (Forst 2017: 309).

To rely on the all-subjected principle opens the door to the "boundary problem" in democratic theory. Thus, Forst clarifies that all persons morally *affected* by our actions have a moral right to justification, and we all have a moral duty of justification to the persons we morally affect. However, the contexts of "political and social justice" are narrower than the moral contexts (Forst 2014: 206). These are contexts of *domination* or *rule* as specific forms of power[79] (ibid.: 201); the circumscribed contexts of a "*political* community of justification" (ibid., emphasis mine), and all the people *subjected* to these contexts, are part of this community. The endorsement of the all-subjected principle instead of the all-affected one is very controversial. However, I do not take position on this issue because it is not pivotal for my use of Forst's theory.

Political communities of justification vary from *domination* to *rule*. The difference (of degrees rather than category) between these rests on the shape of the structure of justification. There is *domination* when this structure is "sealed off," that is, when unjustifiable (non-reciprocal and non-general) relations of power are seen as "legitimate, natural, God-given, or in any way unalterable" or "backed by serious threats" (Forst 2015a: 125). Domination is a context of power where people subjected to it cannot participate in an appropriate structure of justification. There is *rule* when such a structure exists and when power

---

[79] Forst (2014: 206) accepts that his restriction of the context of justice to rule and domination can be framed as a "systemic view: justice is owed only to co-participants in a system of power" (Caney 2014: 163).

is supported by "comprehensive (religious, metaphysical, historical or moral) justifications" (ibid.: 124). It is important to stress that for Forst both forms of domination and rule can be considered as *legitimate* (which does not mean, however, democratic). Indeed, he conceives legitimacy as "normatively dependent": its specific content can rely on many different normative sources ("reasons or motivations for legitimacy"), with variable degree of justifiability (Forst 2017: 133). For example, domination justified by God's will can be perceived as legitimate, as well as rule supported by dynastic lineage. Forst defines legitimacy as "the quality of a normative order that explains and justifies its general binding power for those subjected to it" (ibid.). With this Weberian (and Luhmannian, see Chapter 4) understanding of legitimacy, *democracy* is a specific normative source to fill up the normatively dependent concept of legitimacy.

Democracy, according to Forst, as a "particular form of organization of political rule," rests on a basic moral claim: the right to justification (ibid.). No reciprocal and general justification can claim otherwise: the claim to the right to justification is not reciprocally and generally rejectable. Concretely, this right implies that those who are subjected to a normative order must be its "co-authors" as "justificatory equals" (Forst 2015a: 118/125). Another implication of this right for democracy is that it requires *actual* practices of justification to be in place and some to be institutionalized in order to secure this right. *Hypothetical* justifiability does not suffice in the political realm. If each person subjected to rule can be its co-author through *actual* and appropriate practices of justification, such rule can be called *democratic*. Moreover, Forst stresses the important reflexive character of the practices of justification in arguing that: "Institutionalizations of democratic practices of justification always involve an inherent critical-reflexive dimension that questions these procedures and their results as regards their justifiability" (Forst 2017: 134). Forst refers once again to the reciprocal and general character of justifications when he speaks of justifiability. Both *procedures* of justifications and their *results* are tied to these criteria. If this is indeed the case, as I think Chambers believes too, I must echo her fear about these criteria "creating critical standards that stands above the democratic actions and lives of real citizens" (Chambers 2015: 215). To tie the results of the procedures of justifications to the same standards than the procedures themselves raises some concerns about the relative importance of *actual* justifications over *hypothetical* ones (ibid.). I think Forst would reply with a distinction between "basic questions of justice," where reciprocity and generality apply to outcomes, and "political issues" where these criteria apply only to the procedures of justification. This seems to be what is meant in the following quote:

> Democratic power is exercised through the rule of reciprocally and generally justifiable reasons when it comes to basic questions of justice. Further political issues are decided through fundamentally just (and legitimate) justificatory procedures in which all subjected can participate as justificatory equals. (Forst 2015a: 125)

I will not follow Forst on drawing distinctions between basic questions of justice and further political issues. The relation between democracy and justice is central for him, as he contends that the concept of democracy is "normatively dependent" on the concept of justice (Forst 2017: 135). The demand for the right to justification might be a demand for "fundamental justice"; the one for a basic structure of justification as well (ibid.: 138). However, for my purpose of discussing the normativity of *political* systems, it suffices to accept, with Forst, that: "Democracy, properly understood, is thus the *political form of justice* [...] [it] is not just a, but the practice of political and social justice" (ibid.: 135, original emphasis). Democracy is the political practice of justice grounded in the right to justification. Whether democracy is instrumental to the end of justice does not really matter here. The important assumption is that democracy has a value: it represents the most important normative resource for discussing the normativity of political systems, and for this reason, we can use it without a full-fledged connection to justice. Accordingly, I suggest that the basic normative criteria of reciprocal and general justifiability of claims constitute an appropriate normative ground to develop a theory of *democratic systems*.

Reciprocity and generality as normative compasses for democracy

Following Forst, the granting of the basic right to justification to all people subjected to a normative order, and its securing through institutionalized practices of justification, constitutes the normative pivot between political and democratic systems. The right to justification represents a firm, yet very abstract, normative *boundary* that distinguishes all political systems from democratic ones. Once this boundary is crossed, there is a *continuum* regarding the democratic character of practices of justifications.[80] Importantly, the idea of a continuum must not be taken as a scale to compare and rank the democratic quality of different political systems. It instead expresses the idea that a particular democratic system is constantly fluctuating along this scale. The task of *diagnosis* seeks to identify where (or rather, *how*) a political system is situated on this continuum, in order to detect which practices could push it in the right direction, the *democratic* direction. However, although the democratic horizon is unique (for Forst, as a structure of reciprocal and general justification for binding power), the ways to get there are multiple and diverse. The ultimate aim for all political systems is to get closer to it, but from existing positions and by different means. Therefore, each continuum is *context-specific*; it is relative to the political system under investigation. I aim to develop tools to navigate along this continuum, in diagnosing how existing practices of justification are contextually problematic and how they can be contextually improved.

For this aim, Forst's right to justification is a useful starting point. It offers a normative *threshold* or *minimum*, as there cannot be democratic systems without at least some opportunities of justification. But the granting of this right only settles the beginning of the continuum. The point is not only to have opportunities for justification, but to have opportunities for *reciprocal and general* justification. For Forst, a democratic system ultimately requires collectively binding decisions that are reciprocally and generally justified. Accordingly, the criteria of reciprocity and generality constitute a normative compass: they indicate the direction towards *democratic* practices of justification. While these normative criteria indicate the democratic direction, they do not show how to get there. Therefore, the practical use of this normative orientation requires further normative resources. This section suggests a way to use Forst's normative criteria for the contextual diagnosis of particular democratic systems.

To use reciprocity and generality as basic normative criteria, I need to discuss these in greater detail. In Forst's argumentation, reciprocity

---

[80] This is greatly inspired by Saward (2021: 59), who suggests a continuum above the threshold of what he calls a "democratic minimum."

and generality become normative criteria for the justification of norms or courses of actions because they are *validity claims* inherently raised in any justification of norms or courses of action. Indeed, we understand clearly that when someone claims for a norm (e.g., the interdiction of alcohol consumption or universal suffrage), this claim comes with two underlying assumptions: one, that the claimant accepts this norm to apply to herself too; and two, that she intends this norm to apply to everyone else (or explicitly, to a specific group, such as children or adults). To claim for a norm's *validity* means claiming that "nobody has good reasons to violate this norm": the results is that "both objections and exceptions carry a high burden of justification" (Forst 2011c: 19). For the norm to be "valid," it needs to stand on relevant claims, that is, on "reasons that cannot be reasonably – that is reciprocally and generally – rejected" (ibid.: 20). Put conversely, a norm cannot be valid if it does not rely on reciprocal and general justifications. Forst makes a recursive reasoning: "If one asks *recursively* about redeeming this claim, then this calls for a *discursive* justification procedure in which the address-ee of the norm can assess its reciprocal and general validity" (ibid.: 20, original emphasis). In short, claims to the reciprocal and general validity of some norms demands their reciprocal and general justification.

Forst's recursive move is convincing to me, at least insofar as it applies to *norms*. As norms intrinsically have a collective dimension, I can clearly see the claims to reciprocity and generality they inherently raise. I doubt whether the same reasoning can apply to concrete actions (on this issue, see Benhabib 2015: 781–2), but I leave that question aside. For the purpose of discussing democratic *systems*, suffice to accept the application of Forst's criteria to political *norms* (operating within political institutions and practices). In order to diagnose democratic systems, I thus suggest restricting the application of Forst's normative criteria to the norms structuring political *procedures* and *practices* of justifications (e.g., rules of eligibility). Indeed, these criteria are here relevant as the common normative reference for the assessment of *political* practices and institutions of justifications. Yet Forst contends that these criteria apply to the outcomes of procedures too, at least for "basic questions of justice." This means questioning whether some concrete outcomes are *justifiable* in terms of reciprocity and generality. I remain agnostic on this point, as I am not interested in assessing the *justifiability* of the outcomes of democratic systems, but only of the political structures generating these outcomes.

Regarding the substance of reciprocity and generality, I must clarify how I understand these normative criteria. To start with, *reciprocity* is the procedural expression of equality. According to Forst, it "underscores the equal status and imperative of concrete respect for moral persons as individuals" (Forst 2011c: 20). Reciprocity is actually divided into two criteria. First, *reciprocity of content* is easy to understand and seems to be the least challenged and challengeable of these criteria. It basically means the interdiction of self-exemption for the claimant: "It prohibits unjustifiedly self-regarding claims" (Benhabib 2015: 782). As such, it grounds the process of justification into the realm of morality, yet without relying on any specific moral substance. Consequently, it is the least controversial of Forst's criteria.

Second, the *reciprocity of reasons* is more controversial (see Besch 2020 for a detailed critique). In substance, it means that "no one may simply assume that others have the same values and interests as oneself or make recourse to 'higher truths' that are not shared" (Forst 2011c: 6). I struggle to see how this requirement conceptually emerges from Forst's recursive reasoning. And more importantly, its expected normative work is unclear. In answering to Benhabib (2015) on this latter concern, Forst argues that this criterion rules out "values one may reasonably hold but cannot generalize reciprocally," such as religious doctrines (Forst 2015b: 826). However, I wonder how we can concretely determine that a *claim* respects or not a reciprocity of reasons. That would probably necessitate drawing lines between shareable and non-shareable reasons, hence reintroducing the need for distinctions between particular ethics and universal morality. For this reason, I suggest leaving this criterion aside.

Third, *generality* refers to the scope of applicability of norms: the people that are potentially affected by them. Generality is Forst's label for "universality" (Forst 2011c: 20). The purpose of this criterion is "to prevent the exclusion of those possibly affected and confers the authority of the moral community on the individual" (ibid.). But there is an ambiguity regarding the criterion of generality. Sometimes, it means the inclusion of the affected person's claims in the process of justification: "Nobody may be excluded from the community of justification" (Forst 2017: 28). Yet, often, it also means that "reasons for generally valid basic norms must be *shareable* by all those affected" (Forst 2011c: 6: emphasis mine). The two formulations do not mean exactly the same thing. The former is a *procedural* requirement of inclusion, the latter requires some additional *substance* to determine what is "shareable" and what is not. Or it could be that shareable means reciprocal and general, and a tautology would occur.

According to me, the use of "shareable" reasons serves to pave the way for the possibility of *hypothetical* justification, even though Forst's account appears to be one of *actual* discursive justification. Indeed, his use of this adjective "underscore[s] the (in this sense *counterfactual*) moment of reciprocal and general acceptability – or better, non-rejectability – *independent of the factual* acceptance or nonacceptance of reasons" (ibid.: 21, emphases mine). In using "shareable" instead of "shared" to qualify reasons, and in oscillating often between "justified" and "justifiable," Forst hopes to avoid a conflation of his approach with consensus theories (Forst 2017: 29). As he argues, shared reasons might nevertheless be "one-sided," and that may be proved "in the light of shareable reasons" (ibid.). I understand the use of hypothetical justifiability as an attempt to tie claims to higher expectations than their actual acceptance. And the further requirement of "shareable" reasons within Forst's package of normative criteria precisely enables hypothetical or counterfactual justifiability. Indeed, reciprocity of content (as interdiction of self-exemption) and generality (as inclusion of all-affected) are criteria applying to *actual* justification. They question whether *actual* claims are reciprocal and general and thus actually *justified*. In contrast, the requirement of shareability interrogates whether these claims *could be* shared by all those affected. But how to answer this question? By using the criteria of reciprocity and generality or with external standards? Again, if *shareable* means something other than reciprocal and general, how to substantiate it without external resources? Moreover, I doubt that Forst's justification for the need for shareability really holds. He fears that shared reasons may be one-sided, but this risk is ruled out by the criterion of reciprocity of content. In consequence, I do not follow Forst on a distinction between shareable and non-shareable reasons.

In line with these remarks, what exactly do I take from Forst's theory? I endorse *reciprocity of content* without amendment. I drop *reciprocity of reasons* because I do not see it applicable to claims and in need of extra-procedural moral substance. I accept *generality*, but only as a procedural requirement demanding the inclusion of the all-affected[81] in the actual processes of justification. Hence, I reject a more substantial understanding of generality, because for my purpose of assessing political systems, we do not need to identify if shared reasons are *shareable* according to external standards. Nevertheless, I accept the *counterfactual* (or reflexive) use of these criteria, that is, the hypothetical question of the justifiability of the norms operating within a particular system. But not in order to tie these to greater standard of acceptability, as I suspect Forst's does. I rely on hypothetical justifiability as the best *proxy* in case of absence of actual justifications for political arrangements. As I contend in the next chapter, actual justifications for the shape and functioning of political systems are likely to be absent in many contexts under diagnosis: there might be no actual claims to be assessed by the criteria of reciprocity (as interdiction of self-exemption) and generality (as all-affected inclusion). In such cases, hypothetical justifiability becomes relevant, and it questions whether a particular political arrangement, despite its problematic lack of actual justification, *could be* sustained or rejected by reciprocal and general claims. In the next chapter, I show how to use these criteria for the task of diagnosis.

In order to assess the norms operating within a democratic system, reciprocity and generality serve as abstract critical tools. They are probably too fuzzy (and unclear) to serve as *sharp* critical tools for real persons in actual processes of justifications (Besch 2020: 373; McNay 2020: 41), although I think that everybody could understand and accept the interdiction of self-exemption and the inclusion of all-affected as basic justificatory rules. Nevertheless, this abstractedness may not be problematic for the theorist taking Forst's theoretical abstractions as normative compasses *precisely because they are abstract*, and thus *a priori* relevant for any kind of political context. Once more, abstraction or "thinness" appears to be the price for generalization. Indeed, reciprocity and generality do not provide a detailed metric to assess with certainty whether claims, norms, political arrangements, or individual actions are justified. Nonetheless, they represent basic questions to

---

[81] Recall that Forst considers that in the *political* domain, contra the *moral* one, the all-subjected principle replaces the all-affected principle. I do not take position on this move's relevance, as I take Forst's theoretical core to be valid with both principles of inclusion. Eva Erman's "function-sensitive view" on the boundary problem of democracy (2022: 241) is a promising route to tackle this issue as it argues for the compatibility of the all-affected and all-subjected principles, granting they are "justified vis-à-vis different functions."

interrogate the justifiability of political norms and institutions, at the very least. Questions that I doubt any democratic theorist can avoid when undertaking diagnoses of political systems.

Moreover, Forst's normative criteria have two analytical advantages over the "grounding" of other political principles (e.g., freedom, equality, inclusion, deliberation, etc.). First of all, they prevent at the outset the risk of normative trade-offs between the two cardinal values of freedom and equality.[82] Indeed, as complementary expectations, the criteria of generality and reciprocity do not stand in conflict. Together, they form a critical tool to assess the justifiability of normative trade-offs between *other* principles, such as participation and epistemic quality, by asking: is the prevalence of epistemic quality over participation, in this context, justified by reciprocal and general reasons? Second, as criteria for the validity of *claims*, they are more encompassing than other principles such as equality and freedom. They are not exactly "political" principles, but rather emerge from general morality. These criteria represent a common *procedural* ground to question the justifiability of the claims upholding political principles, equality and freedom among them. They are criteria of validity *for* principles, and thus can stand above and apply to a broad range of principles "that cannot generate their criteria of validity out of themselves in an autonomous way" (Forst 2017: 66). For instance, the principle of inclusion does not itself contain criteria of validity; external resources are necessary to argue that a particular inclusion (or exclusion) is justified. Reciprocity and generality can be such resources in asking: is this exclusion reciprocally and generally justified? But the answer to this question requires much more: for instance, an exclusion could be justified to enable a proper deliberation, or an inclusion might be demanded in order to foster the expertise of a deliberative forum. I discuss in the next section how to combine the encompassing normativity of reciprocity and generality, with the more specific normative expectations operating in political contexts (participation, representation, deliberation, epistemic quality, respect, and many others).

To summarize, reciprocity and generality represent the common "critical questions" for the norms operating within political systems. Yet other normative expectations are necessary to question political

---

[82] To be sure, I do not suggest that there is *necessarily* a trade-off between freedom and equality. But the history of political theory contains several examples of such an assumption (e.g., Nozick 1974).

arrangements. These other norms are more *contextual* expectations, whose endorsement must be justified according to these criteria in specific contexts. Consequently, reciprocity and generality are *context-sensitive* normative criteria that apply to the justification of other norms. Chambers contends that generality and reciprocity are "too indeterminate to have critical teeth" (2015: 215). She is right, but they do not have to carry the entire critical burden. Reciprocal and general justifications only constrain the validity of the claims in support of *other* "critical teeth" (such as inclusion, participation, publicity, accountability, responsiveness, deliberation, representation, and so on) that are much sharper indeed. In the next section, I articulate the requirements of reciprocity and generality with these more contextual normative expectations within the normative layer of democratic systems.

The normative layer: justification criteria and contextual norms

In my understanding, the normative layer of democratic systems is analytically two-fold (see Chapters 1 and 2). On the one hand, there are the criteria of justification of norms and institutions: reciprocity and generality. On the other hand, there are norms and institutions whose contextual enactment is to be justified. The first are invariable, while the second are more contextual: they are *system-specific*. By contextual and system-specific, I mean that in each political context (understood as a system, or for Forst as a normative order) some norms are more at play and/or expected than others. For instance, in the political subsystem of the administration, the norms of efficacy and accountability are more directly at play (and expected) than other norms, such as participation or preference-flexibility. Let's take another example: in the context of party politics, the norms of competition and strategic bargaining are more at play than consensus and mutual recognition, while in the context of a deliberative mini-public, the opposite is likely to be true. The point is that normativity is to a large extent a contextual matter; different systems (or normative orders for Forst) select and mobilize different normative expectations. The main critical question is to what extent these selections and mobilizations of normative expectations are *justified*. The framing of this normative question corresponds, as I understand it, to what Forst calls a "justificatory monism and diagnostic-evaluative pluralism" (2007: 294). There are different principles or norms[83] operating in different normative orders. The criteria of reciprocal and general justification entail the critique of particular normative orders both on these minimal common grounds *and on their own terms*, that is, according to the particular norms operating in these normative orders, insofar as these norms are reciprocally and generally justified.

Accordingly, I suggest the use of two "types" of normative criteria: justification criteria and contextual/systemic norms. Recall in Chapter 2, Saward's account (2021) also distinguished *required* principles (e.g., freedom, equality) from *ordering* principles (e.g., deliberation, representation, transparency). The purpose of this distinction is to maintain a common normative core for democracy, while allowing its variable enactment in different contexts. It enables not only the variability of democratic *means*, but also to some extent of democratic *ends*. In Saward's framework, ordering principles are "a wide range of political principles [that] may be invoked as informing, animating, or defining democratic designs or plans" (Saward 2021: 82). Indeed, these ordering principles enable the task of design in mobilizing clear and detailed expectations according to their contextual relevance to be greatly complexified. Hence Saward draws a list of more than forty ordering principles (ibid.: 156), intendedly as diverse as virtue, choice, expertise, deliberation, non-domination, sustainability, and social justice. For the task of *design*, it is to some extent a question of the designer's choice on the priority in which these principles should be fostered (considering, of course, contextual imperatives). But for the task of *diagnosis*, the aim is precisely to determine which principle(s) are enacted or not (at all or appropriately). Therefore, although I share Saward's distinction of two sorts of principles, I need to use it slightly differently than he does for his design purpose. Moreover, I suggest that since these two levels are conceptually related, Forst's criteria are useful resources for conceptualizing this connection. Thereafter, I discuss Saward's normative framework sharing this similar twofold structure and explicitly justify my deviation from it.

For Saward, the democratic minimum normatively requires the enactment of the principles of *equality* and *freedom* (besides some other

---

[83] Principles and norms are not exactly conceptual equivalents, yet the distinction between them is not analytically useful for this discussion. I take them here as equivalent labels meaning "normative expectations."

"circumstances" such as a community, resources, governance, and a constitution). They are "fundamental" to democracy (ibid.). I agree: democracy cannot do without the enactment of *some kinds* of equality and freedom. However, the purpose (among others) of democracy is precisely to decide *which* form of equality (and sometimes, inequality) to enact, and which freedoms to promote or restrict. Saward stresses the interpretability of these principles: "Think of equality, of outcome, of opportunity, of rights, and so on; think of 'freedom to' and 'freedom from' and their consequent further variations" (ibid.: 84). Nonetheless, Saward fills up his required principles with a very precise content: equal opportunity on the one hand and freedom of expression and of association on the other. He notes that often these freedoms are "not total," nor do they always need to be (ibid.: 56). Indeed, sometimes freedom of expression can become an issue of democratic governance itself (think of conspiracy theories and fake news). I agree that freedom of expression and association are *minimal requirements* for democracy: without the possibility of expressing and associating, any type of democracy is not only normatively discarded, but even functionally impossible since it prevents communication *tout court*. Of course, I also agree that some form of equality is fundamental for democracy, even if I am not sure whether this form is necessarily and always an equality *of opportunity*.

Although the principles of equality and freedom are fundamental, I suggest their normative endorsement is of little help to discuss the contextual relevance and appropriateness of *other principles* ("ordering" principles for Saward). I contend that non-required principles (contextual/systemic normative expectations in my vocabulary) cannot "stand alone": their contextual justifiability depends on other, universal principles, "required" or "cross contextual shared norms" to speak with Saward (ibid.: 66). Indeed, how can we conceive or even solely explain the principle of inclusion without that of equality? In addition, how can we justify the contextual enactment of inclusion under a particular form without reference to equality? I thus suggest that the conceptual relationships between these two types of principles needs to be more explicit. Second, although equality and freedom are fundamental requirements of any democratic system, they do not provide critical tools to assess the enactment of *other* political principles, such as deliberation or representation. The principles of freedom and equality are necessary for the *theoretical* justification of deliberation and representation, but they do not provide a critical reference for the *actual* justification of the enactment of these principles in practical contexts. For instance, one can theoretically question whether the principle of representation fosters equality, but that does not tell us much about the justifiability of a *certain kind* of representation in a particular context. On the contrary, to reflect on whether the specific representativity of (or lack of) a deliberative mini-public is justified by reciprocal and general claims, is to ask a much more critical question.

In my opinion, the point is not to ensure that every norm, institution, or political arrangement features equality and freedom, and even less a particular understanding of these principles. The point is rather to assess, for a particular normative order or system, to what extent the presence or predominance of some "ordering principles" instead of others results from (or at least hypothetically respects) a process of reciprocal and general justification. As Saward notes, "all democratic systems, existing or imaginable, favor some principles over others in their mode of institutionalization" (ibid.: 160). As I am interested in the assessment of *existing* systems, some critical tools are necessary to question the justifiability of these favored principles. This critical question has nothing to do with the appropriate *meaning* and justification of principles (required or ordering). It has to do with the justifiability of their selection, prioritization, interpretation, and contextual enactment. Reciprocal and general justifications limit the scope of acceptable uses of these principles, without tying them to specific *theoretical* justifications. Instead, it gives center stage to the *actual* justifications of these principles in context, by people themselves. In sum, the main difference with Saward's account derives from our respective different aims: the task of diagnosis requires the identification of "problems" with the *actual* operating principles, while the task of design offers more latitude to *choose* principles in order to address these problems.

I must specify (beyond the encompassing normative criteria of reciprocal and general justification) the other principles or norms operating in democratic systems. Three principles are necessarily part of any democratic framework: equality, inclusion, and freedom. However, each in their own way has a special standing that differentiates them from contextual normative expectations such as deliberation, responsiveness, civility, and representation. To start with, *equality* is "inextricable from democracy, whatever particular forms the latter may take in different contexts" (ibid.: 82). There are multiple ways to understand theoretically the principle of equality, and I do not intend to present these here (see Gosepath 2021). My aim is rather to explain how equality is conceived here and where does it operate within the normative layer of democratic systems. Besides encompassing various theoretical forms (formal equality, substantial equality, equality of opportunities, etc.), equality can also *empirically* endorse variable forms in different contexts. I thus take here an important position regarding equality: no form of equality trumps all the others whatever the context is. Accordingly, I do not restrict equality in defending one of these conceptions as the "right" one, I take them all as possibilities of what equality *could be* in variable contexts. My goal is then to ensure equality in the ways people decide upon the forms of equality they favor at a certain time and for a certain place. After all, democracy is about making complex choices regarding concrete applications of the abstract principle of equality, not to fix once and for all what equality means and how it should be enacted. If we could know for certain what equality demands in every circumstance, as some philosophers are keen to claim, there wouldn't be much room for democratic activity.

Therefore, which understanding of equality provides latitude to *decide* about equality? Forst's account clearly favors *relational equality*, as he contends that "all those who are subjected to a normative order should be its co-authors *as equal* participants and normative authorities in adequate justificatory practices" (Forst 2017: 42, emphasis mine). By tying every norm to the burden of *reciprocal* and *general* justification, the principle of equality is procedurally omnipresent in Forst's account. For any claim, the criteria of reciprocity and generality guarantee a minimal presence of equality *within the relation of justification*. Reciprocity ensures that the claims are not one-sided and self-exempting. Generality secures some procedural equality in demanding the inclusion of all-affected individuals. Consequently, in the normative layer of democratic systems developed here, relational equality is invisibly omnipresent, so to speak. It constitutes the normative core of the right to reciprocal and general justification, even though it is not at the forefront as an operative criterion. Equality is thus clearly not a contextual normative expectation such as deliberation or publicity; equality is *always* expected within a democratic system under the form of reciprocal and general justification. However, the contextual enactment of the principle of equality (for instance, equality of opportunity in the education system) remains variable and in need of justification. Furthermore, reciprocal and general claims also apply to the justifiability of some forms of *inequalities*: unequal outcomes, unequal taxation, unequal rights, positive discrimination, etc. To sum my position on equality, extra-procedural justifications of what equality necessarily *must* be reduce the scope of what it *can* be and *should* be in context. In contrast, a relational and procedural equality as enforced by the reciprocity-generality couple allows a greater variety and variation of equality's instantiations in real and changing circumstances.

Relatedly, is the principle of *inclusion*, which is probably the corollary of equality in democratic theory. Democracy is about the inclusion of people but also of perspectives, claims, ideas, narratives, etc. The improvement of democracy demands "more inclusion." Yet it demands other things too (such as autonomy, expertise, deliberation, or "separation of powers") that in their own way sometimes require *exclusion* (or non-inclusion). Not everybody or every claim can be included everywhere: complex organizations need selections. Even the simple fact of associating with a group such as a political party de facto excludes others (because one has to satisfy membership criteria, and not everyone does). The point is that to include is always simultaneously to exclude, and conversely. As Forst puts it, "democracy is a self-correcting enterprise, it establishes forms of justification, but it cannot *fully* establish forms of justification, because every institutionalization is inclusive and exclusive at the same time" (Forst 2021: video). The question of inclusion is present in multiple (not to say *all*) moments or locations of a democratic process. But the answers to this general question depend on variable criteria. For instance, the exclusion of someone from presidential eligibility might rely on his criminal record, while the inclusion of an expert within a deliberative mini-public might be motivated by his specific expertise. However, these variable answers must also be reciprocally and generally justified. The point is that questions of inclusion must be answered in relying on *both* common justification criteria and contextual normative expectations. As discussed in Chapter 6, the principle of inclusion has a special standing within this framework of democratic systems: it is always *a priori* favored over exclusion, but in practice exclusions are often necessary. Therefore, for every political context under analysis (e.g., the parliament, a political party, a participatory budget), the principle of inclusion is at stake: potential exclusions must be justified, and so by reciprocal and general claims. As such, inclusion contrasts with other normative expectations that are only contextually relevant, such as participation, transparency, or consensus.

The last cardinal principle of democracy is, of course, *freedom*. Democracy requires freedoms, among them most certainly the freedom to express oneself and to associate. It probably demands other freedoms too, such as the freedom of conscience and the freedom to demonstrate or even of civil disobedience in some circumstances. Metaphorically speaking, democracy needs the freedom to actively and loudly say "yes, because..." and "no, because..." to political decisions, to ask "why" when the reasons are unclear, and "what about X or Y" when other ideas emerge. Democracy is largely about freedom; it is individual and collective agency within systems of power. Sociologically speaking, power requires freedom; there cannot be power, and therefore any type of political system (democratic or not) without some freedom. At a more abstract level, power but also communication in general emerge only when there is the freedom to shape meaning. That is why individual agency lies at the core of communication (see Chapter 3). In this context, political systems *decide* on freedom: they select freedoms and thus simultaneously expand and limit the possibility of other freedoms. The important question for democracy, paradoxically, is how to select freedoms *freely*, so to speak. I do not review all the possible ways to answer this question, but only explain how it could be answered in this framework of democratic systems.

In Forst's theory, the value of freedom is understood to a large extent in a Kantian sense as "autonomy" and to a lesser extent in a neo-republican vein (inspired by Philip Pettit in particular) as "non-domination" (Forst 2017: 153–162). Moral autonomy is central in his theory of justification, understood as "the freedom to determine one's will in accordance with self-imposed laws" (ibid.: 83). When secured into legal rights and performed through appropriate justificatory practices, moral autonomy grants every individual the right to be treated as an "end-in-herself," as a "justificatory authority of moral norms" (ibid.: 29). When understood in the context of the political system, the principle of autonomy turns into the idea of democracy, which means the "[avoidance of] political arbitrariness (i.e., domination)" *and* "the expression of collective self-determination" (ibid.: 134–135). Non-domination is understood here not solely in the negative sense of non-interference, but also positively as the expression of individual and collective autonomy. Autonomous political self-legislation is for Forst a discursive and intersubjective practice with the right to justification at its core, "namely, the right to be a democratic co-author of the norms that claim to be legitimate ruling principles" (ibid.: 149). Accordingly, Forst understands freedom as autonomy, as a "*relational* freedom of being a codetermining agent of justification within the normative order that binds us" (ibid.: 162, emphasis mine), unfolding through discursive practices enacting the right to reciprocal and general justification.

As for the principle of relational equality, relational freedom as well is *invisibly omnipresent* within the relations of reciprocal and general justification. Hence, freedom as autonomy is guaranteed exclusively through the right of justification, and thus isn't a normative expectation standing independently of this right. As will become clear in Chapter 6, equality and freedom are not *operative* criteria in the diagnostic framework developed here, contrary to inclusion as a general democratic expectation, and various contextual normative expectations (e.g., deliberation, epistemic advancement, transparency). My point is that freedom *itself*, because of its inherence within contexts of power, and normative omnipresence as autonomy within the right to justification, is of little help to orient the diagnosis of democratic systems. Besides few required substantial freedoms, formally guaranteed, one cannot use freedom as a normative compass because it is precisely the material of politics, and that sometimes, the path towards freedom is made of restrictions to it. Moreover, the normative value of freedom is fully covered normatively speaking by the right to reciprocal and general justifications for power relations. Nevertheless, conceptual declinations of the abstractedness of freedom have a greater analytical strength for the task of diagnosis (such as non-domination, self-determination, independence, individual and collective empowerment), even if they themselves remain subject to various interpretations. These sharper criteria can be at play in the task of diagnosing democratic systems, which I develop in Chapters 6 and 7.

Finally, besides (or rather *from*) the cardinal principles of equality, inclusion, and freedom, multiple other normative expectations are potentially at play within democratic systems. These principles are not always at play or expected (at all or saliently) in *every* location of democratic systems. Accordingly, these other normative expectations are framed as *contextual* or *systemic*; different locations (as systems themselves) of the broad democratic system emphasize different normative expectations. The main normative aim is to interrogate the justifiability of particular systems enacting these various normative expectations, favoring some at the detriment of others. Put differently, the aim is to question the flexibility of the democratic ideal in context. The stable normative anchor is the right to reciprocal and general justification; all the rest is versatile material. I mean here that other principles generally associated with democracy (e.g., deliberation, accountability, participation, publicity, representation, competition) are not at play or expected in *every* location of a democratic system. The latter is a complex articulation of all these expectations, that can complement each other or be in conflict in some locations. Moreover, different democratic systems articulate those expectations diversely. This great versatility of the democratic ideal makes the task of diagnosis very complex. Diagnosis thus requires both "universal" normative grounds (the right to justification) and contextual normative expectations substantiating Forst's "diagnostic-evaluative pluralism."

What are these contextual/systemic principles? A few obviously come to mind: representation, deliberation, participation, responsiveness, accountability, transparency. Some are perhaps less evident: consensus, competition, bargaining, epistemic advancement, recognition, respect. Others are related to broader principles of that list: think of reason-giving, listening, consensus, preference-flexibility, and truth-seeking, as more or less intrinsically related to deliberation. Some principles would be more contested as characterizing democracy, but still can retain some reading of it: order, security, stability, prosperity, efficiency, rationality, resistance, virtue, creativity, innovation, precaution, reasonableness, uncertainty. My point is that drawing a list of these principles is a tricky task. It amounts to setting a theoretical distinction between the principles that can be expected by democratic polities as genuinely democratic, and those that obviously have nothing to do with democracy, regardless of the principles that people themselves use to define and value democracy. In addition, it would "freeze" theoretical labels and conceptualizations, and thus interpretations of these principles. Furthermore, who knows how near horizons (with artificial intelligence, big data, metaverse, space colonization, environmental catastrophes, pandemics, energetic and resources scarcity) will impact the principles at play in political systems. New principles may find relevance in the future, or new labels and interpretations of current principles.

At the same time, not anything goes as a *democratic principle*. Some grounds of differentiation are necessary, not in order to settle a definitive list, but to circumscribe a perimeter of relevance. To start with, a source of differentiation questions which principles are *democratic* or not. There is a difference between a principle that is expected democratically and a democratic principle (although a principle can be both democratic and democratically expected). Indeed, a democratic principle has to do with the *political* functioning of the democratic system, not with its outcomes. This echoes a distinction made by Saward between principles of *governance* and principles of *policy* (2021: 83). For instance, the principles of sustainability and social justice appear to me as principles for policies, not principles for the mode of governance leading to these political outputs. As discussed further in Chapter 7, that does not mean that sustainability and social justice do not matter at all for the diagnosis of pathologies in democratic systems, only that they do not matter as principles regulating *democratic processes*. On the contrary, the principles of representation and publicity, for instance, directly regard the functioning of some parts of the democratic system.

There is another major ground of differentiation: What constitutes or not a democratic *principle*. The identification of democratic *principles* must be done by differentiating them from two related elements, *practices* and *functions*. First, principles have to be distinguished analytically from the practice that performs them. A practice is what occurs concretely (e.g., a parliamentary debate), while a principle is a normative expectation (e.g., deliberation) that is fulfilled or not by this practice. Importantly, some conceptual elements such as deliberation can endorse both analytical statuses within the task of diagnosis. It is both a very concrete practice (e.g., in a mini-public) and an ideal to strive for (deliberativeness of the democratic system). However, deliberativeness as a principle can be a normative expectation also relevant for practices that are not deliberation *per se*, such as within a parliament. Second, there is also an analytical difference between the principles enacted by practices and the *functions* performed by practices. For instance, the selection of political performers is a political function, that could enact the principle of representativeness, via the practices of elections or random selections. In order to pinpoint precisely what are the normative expectations operating or expected in a system, principles as normative criteria should not be conflated with particular practices or functions. I discuss further in Chapter 6 how the task of diagnosis operates through the complex relationships between practices, functions, and principles.

To conclude this discussion on these contextually expected democratic principles, contrary to equality and freedom (through the right to justification) and inclusion, I do not draw a definitive list. Saward's suggestive list of more than forty principles (2021: 156) is a great inspiration, providing a basis from which we could disagree on some items and suggest the integration of others instead. Disagreements over such a list are inevitable (but fruitful), and we do not really need a definitive one. Instead, we would certainly benefit from elements of conceptual and analytical demarcations, such as those suggested here above. Through these distinctions, an observer of a political system can set a list for herself, drawing it from her identification of (the interpretation of) democratic principles operating in her context of analysis, and justifying further relevant democratic principles that should be at play in this context. An awareness of the multiplicity of potential democratic principles and the versatility of their interpretation and labelling is essential when using them as critical material for the contextual diagnosis of democratic systems.

Besides not drawing a definitive list of principles, I also leave open the question regarding the *necessity* of some of these principles for a democratic system. I said above that none of them is to be expected in *every* location of a democratic system. But can we imagine that some principles *need* to be enacted in any democratic system? It is likely that some are necessary, such as representation or mass participation, *in the current shape of modern society*. However, can we ascertain with certainty that any political context claiming to democraticness inevitably requires these principles? I am not sure, and thus suggest answering this in a more pragmatic way: some democratic principles are "usual suspects," notably representation, deliberation, participation, responsiveness, accountability, transparency, and perhaps others. It is obvious that a good diagnosis cannot avoid interrogating the enactment (or absence of) these principles.

Conclusion

In this chapter, I deviated from the lack of normative bite of Luhmann's theory, towards more critical resources for the diagnosis of democratic systems. This shift took place within a discussion on power as the constitutive element of political systems. I described his conception of power and highlighted its limitation regarding what makes it normatively acceptable. From there, I discussed Habermas's conception, similar to Luhmann's regarding the sociological dimension, but providing communicative rationality as a normative orientation. Despite the strength of his proposal, its critical bite relies too much on contrasting dubious dichotomies such as systems and lifeworld or strategic and communicative action. Hence, I followed Forst's remodeling of the concept of power along a *continuum* of reasons/justifications. Moreover, by conceiving systems of power as orders of justifications, he provides broad critical tools to assess the justifiability of power relations and political structures in particular. Reciprocal and general justifications are context-sensitive normative criteria to navigate the continuum of democraticness of political systems. They are used as critical "grounds" to assess the justifiability of the enactment of more contextual normative expectations operating within specific parts of political systems. Therefore, this twofold normative layer enables the critical assessment of existing political systems through both universal and contextual normative grounds.

Before closing this chapter, I must make two positions more explicit. First, normativist readers will clearly notice my position regarding the debate in democratic theory about the respective importance of *substance* and *procedure* as normative grounds for democratic legitimacy. Schematically, the substantial or instrumental position holds that the value of democracy resides in the quality of the outcomes it produces (e.g., consensus, truth, fairness, equality, rationality). This position assumes that there exist *extra-procedural* standards of democratic quality (or justice, or rationality, or sometimes a mix of those). The proceduralist position rejects such external standards and restricts democratic legitimacy to the quality of procedures generating these outcomes. I hold here the latter position regarding democracy's legitimacy. In line with Luhmann's hyper-contingency, I do not assume that we can determine stable and universal *external* standards of validity, whether these concern democracy, justice, or rationality. I endorse instead what Saward labels a "pure democratic proceduralism," that is, the idea that "if a given procedure incorporates, at least, the demands of the democratic minimum, then its outcomes are to be regarded as democratically legitimate" (2021: 93).

But I take a different idea of the democratic minimum than Saward. In my account, the democratic minimum is the right to reciprocal and general justifications. Procedures are a kind of practice of justification. The criteria of reciprocity and generality embed the "substances" of relational equality and relational autonomy: to be *democratic*, practices of justification (procedures among them) must feature these two criteria of justification. Consequently, this pure proceduralism is clearly a case of "procedure-with-substance," as Saward puts it (ibid.: 97). Moreover, these two criteria of justification are only *minimal* grounds for the democraticness of procedures: other democratic principles are to be enacted through procedures depending on the context, such as deliberation or publicity. This position is contestable, but it is arguably compatible with the sociological grounds endorsed here. Furthermore, it has the advantage of being a cautious, skeptical, and normatively minimalist stance. Its claim can be reframed more modestly: *if* we do not or cannot agree on what these extra-procedural standards are (as it is likely to be the case among both theorists and democratic citizens), we can still agree to disagree on these, yet agree on a very minimal procedural basis, reciprocity and generality, that serves to express and confront our disagreements when claiming for some standards instead of others. To be clear, I am not claiming that we can be certain that there are *not* extra-procedural standards of validity. I am simply reasoning from the suspension of both certainties: that there are some on which we can all agree, and there are those on which we cannot. From this agnosticism, we could follow both paths. I chose the more prudent one: I question here the democratic quality of political *procedures* of justifications through procedural criteria, not of their outcomes through extra-procedural standards.

Second, I must justify further the connection between Luhmann and Forst's diverging accounts. I anticipate here a straightforward objection: are these two theories really compatible? The interrogation is legitimate: Luhmann would hardly have agreed on Forst's normative grounding, and Forst is likely to reject the normative indeterminacy and hyper-contingency of Luhmann's account. However, besides this irreconcilable divergence, this chapter has displayed important (and perhaps surprising) affinities between these two authors: the ontological centrality of communication, the relational conception of power, reciprocity as the core of morality, a society differentiated in multiple social systems as normative orders, and the immanence of critique oriented towards the existing norms ruling these systems. It is likely that Luhmann would have rejected Forst's normative "monism," favoring a more groundless constructivist and pluralistic approach. But it is precisely because such an approach left me at a dead-end that I investigated elsewhere; not to find something diametrically different, but to complete what was missing. In that regard, Forst provides a useful complement.[84] Do the tenets of Forst's theory invalidate Luhmann's sociological depiction of political systems? I don't think so: Forst' sociological background appears to me quite similar (although less developed) to Luhmann's. In the end, the conceptions of Luhmann and Forst may not be fully compatible, but they are to some extent, and probably enough to represent complementary inputs for the construction of a theory of democratic systems.

---

[84] Again, one may ask: Why Forst? Well, because he deeply investigated an important step of the journey: the step from a sociology of power to the grounding of normative criteria to assess the justifiability of power. Alternative candidates for this grounding certainly exist, but among our contemporaries, Forst is arguably not the least important. Shall I contrast the value of Forst's account to those? Ideally, yes. But that would require more than another chapter. Is my Forst-inspired normative move good enough to contribute to the development of a theory of democratic systems? Provisionally, yes: it opens a promising horizon. It may turn out to be a dead-end, but that would be a great result triggering a reorientation towards more promising candidates of normative grounding.

Democratic systems: sketching complexity

Democracy can legitimately look and feel very different – different practices in different sequences, intended to enact different principles, in order to meet different challenges – from one context to another. (Saward 2021: 112)

If we assess practices and their institutional combinations in light of their normatively democratic functions, we will be better placed to frame, theorize, and assess the many emergent possibilities for democracy in complex societies. (Warren 2017: 51)

In this chapter, I develop my own theory of democratic systems, on the grounds developed in the previous chapters. As a reminder, Chapters 1 and 2 discussed the current state of the literature regarding deliberative/democratic systems, focusing on six questions essential to building a theory of democratic systems. In Chapters 3 and 4, I explored systems theory for external resources to inspire original answers to these questions. In Chapter 5, I rejoined democratic theory while exploring some normative grounds of democratic systems that are compatible and complementary to systems theory. In this chapter, I put the pieces together by attempting a re-articulation of the conceptual elements discussed in the previous chapters within an original framework of democratic systems. The following core elements of a theory of democratic systems ultimately serve as conceptual and analytical grounds for a diagnostic tool of democratic problems, a task I tackle in the next and final chapter. I proceed in this chapter by giving an original answer to the six questions posed in Chapter 1 and replied with the literature in Chapter 2. Following Chapters 3, 4, and 5, I particularly rely on Luhmann's sociological conception for the *descriptive layer* and on Forst's normative grounds for the *normative layer*. After replying in detail to each of these questions, I take position on the place of deliberation and deliberative systems in the framework of democratic systems.

Observing and mapping political systems: the descriptive layer

The observation and diagnosis of political systems must rely on an analytical framework: a conceptual system indicating what to look at in empirical reality. The potential for generalizing the framework and its elements is relative to its level of abstractedness. Indeed, concrete descriptive elements such as "parliament" and "competitive elections" cannot as such compose this general framework, they are only contextual instantiations of some of its abstract common features (such as the function of legislation and selection of political performers, respectively). Consequently, the descriptive layer must be *context-sensitive* enough to encompass a wide variety of political realities that could be and could be made more or less democratic. Put differently, it has to be sensitive to contextual particularities, such as the selection of performers through sortition instead of election (or combinations of both). However, the descriptive layer must feature clear and relevant differences to bring enough contrast within the whole that it aims to sketch. The more the descriptive layer balances these two conflictual requirements (context-sensitivity and common distinctions), the greater its analytical capacity to observe and map all kinds of political systems. Moreover, this observation and mapping task should focus on *political* systems rather than *democratic* ones. Every political system is *potentially* democratic; the point of diagnosing problems is to uncover how and to what extent it is and can be more democratic. But one cannot produce a faithful *description* of a political reality by observing it with specific normative expectations (democratic ones here). The task of diagnosing political systems in *democratic* terms requires further normative resources and must remain analytically distinct from that of mapping *political* systems. Therefore, within each question below, the focus is brought back to the *political* rather than the *democratic* dimension.

If deliberative/democratic systems are composed of parts, what are these parts "made of"?

In Chapter 2, I described how the main accounts of deliberative and democratic systems answered this question. They share a focus on *practices* instead of *institutions*. This shift in focus aims to highlight the agency of actors within democratic systems, often undermined by the focus on institutionalized structures. In addition, institutions are themselves a special kind of practice. As Saward insists, all institutions are practices, but not all practices are institutionalized (2021: 70–73). Similarly, Bächtiger & Parkinson (2019) place the emphasis on *communicative* practices, taking "memes" (i.e., units of meaning) as the stuff of politics. They argue that memes shape practices; practices are thus communicative processes of collective meaning-making. In line with Luhmann's theory of communication and social systems, I endorse a position close to Bächtiger & Parkinson's on practices representing what political systems are made of.

For systems theory, every social system is made of *communication*. This should not be understood in a reductionist vein, such that the lower "level" of social systems is communication. Rather, *everything* in a social system, from the system itself to each of its operations is a form of communication. Communication is an emergent phenomenon: it emerges from interacting elements that are not communication themselves, such as individuals and some of their actions. Individuals alone cannot communicate, they interact through specific relations: systems of communication (that is, *social* systems). Communication can take many different forms: language, gesture, image, power, money. It has always a *purpose*: generally speaking, this purpose is social coordination. However, this general purpose endorses different forms in different types of systems: basic coordination in small inter-action systems and societal functions such as producing collectively binding decisions in broad systems like the political system. Of course, in a political system, communication has many more specific purposes contributing to the broad goal of decision-making, such as agenda-setting or implementation. The point is that the political system, as with any other social system, is a system made of communication, with its own purposes and specific features.

It is important to say few words on why political systems are *not* made of *actions*. For systems theory, there are two types of socially relevant action: communicative acts (that is, any involvement in communication attempts) and non-communicative acts (typically, actions resulting from the process of communication, but also solitary acts that can be topics of communication). Communication (emerging from communicative acts) is a "proposition of selection, an incitation" (Luhmann 1991: 134–35, my translation) orienting action without constraining it. The distinction between communication and action portrays the respective importance of structure and agency in social relations. Communication sets, stabilizes, and transforms structures of expectations, hence premises of behavior. Actions fulfill or deceive expectations, hence fuel the process of communication with individual agency. The point is that a large part of the action depends on the communication system from which it results. The intentionality of the actor is somehow reduced: to her own communicative utterances, to her acceptance or rejection of the communicated meaning, and to her compliance with or deception of the communicated expectations through her resulting action(s). Therefore, political systems are not networks or sequences of individual and collective *actions*. They are networks or sequences of *communications* that enable and orient individual and collective actions.

Theoretically speaking, the distinction between action and communication is fundamental. Analytically speaking, however, communication is hardly observable as such. To be observed or to observe itself, a communication system appears as a system of action: "It is only as action that communication is fixed as a simple element occurring at a specific moment" (ibid., my translation). Accordingly, we can observe actions (both communicative acts and non-communicative acts) as representational simplifications of the communication processes through which they occur. Hence, we always need to consider the communicational context of actions. The concept of "practices," widely endorsed in the literature, should be understood along these lines. Practices as social actions are the *visible* form of communicative processes of social coordination. When we theoretically distinguish some practices, we actually contrast clusters of communication oriented towards a purpose. For instance, the practice of voting is a communicative act whose purpose is to select someone or something among alternative options. Voting is a solitary action (selecting an option, filling and then dropping a ballot in the ballot box) that is actually a communicative act because it takes place within a system of communication for which this selection is meaningful. Voting is a practice only because it is meaningful and consequential for a communication system; in this case, a political system for which voting means something specific and has consequences. No practices are independent from communication systems. Analytically speaking practices must always be contextualized within the broader communication system in which they take place. Concretely, this means that practices always have a specific purpose within a communication system, they have a *function*.

We can now specify what *political practices* are. At the outset, the theory of system differentiation prevents us from conceiving fixed boundaries of the political. There is no *essence* of the political, only a basic *form* of political communications. Does a particular communication have to do with the current or potential exercise of power? That is the abstract filter (the *code*) that constitutes the flexible boundaries of the political system, enabling any issue to be potentially *politicized*, that is, thematized as requiring binding decisions. Generally speaking, these are political communications, which basically constitute the political system. They can take multiple forms and are clustered as practices within the different communication (sub-)systems constituting the broad political system. We now need to interrogate the *differences* between these political practices in order to bring more contrast and clarity within political systems.

On which grounds can we distinguish the system's parts?

Distinctions are fundamental because the analytical depiction of a system depends on the contrasts that we can bring to light. A social system such as the political one is internally differentiated in distinct systems. Theoretically speaking, there are three types of social systems, each with a specific mode of inclusion of communications: interaction (presence), organization (membership), and functional systems (function performance). The political system is a broad functional system, focused on the decisional function, encompassing a few subfunctional systems (e.g., politics and administration), multiple organization systems (e.g., political parties obviously, but also parliaments or mini-publics), and countless interaction systems (e.g., street demonstrations, political discussions at the bar). Each of these systems has different basic preconditions and purposes, and therefore (re-)produces specific structures of expectations and norms of behavior. The general distinction between these *types of systems* helps to contrast *types of parts* of political systems. Each type represents a different kind of cluster of political communications/practices.

However, we need much more contrast than these three types can provide, and we need contrast specific to the political system. We must distinguish these communications/practices according to their specific form in political systems. On this aspect, I rely partly on Saward's practices matrix (2021: 76). Putting practices at the heart of his theory, he distinguishes between *institutionalized* and *non-institutionalized* practices.[85] He defines institutionalized practices as "bounded sets of practices that have a recognizably organized form and a comparative continuity" (2021: 70). The *organized* form of institutionalized practices means, in systemic terms, that the operations of such communication systems are limited by inclusion rules (membership) and programs (conditional and teleological) as operational criteria. For example, the practice of voting is limited to some people (e.g., adults, citizens), and it operates according to specific programs (e.g., conditions for the formal validity of the ballot). For systems theory, institutionalized practices generally regulate the operations of *organization* systems.

Saward also stresses the feature of the *continuity* of institutionalized practices. In the language of systems theory, *stability* (and thus reproduction) is indeed the purpose of institutionalization: institutionalized practices stabilize and reproduce behavioral expectations. This stabilization can be more or less formal, even customs and oral traditions can be forms of institutional stabilization. But in a functionally differentiated political system, the most important form of stabilization is as *positive law*. It secures general compliance through law, relying only latently on political power. As positive law, an institutionalized practice is temporarily depoliticized, it legally holds at

---

[85] The use of the verbal form institutiona*lized* invites us to think that practices were *preexistent*, and then have been made institutional. Although it is often the case, sometimes institutionalization aims to *create* the practice instead. Therefore, it might be less confusing to use the adjectival form of *institutional* or non-*institutional* practices.

the moment. But simultaneously, what holds as *positive* law is contingent and evolves along decisions. Positive law thus stabilizes political practices in guaranteeing simultaneously their continuity and a general compliance to these, *and* their potential transformation. Indeed, practices institutionalized as positive law are inherently contingent and presuppose the existence of institutional opportunities for being transformed. And these opportunities are *procedures*: a type of institutionalized practice aiming at the modification of a previous situation.

Procedures refer to *how* things are done for a certain purpose. They are, in systems theory, *operations* that simultaneously produce change and continuity: they structure transformations. For instance, the procedure of election creates a new reality (a selected sample of political performers), but it does so in a stable and reliable way. Procedures are a special kind of institutionalized practice that contrasts with "substantial" laws (e.g., the interdiction of alcohol consumption for children). To take an example more related to the political system: a formal condition of eligibility (such as being a citizen) is a practice institutionalized as positive law, but it is not a procedure. It is a substantial criterion to participate in the procedure of election. Broadly speaking, political procedures aim at the (trans-)formation of substantial institutionalized practices. As Saward notes, their "ultimate function is to make collective decisions" (ibid.: 91), but they can have smaller decisional functions such a selecting decision-makers.

In my view, procedures are practices *always* institutionalized as positive law, otherwise they cannot fulfill their task of *stabilized* transformation. When defining procedures, Saward gives the example of a dictator discussing a matter with his close advisers, and then making a decision (2021: 92). I disagree on qualifying this example as a procedure. In this example, only the dictator's willingness seems to determine what occurs in the sequence of events. Nobody (including, for instance, one of the dictator's advisors) can rely on this "procedure" and claim that the way things were done didn't respect what was supposed to happen. A procedure exists only if it *formally* institutionalizes expectations. If it does not, this practice is simply a widespread habit or a tradition that may well be socially expected, but whose compliance is not secured by positive law. Take, for instance, the Swiss "Magic Formula" which determines the number of seats to the federal government for each main party: it is clearly an institutionalized practice, but it is not a procedure that is legally binding. It rests instead on a more or less tacit agreement between Swiss political parties and derives from a shared understanding of the consociational nature of the Swiss political system. For systems theory, procedures are *reliable* ways to guarantee operational and normative stability for change, and more particularly decision-making in the political system. Procedures are reliable because they rely on positive law. There are then major differences between procedures and other kinds of institutionalized practices.

Accordingly, non-institutionalized practices are not procedures either. However, as Saward contends, non-institutionalized practices can contribute to or impact procedures. Examples of non-institutionalized practices are typically what occurs in what Habermas calls the public sphere and what Saward refers to as the "protected public spaces of debate and discussion" (ibid.: 100). There, practices such as demonstrating in the street or debating in a claimed public space are not institutionalized, but they can impact procedures. For example, demonstrations can target decisional procedures themselves (e.g., demonstrations against the use by the French government of the constitutional article 49.3 to bypass parliament). Non-institutionalized practices can also be less straightforward, such as informal talks along and within a formal decisional venue (Saward even takes "gossip" and "greeting, shunning, chatting" as examples). Such informal talks can, for instance, occur at the margin of a parliamentary debate. Informal talks are not what parliamentary procedures aim to stabilize, parliamentary procedures stabilize the operation of the parliament as an organization system (who participates, with which prerogatives, when, etc.). Yet the topics of such informal talks are often these procedures, and they can produce strategic moves within procedures. When analyzing procedures, it is therefore important to consider the non-institutionalized practices occurring along or between them.

In consequence, I endorse a slightly different understanding of procedures than Saward's. As I see it, procedures are not *processes* or *sequences* made of practices institutionalized or not. Procedures are the steps or elements secured by positive law that occur *within* broader processes or sequences of operations, processes that also include other types of institutionalized practices and non-institutionalized practices. This conceptual difference is important to understand that procedures stabilize only *a part* of much more complex processes or sequences. The analysis of the functioning of complex political systems requires a focus on procedures *and* other types of institutionalized practices *and* non-institutionalized practices, *and* on the relations between them. Analytically speaking, a sequence or process of decision-making encompasses all these elements, not only procedures. Moreover, by taking each procedure as a single step in decision-making, one can see more clearly how each step is (dis-)connected from one another and question this connectivity. For instance, a procedure may or may not be formally conditioned on a previous procedure. The ordering of procedures can be stabilized by positive law, but it may also be simply a matter of tradition. The point is that these conceptual distinctions, and notably the restriction of procedures as formally legalized steps of decision-making, enable a more complete and subtle investigation of actual *processes* of decision-making.

Theoretically speaking, we could imagine a political system without any procedure, with only decisional processes that are not stabilized as positive law, for instance, a tradition of asking certain transcendental entities what to do. Perhaps, we could even imagine a democratic system that does well without procedures, with decisional processes stabilized only by tradition, customs, and habits, or even a form of spontaneous collective self-governance such as those dreamed of by some anarchists. But there are great added values of procedures over these other forms of stabilization: their reliability (everybody can observe and rely on the procedure as it is formally established) and external securing by law (procedural breaches are broadly speaking illegal). Moreover, as means of transformation, procedures are likely to be themselves subject to procedures of change precisely because they rely on *positive* law.

These added values of procedures do not imply that every opportunity for change must have the form of procedure, nor that extra-procedural opportunities for change must be discarded. For instance, social movements and civil disobedience are crucial means of systemic transformation too. The flexibility of political systems also depends on their structural openness towards other forms of triggering change, only some of which can be secured further as procedures. However, the mere existence of procedures, *by their form only and whatever their specific content is*, already represents a precondition and a step towards a democratic political system.[86] Indeed, the generalization of procedures as

---

[86] On this basis, one might discard *populism* as a form of democracy. Indeed, populists generally claim to truly speak in the name of the people *independently of procedures* and draw their legitimacy from mass mobilization rather than decisional procedures (see Saffon and Urbinati 2013).

positive law makes them legally reliable for every subjected individual. It ensures that political decisions are taken via a path that is broadly structured, predictable, and visible. The mere existence of procedures does not make that path democratic, however; procedures themselves must be democratic. But the fact that there are procedures, and not only ad-hoc or traditional ways of making decisions, is a *democratic precondition*. While I endorse a kind of pure proceduralism (see Chapter 5), I do not defend procedures *normatively* as a better source of legitimacy than more substantive approaches. I only take procedures as (so far) the most reliable and revisable form of stable transformation of political systems.

Now that we have more contrast about what is part of a political system (procedures, but also institutionalized and non-institutionalized practices), we can tackle the issue of the broad analytical representation of such a system, hence the question of how these practices are *clustered* as different ensembles. As discussed in Chapter 2, two representations have been advanced in the literature: *spatial* and *temporal*. Both have their strengths and weaknesses, and I do not think one is necessarily better than the other. Moreover, both seem to claim for the "right" representation whether as a map of spaces or a sequence of steps. In that regard, I share strong affinities with Saward's context-sensitivity and focus on active sequenc*ing* and layer*ing*, rather than on the *right* representations of sequences or spaces. The idea is more to provide conceptual tools to distinguish elements of a decisional sequence or a political space, rather than claim that a particular sequential or spatial representation is the correct one. To do so, I contend that the analytical task of represent*ing* political systems needs a clear analytical anchor, which systems theory clearly provides: functions.

Drawing distinctions within a whole starts from what unifies its difference. A functionally differentiated political system focuses on the function of issuing and implementing collectively binding decisions. Every operation of the system is related more or less directly to this broad purpose. Decision-making is what the system *as a whole* does continuously. Consequently, it is incorrect to assume that there is a precise decision point, whether as a space or as a moment. Similarly, it is misleading to take collective decision-making as *one* of the functions of a political/democratic system, as Warren does (2017). Instead, the broad function of "decision-making is distributed through a division of labour," within a system made of countless decisions, where each decision is a premise for further decisions (Luhmann 1982: 94). That is what makes a political system a *complex* and *dynamic* system. What we usually take as "the decision" (from the government or parliament, for instance) both results from several previous decisions and is itself a premise for the multiple decisions leading to its concrete implementation or further contestation. Nonetheless, for analytical purposes, it is important to bring contrast within this continuous function of decision-making. That is what spatial and temporal metaphors actually do: they cluster types of contribution to decision-making. But they do not, so far, explicitly put *functions* at the heart of their analytical strategy of differentiation. What really distinguishes these spaces or moments are indeed the specific tasks that they perform. By focusing on the different (sub-)functions that contribute to the broad function of decision-making, we can depict a *systemic* representation of the political reality. Accordingly, the descriptive mapping of political systems must contrast their different *functions*: they represent the most context-sensitive (since they can be performed by various practices) *and* common basis of representation (since all political systems perform these functions).

For both the spatial and temporal representations, spaces or steps were stated without much justification (see Chapter 1). In Chapter 4, I discussed the internal differentiation of the political system according to Luhmann's systems theory. Although there is no set form of internal differentiation, modern political systems tend towards a common basic internal differentiation along two dimensions: vertical and horizontal. Vertical differentiation is easily understood as "levels" and relations of governance. Importantly, distinctions between levels and the institutionalization of these distinctions already forms a question about democraticness. Indeed, the institutionalization (often under a constitutional form) of differentiated prerogatives and relationships of governance between the national, regional, and local levels is a major step towards the self-governance and political autonomy of these levels. It opens the possibility for each of these levels to become a political system on its own, with its own democratic potentials and pitfalls. In the next chapter, I discuss in detail how the vertical dimension of internal differentiation can be used for the *diagnosis* of existing political systems. For now, however, I focus on horizontal differentiation, as spatial and temporal representations of political systems generally unfold on this dimension.

Political systems are also internally *horizontally* differentiated; they develop internal complexity to process and respond to external complexity. From a systemic perspective, these broad differences are *subsystems*, stabilized by procedures and other institutionalized practices, and with specific inclusion roles and organizational programs. What differentiates these subsystems is their specific *function*, that is, how they contribute to the broad political function of decision-making. Modern political systems generally feature three subsystems: politics, administration, and the public. The functions of politics are to *select political performers* and to *determine the decision premises* for actual decisions produced and implemented by the administration. In this subsystem, issues that require binding decisions are filtered and structured, decision-makers are selected, and broad orientations are decided. Furthermore, the subsystem of politics has a symbolic function. Through its wide visibility, it constitutes the main point of observation and description of the political system: politics is what people most directly perceive of the political system. Therefore, its function is also to represent the system as a whole and produce a *symbolic legitimacy* for the global acceptance of the entire system. The functions of the second subsystem, administration, are *legislation*, that is, the transformation of broad decisions into detailed applicable rules, and their *implementation*. Administration is also the place where political and legal systems interpenetrate, allowing the self-limitation of the former through positive law. The third political subsystem is the public. Its functions are *observation* and *orientation*. As the addressee of decisions, the public *observes* the administration and politics, which impacts their own operations. In addition, being outside both of these subsystems, the public observes society as a whole without an institutionalized lens. The public thus centrally contributes to the thematization of political issues. Although thematization can be triggered by politics and administration, it needs to find resonance among the public to become a stable political theme. Therefore, the public *orients* the political system. Of course, the public also "participates," that is, it interacts with politics and administration in multiple ways, and these opportunities of interactions constitute *connections* between these subsystems. The question of connections is the object of the next section.

These three subsystems constitute the basic internal difference of modern political systems, and therein lies a precondition for democracy. Of course, the extent and shape of the actual differentiation of these three subsystems is variable and profoundly impacts the democratic quality. But the point is that these three functional subsystems compose a common basis of *representation* of modern political systems. Since that functional representation may appear to be spatial, it is important to understand that each of these subsystems encompasses a special kind of communication, related to their respective *function*. Therefore, this threefold distinction does not cluster actors and organizations, attributing them specific tasks. Instead, the functional representation clusters types of contributions to the political activity, that can *a priori* be performed by various kind of actors and organizations. Indeed, some actors perform several different functional roles. Take, for instance, the head of government and its ministers: they contribute to both politics and administration.

In in this functional representation, the temporal dimension is underlying, as the performance of each function depends on multiple interactional *processes*. However, there is no beginning or end point of the system, only constant cyclic and recursive processes of mutual influence. The political system as a constant decisional process does not start with agenda-setting to finish with implementation. Indeed, all these subsystems perform their own functions continuously and simultaneously. A temporal representation emphasizing a start and a beginning, and a right order of previous and next "steps" of decision-making, cannot serve as a faithful analytical depiction of the system. Because they focus only on one dimension of systemic reality, neither spatial nor temporal representations are appropriate to describe political systems. On the contrary, a functional representation combines these two dimensions, hence articulating the stability (structural differences) and dynamism (processes of interaction between these) characterizing a system.

The functional representation provides commonality as a starting point precisely as a way to uncover contextual specificities. As the analytical anchor, functions are used to structure the analysis: we interrogate how these functions are contextually performed within a system. To do so, spatial and temporal representations allow us to focus on some aspects of the system. Without exception, some "spaces" and "sequences" are more or less institutionalized in every concrete political system. The *spatial* representation is useful for mapping stabilized differences and relationships between (sub-)systems and between organizations, and the practices institutionalized to perform their respective functions. Take, for instance, the parliament as an organization system: it is a space stabilized by institutional practices (often constitutional) and most of its operations are proceduralized in order to perform its function of legislation. The spatial representation enables us to map the different "spaces" (as systems themselves) shaping a systemic architecture, in order to investigate the relations (both horizontal and vertical) between them. The question that the spatial representation asks is about the *stabilization* of differences and relationships. This is the *structural* question.

The temporal representation is useful for uncovering the interaction *processes* between structural differences. It investigates the chronological order of the performance of functions by specific spaces and practices. Take, for instance, the "popular initiative" in Switzerland as a sequence made of different practical steps (signature gathering, parliamentary scrutiny, popular vote). Importantly, these institutionalized steps are not exhaustive of the sequence: the public debate that it triggers is central to this sequence and is perhaps even the most important step (see Parkinson 2020 on this point). Therefore, the sequential representation questions what occurs *before, during, along*, and *after* an institutionalized process. It highlights how things really go in practice within political systems; for instance, which non-institutionalized practices fuel or hinder an institutionalized sequence. This is the *processual* question.

In a complementary vein, the structural and processual questions ask how political spaces and sequences are structured and operate, through which practices, *and for which purpose*. The different spaces and sequences themselves have functions, as well as their different parts or steps as practices. The mapping of a political system is the mapping of the multiple functional differences stabilized as spaces or sequences, by procedures and other practices. Therefore, the functional representation serves as a reference point to uncover what the existing spaces and sequences (and their constitutive practices) are *expected* to perform. Concretely, it implies a two-fold question: it interrogates which spaces, sequences, and practices perform the basic political functions, and conversely, it questions what functions are performed by the existing spaces, sequences, and practices. The generic functional representation of the political system is a counterfactual reference to map the *actual* shape and functioning of a particular system and to operate a grounded normative critique. Consequently, I reject the pursuit of the *right* sequences or spatial articulations; I instead endorse research into *better* articulations from the identification, through a functional representation, of the existing articulations.

If the system's parts are connected in complex ways, how can we conceptualize these connections?

With these insights on how political systems are internally differentiated and how we can map these functional differences along spatial and temporal representations, we can discuss now how these "parts" are *connected*. In Chapter 2, I discussed two metaphors of connectivity present in the deliberative/democratic systems' literature: *transmission* and *coupling*. Systems theory clearly favors the latter and explicitly rejects the former (see Chapter 3). Systemic connections do not involve the transmission of inputs and reception of outputs. Systems are operationally closed, and everything coming from outside is a perturbation that may or may not be tackled by the system, from its own perspective and through its own operations. As social systems are made of communications, the transmission metaphor is rejected as unfit to characterize the phenomenon of communication. To be precise, communication is an interactive *construction* of meaning, not the *transfer* of meaning from one place to another. This is the case between individuals, and it applies to social systems as well. There is no transmission of meaning (in the political system, under the form of influence, for instance) between political subsystems; there are processes of communicative co-construction of meaning. The issue of connectivity must be understood from that perspective: what is connected are ultimately *communications*. In the political system, these communications are relative to power, as a symbolically generalized medium of communication.

The question of systemic connectivity is first and foremost about what *stabilizes* connections between some communication systems. Importantly, stabilized connections between two systems do not necessarily prevent other opportunities for mutual impact. A communication can connect to a system if it is relevant for itself, according to its own code and programs of processing external perturbations. Therefore, there can always be perturbations impacting the system, even if no structure of connections is in place to do so. However, the analytical question of systemic connections mostly regards *stabilized* communications, that is, the structures in place whose precise *aim* is to connect,[87] or the absence of structures where we expect a connection to be stabilized.[88] This is why, in systems theory, connections are conceived as *structural couplings*: relatively stable ties of communication where each part knows more or less how the other part will interpret and react to its perturbations. This allows both parts to stabilize their expectations[89] and therefore to coordinate. Structural couplings sometimes lead to "interpenetration": a system conditions part of its activity on some operation of another system. This is typically the case for a sequence that is fully proceduralized; the performance of each step is conditioned to the performance of the previous ones. Without undermining the importance of "micro" and unstabilized connections, as highlighted by Hendriks et al. (2020), I focus here on how to comceptualize connections and diagnose disconnections between *systems* (functional, organizational, and interactional). I then tackle the question of connectivity through the concept of *structural* couplings.

Structurally coupled systems mutually influence each other with variable intensities. The metaphors of *tight* and *loose* couplings are used in systems theory to qualify these intensities. The difference between tight and loose coupling regards whether the influence is respectively *continuous/sudden, significant/negligible, direct/indirect,* and *immediate/ eventual*. In democratic theory, decoupling, and loose and tight coupling have been employed normatively to qualify a desirable state of the system and to define systemic pathologies (see Mansbridge et al. 2012; Hendriks 2016). I both agree and oppose this normative use. On the one hand, I agree that the shape and extent of coupling between systems (and parts) largely determine how they operate, and therefore that coupling is a central dimension for diagnosis and contextual transformation. On the other hand, I disagree (in line with Hendriks 2016) on taking "loose coupling" as a set standard of connectivity, and on conceiving "tight coupling" and "decoupling" as systemic pathologies.

---

[87] Sometimes, nevertheless, some stabilized connections are no longer appropriate to perform their job. For instance, the growing reluctance towards political parties as connective organizations between the public and politics shows that perhaps other mechanisms must be stabilized in order to connect these two spaces.

[88] To be sure, this does not rule out the relevance and importance of ad hoc solutions in cases where a connection urgently needs to be set. But the issue of systemic connectivity is primarily about the stabilization and reliability of connections.

[89] This is why influence is always *mutual*: the reaction of a system to a communication from another one recursively entails either a reinforcement or change of expectation of both systems.

Sometimes, decoupling might be what is needed: for instance, a decoupling of politics and the judiciary, in avoiding notably the selection of judges by the executive. In other cases, tight coupling might be necessary to ensure a significant, direct, continuous, and immediate impact from one system to another. For example, the institutionalization of permanent and consequential mini-publics regarding environmental issues might be required due to the emergency and gravity of the situation, hence coupling *tightly* the subsystems of administration and the public.

Instead of taking coupling intensities as normative standards, I instead suggest that the distinction of coupling intensities is helpful in two related ways. First, to *describe* the reality of existing couplings in specific systems along the above four differences. Second, to *diagnose* whether a particular coupling is contextually appropriate, for instance, whether the mutual influence between two coupled systems is negligible when it should be significant. This enables this coupling to be redesigned to make the influence more significant.[90] Accordingly, I do not take loose coupling (and other intensities) as a *normative standard* for the connections of systems, but as *indicators* to describe and diagnose the existing connections.

Now, recall Neblo & White's (2018) conditions of connectivity for the successful functioning of a deliberative democratic system discussed in Chapter 2: awareness, translatability, receptivity, flexibility. I understand these conditions as *standards* of connections between parts. I don't follow this normative path, for reasons mentioned above.[91] However, two of these four conditions of connectivity add considerable value. The conditions of awareness and receptivity characterize the broad phenomenon of coupling: to be (and stay) aware and receptive in order to avoid gaps in "communicative chains" (2018: 449). Yet the awareness and receptivity of a particular system is always *selective*. The whole point of coupling is to stabilize this selective awareness

---

[90] Again, the institutionalization of coupling stabilizes these connections, notably through procedures. I think that for Hendriks (2016) one of the added values of "designed coupling" over more "self-generated couplings" is precisely to offer *procedural guarantees*.

[91] As with the normative use of coupling intensities, these conditions tend to produce a rigid and caricatural depiction of how a democratic system should be internally connected. For instance, in some cases of coupling, it is not desirable that the "receiving system" responds with flexibility. A system always has some flexibility to respond to external perturbations, but the aim of coupling is to limit this flexibility in order to stabilize mutual expectations.

and receptivity. These two conditions do not add much to the variables of coupling's intensity presented above (sudden/continuous, negligible/significant, etc.). However, the conditions of *flexibility* and *translatability* both point towards other important dimensions. Flexibility is for Neblo & White the latitude of reacting in different (even creative) ways to a connection. In systems theory, this question echoes *interpenetration* as a type of structural coupling, where one system's operations *depend* on another, without much latitude to react differently than expected. I therefore suggest the distinction *rigid/flexible* to cover this dimension as an important feature of couplings. It questions the latitude of freedom that one system has in reacting to another's perturbations.

The condition of *translatability* also highlights an important issue raised by Bächtiger & Parkinson (2019): How can we reconcile the two contradictory expectations that a democratic system "faithfully transmits ideas, yet also transforms them" (Parkinson 2018: 441–442). The authors suggest a "memetic account of transmission" to reconcile these two conflicting requirements. Nevertheless, while I agree that transmission and transformation are opposed expectations, it does not create a "dilemma" for which their memetic account is a necessary *via media*. The systemic perspective itself suggests a more straightforward answer to reconcile transmission and transformation: they do not have to occur simultaneously and for the same connections, they are distributed, as are the functions and principles of the system. As some parts are tightly coupled and others loosely coupled, some connections aim for the faithful "transmission" and "reception" of communications, while others aim for greater transformation. The distinction *transmissive/transformative* is taken as another additional variable characterizing systemic connections. We now have a conception of systemic connections as structural couplings, and six distinctions to describe existing couplings.

In modern political systems, the three subsystems are structurally coupled and even interpenetrate at some points. For instance, the administration generally conditions some of its operations on the premises of decisions produced by politics. But the connections between these subsystems vary greatly from one particular political system to another, and this variation deeply impacts their legitimacy and ultimately their democratic quality. Take, for instance, the structural coupling between the public and politics: if the connection is negligible and indirect, let's say through the sole existence of consultative mechanisms triggered by the government once in a while, then this coupling is quite loose between these two spaces. In that case, the public can hardly perform its function of orientation of the whole political system. In contrast, the existence of recall procedures could be a significant, direct, and immediate connection that tightly couples the public with politics and administration. However, it might be argued that this connection is *too tight* and thus prevents the operational autonomy of both politics and administration. But this would depend on whether a functional equivalent to this undesirable tight coupling exists, such as a procedure of impeachment internal to politics or the administration. My point here is to illustrate how the focus on connections, both broad and more specific, and their description with the six coupling features, already says a lot about the functioning of a system. If we agree with Luhmann that political legitimacy has to do primarily with the good functioning of the system in a complex environment, the analysis of systemic connections is a pivotal element of diagnosis.

In what follows, I briefly discuss how the analysis of connections is important for the diagnosis of democratic systems. To start with, Hendriks et al. (2020) identify three disconnects characterizing contemporary democratic systems: between citizens and elected representatives, between citizens and administrative policy-making process, and among citizens themselves. The authors implicitly endorse here the systemic differentiation between politics, administration, and the public. It is indeed at the level of these functional subsystems that the question of connection must be tackled first, before confronting more specific connections at lower levels, for instance, between organization systems such as political parties and the parliament, or between the steps of a decisional sequence. Although I broadly share Hendriks et al. "diagnosis" of these three major democratic disconnects, I suggest another way to perceive this situation. In the political systems that probably inspired their diagnosis (Western liberal regimes I guess), citizens, elites, and policy-making processes are in fact deeply connected (they have probably never been so connected throughout history). The problem is thus not a matter of *dis*connect, but precisely of *mis*connect. If political parties do not connect citizens and elites as expected, there might be other means to do so, already at play or in need of creation. In systemic terms, these are functionally equivalent means to connect citizens and elites. Besides pointing out the absence of connections that should exist, the point of diagnosis regarding connectivity is mostly to identify *misconnections*: inappropriate coupling intensities, functionally deficient connections, normatively problematic connections, etc. It is also the occasion to remind ourselves that the primary aim of connections is to contribute to the performance of a function. Connections between systems allow them to fulfill their specialized task. Connections themselves do not have a *specific* function, they are only necessary for each system's function. What orients and stabilizes connections for a system is always the performance of its function. Therefore, it is important to know to which function(s) a particular connection contributes in order to diagnose a potential misconnection and imagine functionally equivalent ways for it to perform better.

To conclude this section, I answer the three questions regarding systemic connectivity raised in Chapter 2. First, *what are systemic connections theoretically?* They are structural couplings, whose shape and intensity vary along six dimensions characterizing mutual influence: sudden/continuous, negligible/significant, indirect/direct, eventual/immediate, rigid/flexible, and transmissive/transformative. With this conception, I thereby reject "consequentiality" as a normative criterion for democratic systems (see Chapter 1). Indeed, the complexity of connections and the variability of mutual influence prevents our expectation that each part of a system be consequential on another. The six features of couplings capture the versatility of consequentiality in a more detailed and context-sensitive manner. Second, *which connections actually matter in a democratic system?* Both micro and macro connections matter. But the task of diagnosing systemic deficiencies focuses primarily on *stabilized* connections, that is, on structural couplings. This focus aims to diagnose structural problems in need of a solution, instead of problematic particular moments of connections. Third and finally, *which connections are desirable or not?* I reject a perspective of "ideal configurations" of connections, such as loose coupling, and the pathologization of decoupling and tight coupling. Instead, I endorse a more context-sensitive approach to the desirability of connections. In this section, I argued that a large part of this question can be answered by interrogating what is *functionally* expected from a particular connection. But this is not the entire story; as Saward suggests, connections enact *principles* as well (2021: 103). If this is indeed the case, the desirability of connections also depends on the principles they enact, an issue I tackle in the second part of this chapter.

What are the boundaries from and connections with other systems?

It is important to discuss the issue of "external" boundaries and connections. Any political system, whether a local government or a supranational organization, is embedded in an environment. Within its environment, several other functional systems are present, some of which it has strong connections with. I discussed in Chapter 4 the differentiation of the political system from and coupling with the legal and economic systems, since they are its most important neighbors. Other systems deserve such a mention: the education, scientific, religious, and mass media systems. In some contexts, other systems are important to understand the functioning of the political system, such as, for instance, the "criminal system" or the military system. Here I will not develop their specificities and how they can impact political systems, but depending on the political context under diagnosis, some of these are central to the analysis. As a general comment, I contend that the freezing of boundaries and connections between these social systems as right or normal configuration and "pathologies" is misleading and over-simplistic. To reify the boundaries of political systems with other social systems is to misunderstand the nature of social systems; they do evolve, and they *must* do so. There is no "ideal configuration" of the society and its subsystems. The boundaries and connections of the political system with its environment must remain flexible, and this flexibility is a democratic precondition. Simultaneously, in order to stabilize and legitimize its operations, a political system must constantly state its main boundaries and connections, and self-limits with these through positive law (often under a constitutional form), which is also another democratic precondition.

The description of any political system requires a contextual understanding of its environment through the tools developed above regarding connections. The diagnosed "pathologies" of differentiation and connections are contingent. For example, there might be times when the economic and the political systems must be tightly coupled to prevent or solve an economic crisis, and other moments when society benefits from loosening this coupling to unleash capitalism's force for quick development. Or there can be moments where some sectors of the economic system become so powerful that they have the capacity to perform activities so far monopolized by states (e.g., SpaceX's space programs). In this case, the structural couplings between the political and the economic systems face deep mutations. Take also the emergence of new kinds of actors that belong to multiple functional systems at the same time (e.g., Google, which is a private company, but also a major actor in the scientific, educational, and mass media systems). Such evolutions of the current functional differentiation could impose a complete redefinition of the boundaries and connections between these systems. I can only briefly suggest here the importance of investigating the concrete environment of a particular political system and the manner in which one might carry out its diagnosis.

Nonetheless, I focus on the case of the *mass media* system, as it is particularly important for the political system. The mass media system is characterized by its unprecedent capacity for the diffusion of communication, such that the meaning it conveys (through the information/non-information code) is potentially known by everybody (Bourgne 2017). Its function is to "orient the self-observation of the society" (Luhmann 2012 in Bourgne 2017: 497, my translation), that is, to build a representation of a common reality as a "transcendental illusion" (Luhmann 2012 in Rabault 2015: 210). Historically, mass media has supplanted religion as the main source of societal self-description, after science failed to do so by being mostly only accessible to itself.[92] In fact, the success of mass media comes from its ability to enable the co-existence of several partial semantics, including scientific truth and religious faith, and, paradoxically, to do so through a *common semantic* (Rabault 2015). Hence, the mass media does not need to produce consensus, but only a background objectivity, a "latent daily culture" that facilitates the development of compatible communications by other systems (Luhmann 2012 in Rabault 2015: 210). The problem of mass media is not *truth*, but *selectivity* (Bourgne 2017: 497): it needs to select what is information or not, and it does so autonomously. As a result of this inherent selectivity of mass media, there

---

[92] Media themselves are now the main vector of penetration of scientific knowledge into society, through a simplification of its complexity (i.e., popularization of science) (Rabault 2015: 215).

is an ever-present suspicion of manipulation, yet it remains society's main source of self-description.[93]

The mass media is important for the political system in several ways. Its acknowledgment and replication of the plurality of world views is essential for the display of the diversity of opinions regarding political issues. The imperatives of objectivity and neutrality characterizing journalism (Rabault 2015: 209) claim to describe reality as it is, serving as a common ground for opinions to deviate. In the public debate, particular opinions are mostly articulated in reference to the reality presented by the media, and they rely much less on scientific evidence.[94] In addition, media do not only describe the factual reality of society, they also contribute to its structuration in themes, selected and prioritized (ibid.: 215). Therefore, "agenda-setting" as an important task of the political process cannot be understood solely as a political step, but as something largely performed and oriented by the mass media.[95] As Luhmann notes, "news reports in the media usually demand a response within the political system" (2000: 67). Moreover, the mass media also contributes strongly to the relaying and even creation of *moral* communications. With their focus on "scandals, crimes, corruption, etc. [mass media] sets the moral mood of society, in other terms, a common moral world" (Rabault 2015: 215, my translation). As such, mass media is an important source of moral stabilization and reproduction of a society that is *not* morally integrated.[96] Mass media push simultaneously in two opposite directions: moral homogeneity and moral pluralism (by their openness towards multiple semantics). To summarize, in modern society, the political system and the mass media system are structurally coupled quite tightly, to the point that each produces constant perturbations for the other.

[93] The issue of conspiracy theories must then be understood as a *structural* phenomenon in modern society.

[94] With the introduction of fact-checking in mediatized political debates, media themselves become the "referees" regarding scientific evidence, deciding which statistic is "correct."

[95] Mass media produces the *tempo* of society, by selecting information as new, no longer new, or redundant (Fortier 2013: 2). Mass media set the past and present common to all of society.

[96] Mass media are probably more effective than the legal system (nowadays largely independent from morality, yet a primary source of normative stabilization) in that regard because they can communicate moral norms without having to guarantee their compliance (Luhmann 2012 in Rabault 2015: 215).

The general implication of these illustrative remarks is that we cannot investigate the functioning of a specific political system *in isolation*, that is, without uncovering the influence over it from its closest neighboring systems such as law, economy, and the mass media. Regarding the latter system, we cannot take it as a *part* of the political system or as an internal connector between its parts, nor as simply something external that contributes to it notably by making political issues more visible, publicizing political claims, and by being the main locus of the public debate. The mass media and the political system function in close conjunction, with contextual variations. The point is that there cannot be diagnoses of political systems without an explicit awareness of their specific connection with the mass media. The same goes for law and economy, and to some extent to religion, science, and education. Nowadays, *social media* as a new kind of system, relatively autonomous from the mass media, is a major disturbing neighbor of the political system. Tomorrow, the *metaverse* could do the same through a profound virtualization of political activity. No serious description and diagnosis of political systems can avoid discussing their fluctuating boundaries and connections with other social systems.

Summary

In the first part of this chapter, I proposed a *descriptive layer* of political systems by taking position regarding the questions I deemed necessary for a framework of democratic systems (see Chapter 1). I presented the main conceptual contours necessary to observe, describe, and map political systems. In line with systems theory, these features revolve around several conceptual and analytical distinctions. They undoubtedly remain abstract, but only these differences are common to all political systems and can endorse multiple contextual forms. To summarize, the distinctions characteristic of the political system are the following:

    A.   Constitutive features of political systems:
- *Basic element: political communications*, apparent as political practices, whose meaning is relative to the current/potential exercise of power (i.e., the government/opposition political code).

- *Types of political communications/practices*: procedures / other institutionalized practices (rules, traditions, etc.) / non-institutionalized practices
- *Types of constitutive parts as systems*: interaction systems / organizations systems / (sub-)functional systems

B. Analytical representations of political systems
   - *Vertically*: institutionalized levels and relationships of governance
   - *Horizontally*:
     o External: Functional differentiation and connections with other social and political systems
     o Internal: Functional differentiation
       i. *Politics*: with the functions of selection of political performers, elaboration of decisions premises, symbolic legitimacy
       ii. *Administration*: with the functions of legislation, implementation
       iii. *Public*: with the functions of observation, orientation
   - For the focus on specific dimensions of the system:
     ➢ The structural question: representation as functional *spaces*
     ➢ The processual question: representation as functional *steps*

C. Connectivity of political systems
   - *As structural couplings*, with six features characterizing mutual influence: sudden/continuous, negligible/significant, indirect/direct, eventual/immediate, flexible/rigid, transformative/transmissive. Applicable to:
     ➢ Internal connections: between the subsystems, organization systems, and interaction systems
     ➢ External connections: with other political systems and with neighboring functional systems (economy, law, mass media, religion, education, science, etc.)

This list of analytical distinctions may sound trivial, but it suffices to describe the broad functioning of *any* political system and to open the way for more detailed assessments. Before tackling the question of the normative layer necessary to assess and diagnose political systems, it is important to highlight all the elements that represent *preconditions* for democratic governance:

1. Functional differentiation of the political system from its environment;
2. Some flexibility for the differentiation and connections of the political system with its environment;
3. Constant fluctuation of the self-limitation of the political system;
4. Structural abstraction regarding what are political/non-political issues;
5. Generalization of power as positive law;
6. Some institutionalization of the levels and relations of governance (vertical differentiation);
7. Basic functional differentiation between politics, administration, and the public, entailing the differentiated inclusivity of roles and issues (horizontal differentiation);
8. Some institutionalization of structural couplings between these three subsystems, with variable coupling intensities;
9. Stabilization of horizontal internal differences (represented as spaces or steps) by institutionalized practices (notably procedures) and non-institutionalized practices; and
10. Widespread existence of procedures as main practices of transformation of institutionalized practices

These elements constitute *systemic preconditions* for any democratic continuum, or so I claim. They represent basic grounds on which democratic systems can develop. However, to navigate along the democratic continuum, we need additional normative resources. In the second part of this chapter, I take position on what these normative resources are and how to use them for the diagnosis of political systems in democratic terms.

Towards democratic systems: the normative layer

The descriptive layer enables a reliable, common, and context-sensitive observation and representation of political systems, notably because it is exempt of normative presuppositions. This absence forced me to find external yet compatible normative resources (see Chapter 5). From these resources, I conceptualize thereafter a normative layer that is compatible and complementary with the descriptive layer. To do so, I first answer the two questions discussed in Chapter 2 regarding the composition and application of the normative layer. I conclude in tackling the issue of what is the place of deliberation and deliberativeness in the normative layer.

What kind of criteria should the normative layer be comprised of?

As discussed in Chapter 2, most accounts of deliberative/democratic systems fill the normative layer with "functions" as normative criteria. Broadly speaking, functions are taken in this literature as *goals* that the system must perform. It is not surprising that a functionalist semantic emerges within the systemic approach to democracy. Given their centrality for the general understanding of systems, *functions* naturally appear as pivotal elements of deliberative/democratic systems. Except for Warren (2017), sets of functions are mostly stated, without much justification of why *these* functions are stated and not others. This has led to a multiplication of lists of functions as diverse as epistemic advancement, mutual understanding, collective will formation, empowered inclusion, agenda-setting, collective decision-making, accountability, ethical function, constraining sovereignty, responsive outcomes, and others. Some of these are *democratic*, while others are instead *deliberative*: a distinction further complexifying the understanding of functions. It is unlikely that all these examples of functions constitute *democratic* functions. Some are instead *political* functions, which can be performed more or less democratically (e.g., agenda-setting). To have sharp *democratic* criteria, these must be distinguished from more generic *political* functions. Moreover, if some of these examples are indeed democratic functions, their normative nature needs to be highlighted further, notably regarding their relationships with classical democratic principles of equality and freedom. To develop a diagnostic tool for democratic systems, we need clarity on what functions are and what distinguishes them from other essential concepts such as practices and principles. This is necessary to advance some normative criteria to apply and suggest explicit rules of application. The relationship of these criteria with the political functions constituting the descriptive layer is crucial to that end. Here I take position on how to distinguish *political functions* from *democratic principles*, and I articulate them in a theoretical framework of democratic systems.

A. The functional distinctiveness of democracy

Functions are the core feature of systems: they are their *raison d'être*. Every communication occurring within a system is primarily oriented by its function. Analytically speaking, when distinguishing systems (subsystems, organization systems, interaction systems), the first analytical indicator is their distinctive function. Hence the centrality of functions as an *analytical anchor* in the descriptive layer. In modern political systems, three subsystems perform different functions. We can bring contrast within political systems by distinguishing the functions of *politics* (selection of political performers, elaboration of decision premises, symbolic legitimacy), *administration* (legislation, implementation), and the *public* (observation, orientation). Modern political systems "only" need to perform these functions, and as argued, this differentiated performance is a crucial precondition for democratic systems. But this sole performance has not much to do with the democratic quality of a political system; each of these functions can also be performed in a non-democratic manner (e.g., the selection of political performers can be done by arbitrary designation from a dictator). As a reminder, democratic quality varies along a continuum, and one that is moreover context-sensitive. Consequently, we need *more* than the above-listed democratic preconditions, that is, clear normative elements that push further in the democratic direction. And we need more than these mere political functions; we need *democratic* criteria to assess the performance of these *political* functions.

The question now is what are these distinctive democratic elements. The more straightforward route is to consider that a democratic system, as opposed to all other types of political systems, has one or several *distinctive and additional* functions. A democratic system has to do something more, it has other goals than "just" producing collectively binding decisions (through the basic political functions). If the democratic system has a specific function, I see here two potential candidates. One that directly comes to mind is *inclusion*. There will not be much disagreement with suggesting inclusion as the (or a) democratic function. For instance, Mansbridge et al. define three functions of the deliberative system, one of them being the *democratic function* defined precisely as the "inclusion of multiple and plural voices, interests, concerns and claims on the basis of feasible equality" (2012: 12). A similar position is held by Warren (2017) with *empowered inclusion* as a cardinal democratic function, probably the most distinctively normative of the other functions of *collective agenda and will formation* and *collective decision-making*. Inclusion is certainly one of the most distinctive features of a democratic system. When asking to ordinary people what democracy is, there is a great chance that their reply will contain something like "*every*body" or "*every* citizen." Inclusion thus inevitably has a special standing within a theoretical and normative framework of democratic systems. But can inclusion really be taken as the democratic *function*?

If we take "function" as conceptualized by systems theory, that is, as what *orients* the systems' communications, inclusion does not perform that job in a democratic system. It does not *orient* communications towards a specific purpose such as the functions of legislation or implementation. Functionally speaking, inclusion is not a specific purpose, it is a general concern for the differentiation of any social system: inclusion *differentiates* communication systems through diverse inclusion criteria. As in any social system, inclusion is a *general problem* that requires criteria to determine what and who is in or out. Inclusion/ exclusion from a functional system is primarily determined by the performance of a specific function (e.g., decision-making). As argued in Chapter 4, inclusion cannot be absolute, or in systemic terms, undifferentiated. The selection of both issues and people operating in the political system is necessary for its functional differentiation from other systems. Within the political system too, each subsystem has different criteria of inclusion/exclusion (e.g., compare the public and the administration). Accordingly, inclusion is not functionally specific to a *democratic* system: in all types of political systems, there is the issue of which themes and persons are included or not.

Although inclusion is not the/a *function* of democratic systems, it *normatively* has a special standing. The specificity of inclusion in the democratic system is that it is *always* favored over exclusion: there is a structural "bias" towards inclusion, and this is what makes it a *principle/norm* (a normative expectation). Contrary to contextual normative expectations (e.g., deliberation, see Chapter 5), the expectation of inclusion is always present, it is a general problem in all political subsystems and organizations of the democratic system. Inclusion, as a general democratic principle must always and in all political subsystems be *a priori* favored over exclusion. Inclusion is, in democratic systems, a pervasive normative expectation. As such, attempts to increase the inclusiveness of any venue of the democratic system generally push towards greater democraticness. However, exclusions or limitation of inclusions can be justified, and in a democratic system, sometimes *must* occur and be justified. Inclusion is not a *function* of the democratic system, it is a general and pervasive *principle* that imposes a burden of justification for its breach. As such, inclusion is a central normative element of the self-description of the political system as democratic, but not its distinctive function.

A second candidate for the democratic function is *justification*. As described in Chapters 3 and 4, the modern political system is characterized by contingency and the awareness of its contingency. Things change constantly outside and inside the political system, which institutionalizes opportunities of change with procedures notably. In addition, it stabilizes its operations and its self-description through certain principles, one of these being inclusion, but also many others, such as representation, deliberation, accountability, transparency, non-domination, truth-seeking, etc. Following Forst, I argued in Chapter 5 that justification is the *normative* core of democratic systems and that it applies to these more "contextual" normative expectations. The mobilization of these contextual norms serves precisely the democratic principle of justification; they justify practices (e.g., parliamentary voting) with something more distinctively democratic than the specific political function they perform (for instance, legislation). In line with the assertion that justification is democracy's normative core, I contend now that justification is the specific *function* of the democratic system. Contrary to non-democratic systems, a democratic one constantly needs to *justify* its operations, or stabilize/institutionalize justified ones.

Communications occurring in *political* systems can connect because they all perform the broad function of decision-making. But

in *democratic* systems, communications fail to connect appropriately if they are unjustified. More than inclusion, deliberation, or representation, what a democratic system is always expected to do is to
provide a suitable justification for each of its operations. The broad system of democracy has as its *specific* purpose justification. Democracy is a self-justificatory system: this is its true distinctiveness. While
political legitimacy functionally demands self-legitimization (see
Chapter 4), democratic legitimacy requires self-justification. As a
functional system, democracy recedes when it ceases to perform its
function of justification. Conversely, democracy thrives when rein-
forcing its capacities for collective justification. The normative apex
of democratic systems is to be *democratically self-justified, self-diagnosed, and self-corrective.* The normative centrality of justification for
democratic systems makes this feature the pivotal distinctiveness of
democracy. This leads me to take justification as a *function* within a
theoretical framework of democratic systems, in order to analytically capture and highlight its pervasiveness.

Justification is an *additional* function to collective decision-making
and its political sub-functions (selection of political performers, elaboration of decision premises, symbolic legitimacy, legislation, implementation, observation, orientation): an addition that incarnates the
specialty of democracy. Concretely, the democratic function of justification occurs *simultaneously* with the normal functioning of the political
system, that is, the constant performance of these political functions.
Justification is a function that take place *within* or *along* the performance
of these subfunctions. This means that the specific operation of each
subsystem (e.g., the function of legislation in the subsystem of administration) carries the burden of justification. The function of justification is *pervasive* within the entire democratic system; it applies to all its
features. At the broader level, a democratic system's particular external
(its constitutional self-limitation) and internal differentiations have to
be justified. At an inter-individual level, the mutual expectations and
subsequent interactions of people in relations of power stand also in
need of justification. Justification impacts all political functions (e.g.,
legislation), the practices performing these functions (e.g., parliament),
and the norms/principles stabilizing expectations regarding this performance (e.g., deliberation). It tends to create a new and more specific
code for the democratic system: the thematization of political structures and operations as *justified/unjustified.*

B. The conceptual articulation of functions, principles, and practices

I explained in Chapter 5 why justification is the normative core of democratic systems and how it applies to other normative principles. As I take it now as the distinctive *function* of democratic systems, it is essential to explain the analytical implications of this conceptual move. To that end, I first need to make clear the general conceptual relationships between *functions*, *principles/norms*, and *practices*, simplified in Figure 2.

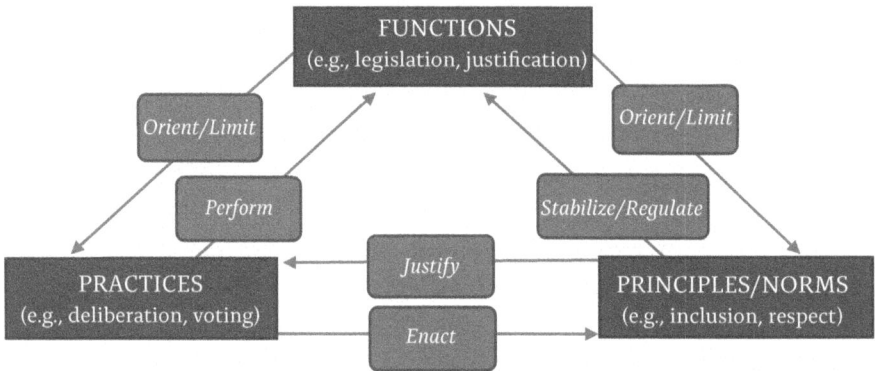

FIGURE 2 The conceptual articulation of functions, practices, and principles in a democratic system

First, *practices and principles* are intrinsically imbricated. Practices enact principles (Saward 2021: 83–85). Principles come to life through practices: "A principle only has a reality or a presence by virtue of enactment" (ibid.: 84). For example, universal suffrage in elections enacts the principles of political equality and inclusion. In this "performative" perspective, principles exist only insofar as they are performed/practiced.[97] Principles also have effects on practices since these are "structured according to different principles" (ibid.). In a systemic vein, this means that communications (practices) are clustered within systems that operate according to specific normative expectations (principles). I agree, but practices aren't exclusively nor primarily oriented by principles but by a function; the "telos of the practice" (as Saward puts it) is firstly the function it aims to fulfill, not the

---

[97]   I agree, but in a systemic understanding, principles can also be "topics" of communication independently of their practical enactment. Their meaning can also be performatively shaped *discursively*; as practices are communications clusters (see section 1 of this chapter), *communications* actually enact principles.

principles it enacts in doing so. Take the practice of representation. As Warren notes "representative relationships overcome the limitations of time, space and complexity" (2017: 48), hence what he calls empowered inclusion is notably enacted. However, the practice of representation enacts inclusion *because* it performs the function of legislation. Outside the context of a *political* function, the practice of representation may enact some forms of inclusion (e.g., symbolic, social, cultural) but not political/democratic inclusion. The relationship between practices and principles is never independent from their functional purpose. Hence, practices are not political unless they perform political functions.

Moreover, agreeing with Warren, political practices are not "inherently democratic" (ibid.: 45). And agreeing with Saward (2021), political practices are democratic when they enact democratic principles. Accordingly, to be democratic, a practice must perform a political function *and* enact one or several democratic principle(s). This understanding of democratic practice is *to some extent* compatible with Felicetti's definition of democratic practices as "an array of human activity that addresses political problems and is centrally organized around a shared practical understanding that is inclusive and egalitarian" (2021: 1589). Although the normative horizon of democracy demands some inclusiveness and equality, several democratic practices (e.g., expert committees, mini-publics) are not *fully* inclusive and egalitarian, yet they enact other democratic principles (respectively expertise, deliberation). Accordingly, a practice is never fully democratic; it is a matter of continuum and not of dichotomy. A practice enacts *some* democratic principles; it is then democratic *to some extent*. Principles also justify practices; a practice is *normatively* relevant because it enacts a particular democratic principle. For example, the practice of periodic election is oriented by its function of selecting political performers and justified by enacting the principle of accountability in opening the periodic possibility to sanction the performers in office.

Second, *functions and principles* are often conflated in the literature because both express a kind of *goal*. But these goals are of a different nature. Functions determine *what* is to be done by practices (e.g., orientation, legislation, etc.), principles regulate *how* it should be done by practices (inclusively, deliberatively, etc.). While practices are oriented towards the performance of a "goal" (function), principles are essential to regulate and stabilize this performance *in a specific way*. They provide a normative orientation and a *justification* for practices. In a systemic vein, systems enact principles to stabilize their operations under a specific form, hence structuring the expectations of the system's actors. Whether as abstract principles or specific rules, the purpose of principles is always to regulate and stabilize the performance of a function in a certain way. They are not the goal themselves (the function is), they are *additional expectations* for the reach of the goal. Conversely, the function to be performed limits the principles that could regulate and stabilize the practice. For instance, if the practice of election has for a function to select political performers, it can enact, and is expected to enact, *some* democratic principles but not all of them: arguably, participation and competition rather than expertise and consensus. For the same function, take the practice of random selection; it could conceivably enact the principles of equality of chances and descriptive representativity, but not participation and popular sovereignty. A practice can enact several principles but cannot enact every principle. Plus, some are more *saliently* expected depending on its function. Thus, the function *orients* the principles that could be enacted by the practices. A significant part of context-sensitivity in the enactment of principles is here *function*-sensitivity. For analytical purposes, the point of distinguishing functions from principles is to open the possibility that common political functions can be performed by variable practices enacting *different* democratic principles.

Third, *functions and practices* are understood in a means-ends relationship: function is a stable *goal* fulfilled by a range of possible practices as functionally equivalent means. A function limits the set of practices that can perform it (e.g., the practice of election cannot presumably perform the function of implementation but effectively performs the function of selection of political performers). The performance of a function by a particular practice inevitably has implications in terms of democratic quality. Majoritarian election, designation, and random selection are functionally equivalent practices for the function of selection of political performers, they do exactly the same job. But they do it very differently; they have different criteria of inclusion (respectively everybody can be candidate, a short-listing of relevant candidates, a sampling of the whole population) and of decision (aggregation, meritocratic choice, sortition). Here, principles intervene in the relationship between practices and functions. Principles serve to normatively *justify* a practice *beyond its function*. Principles hence are normative criteria to assess the respective merits of functionally equivalent practices (e.g., the principle of inclusion is better enacted by the practice of election than designation). However, the latter can arguably better enact the principle of expertise than election. Here we face a *trade-off* between two democratic expectations: inclusion and expertise. Two practices (election and designation), performing the same function (selection of political performers), have different merits in terms of the enactment of principles (inclusion and expertise). One is not *a priori* better than the other. Hence, the justification must go on to assess which practice must be favored in a particular context, and other principles might claim relevance in the trade-off. Why this practice, for that purpose, here and now, enacting these principles, instead of this other practice enacting other principles? The conceptual core of democratic systems as functions-practices-principles questions the *contextual justifiability* of the multiple normative trade-offs composing complex democratic systems.

This conceptual articulation of functions, practices, and principles combines the commonality of broad goals (political functions) with the variability of both democratic *means* (as practices) and democratic *ends* (as particular regulations of political functions through different democratic principles). It allows the conception that democratic systems can be made of different practices enacting diverse democratic principles while performing the same political functions, and still remain recognizably yet distinctively *democratic*. This conceptualization paves the way for the development of fine-grained and context-sensitive analytical tools for the diagnosis of whole democratic systems.

C. The contextual justification of democratic practices

With this understanding of the relationships between functions, practices, and principles, we can question how the pervasive function of justification interacts with contextual principles. Justification is a practice inherent in any relation of power (see Chapter 5). The political system is characterized by the medium of power, necessary for the production of collectively *binding* decisions. Hence, power is pervasive in the political system, and so is justification. By qualifying power as pervasive, I highlight that power does not come to existence with collectively binding decisions, it occurs in the overall variety of political communications, such as executive decrees or claims raised in mini-publics. Each of these political communications are *practices of justifications*; they aim to motivate others to fulfill certain expectations. In a democratic system, these practices of justifications (or relations of power) bear a burden of justification, they can be more or less justified. Taking justification as a function involves the generalization of this burden of justification to *all* relations of power (e.g., majoritarian elections of political performers, parliamentary committee hearings, acts of civil disobedience, and countless others). To put it in an autological form, relations of power as *practices of justification* demand the *justification of practices* in a democratic system. Therefore, the specific practices performing a function (e.g., legislation) require justification.

This is where the distinction within the normative layer operates between the common normative core (reciprocal and general justification) and contextual normative expectations (accountability, representation, deliberation, epistemic quality, etc.). These two normative sources serve to justify (and critique) the practices performing the functions. Recall that "good" justifications must feature reciprocity and generality. But these two criteria only constitute a threshold of *minimal justifiability*; if some practices cannot be justified by reciprocal and general claims, they cannot be democratic, even though they perform political functions. As such, these two criteria serve as a filter between democratic practices and those that are obviously not. For instance, the granting of voting rights to only a very specific socio-economic category of the population, let's say only to people holding a PhD, supported by the claim that "they are more competent," is likely to breach these two criteria. However, this *direct* application of reciprocal and general justification only enables non-democratic practices to be sorted out, and mostly very obvious ones at that. While the test "democratic/non-democratic" is important, the task of diagnosis of democratic systems aims for much more subtlety and incisiveness. Often, the question will not be whether a particular practice is democratic or not, but whether a particular democratic practice appropriately fits its functional context and should be preferred to a range of functionally equivalent democratic practices. Put differently, the question is whether a particular democratic practice (e.g., a referendum) is *contextually* justified. And for this purpose, we need to use the criteria of reciprocal and general justification *indirectly*. We must use these in relation to contextual principles/norms.

Principles support and justify particular practices. For example, inclusion justifies universal suffrage or representation (as a norm) supports elections. One part of the contextual justifiability of a practice depends on the function it aims to fulfill. But the other part depends on the norms it enacts. The enacted norms justify the practice: universal suffrage (rather than census suffrage) *for* inclusion, equality, etc. Some (most) practices enact several norms simultaneously; a randomly selected mini-public can, of course, enact deliberation *per se*, but also respect, civility, recognition, authenticity, epistemic advancement, consensus, reason-giving, representation, publicity, equality, inclusion, etc. When some norms are enacted by a practice, others are not. In the systemic perspective, the enactment of some democratic norms instead of others is not a problem since this approach does not require *each* principle to be enacted by every practice. What might be problematic is when the enactment of some democratic norms *prevents* the enactment of others. The enactment of deliberation (as a norm) is famous for running against inclusion, as the practice of deliberation faces some practical limitations. As another example, epistemic advancement (or truth-seeking) can prevent a faithful representation of all perspectives and demographic categories, as sometimes it is necessary to speak "among experts," and even among minimally "like-minded" experts.

The general point is one already made by Warren (2007) and Thompson (2008) regarding deliberation, and Mansbridge et al. (2012) regarding deliberative systems; *trade-offs* between deliberative principles are inevitable within a deliberative system. I apply the same reasoning for democratic principles within democratic systems. The "full menu" of democratic principles, to reframe Chambers' metaphor (2017:167), is hardly achievable in most locations of a democratic system. Of course, broadly speaking, the more of these principles are enacted by a practice, the better. But within complex empirical realities, conflicting principles and thus trade-offs between them are inevitable.[98] This is why the approach to improving democracy cannot simply be a maximalist one, aiming for a proliferation of democratic practices and institutions, maximizing democratic principles within each of these venues. Democracy as a complex system must function efficiently and

---

[98] There can also be trade-offs between different instantiations of the same principle, such as between *substantive, descriptive, formal,* or *discursive* types of representation.

coherently; its improvement cannot simply be a chaotic proliferation but needs to be a structured and coherent development of more or less functionally specialized, ordered, balanced, complementary, and appropriately connected practices enacting some democratic principles and not others.

In this reading of the complexity of democratic systems, not every democratic expectation *can be* nor *must be* satisfied in every venue. Hence, a division of labor and normative trade-offs are central to the empirical fulfillment of the democratic ideal and to the analytical endeavor of locating democratic problems and concrete opportunities for improvement. Similarly, Warren (2007) considers that each part of the system has its own strengths and weaknesses. Specific parts cannot always achieve simultaneously conflicting goals, which imposes trade-offs between these goals. As Thompson argues, when trade-offs arise, we need "to decide under what conditions which value should have priority, and which combination of value is optimal" (2008: 513). In some cases, this decision is easily made by referring to concrete functional needs; if a specific expertise is requested for legislation, epistemic advancement might naturally trump other norms in the trade-off. But in other cases, the function may not be sufficient to make a decision: if, for example, no value automatically trumps another. For example, should the representativity of a parliament trump its deliberative quality? The number of elected representatives certainly enhances the parliament's representativity of the constituency, but it simultaneously makes deliberation practically impossible. The reference to the function of legislation does not provide a straightforward solution to this trade-off between representation and deliberation, hence further *justification* is required. The prominence of some norms over others cannot be settled theoretically once and for all. Instead, it requires *contextual justification*. Some contexts might favor deliberation while others would give priority to representation; both options are democratically acceptable, as long as reciprocal and general justifications sustain them.

In real-life settings, it is unlikely to find *actual* justifications for political practices and institutions (in contrast with political outcomes), even less so regarding the norms that support them (see Chapter 5). Concretely, the favoring of representativity over deliberation in the parliament is a trade-off generally *not* sustained by actual justification. Instead, the specific shape of existing political systems depends largely on underlying "justification narratives" deeply rooted in social and philosophical history, such as contractualism, nationalism, utopia, progress, etc. (Forst 2018: 57–61). These narratives are much too broad and empirically intertwined to be reliable grounds for a reconstruction of *actual claims* advanced to justify particular political arrangements. Existing institutions enact normative trade-offs, but there are often no explicit claims we can rely on to assess whether these trade-offs are justified or not. There are no directly available claims saying: "Parliament should favor representativity at the detriment of deliberative quality because…" These might emerge from an interpretive empirical reconstruction, but the *actual* justification of existing political practices and institutions is not always an empirical reality. In these cases, for the aim of diagnosing political systems, we need to rely on the *hypothetical* justifiability of normative trade-offs. This does not prevent the development of practices and institutions of *actual* justifications in democratic systems. But when actual justifications are missing, hypothetical justifiability in terms of reciprocity and generality serve as the best *proxy* for the assessment of political arrangements. When assessing political institutions such as the parliament, we must thus interrogate what *could be* the reciprocal and general reasons supporting or rejecting the particular trade-off it embeds.

Contextual norms can trade-off among each other, such as in the above example. But importantly, in a democratic system, contextual norms *always* trade-off with the general norm of inclusion. In any system (whether subsystems like the administration, organization systems such as parties, or procedures such as elections), the question of inclusion is posed: Who and what should be in/out? This general question triggers trade-offs. Ideally, inclusion should be maximal: it is an *a priori* expectation for any democratic practice. However, inclusion must often be restrained to enable each system to process only a selective part of external complexity, according to its own function. Moreover, inclusion can also be limited in order to allow the enactment of other democratic norms: deliberation, of course, but also arguably civility, authenticity, mutual understanding, efficacy, epistemic advancement, arguing, consensus, rationality, professionalism, and others. The trade-off with inclusion also faces the burden of justification, making exclusions justified for the enactment of other democratic norms. Consequently, system-specific criteria of inclusion are possible in the different parts of a democratic system.

To summarize this section, I argued that the normative criteria of democratic systems should be understood in a complex threefold relationship between practices, functions, and principles. In short, this relationship is: the enactment of democratic principles by practices performing political functions. By conceptually distinguishing these three core elements, we can tackle the task of diagnosis with more clarity and nuance. The general aim of diagnosis is to assess the adequacy of existing practices, by referring to both their functional purpose and their normative fulfillment. Put differently, it targets the *contextual justifiability* of existing practices along these two dimensions. In this framework, justification is taken as the distinctive democratic function, applying to each political feature. Inclusion is the general principle of democracy, *a priori* favored for every democratic practice, but whose deviations must be justified. Contextual norms/principles justify specific practices, but often face *trade-offs* with each other.

The normative layer is then twofold: justification criteria (reciprocity and generality) and more contextual normative expectations[99] that can trade-off with each other. This complex normative layer is well suited to the analytical core of democratic systems defined by the relationship between practices, principles, and functions. It maintains democracy's normative distinctiveness and the flexibility of its variable enactment in diverse political contexts. A further normative implication is that the enactment of democratic principles by practices is not enough normatively speaking; the justification of *these* practices enacting *these* principles and not others is also a crucial democratic issue. Democracy's horizon requires the constant self-justification of its own democratic practices of justification, a point developed in Chapter 7. Finally, as the normative layer also places *political functions* at its core, the normative layer is clearly compatible and analytically connectable with the descriptive layer of democratic systems (see the first section in this chapter). In the next section, I suggest elements for the application of the normative layer and describe in Chapter 7 how to articulate the descriptive and normative layers of this framework of democratic systems for the task of diagnosis.

---

[99] I do not provide an exhaustive list of these contextual norms, but it could certainly include things as diverse as civility, recognition, efficacy, representation, rationality, competition, cooperation, integrity, deliberation, truth-tracking, moderation, reflexivity, consent, accountability, responsiveness, hierarchy, innovation, contestation, and many others. See Chapter 5 for more details.

How does the normative layer apply to the parts, connections, and/or the system as a whole?

The systemic approach to democracy brings back theoretical debates and empirical inquiries at the level of the whole system. In reaction to deliberative democracy's over-focus on single and isolated deliberative venues, this re-scaling was an important motivation for its systemic turn. The systemic approach contends that what matters *ultimately* is the democratic quality of the *whole* system, and not of its composing parts. The representation of the whole system usually depicts a national political system, composed of multiple institutions and practices. But systems theory insists that systems are made of systems and that parts are systems themselves, hence what is whole and what is part always depends on which political system one intends to work on. Indeed, while the national political system is often taken to be the whole, it can represent a part in the analysis of the global political system. In the same way, a transnational network of advocacy can be a part of the latter analysis, or it can itself be the whole under analysis. The descriptive layer conceptualized here is flexible enough to be applied to the overall diversity of political "wholes." Here, Saward's (2021: 109–110) distinction between *whole-systemic* and *part-systemic* is enlightening. As I understand it, whole-systemic analysis covers the whole functional unity of a political system, that is, all its subfunctions, whatever its level of governance. The classic example is the national political system, but it also applies local and supra-national systems. Part-systemic analysis focuses on one part of the function system, such as the entire subsystem of administration or an organization system such as the parliament or political parties. In order to be *systemic* in kind, part-systemic analysis cannot study specific systems in isolation, it must investigate their external and internal differentiation and subsequent connections.

That caution being heard, I agree with Dryzek that "the systemic test should take priority" (2010: 82) over assessments of institutions in isolation. However, it would be a misleading to assume that we can assess the democratic quality of political systems without investigating how their parts are shaped, function, and interrelate. Once again, the understanding of a system depends primarily on the analysis of its external and internal differentiation and connections between these differentiated parts. We need to distinguish parts to question how they normatively contribute to the whole. Consequently, in order to assess the democratic quality of a whole political system, we have to investigate *if* and *how* its parts perform political functions and enact democratic principles.

The qualifier we work with here is *democratic*; it normatively qualifies the whole, the systemic level. Systems are emergent phenomena; they are something other than the sum of their parts (see Chapter 3). Democracy is an emergent system (what Parkinson calls a "summative" quality), it is not the *addition* of democratic parts (see Chapter 1). Accordingly, the qualifier "democratic" does not properly apply to its parts. Of course, we commonly qualify the parliament, for instance, as a democratic institution. But in the systemic perspective, analytically speaking, the parliament is an institution *of* a democratic system. It is democratic in the sense of enacting *some* democratic principles (e.g., representation, deliberation, bargaining, competition, civility, integrity, etc.). And it enacts these principles to variable extents. Hence, it is never fully democratic (in enacting all the possible democratic principles in the best possible way), nor should it be.

To qualify practices and institutions as democratic conceals the *specific* democratic principles they enact, hence their distinctive and limited contribution to the whole system. I am also reluctant to qualify institutions by their most salient enacted principles, such as considering the parliament as a *representative* institution. It does enact representation, moreover a special kind of representation (delegative mostly), but it also enacts other democratic principles. To label practices and institutions by their most saliently enacted principle occults the other principles at play in these venues. Analytically speaking, the aim is precisely to question the multiplicity of enacted principles and the justifiability of the contextual favoring of some over others. Therefore, I summarize this paragraph with an addendum to an assumption of Mansbridge et al. (2012: 5, emphasis mine): "The system should be judged as a whole *in addition* to the parts being judged independently" *but with different normative criteria.* Democratic as an emergent property qualifies the whole system; contextual normative expectations (e.g., deliberation, inclusion) serve to qualify the specific democratic contribution of the parts.

From these considerations, I sketch the foundations of what Dryzek would call a "metric to assess the performance of the system *as a whole*" (2017: 621, original emphasis). Elements of this metric are tentatively developed in the next chapter as a clear diagnostic strategy, by articulating the descriptive and normative layers for that purpose. For now, I focus on the basic *application* of the normative layer. After the descriptive phase, the normative assessment starts by interrogating the minimal justifiability of the identified practices. There we question whether a particular practice is or could be justified by reciprocal and general claims. It enables practices that are not minimally democratic to be ruled out. Among these, the second step identifies the democratic principles that are actually enacted by these practices in each functional part of the system under analysis. Concretely, this step uncovers the distribution of democratic principles within the system: the "normative division of labor" so to speak. The third step regards the justification of the potential trade-offs between the principles enacted by practices. By doing so, we must consider the democratic principles that are saliently expected or could reasonably be but fail to be enacted by the practice in question, potentially revealing an inadequacy between the specific practice and the expected democratic principles.

A further difficulty in assessing trade-offs is that their justifiability depends also on what occurs in other parts of the system. It depends on the fact that other parts can "balance" (Warren 2007), "compensate" (Dryzek 2009), or "complement" (Mansbridge et al. 2012) this trade-off. The respective weaknesses and strengths of the parts can complement one another: for instance, parts that "generate consensus should be balanced by those that harbor and refine dissent" (Warren 2007: 287). If we combine this analytical feature of complementary/balancing relations *between parts* with the idea of normative trade-offs occurring *within parts*, we understand that trade-offs themselves are what is supposed to be balanced. Concretely, the justifiability of representation trumping deliberation at the parliament also depends on whether deliberation is enacted or not in another location, which would "balance" its weakness at the parliament.

Importantly, a part's strength can only balance another's weakness if they share the same purpose, that is, the same function. It must be a balancing of the same thing, so to speak. Indeed, the enactment of deliberation in a part "somewhere in the system" (let's say in the orientation phase) is not enough to counterbalance its absence at the parliament during the legislation phase. For instance, the deliberation within an agenda-setting mini-public cannot balance the lack of deliberation of the legislating parliament. However, the legislative work of special-ized parliamentary committees can balance the lack of deliberation at the plenum. The implication is that, in order to count as "balanc-ing," two parts must perform the same function (here, legislation) and be appropriately connected (here, structurally coupled through formal procedures). If these two conditions are not met, the lack of delibera-tion in one part would not genuinely be compensated by another part; a deliberation within the administration for the implementation of a pol-icy cannot balance the lack of deliberation within the parliament. The application of the democratic normative criteria to specific parts of the system must proceed according to these three analytical steps: *testing of the minimal justifiability of practices, identification of the normative distribu-tion, and justifiability of the trade-offs and balancing relationships.*

Regarding connections, when conceived as structural couplings, they do not enact principles *themselves*. Indeed, structural couplings enable *functions* to be performed by practices (see the first section in this chapter). Depending on the features of their couplings, practic-es can perform their respective functions with more or less success. For instance, the structural coupling between the public and politics enables the performance of their function (respectively observation and orientation, selection of political performers, and elaboration of decision premises). *If* these systems are structurally coupled, through the practice of election, for instance, politics can enact representa-tion and inclusion, and the public can enact participation. Let's take another example: a randomly selected mini-public is implemented in order to propose an agenda to executive politics. As such it per-forms the public's function of orientation (here specific agenda-set-ting). The mini-public performs agenda-setting *if* it is appropriately coupled with executive politics. But this coupling is not *itself* enact-ing representation or inclusion, the mini-public does. Nor is this cou-pling enacting responsiveness, executive politics do if they consider the agenda proposed by the mini-public. The point is that connections as couplings do not enact democratic principles, they enable demo-cratic principles to be enacted by practices (here the mini-public and executive politics). Depending on the coupling's features, some dem-ocratic principles can be more or less enacted. The couplings' quality facilitates or restricts the enactment of principles by connected prac-tices. Accordingly, connections as structural couplings are *not* assessed with democratic principles, but with couplings' features enabling the functioning of the practices. Once again, decisiveness and consequentiality are not normative criteria (i.e., democratic principles) to assess connections. In my framework, their critical work is covered in greater detail and with much flexibility by the six features of coupling that apply to every connection within a system.

To summarize, the assessment of a political system as a whole in democratic terms requires us to consider how it is internally shaped and differentiated, which practices perform which functions, and which principles are enacted or not. Moreover, the systemic dimension of this assessment is displayed through the evaluation of the normative trade-offs embedded in these practices, the potential relations of compensation/balancing of these trade-offs, and the features of coupling between these different practices. The point of such an assessment is not to state that a system *is* democratic, nor that is inclusive or deliberative, for instance. Instead, the goal is to determine *how* it is democratic, by uncovering its specific and selective enactment of democratic principles such as inclusivity and deliberativeness in particular locations. As a reminder, the democratic quality is taken here as a continuum rather than a democratic/non-democratic threshold. The normative layer developed here interrogates the current position of a political system on this continuum and determines how to shift it towards greater democraticness.

What about *deliberative* systems?

Before concluding this chapter, I discuss the implications of the suggested framework of democratic systems for deliberation and deliberative systems. This overall research was triggered by a systemic turn in *deliberative* democracy, a systemic inspiration that also fueled more "ecumenical" (Saward 2021: xix) approaches to democracy, notably Warren (2017) and Saward (2021). These approaches explicitly criticize the predominance of the model of deliberative democracy in democratic theory. According to Warren, democratic theory is pervaded by "model thinking": the tendency to focus on one feature (for instance, deliberation or representation), to assume its ability to deal with all the problems relevant to democracy, and to define an entire model of democracy around it. Deliberative democracy is directly targeted by this critique. For Saward, deliberative democracy's "asserted generality and encompassing nature ignores or downplays non-deliberative components of a democratic system" (ibid.: 21). Deliberative democracy's systemic turn precisely acknowledged the assumption that "democratic systems also require much more" (ibid.) than deliberation. They thus welcomed non-deliberative practices (and even anti-deliberative practices) as contributing positively to ... *deliberative* systems. The deliberative quality, disaggregated into deliberative normative criteria to be distributed along the system, remained their normative horizon. Through this move, deliberative democratic theorists "have found a way to continue to privilege deliberation over other democratic values" (ibid.: 22). Moreover, they erected deliberative systems as something *other* than democratic systems, something that can be democratic or not. This is clearly illustrated by Parkinson:

> To be democratic, a deliberative system needs to be both plugged into the experiences, narratives, deliberations, claims, even the symbols and language, of the relevant demoi at one end; and plugged into the "power socket" at the other, by being decisive in some way. (2018: 436)

This position[100,101] appears to me as a conceptual subversion of the central question of whether and how democracy should be deliberative. The question becomes instead how deliberative systems can be democratic, shifting the spotlight from *democratic* to *deliberative* systems. If this predominance of deliberation is obvious in democratic theory, it is not necessarily misplaced. Through the lens of the systemic framework developed here, I envision three main explanations for the prominence of deliberation within the normative ideal of democracy.

A. Deliberative democracy: a misplaced predominance?

A first possible explanation of deliberation's prominence in democratic theory lies in the fact that, like any political and social system, democracy is a system of *communication*. Deliberative democracy and social

---

[100] This quote shows an Habermassian understanding of democracy: the coupling of the public sphere with the communicational lifeworld on the one side and the power system on the other side (see Chapter 5).

[101] If the deliberative system is something *other* than the democratic system, what it represents is sometimes unclear. Is it something close to the Habermassian "public sphere" that should be connected to the power system? In which case the deliberative system is always *political* or *politically oriented*. Or is it something like the "lifeworld" that is not bounded to the political system but infuses all the existing social systems (economy, law, education, religion, etc.)? Parkinson's (2018) favoring of the term deliberative *society* over *system* strengthens the relevance of this interrogation.

systems theories share the centrality of communication. However, as Parkinson argues, deliberative democratic theorists "have surprisingly little to say about the mechanics of human communication" (2019: 1). Moreover, he points out that the theory of deliberative democracy is often misleadingly built "on the back of a normative theory of communication" (ibid.) drawn from a misreading of Habermas's theory of communicative action. Parkinson forcefully reminds us that the ideal speech situation articulated *pragmatic* presuppositions for communication, hence was not a *normative* theory of communication. Indeed, deliberative democratic theorists have focused mostly on why and how communication *should be* deliberative, without relying much on "an *empirical* theory of communication" (ibid.: 5, original emphasis). As a consequence, as Bächtiger & Parkinson note, "normative standards and descriptive claims are often intertwined" in most deliberative systems accounts (2019: 83).

A reason for this intertwining is that the theory of deliberative systems uncovers the "implicit normative standards already at work in modern democracy" (Neblo 2015: 17). It describes at length how political/democratic communication operates in modern society and which norms actually regulate it. By doing so, the deliberative system approach has (or at least had) a tendency to read the overall political/democratic communication *through a deliberative lens*, to the point where it could be suspected that the label "deliberative system" is used as a synonym for political/democratic communication. The conflation is understandable since most of the other models of democracy give much less importance to communication, nor are they generally built upon sociological grounds that put communication at their core. To exaggerate slightly, deliberative democratic theorists acted as if communication was *their* thing, mostly because non-deliberative democrat theorists considered that communication was *not* their problem. Furthermore, deliberative democrat theorists did so without always highlighting the fact that deliberation is only *one* mode of communication occurring in political systems and desirable in democratic ones. A major exception is Bächtiger & Parkinson (2019), who clearly distinguish deliberation from other modes of democratic communication such as story-telling and bargaining, thus resisting the tendency to "inflate the concept of deliberation to the point that it encompassed all kinds of communicative acts" (ibid. 23). I accept their restriction of deliberation as a distinct mode of communication characterized by reason-giving and listening. Accordingly, the adjectival and norma-tive use of *deliberative* is here restricted to these two "deliberative prin-ciples."[102] Analytically speaking, *deliberative systems* are hence specific communication systems with reason-giving and listening as distinc-tive features. Deliberative systems thus defined are not inflated as syn-onyms for "democratic systems" nor "political systems." A restricted definition I endorse here.

A second explanation for the deliberative predominance, from the perspective of the framework developed here, relates directly to the normative distinctiveness of democracy. Relying on Forst's theory, I argued that democratic systems, in contrast with other political sys-tems, have a pervasive function of *justification*. With the centrality of justification within the practice of deliberation (whether we label it reason-giving, argumentation, communicative rationality, etc.), the prominence of deliberation within democratic theory is quite under-standable. Indeed, deliberative democracy as a normative ideal ulti-mately aims for the actual justification and mutual justifiability of political procedures and outcomes. Joshua Cohen's classical defini-tion of deliberation clearly puts justification at its core: "Justification through public argument and reasoning among [...] citizens" (Cohen 1989 in Bächtiger & Parkinson 2019: 2). Moreover, deliberative democ-racy is by far the model of democracy that puts more effort into devel-oping normative criteria for appropriate procedures of justification. Furthermore, deliberation is probably the ultimate practice (so far) for performing mutual justification in the best possible way (without assuming it is perfect either). This is Forst's position when he con-tends that:

> We have to analyze power relations along a spectrum extending from its exercise through the justificatory quality of reasons shared among deliberating persons, at one end, to the limiting case of its exercise by way of physical force, at the other, which in its extreme form lies outside of the realm of power, being instead a reflection of the lack of power. The reality of the exercise of power usually falls somewhere in between, and the main object of analysis is the noumenal character of the social relations or events in question: What are the justifications that move persons? (2018: 50)

---

[102] One can wonder if the principles of reason-giving and listening must occur *simultane-ously* to qualify something as deliberative. Otherwise, reason-giving and listening could stand as principles *on their own*.

This quote puts deliberation at one end of the continuum for the justification of power relations. But it also expresses that justification is a much broader phenomenon than deliberation, and that other democratic practices such as election, governmental decrees, referendums, and representation are *also* practices of justification. Indeed, these practices provide justification/reasons for the exercise of noumenal power (see Chapter 5). The democratic norms they enact (or fail to enact) are motivations for the acceptance (or rejection) of power. In consequence, at least within this framework, justification cannot be equated with deliberation; we must see deliberation as *one* practice of justification, albeit certainly the best one at our disposal. We can thus understand why deliberation as the best practice of justification has been granted such a normative predominance within democratic theory. This led to the normative horizon of justification being conflated with that of deliberation, ultimately conflating deliberative systems with democratic ones.

A third possible explanation has to do with what systems theory takes as a specificity of modern society: the awareness of its contingency, leading to its *reflexivity* and self-thematization as a system in a changing environment. The modern political system (as with other social systems) largely refers to itself and is even openly self-critical. The capacity for critique is certainly a central condition for a *democratic* political system. For Forst, the right to justification directly implies the necessity for a critique of existing justifications, and vice versa. Indeed, as he contends: "Built into the idea of democratic justification then is the possibility of self-critique and recursive questioning whether any concrete justification *could have done better* – not: was ideal" (Forst 2001: 373, original emphasis). This quote highlights the *self-corrective* character of a democratic system. The deliberative systems approach also stressed this important feature, under the label of *meta-deliberation* (Thompson 2008). Notably, meta-deliberation was recognized by Dryzek & Stevenson as a core component of deliberative systems and defined as "the capacity of a deliberative system to examine itself and if necessary transform itself" (2014: 29). The authors also contend that *meta-deliberation* and *reflexive capacity* are synonymous (ibid.: 35–36). In a more detailed discussion on meta-deliberation, Holdo's less exaggerated formulation suggests that meta-deliberation "[serves] a reflective function in the deliberative system," a function of "critical reflection" (2020: 108). The point is that there is an evident tie between the necessity of self-critique or self-reflexivity deriving from the democratic function of justification and the practice of meta-deliberation's great capacity to perform it.

However, once again, just because deliberation is probably the best practice to put the system into question in order "to detect its own deficiencies and improve" (ibid.: 116) does not imply that this task is devolved entirely to the practice of deliberation and must exclusively occur under a deliberative form. We can think of the importance of social movements or civil disobedience to alert a democratic system to its deficiencies. In line with the deliberative systems approach, Holdo is aware of that fact in arguing that "meta-deliberation may take place in a variety of contexts and taking a variety of forms that may not traditionally have been seen as deliberation" (ibid.: 107).[103] But to talk of meta-*deliberation* is once again to push towards a reading of non-deliberative practices such as contestation as serving so-called "deliberative functions." Moreover, critical self-reflection does not have as its sole *object* deliberation,[104] it has as its object the democratic system as a whole and all its potential deficiencies (lack of representativity, unjustified exclusions, inappropriate coupling between parts, etc.). Therefore, I follow Thompson's initial suggestion about the role of meta-deliberation. As described by Holdo, "Thompson sees meta-deliberation as a process of addressing the role and place of different forms of democratic politics, including deliberation, in the larger democratic system" (ibid.: 110). Defined as such, meta-deliberation can be decisive for assessing trade-offs between democratic principles. It might even be necessary, as Holdo argues (ibid.: 115), to actually assess the justifiability of poorly democratic practices such as confrontational protests.

Understood with this purpose, critical self-reflection (under the form of meta-deliberation but not exclusively) is crucial for the self-steering and improvement of democratic systems. But it shall not

---

[103] Similarly, we can see meta-deliberation as an emergent phenomenon (or summative for Parkinson), made of multiple elements that do not only include deliberation *per se*. But this would subsume something broader (critical self-reflection) under the conceptual banner of meta-deliberation as its best way to perform it.

[104] See how Holdo defines meta-deliberation: "to discuss how we discuss" (2020: 107), restricting its use about the deliberative quality of the deliberative system. Moreover, he also restricts to some extent the reflective capacity to the object of deliberation: "Reflective capacity refers to a society's ability to see problems of communication, and deviations from values such as inclusion, public-mindedness, and sincerity that are central to deliberative theory, as indicating systemic deficiencies" (ibid.: 115).

be restricted to deliberation as an *object* of critique or as a *means* of critique. I do not deny that often the deliberative quality is the object of critical self-reflection, nor that meta-deliberation is possibly the more powerful means to that end. On the contrary, I am deeply sympathetic to Landwehr's suggestion of institutionalizing democratic meta-deliberative venues to enable "reflective institutional design" (2015: 38). This "addition" of meta-deliberation in the system, about the system as a whole, could be a very beneficial thing in most political contexts. However, the reflective critique of political systems also occurs through diverse means such as "wearing a T-shirt" contesting a political feature (as Holdo argues), elections bringing to government a party whose program is a deep transformation of the system, a popular initiative demanding an important constitutional change, and, of course, a bunch of randomly selected ordinary people with enough time to deliberate on the system's deficiencies. Again, it is a matter of degrees; the latter is probably the best means at disposal for the critical self-reflection of the democratic system, but it does not exhaust the capacity of systemic reflexive critique. The point is that meta-deliberation cannot be conflated with the broader phenomenon of critical self-reflection, if these other forms of critique are to be considered as contributing to a democratic system's reflexivity.

Taking stock of these three hypotheses about the deliberative predominance in democratic theory, I conclude that it is not totally misplaced. The rationale is that the practice of deliberation is intrinsically attached to the nature of political systems (i.e., communication), the specific function of democratic systems (i.e., justification), and its self-corrective capacity (i.e., critical self-reflection). Accordingly, the deliberative predominance in democratic theory is perfectly understandable, as it derives from a natural conflation of the "deliberative" and "democratic" normative horizons. Indeed, this chapter's depiction of the normative horizon of democratic systems is very close in many respects to "deliberative democracy." Ultimately, democratic systems are self-justificatory and self-corrective political systems. No doubt the practice of deliberation is pivotal along the way to this democratic horizon. Nonetheless, since democratic systems range along a continuum, some democratic systems perform less well regarding their justificatory and self-reflexive capacities. These systems simultaneously are less "deliberative." Of course, strengthening their deliberative quality, or rather the deliberative quality of some of their parts and their connections with other important venues, may improve their overall democratic quality. However, what is perhaps particularly missing in a specific democratic system is instead representativity, inclusion, or accountability, not deliberation.

A democratic system could perform well deliberatively speaking, but not regarding other democratic principles. Bächtiger & Parkinson (2019) take the example of "authoritarian deliberations" occurring in China. In this case, what the political system under scrutiny lacks, to get closer to the democratic horizon, is not deliberation, but probably responsiveness, accountability, and an appropriate coupling with decision-making in order for deliberation to have concrete political effects. My point is that, *analytically speaking*, there is no sense of having deliberativeness as the driving normative horizon towards which we should aim. The routes towards the democratic horizon are not always made of more deliberation (or deliberativeness). To take deliberative democratic systems (or deliberative systems *tout court*) as the normative horizon for democratic systems blurs that fact and orients the identification of problems and the proposal of solutions towards deliberativeness, although this is not always what is at stake in a political context. In the next section, I argue further why deliberativeness should remain analytically distinct from democraticness. I then suggest how we should use deliberation and deliberativeness in the task of diagnosing political systems. I conclude by discussing the relevance of the distinction between deliberative/non-deliberative democratic systems for the diagnostic framework developed in Chapter 7.

B. Deliberation and deliberativeness within democratic systems

First, I oppose the tendency of the deliberative systems approach, especially in initial accounts, to subsume democratic principles (e.g., respect, accountability, epistemic improvement) under the deliberative banner as disaggregated components of *deliberative* quality (the more striking example being inclusion, see Dryzek 2009 and Mansbridge et al. 2012). Deliberativeness *as a normative expectation* must be restricted to what makes the distinctiveness of deliberation *as a practice*: reason-giving and listening. This is not to say that deliberation is not well-suited for generating respect and recognition, tracking truth, and including representative perspectives on a complex issue. But analytically speaking, these democratic principles are not deliberative, since they can be enacted independently of the practice of deliberation. Bächtiger & Parkinson explicitly recognize, for instance, that inclusion is not "uniquely a deliberative virtue" but "a general democratic virtue" (2019: 9). They read inclusion through a deliberative lens, "blending the timbres of deliberation and inclusivity" (ibid.) to describe how inclusion could be enacted in deliberative systems under the form of a broad, deep, and clear inclusion of *perspectives*. However, this is a reduction of the multiple ways in which inclusion can be enacted in democratic systems. As they note themselves: "Focusing purely on memes, discourses, or storylines obscures the fact that these are *people*'s positions, people's claims, grounded in people's experiences of collective life" (ibid.: 112, original emphasis). Democratic inclusion *also* demands the inclusion of people of flesh and blood in some venues, not only of their perspectives, ideas, and preferences. Therefore, inclusion must stand alone as a democratic principle to analytically contrast different forms of inclusion that can trade-off in many democratic venues. Furthermore, inclusion must stand alone to identify its potential trade-offs with deliberation or other democratic expectations. The same goes for all other democratic principles, including deliberativeness. If democratic principles such as deliberativeness or inclusion are blended together, we analytically lose track of their unique critical potential.

Second, I clarify what deliberation and deliberative characterize in my framework of democratic systems. Deliberation is first of all a *practice*, whose distinctive core is reason-giving and listening as argued by Bächtiger & Parkinson. I also follow the authors (borrowing Saward's expression) on the "shape-shifting" character of deliberation: "Deliberation not only 'shape-shifts' according to different goals and contexts, it is also transformed by creative agents in situ" (ibid.: 15). I agree that the practice of deliberation takes place under diverse forms in different contexts and depending on the "goals" of deliberation. Nonetheless, at the conceptual level, I reject Bächtiger & Parkinson's distinction of five *deliberative* goals: epistemic, ethical, emancipatory, transformative and clarifying, and legitimacy-oriented. In my framework, "goals" for practices (including deliberation but also many others such as contestation or elections) are divided into two types: political functions and democratic principles. The practice of deliberation can thus perform several political *functions* (e.g., orientation, elaboration of decision premises, legislation, etc.) and in doing so it can enact some democratic principles (e.g., epistemic advancement, mutual respect, etc.). With this conceptualization, we can analyze the contextual appropriateness of a specific form of deliberation according to both the political function it performs and the democratic principles it enacts or fails to enact.

Deliberation can also be taken as a democratic principle itself that serves to orient and justify other political practices, such as parliamentary debates, commission hearings and inter-party negotiations. In some contexts, deliberation can then also be mobilized as a principle, representing the expectation of some deliberativeness of the practice in question, that is, the simultaneous enactment of reason-giving and listening. This rejoins the counterintuitive and contested assumption of the systemic approach to deliberative democracy according to which *non-deliberative* practices and institutions can perform deliberative "functions," or more accurately, can enact the deliberative principles of reason-giving and listening. However, with such a restriction of deliberative principles (to reason-giving and listening), this counterintuitive assumption still holds yet also loses much of its impetus. In the classical example, protests (as not being the practice of deliberation) can still perform a deliberative function (inclusion) by loudly exposing a striking lack of inclusion of people or perspectives in the decisional process. With inclusion not being taken here as a deliberative principle (but as a democratic one), this example no longer supports the assumption. But we can see a protest (not being deliberation) as nevertheless *providing reasons* for its demands, hence enacting deliberativeness as a principle, among other *democratic* principles. The point is that if deliberation as a practice and as a normative expectation is to be used as a sharp analytical tool in a diagnostic framework of democratic systems, it must retain its distinctiveness and not subsume all the other democratic features and expectations under its conceptual and normative banner. The dilution of deliberative expectations does not serve its unique normative and critical potential, while undermining others.

In conclusion, what about the relevance and usefulness of the label of *deliberative systems*? It depends. If the ultimate claim of deliberative democratic theorists is: "Deliberation is essential to democracy" and thus that: "Democracy must be deliberative" (Curato et al. 2017), *otherwise it is not democracy at all*, then why would the normative horizon be *deliberative* systems instead of *democratic* systems? If democratic systems are defined, largely yet partly, by the necessary presence of deliberation as a practice and/or its enactment as a principle, then there is no point in speaking of deliberative systems. The normative horizon, to which deliberation and deliberativeness are essential features, is democratic systems *tout court*. Hence, the task is precisely to investigate where deliberation is an appropriate and necessary practice and where deliberativeness is a relevant normative expectation. Indeed, the burden of the argument falls on deliberative democratic theorists to justify why a complex democratic system including non-deliberative elements (as they claim in the systemic approach to deliberative democracy) can still be labelled a *deliberative* one.

The only reason I see, with Bächtiger & Parkinson (2019: 69), of characterizing a democratic system as deliberative is that this feature is particularly *salient*. So, would deliberativeness be *empirically* salient in a democratic system that is labelled as deliberative? It would be surprising that within a perfect democratic system imagined by deliberative democratic theorists themselves, deliberativeness would be more salient than other democratic expectations such as representativeness or inclusiveness. Would deliberativeness instead be *normatively* salient within democratic systems? Again, this would entail seeing deliberativeness as a greater democratic expectation than inclusion, representation, accountability, etc. Since deliberation is the practice that best performs the function of justification, it might be legitimate to grant it such a privilege. However, in my framework of democratic systems, that would lead us to favor the enactment of deliberativeness over other democratic expectations in all cases, and regardless of the actual expectations of people in democratic polities. And thus, that would ultimately undermine the function of justification itself by bypassing the need for the contextual justification of the priority of deliberativeness over other democratic expectations. To summarize, assuming that deliberation or deliberativeness is necessary to democracy does *not* imply that it is empirically salient in a perfect democratic system; that it is normatively salient in democratic systems; that it has a generalized priority over other democratic expectations in normative trade-offs; and therefore, that a genuine democratic system could legitimately be labeled as deliberative.

In contrast, if the ultimate claim of deliberative democratic theorists is instead: "Democracy is certainly possible without much deliberation, but [...] democracy with a deliberative timbre is a better one" (Bächtiger & Parkinson 2019: 160), then we can indeed speak of a particular kind of democracy, *deliberative democratic systems*. This label can indeed characterize *a type* of democratic system where deliberation and deliberativeness are empirically salient, and *a kind* of normative ideal of democracy where these are normatively salient. I do not reject this approach to what democracy should look like, but I question its potential regarding the diagnosis of democratic problems in existing political systems. Indeed, as suggested in this book's introduction, the endorsement of deliberative democracy as a normative model is a very consequential perspective, driving focus and attention towards *one* particular feature and expectation of democratic systems. From this perspective, diagnosed problems and suggested solutions are likely to gravitate around deliberativeness and deliberation. In contrast, I have favored a more agnostic, open-ended, and context-sensitive approach. My aim is to diagnose *any* democratic problem a political system could face (e.g., lack of responsiveness or representativity, inefficient coupling between two parts of a system, undifferentiated inclusion or unjustified exclusion, etc.), in order to open the road for multiple kinds of possible solutions. To speak of *deliberative* democratic systems leads us to read problems and solutions in a deliberative vein. Notably, it apparently leads us to assess non-deliberative elements in terms of their deliberative contribution to the system. Given the complexity and variability of the fulfillment of the democratic ideal, this perspective appears too narrow and unfit for the challenge of contextual diagnosis.

Finally, besides being unfit for the task of diagnosis as I see it, is the distinction of *deliberative democratic systems* from *non-deliberative democratic systems* really useful analytically speaking? As noted in Chapter 2, Bächtiger & Parkinson (2019) justify this distinction to make sense of political systems that are deliberative but not democratic, and systems that are democratic but not deliberative. In contrast, I take democratic systems as ranging along a continuum *without* such a sharp distinction (there is no threshold where democratic systems become deliberative). In my account, a *deliberative system that is not democratic* and a *democratic system that is not deliberative* both range somewhere on the democratic continuum.[105] Both are types of democratic systems, they clearly both

---

[105] One could ask provocatively: If we take democratic systems as ranging along a continuum, which of the two following cases would rank higher on this continuum: "a deliberative but non-democratic system" or "a democratic but non-deliberative system"? If deliberation is so central to democracy, it is not obvious at all that the latter would rank higher than the former. The purpose of this question is to strengthen my assertion that the distinction between deliberative and non-deliberative democratic systems is not actually that relevant for the task of diagnosis.

have *some* democratic features, and both have very obvious important deficiencies. Both need to be improved, one with "more democracy," the other with "more deliberation." But by *not* drawing a distinction between deliberative and non-deliberative systems, we are pushed to go much deeper than this basic diagnosis.

On the one hand, it enables us to ask: What does *the deliberative but non-democratic system* require to be more democratic (perhaps more representation in some venues, accountability, a better coupling with decision-making) and where and to what extent would its deliberative quality have to be traded-off in order to enact these other democratic expectations. On the other hand, it questions: What does *the democratic but non-deliberative system* require to be more deliberative; where, how, under what practical forms, towards which functional goals, coupled to which other venues, would deliberation make such a system more democratic. Let's take an example: a representative liberal democracy is a democratic system, although, of course, not a perfect one. Probably, it has a poor deliberative quality, although it inevitably features *some* deliberativeness. What would be the analytical value in qualifying this system as deliberative or non-deliberative? None, because the point is not that this system become more deliberative (enough to reach an arbitrary threshold to be qualified as deliberative enough), the point is that it become more democratic, and in this case that occurs through it being more deliberative *in specific locations*. And the goal is precisely to identify those locations where deliberation is missing and could improve the overall democratic system. The dichotomization of deliberative versus non-deliberative systems distracts us from the complex endeavor of context-sensitive identification of democratic problems.

In line with these remarks, I do not use the label of "deliberative (democratic) systems" in the framework developed here. Its normative horizon remains *democratic systems*, to which deliberation as a practice and as a principle is a pivotal feature to drive diagnoses of democratic systems. Consequently, I contend that democratic systems are not inherently deliberative, but *justificatory*. Deliberation being arguably the best practice of justification, the capacity of democratic systems for justification is generally enhanced by deliberation as a practice and as a principle regulating other practices, *where its salience is justified*. To diagnose democratic systems with the sharp critical tool of deliberation (among other sharp critical tools) allows us to interrogate the contextual need for deliberation with more nuance and awareness of the other democratic principles that should simultaneously be expected and could trade-off with some practical enactment of deliberation.

Conclusion

The complexity of democratic systems cannot be fully grasped, but only reduced to a conceptual system. This chapter contributes to that end by depicting in the best way possible the core descriptive and normative features of democratic systems, and by building a descriptive layer that mirrors cross-contextual limitations (hence reveals contextual possibilities) and a normative layer allowing the comparison and assessment of these possibilities. Section 1 displays the main characteristics of functionally differentiated political systems and their analytical representations. In addition, it draws from the commonality of modern political systems' several preconditions for democratic systems. Section 2 focuses on the normative distinctiveness of *democratic* systems, revolving around its pervasive function of justification. It argues that practices must be sustained by reciprocal and general justification in order to be minimally democratic. Moreover, it contends that functionally equivalent practices can be compared in terms of the contextual democratic principles they enact. Trade-offs between these principles must be assessed through reciprocal and general justifications supporting their enactment. In this way, choices over democratic practices can be genuinely *democratic*. Finally, I conclude this chapter by taking a firm position regarding the place of deliberation and deliberativeness in this framework of democratic systems. They remain crucial *means* to the normative end of democraticness. Figure 3 below illustrates and simplifies this chapter's core claims.

From the democratic function of justification, the necessity for critical self-reflection emerges recursively. As I argue in the next chapter, this task can be enhanced by the development of a diagnostic scheme for political systems. The framework of democratic systems developed in this chapter constitutes the groundwork for building a context-sensitive diagnostic strategy for political systems. The next chapter suggests how to use it for diagnosing the specific problems of actual political systems. This requires taking seriously the idea that problems vary depending on contexts, and that it is crucial to be able to identify those in order to design appropriate solutions.

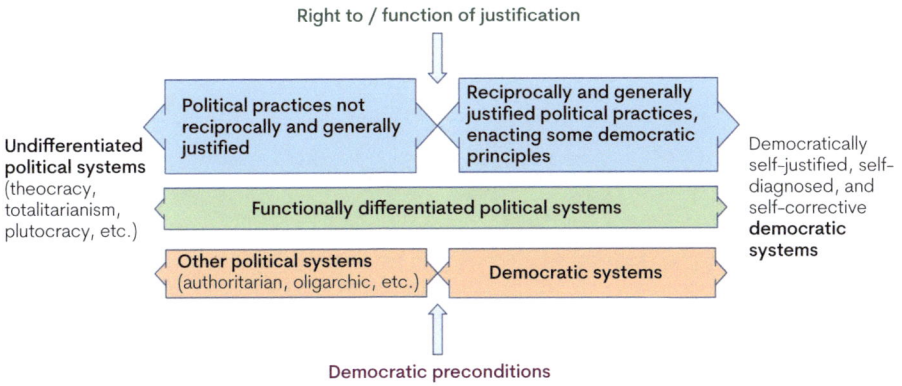

FIGURE 3 The democratic systems continuum

Towards the democratic diagnosis of political systems

7

Le rôle du philosophe actuellement, c'est d'être non pas le théoricien de la totalité, mais le diagnosticien d'aujourd'hui. (Foucault: 1979, audio)

In every society in many arenas, the reality of collective decision-making falls far short of the democratic ideal in countless ways. [...] But there is no once-and-for-all solution. Instead, approaching the democratic ideal requires political practices of continuous democratic innovation. (Fung 2012: 609)

Democratic problems cannot be addressed by once-and-for-all and one-size-fits-all solutions (Fung 2012; Warren 2017; Saward 2021). The impetus for the systemic turn in democratic theory was precisely to stop the search for "perfect" institutions or democratic innovations that would solve every issue and fit within every political context. Moreover, context deeply matters; solutions must "fit" their context. It is then crucial to start, as Archon Fung suggests, from the "highly imperfect contingent and historical circumstances in which societies actually find themselves" (Fung 2012: 610). In particular, he stresses the need to identify "the governance problems of particular societies *as they are*" (ibid., emphasis mine). I couldn't agree more; the centrality of political systems' *contingency* and the ambition of diagnosing their *particular* shortcomings is the common thread of this book. Its ultimate aim is to contribute to the development of a context-sensitive diagnostic tool to uncover the *specific* democratic problems of political systems.

This chapter starts by assuming that, so far, current democratic problems are *not* identified from a systematic and context-sensitive diagnostic framework. It argues that such a framework would have an added value, notably by constituting a common ground to generate and confront different perspectives about what is actually problematic. In the second part, I discuss what could be the theoretical contours of such a diagnostic tool, by suggesting some practical guidelines for the task of diagnosis. Based on the account of democratic systems developed in the previous chapters, these guidelines rely on an articulation of the descriptive and normative layers. I conclude with a discussion on who diagnoses and the necessities of diagnosis in a democratic system, by arguing that the task of *democratic diagnosis* is a direct implication deriving from my account of democratic systems as a crucial dimension of the democratic ideal. This chapter's discussion is broadly speculative and forward-looking, as it serves to pave the way for two further major agendas: first, to develop a detailed and operational metric for the scientific diagnosis of political systems in democratic terms, and second, to envision the creation and empirical testing of *democratic* venues where citizens can diagnose the democratic shortcomings of their own political systems and do so on their own terms and according to their own expectations.

Diagnosis and context-sensitivity

It is self-evident that democratic systems face many problems.[106] As with any other social system, democracies always encounter perturbations they must cope with. An essential goal of democratic theory is to help identify and solve the challenges faced by democratic systems. The empirical literature on democracy has long identified major democratic problems such as political apathy (Rosenberg 1954) or political

---

[106] Importantly, I do not speak here of problems of *democracy* (as a generalized conceptual entity) but of *democratic systems* (as concrete and contingent empirical phenomena). Although endorsing democracy as the normative horizon for political systems, I do not consider here theoretical and generalized problems of democracy as a normative ideal, such that democracy allegedly produces ignorant citizens and therefore must be replaced by some form of epistocracy (Brennan 2016). In a nutshell, I focus on diagnosing *democracies* not *democracy*.

distrust (Dalton 2004).[107] The literature in democratic theory also contains multiple assertions regarding "democratic deficits" (Warren 2008; Fung 2012), "democratic malaise" (Newton & Geissel 2010), or deliberative democratic "pathologies" (Mansbridge et al. 2012). Examples of these democratic problems[108] are very diverse: lack of responsiveness (Warren 2008), unclear citizens' preferences and lack of state capacity (Fung 2012), and entrenched partisanship and institutional domination (Mansbridge et al. 2012). A literature review tracking the whole diversity of potential democratic shortcomings is far beyond my reach here, nor properly useful for my current purpose. Indeed, my aim is not to come up with an exhaustive list of pathologies potentially affecting democratic systems. Rather, my objective is to suggest ways to investigate the specific complexity of political systems and to identify *their* problems both with common lenses and in their own terms. Put differently, I focus here on *diagnosing* as a process rather than *diagnoses* as the outcomes of this process. Therefore, I start from the contestable assumption that democratic problems can be identified through a *context-sensitive diagnostic framework for political systems*. By that, I mean a conceptual system to map existing political systems and identify their specific democratic deficiencies. This assumption's corollary is that such a diagnostic framework would be useful for the democratic improvement of existing political systems.

The academic literature on democracy analyzes empirically and theoretically what the problems of democracies are. There are multiple examples of identified democratic problems, from populism to corruption and from the tyranny of majority to excessive bureaucratization. Furthermore, empirical scholars lead sound comparative analyses and case studies about the current shape of specific political systems in terms of their democratic quality. However, as noted by both Warren (2017: 41) and Saward (2021: 7–11), political science generally proceeds from a fixed idea of what democracy is supposed to be, with a particular institutional architecture in mind ("competitive electoral democracy" according to the former, "liberal or representative democracy"

---

[107] The fields of comparative politics and democratization nowadays emphasize "democratic backsliding" as a general tendency towards more authoritarian regimes (Bermeo 2016). However, this unfortunate trend encompasses multiple and diverse problematic realities that would benefit from their own diagnoses.

[108] I take here *problems* as a generic term encompassing multiple labels with similar meanings: pathologies, deficits, shortcomings, deficiencies, failures, etc.

according to the latter). Democratic problems are generally understood as deviations from this common architecture. Nonetheless, it is true that measurement and comparative tools such as Varieties of Democracy (V-Dem) are becoming more and more complex and context-sensitive as they embrace democracy as a continuum, various models of democracy (electoral, liberal, participatory, egalitarian, and deliberative), and the disaggregation of democracy's features to reach more fine-grained measurements (Coppedge 2023). Systemic features such as complementarity and trade-offs among democratic components are also increasingly included within measurements tools such as the Democracy Matrix (Lauth & Schlenkrich 2020). Arguably, the empirical measurement of democratic quality is getting progressively more *systemic* and *context-sensitive*.

However, we can wonder whether this new generation of measurement tools is systemic and context-sensitive *enough*. For instance, in the case of V-Dem, the same criteria are applied to every political system (e.g., elections, political parties, deliberation, the media, legitimation, the judiciary). These democratic expectations are hence common for every democratic system, even if they can be fulfilled through diverse democratic "fashions" or ideal-typical models (electoral, liberal, deliberative, participatory, egalitarian). The resulting measurements of specific democratic systems relate to these five architectures, which emphasize diverse democratic styles, but which all remain characterized by the same general expectations. Indeed, all five models expect the (variable) fulfillment of the same set of practices and institutions, featuring a fixed functional differentiation (externally and internally) and structural couplings, and enacting the same democratic principles.[109] Of course, common criteria are necessary for *measuring* the democratic quality of political systems and to make *comparisons* among them. Arguably, the complexification of these measurements, their increasing systemness and context-sensitivity enable us to identify some specific democratic deficiencies. However, these are *still* deficiencies relative to a quite rigid, yet contingent, democratic architecture. Without undermining the growing quality of these measurement tools, I contend that there is still some room for improvement in order to detect *specific* democratic problems of contingent political

---

[109] Furthermore, core democratic principles such as "self-governing" (Geissel 2023) are also generally neglected.

systems. My goal in this chapter is to provide the theoretical grounds, rationales, and expectations for a much more context-sensitive and systemic effort of democratic diagnosis.

Furthermore, it could also turn out after all that *measurement* and *diagnosis* are slightly different empirical tasks. I attempted to show in previous chapters that the complexity of political systems and the contingent instantiations of democracy demand a context-sensitive approach to diagnosis. It requires working with flexible sets of practices, principles, and functions operating in multiple and diverse kinds of political systems. Accordingly, the task of diagnosing may not be synonymous with that of measuring: the question is not *how much* it is democratic, but rather *how* it is democratic, or fails to be so. In contrast with measurement, diagnosis does not have a ranking or comparative purpose, but a *discovery* and *critical* purpose. It represents a self-reflexive movement not an objective standpoint. Consequently, *systemic diagnosis* demands a different approach, tailored from a systemic understanding of political reality and democracy, thus putting contingency and continuous transformation at its core.

Etymologically, to diagnose means to distinguish, to discern. *Dia* means in ancient Greek "through" or "between"; *gnostic* means "known" (OED 2019). A diagnosis is thus a process to know, to distinguish something from something else. In this context, "something" is a democratic problem. Accordingly, a diagnosis is here understood as a *process to distinguish problems*. By diagnosing democratic problems, I mean detecting what is wrong here and now in democratic terms. This common-sense understanding demands more contours. To start with, *here and now* refers to the political system under critical analysis. In the systemic perspective, the relevant object for analysis is read with the systemic lens developed in the previous chapters. The target of diagnosis is always a system or part of one in its environment. For instance, it can be a local political system or the relationships between the administration and the public at the regional level of governance. Accordingly, the context of analysis is always distinguished through particular differences between a system and its environment. That is, for instance, the differences and relations of a local political system with its own environment made of other local political systems, and with regional and national political systems. The precise aim of what I labelled the *descriptive layer* is to orient the identification and sketching of the "here and now," that is, the political system under investigation in its contextual environment.

Moreover, what are here subject to diagnosis are systemic *structures* and *processes* (including procedures), not *substantial outcomes* emerging from these. In line with the pure proceduralist stance adopted in this book (see Chapter 5), the focus is set on the "procedural" dimension of democracy, that is, on the structures and processes of justifications that produce more or less justifiable outcomes. What is problematized is not the justifiability of these outcomes, but the justifiability of what has generated them. Therefore, the diagnosis of political systems shall be distinguished from the diagnosis of its outcomes. In addition, it shall also be distinguished from the diagnosis of political issues operated by the political system. Indeed, the political system (whether democratic or not) actually identifies problems within society as a whole and thematizes these as political issues. The framework proposed here targets the *functioning* of political systems in democratic terms, not their specific political problematization of societal reality. To illustrate this distinction, take the example of the French *Conseil National de la Refondation*, an allegedly "democratic innovation" set in Fall 2022 by the French government in order to, among other things, "set a common diagnosis [...] on five issues: employment, education, health, old age, and the ecological transition" (Borne 2022, my translation). This new venue has a diagnostic purpose, yet it does not target the functioning of the French political system, but societal issues that have a political saliency.

My target for diagnosis is the political system itself, not political issues. Of course, if the political system fails to diagnose society appropriately, for instance, by not thematizing the environmental crisis as a major political issue, this represents an important cue on the political system's democratic failures. It signals that the political system probably has major problems in its democratic functioning, yet it does not point out precisely what they are. Hence, the focus of diagnosis is here on the features of its (dys-)functioning that led to the misdiagnosis of society. And this (dys-)functioning must be assessed by relying on *democratic* principles: other relevant societal expectations, such as sustainability and social justice, are not part of the normative material to diagnose political systems (see Chapter 5 and Saward 2021 for the distinction between principles of *governance* and principles of *policy*). However, the failure to thematize sustainability as a democratic expectation, or its disparity of resonance between the public and politics, are important symptoms of democratic problems that must be assessed by relying on democratic principles (e.g., inclusion, responsiveness).

Now, regarding *what is wrong*, a few remarks are necessary to interpret what "wrong" means here. At the outset, there is no *right* form that democratic systems must take. There is no common architecture of practices and institutions that inevitably constitutes the core of any democratic system. If we accept that the shape of democratic systems can be sensitive to contexts, that their articulation of democratic features can vary, even slightly, we must agree that what is needed in a democratic context is not always the same thing. In a nutshell, the democratic horizon is not crystal-clear. There is no "universal recipe" for democracy. That is, of course, an assumption, contrasting with a radical universalist position that I think nobody really holds. Even well-established democratic systems are still trying to improve their own recipe for democracy, adding new ingredients and removing old ones. There is no "right" recipe; some are good enough yet *a priori* perfectible and many are really problematic and require deep transformations. To pursue this culinary metaphor; some lack salt, others are under- or over-cooked, and a few did not have good ingredients in the first place or they were incorporated in the wrong order. My aim is to diagnose these *specific* problems.

Although there is no fixed, common, and clear recipe, it cannot be said, however, that *anything goes*. Some ingredients are broadly essential to all the variations in the democratic recipe. They form a perimeter within which the shape of democratic systems can fluctuate. There is in the first place a basic feature constitutive of the political: the functional need to take collectively binding decisions. This specialized aim provides the opportunity for the development of further functional requirements and limitations to possible political forms, which we have already discussed at length in previous chapters (e.g., the political functions of legislation, implementation, selection of political performers, etc.). In addition, from the basic shape that modern political systems tend to have, there are a few common preconditions for the development of their democraticness. Moreover, there is a common normative horizon (the performance of reciprocal and general justification through democratic practices), although ways and paces of navigating towards it vary deeply. And finally, there are multiple democratic principles that are to be enacted by political practices, through multiple combinations, variable interpretations, and degrees of saliency. These features constitute the commonality of democratic systems. Besides these, democratic systems can endorse multiple forms and fulfill variable levels of democraticness. Put differently, they can be democratic "in their own way." And all of them are *a priori* imperfect, and thus potentially perfectible.

This is captured by the idea of a *continuum* along which the democratic quality of a political system fluctuates. The democratic continuum is *not* used here to measure and rank the democraticness of different political systems. Nor does it take a particular practice (such as elections, mini-publics, or referendums) as an indicator or a threshold for one level of democraticness. The continuum is not a single scale where a practice (e.g., a randomly selected mini-public) is *always* better than another (e.g., the governmental designation of an expert panel). If we compare the normative value of these two practices, we would probably conclude that the former effectively enacts the democratic principles of deliberation and some forms of representation, participation, and inclusion; while the latter performs deliberation just as well and probably better regarding epistemic advancement and efficacy, but is clearly less inclusive. In some political contexts, the (temporary) technocratization of governance through expert bodies might be a step forward on their own democratic continuum (for instance, when the state is totally ineffective and paralyzed by deep divisions and generalized corruption), while it would certainly entail a step backwards for many other systems. Accordingly, what is an appropriate solution in one political system is not necessarily well-suited in others. Similarly, what is a problem in some political contexts (e.g., technocratic governance) might be a solution in others, and vice versa. Consequently, there are democratic *continuums* that point towards the same broad normative horizon, but where solutions *and problems* are context/system-specific.

Of course, two practices such as these can be *complementary*, as each can contribute to diverse aspects of the overall functioning of a democratic system. But they are not *necessarily* complementary, they can also be conflicting, for instance, if they share the same prerogatives in performing the same function. Simply put, if both the mini-public and the expert body are expected to decide on the same issue, a functional dead-end could arise in which it is not clear which decision is actually binding. An *articulation* (i.e., the ordering or sequencing) of these two venues is thus necessary, or a selection of one instead of the other. The point is that the improvement of democracy cannot always be to *add* more democratic institutions and venues, it is also about making choices, selecting more appropriate practices, replacing inappropriate ones, prioritizing some over others, ordering their functioning, and connecting them in the best possible way. The purpose of context-sensitive diagnosis of democratic problems is precisely to determine whether a problem can be simply addressed by adding something new (e.g., a mini-public), or if it requires the replacement of something already in place (e.g., a technocratic body), or if the solutions reside instead in a better connection between these two venues. Consequently, context-sensitive diagnosis aims to *problematize* existing political architectures in quite a nuanced and fine-grained way. In this diagnostic framework, democratic problems are taken as largely context-specific, hence the need to develop ways to identify and frame them through a common semantic of problematization.

The task of diagnosis aims to uncover *specific* problems. These must be contrasted from what I call *generic* problems. All the examples mentioned above, from political distrust to the tyranny of majorities are generic problems. But not in the sense of being common to every democratic system, rather in the sense of being a conceptual generalization of a broad range of diverse and complex problematic realities. For instance, populism as a generic democratic problem[110] (by its rejection of political pluralism, bypassing of intermediary bodies and procedures, and anti-elites/anti-system discourses) emerges from diverse sources, takes multiple forms, and represents variable challenges in different political systems. Diagnosis does not aim at identifying the presence and salience in a political system of generic problems such as populism, but rather at uncovering its specific contextual roots and manifestations within the architecture of a particular system. Diagnosis aims, for instance, to understand the institutional features conducive to populism in a particular system and its contextual entanglement with other generic problems (e.g., post-truth politics, conspiracy theories, rampant corruption, political polarization, or "speech corruption" for Warren 2023). Populism flourishes in some societal circumstances

[110] I am not claiming that populism is necessarily a democratic problem *per se*. If a populist political party wins the elections and respects democratic procedures once in power, it is debatable whether it undermines the democratic system. But populism is always a *symptom* of potential democratic problems, in that it claims that something is wrong in the democratic system (with manipulative intent or not), and some people do agree with such a claim.

that are not *all* directly related to the functioning of democratic systems (e.g., features of the mass media, economic conditions). But some features of the architecture and the functioning of particular democratic systems are supposedly more conducive to the development of populism on some societal fertile grounds.

Take, for instance, Italy; in September 2022, an extreme right and arguably neo-fascist movement won the general elections. The architecture of the Italian democratic system is not exclusively to blame; however, it is likely that it at least partly contributed to the situation. Indeed, populist discourses thematize precisely that there are problems "in the system," and in the political system in particular. Whether or not this is actually the case, the fact that many citizens backed this discourse by voting in favor of this party reveals that there may indeed be problems. Hence, this populist victory is an important cue that something is *potentially* wrong in the Italian democratic system. But the question is *what*. Where and what are the problems in this case? Is the institutional architecture unfit for its actual environmental complexity? Which institutional features are problematic? The electoral process? The misconnection between elites and citizens? The lack of public debate and/or participatory mechanisms? The inappropriate coupling of these mechanisms to politics and the administration? The aim of diagnosis is to structure this questioning, that is, the problematization of the architecture and functioning of a democratic system.

A populist victory such as in Italy is a huge and alarming *symptom* of potential democratic problems, but it does not directly indicate which features of the Italian democratic system are problematic and in need of transformation. Of course, empirical investigations do question the features that are more conducive to populism: quantitative approaches do so in causal and probabilistic terms, and qualitative case studies thoroughly investigate what occurred in specific cases such as this one. However, they generally do so with a particular perspective on what democracy is and *should* look like, with presuppositions on what is problematic and what is not. The point of a diagnostic strategy is to use reliable analytical tools and semantics to make explicit the presuppositions on *why* and *how* something is a problem for a particular democratic system *now*. Without denying the relevance and concrete saliency of generic problems as analytical categories for the (theoretical and empirical) problematization of democratic systems, the task of diagnosis must ideally refrain from reading the problems of democratic systems through the lens of a pre-established list of potential pathologies or symptoms. Otherwise, diagnosis becomes dependent and vulnerable upon contested conceptualizations of these generalized problems and upon their contextual connotations. The diagnosis of a particular system should be alerted by obvious problematic symptoms such as populism, and it can draw inspiration from the problems empirically identified in other contexts to orient the diagnosis towards likely pathologies. But it should not stick to *them* and should avoid trying to detect *these* generic problems and symptoms; it must operate through a more systemic and context-sensitive analytical apparatus.

In consequence, the critical apparatus of the diagnostic framework should not rely too much upon pre-established generic problems, but rather be grounded upon the normatively neutral semantics of systems theory. This would enable specific problems to be framed and discussed with a shared language and confront different interpretations of the same problems. Furthermore, this would provide room to identify *new* kinds of problems that the focus on pre-existing pathologies could have occulted. Accordingly, "democratic problems" within a context-sensitive diagnosis framework are framed in systemic terms: problems regard the (mis-)performance of *functions* by *practices* enacting *democratic principles*. Problems are framed at this level of conceptual abstraction through specific problematizations of the threefold relationship between functions, practices, and principles.

For instance, a democratic problem could be that the political function of legislation is exclusively performed through practices such as poorly representative institutions and designated technocratic bodies, which thus fail to enact the principles of representation, inclusion, and equality; and even if these practices do enact the principle of deliberation effectively, this trade-off may lack appropriate justifications and/or compensatory relationships. This also shows how "problems" are mostly problematic in a specific context: in this example, the practices themselves are not problematic, the lack of justification for the trade-off they embed and the absence of compensatory relationships for it make them contextually problematic. Finally, this illustrates the fact that problems are deeply interconnected. The deficit of inclusion and representation in one venue such as a technocratic body is not only problematic in itself but also because this deficit is not *compensated* for in another venue performing the same function (i.e., legislation).

Accordingly, the design of possible solutions varies greatly depending on whether these problems are taken in isolation or in conjunction. The diagnosis of political *systems* demands that we consider the connections between problems occurring in diverse venues and the eventual compensatory and conflicting relations between them.

With these elements detailing the objective of diagnosing the deficiencies of political systems, one can already get a feeling for what can be expected from this enterprise. Briefly, the development of such a framework should enable *specific* problems to be located and thus orient the design of *specific* solutions. It assumes that a better specification and understanding of problems enables the creative design of better solutions. The diagnosis of problems should operate through a common semantic flexible enough to be applicable to all kinds of contexts, without holding up any normative presuppositions on what democracy should look like institutionally speaking. It must be flexible and context-sensitive yet rely on a clear common analytical and normative core. Such a diagnostic framework would *not* be related to its context of application in the sense of being tailored accordingly, but only *sensitive* to any relevant context of analysis.

In addition, such a diagnostic tool should detect the democratic deficits of political systems *systematically, explicitly, comprehensively,* and *reflexively.* First, the diagnostic framework must be systematic in the sense of applying the same robust and clear analytical apparatus to diverse political contexts, in order to bring, if not "objectivity" for the produced diagnoses, at least commonality in the ways to proceed. Second, the aim to be explicit would provide transparency on why alleged problems are actually problems, how they are problems, and how we know that they are problems. This makes particular diagnoses tractable, and thus more easily and constructively contestable. Third, diagnosis must be able to identify *all* the potential major problems faced by a political system. Its reach must be comprehensive enough to detect all kinds of problems and not steer attention solely towards some of them. Fourth, it has to be reflexive, not only in the sense of being attentive to context[111] but also in the systemic sense of self-reference and self-observation (see Chapters 3 and 4).

---

[111] Saward discusses the need for design to be *reflexive*, demanding that design be "closely attentive to the character of the context for which specific designs are being developed" (2021: 112). In this sense, reflexivity clearly captures the need for the *context-sensitivity* of the diagnostic framework.

Diagnosis must be a contextual enterprise as well: people should have opportunities to diagnose *their* political system. Ultimately, the diagnosis of democratic systems is *self-diagnosis*, which is potentially *democratic* diagnosis. I return to this crucial feature of reflexivity in the detailed section discussing *who* diagnoses and the role of diagnosis in a democratic system.

Such a diagnostic framework, with these strong desiderata, does not currently exist, or so I assume relying on a partial reading and understanding of the relevant literature. In what follows, I would like to support this assumption in discussing the few contributions heading towards a similar aim. To start with, Fung's pragmatic conception of democracy claims to offer "*a diagnostic model* and a menu of institutional alternatives" (2012: 623, emphasis mine). But Fung's diagnosis is largely made *en passant*, by stating four major deficits of democratic governance: unclear preferences of citizens, blunt signals from politicians and parties, tyranny of powerful minority interests, and lack of state capacity. Although these deficits are undoubtedly potential major problems, simply stating them does not provide any information on how to diagnose these (and others) in context. Fung's conception being mostly suggestive of a path to pursue (although he has much more to say on the "menu" of alternative solutions), he does not provide many guidelines to identify problems in practice.

Another major contribution in that regard is that of Warren's problem-based approach to democratic theory (2017). At the outset, it is important to stress that it aims towards "constructing democratic *theories*" (ibid.: 39, emphasis mine), although Warren also claims to provide a "context of functional questions so we can understand the strengths and weaknesses of each kind of practice from a democratic perspective" (ibid.: 45). As with Fung, the assessment of possible *solutions* takes center stage, while the identification of *problems* is left largely undiscussed. This is mostly due to Warren's theoretical identification of "problems" as "normative functions" (e.g., empowered inclusion, collective decision-making). While I challenge in Chapters 2 and 6 Warren's conceptual apparatus on several points, I now raise additional doubts on whether his framework is suited to "frame democratic *problems*, possibilities, and *deficits* in complex polities" (ibid.: 39, emphasis mine) *other than the three basic democratic "problems" he suggests*. Although his framework is successful at tracking the *theoretical* strengths and weaknesses of *generic* practices, and thus *theoretically* compare "functionally equivalent solutions to problems of democracy" (ibid.: 51), it is less clear how it could be used to detect specific problems and assess the relative merits of contextually relevant functionally equivalent practices within concrete political systems. Once again, if specific problems are not pre-defined, as I do not think they should be, we still lack a framework for their concrete contextual identification.

A final major contribution on that regard is Saward's (2021). Although he focuses clearly on the task of design, he nevertheless gives a few indications on the task of diagnosis. He explicitly mentions the issue of the "identification or diagnosing of a problem that needs solving" (ibid.: 130). On this issue, Saward stresses the multiplicity of actors undertaking the task of problem identification, mentioning the importance of social movements, governments, and research work in this endeavor. In line with his contextual approach, the author insists that the identification and definition of problems "will always be open to debate" (ibid.: 113). Saward goes on to say, regarding the identification of social needs: "There is no entirely objective way of identifying these needs, though in most contexts there will be prominent inter-subjective pointers" (ibid.: 115). I agree; different actors might have diverging interpretations on the framing, saliency, and even the problematic character of "problems", and there is probably no way to reach absolute and consensual objectivity on the matter. But this is precisely why we need to put much more effort and transparency in *how* we arrive at considering something a problem. We must attempt to bring some commonality to the way we problematize political reality; we require (or at least could benefit from) a common framework through which we could frame our variable interpretations on the matter. We need to have recourse to a shared language to express disagreements, not necessarily to settle them, but to have common grounds to confront them. I contend that the systemic conceptual framework and semantics could constitute such grounds.

Besides stressing the difficulty in identifying problems, Saward suggests a few "guiding questions" that help us do so. They are part of a "step-by-step guide to democratic design" (2021: 161), including two guiding questions directly related to the diagnosis of problems. One question regards the identification and definition of "the territorial or functional unit, network or community for the design work" (ibid.: 162). This regards the choice of the system under analysis and its broad description. In the framework of democratic systems developed in this book, this refers to the work of what I called the descriptive layer. Indeed, it provides the conceptual distinctions necessary to describe the specific shape of the chosen system. Saward suggests several interesting questions for a detailed description of the system under investigation, such as "what institutionalized practices, etc., have had a longer or shorter-term presence in X historically?" (ibid.: 113–118). I discuss some of these questions in the next section while suggesting my own guidelines for diagnosis.

More importantly, Saward's second guiding question regards the identification of the "set of democratic principles (required and ordering) to be realized or enhanced: (a) required principles in the light of the demands of the democratic minimum and (b) ordering principles in the light of the specific democratic challenges or problems to be addressed or prioritized" (ibid.: 167). This question is more directly related to the problematization in democratic terms of the political reality under analysis. It problematizes it with direct reference to democratic principles, by asking in short: Which democratic principles must the designer try to prioritize through her proposed design. Saward illustrates this question by identifying the lack and vulnerability of the required principle of *equality* in the UK's political system, notably because of the lack of "equality of representation" in parliament. Similarly, he identifies the ordering principles of *citizen participation* and *citizen engagement* as particularly in need of enhancement in the British context.

The identification of these endangered or failing principles is justified by Saward, yet he suggests that the designer has some latitude to *choose* which ordering principles his design attempts to enhance. For the task of diagnosis, such latitude is absent precisely because diagnosis targets which principles are enacted or not (or not appropriately) and must be improved or traded-off. Saward's identification of democratic problems is arguably appealing, although it is inevitably interpretive. However, it is also largely "unguided." And I think that the task of diagnosis is complex enough to merit some guidelines. The problematization of democratic systems demands a guiding structure. Furthermore, Saward focuses exclusively on principles to be enacted, without considering their relationship with the function(s) that these principles are expected to regulate, nor the justifiability of their saliency or trade-offs with other principles, nor potential compensatory relationships between democratic venues. Indeed, diagnosis cannot stick to the identification of democratic principles to be enacted but needs to uncover the enactment of *some* principles by *some* practices in the *specific* context of the function that orients them. Therefore, problems are not only the lack of enactment of equality of representation in parliament, for instance, but its lack of enactment within the function of legislation, unjustified by a legitimate trade-off with other principles, and uncompensated by other practices performing the same function.

Accordingly, I suggest that the identification of problems must go beyond the enactment or not of democratic principles. What is at stake is the contextual appropriateness and justification of the enactment of *some* principles instead of others in particular venues. Put differently, what makes particular practices more or less democratic is not only whether they enact democratic principles, but to what extent they enact the "right" democratic principles at the right moments and in the right locations within the system. If democratic principles are distributed within a democratic system, the target of a *systemic* diagnosis is the relevance of this distribution. The problematization of this normative distribution relies on the identification of the functional differentiation of practices (i.e., the functions that these principles regulate through practices). It then questions the minimal justifiability of these practices in terms of reciprocal and general justifications. It follows by interrogating the justifiability of the trade-offs between the democratic principles enacted or not by these practices, with a careful consideration of which principles are saliently expected in a political context. It ends with the consideration of potential "balancing" practices, granted that they perform the same function and are appropriately connected with the "balanced" practice. For these reasons, the complexity of identifying democratic problems in a systemic vein demands a more fine-grained "guide" to the identification of problems. In the next section, I tentatively suggest the contours of such a diagnostic guide.

Guidelines for the task of diagnosis

The task of diagnosing complex political realities in democratic terms would benefit from guidelines to orient and structure this diagnostic process. That would make the identification of democratic problems and their framing more clear, consistent, and tractable. I suggested that the framework of democratic systems proposed in the previous chapter could provide the conceptual building blocks and analytical tools to develop a context-sensitive diagnostic strategy for political systems. Concretely, the following diagnosis framework articulates the descriptive and normative layers of democratic systems developed in previous chapters. Thereafter, I display the main elements to be interrogated in chronological order through the diagnostic process and highlight the main "guiding questions," to borrow Saward's terminology. The aim of these suggested guidelines is to structure the process of problematization of democratic systems.

1. The selection of the political system to be diagnosed

The task of diagnosis logically starts from a selection of a political reality to problematize. The first question is then: *What is the political system under diagnosis?* Remember that a system is made of communications. These are clustered in three types of systems, each with its own mode of differentiation/inclusion: interaction (presence), organization (membership), or functional systems (function performance). Only the two latter types of systems (organization and functional systems) are well-suited to be diagnosed by the suggested diagnostic tool. Indeed, interaction systems (e.g., a political discussion at the bar, a demonstration in the street) are too elusive and unstable to be relevant objects for a diagnosis aiming towards their improvement. However, they certainly matter for the analysis of more structured political systems (e.g., organizations such as the parliament or broad functional systems such as the administration), since the former are more or less connected with the latter, or should be in some cases. Among organization and functional systems, there are multiple types of relevant candidates for diagnosis: from local or national political systems to multilevel governance systems, as well as specific organizations like political parties or whole sub-functional entities such as the administration or the public, or even specific structural couplings such as between the parliament and the executive government. Relying on Saward's distinction between *whole-systemic* and *part-systemic*, the former covers the whole functional unity of a political system, while the latter focuses only on one part of the function system. Both are relevant candidates for diagnosis. Thus several *analytical entry points* exist: the broad political system, whole functional subsystems (e.g., politics), particular functions (e.g., implementation), specific organizations (e.g., a mini-public), or important connections (e.g., the coupling between the public and the administration).

The selected system of communication must be *political*, that is, related to the current or potential exercise of power. To be sure, in a functionally differentiated society, political communications refers primarily to collectively *binding* decisions enforced by power, whether it occurs under the form of arbitrary domination or legitimized positive law. Therefore, the more evident targets for a diagnosis of democratic deficiencies are "traditional" political systems such as states or subnational political entities. Nonetheless, the diagnostic guidelines developed here are likely to have a critical potential beyond the political system strictly understood as functionally differentiated from other social systems. For instance, these guidelines could be inspiring for the diagnosis of the internal governance of private companies. With some adaptations, these guidelines could even apply to the "workplace democracy," in order to identify the democratic shortcomings of internal processes of collective decision-making. Hopefully, the proposed framework of democratic systems is flexible enough to be adapted to social contexts that are not primarily driven by political functions, but where internal governance can nevertheless be more or less democratic. The following guidelines are broad-brush and indicative: one reason for this is precisely to make them flexible enough to be applicable to diverse political contexts.[112] The first step of diagnosis is thus the choice of a political system according to these broad criteria. Beyond these, this selection is a matter of analytical choice.

2. The external differentiation of the system

After the identification of a political system to be diagnosed (for example, the Canton of Geneva, or the multilevel and transnational governance of the Great Geneva region; or the Federal Assembly of the Swiss Confederation), the next task is to give it contours by contrasting it with its environment. This environment comprises a *political*

---

[112] It is important here to make the conceptual distinction between context and contingency explicit, as a political system is both contingent and represents a specific context of analysis. *Contingency* refers to something with a form that could have been otherwise. *Context* refers to a partial reality under analysis, it expresses the limitation of the scope of an observation. Features of a context can be more or less contingent. Systems are contingent structures and processes of differentiation from an environment; a context of analysis is then a particular difference between a system and its environment.

environment and a *societal environment*. From the point of view of the political system under investigation, these two types of environment are blended as solely *its* environment. But to orient and detail its description, this analytical distinction is useful.

To start with the *political environment*, as discussed in Chapter 4, any political system is a part of the broader political system (world politics we might say). For instance, national political systems are segments of world politics, and regional political systems are segments of national political systems. Each political system is more or less differentiated horizontally and vertically from its political environment. The first analytical question regards the vertical dimension: *How is the system situated within institutionalized levels and relationships of governance?* This indicates the formal boundaries and limited prerogatives of the system. It also opens the way for the diagnosis of its structural couplings with other political systems at other levels of governance. By highlighting its specific inclusion roles, institutionalized procedures, and stabilizing principles, this question allows the distinctiveness of the system as a political system on its own to be grasped. The second analytical question regards the horizontal dimension: *How is the system differentiated and structurally coupled with other political systems at the same level of governance?* This enables us to understand how the system is situated, self-defines, and interacts with its "peer" systems.

Now regarding the *societal environment*, each political system is embedded in its own societal environment. It is always differentiated from it to a variable extent: some are firmly differentiated from the religious system, while others are tightly coupled with it. The same goes for the economy: the extent of structural coupling between the political and economic systems says a lot about their respective autonomy. If the former is largely under the domination of the latter, what Mansbridge et al. (2012) call "social domination," it can hardly develop its democratic potential. And conversely, if the economic system is completely steered by the political system, it is no longer a system on its own and cannot perform the function it is specialized at. The political system would then cease to process thematized issues relative to the economy and instead becomes an encompassing system of control of *all* issues (the extreme scenario of a total absence of self-limitation from the political system is totalitarianism). It is therefore important to situate the political system regarding the other social systems that compose its societal environment (economic, legal, religious, educational, mass media, scientific, etc.). Major problems faced by the political system, or posed by it, can be sketched from the analysis of its differentiation and structural couplings with its societal environment. The important question is then: *How is the political system differentiated and structurally coupled with other functional systems?* By answering this question, one can observe and describe a significant part of the specific complexity of the political system under diagnosis. By displaying the external differentiation of the political system, we are able to diagnose whether there are broad obstacles to the development of its democratic quality. The answers to these questions enable us to examine the extent of its fulfillment of some major *democratic preconditions* (see Chapter 6):

- Functional differentiation of the political system from its environment;
- Some flexibility in the differentiation and connections of the political system with its environment;
- Constant fluctuation of the self-limitation of the political system;
- Structural abstraction regarding what are political/non-political issues;
- Generalization of power as positive law; and
- Some institutionalization of the levels and relations of governance (vertical differentiation).

If these functional preconditions are not met, it is unlikely that political practices would enact many democratic principles. For instance, without the *generalization of power as positive law*, democratic procedures cannot become the main operations of democratic systems and therefore stabilize the enactment of democratic principles. Another example, without the *constant fluctuation of the self-limitation of the political system*, the intrinsic dynamism of democratic systems is simply obstructed, freezing political activity into fixed boundaries. These democratic preconditions interrogate the existence of the possibility for democraticness. Analytically speaking, these are questions to be posed at this stage of the diagnosis process. Their answers are not dichotomous, of course, but a matter of degrees. Nonetheless, they provide clear indications on the specific opportunities and obstacles for the development of the democratic quality.

3. The internal differentiation of the system

Each political system is internally differentiated. Its specific functioning largely depends on the "division of labor" of its communications.
There is a basic functional division of labor that is enacted to a variable extent by every modern political system: the functional differentiation between politics, administration, and the public. Some political
systems may not feature this differentiation, which constitutes an
important obstacle towards their potential democraticness. In most
cases, however, the question is not whether this internal differentiation exists, but rather: *How is the political system internally differentiated in
functional subsystems of politics, the administration, and the public?* Several
more detailed descriptive questions are implied by this broad question:
What are their respective inclusion criteria; to what extent can they
perform their specialized functions autonomously; how are they structurally coupled with each other; what are their main mechanisms of
mutual influence; to what extent is mutual observation enabled or pre-
vented (and mediated by mass media); what are the specific principles
and expectations (if any) operating in these subsystems. The answers
to these major questions provide more concrete contours to the internal shape of the political system under investigation.

However, the task of diagnosis enables and demands a more detailed
picture of the system. We cannot restrain the analysis of the system
solely to the relations between its main subsystems. We need to reach
the level of concrete *practices*, as, ultimately, they are the object of diagnosis and of potential transformation. It is at the level of practices
that malleability resides and (re-)design can unfold. The identification
of political practices relevant for the analysis can proceed in two complementary ways: through *spatial* and *temporal* representations of clusters of practices.[113] The focus on the spatial representation displays the
main practices performing specific functions. For instance, by focusing on the function of legislation, the spatial representation describes
the main practices performing it (e.g., parliamentary work, executive

---

[113] One of Saward's guiding questions covers to some extent the identification of operating
practices: "What institutionalized practices, etc., have had a longer or shorter-term presence in X historically?" (2021: 114). A major difference is that Saward's question does not
relate practices to their function and thus does not systematically grasp the broader goal
of the practice. Another difference is that Saward's question adds value in interrogating *long-* versus *short*-term presence of the practices, enabling potential inertia towards
change or dynamics of change to be identified.

agencies, referendums) and their location within the system. In particular, representing clusters of practices as spaces emphasizes the structural dimension of systems; it targets the stabilization of differences and relations between practices and therefore tracks mostly institutionalized practices (procedures in particular). The precise question it asks is: *What are the stabilized practices performing X and/or Y function(s)?*[114] The answers to this question produce a spatial representation of practices performing the same function or different functions.

In contrast, the temporal or sequential representation focuses on the dynamism of the system, tracking its operational *processes*. It reads the performance of functions by practices in chronological order, that is, *sequentially*. It displays a chronological sequence of practices performing functions. The sequence of practices under analysis itself performs a broad function, for instance, collective decision-making (the function of the political system) or the selection of political performers (a function of the subsystem of politics). From this broad function, the aim is to analyze its internal sequencing, that is, its chronological division in multiple sub-functional steps performed by various practices. Such a temporal representation highlights how functions are sequentially organized in different practices and how the performance of some of these is conditioned by others. The sequential representation thus tracks the operative processes of political systems. Its precise question is: *How are the practices performing X and/or Y function(s) displayed sequentially?* This question attempts to grasp not only institutionalized practices but also more informal practices that contribute to or impede the operation of institutionalized practices. The answers to the above questions regarding the internal differentiation of the political system in clusters of connected practices allows us to interrogate to what extent some major *democratic preconditions* have been fulfilled. These preconditions include:

- A basic functional differentiation between politics, administration, and the public, entailing a differentiated inclusivity (horizontal differentiation);
- The stabilization of horizontal internal differences (represented as spaces or steps) by institutionalized practices (notably procedures) and non-institutionalized practices;

[114] Importantly, it might be necessary to ask the reverse formulation of this question in order to identify, when assessing the concrete practices at play in a particular system, *to which function(s) do the existing practices contribute?*

- Some institutionalization of structural couplings between these three subsystems, with variable coupling intensities; and
- The widespread existence of procedures as main practices of transformation of institutionalized practices.

Furthermore, the structural and processual questions about functional clusters of practices open the path to more critical analyses. First, they enable the identification of connections between detailed functional spaces or steps (e.g., the connections between a deliberative mini-public and the executive authorities through a mandatory consideration of its recommendations). Identified connections can then be interrogated regarding their intensity of coupling, a critical task I detail in the next section. Second, these questions pave the way for the identification of the specific principles enacted by those practices, the trade-offs they embed, and the justifications that support them. From there, we can examine the contextual justifiability of the existing practices and envision normatively superior functionally equivalent solutions. These crucial elements are treated thereafter.

4.   The (mis)connections of the system

Now that we have provided questions to guide the identification of the constitutive differences of the system under diagnosis, we can turn towards the critical analysis of the connections between these differentiated elements. As argued in Chapter 6, systemic connectivity is best understood as *structural couplings* between elements. Whether we talk of connections between whole social systems (such as the political and economic systems) or connections between practices (such as a mini-public and a referendum), the analytical concept of structural coupling operates similarly. The first question to be asked is: *What are the structural couplings between the differentiated elements?* This question applies to all the features of differentiation highlighted above: between the political system and its political environment (both vertically and horizontally), between the political system and its societal environment, between the subsystems of the political system, and between the stabilized practices of the political system (analytically displayed as spaces or sequences).

The distinctions structuring the assessment of structural couplings are also the same for any type of connection between systems. As a reminder, these distinctions qualify the intensity of coupling and therefore indicate the kind of mutual influence between systems. There are six distinctions characterizing mutual influence: *continuous/ sudden, significant/negligible, direct/indirect, immediate/eventual, rigid/ flexible*, and *transmissive/transformative*. Even though framed as dichotomies, these features of couplings are matters of degrees. Moreover, although influence is *mutual*, it is not necessarily *symmetrical*. Indeed, the influence of one system on another can be significant, while the reverse influence is negligible. Consequently, the intensity of structural couplings must be qualified for both sides of the connection, and its appropriateness must be assessed accordingly. As we can recall, there is no general standard of appropriate coupling. On the contrary, each coupling must be assessed on its own, and the appropriate intensity of one coupling could be very different from another. To illustrate, the coupling between social movements and politics might need to be transmissive, significant, and immediate, while the coupling between the parliament and executive agencies might need to instead be transformative, continuous, and flexible. The point of these six distinctions is to detail the shape of existing connections in order to further interrogate: *What do we expect from the existing and potential structural couplings between differentiated systems?*

Connections do not perform functions themselves, nor is connectivity a specific function; it is instead what makes "systemness." Connections are crucial to the performance of each function. Consequently, the expectations regarding the intensity of couplings depends first of all on the functions expected to be performed by coupled practices. For example, the connections between the public and executive politics perform conjointly the function of orientation (by the former) and the functions of elaboration of decision premises and symbolic legitimacy (by the latter). Therefore, the specific coupling intensity between the two must ideally enhance these functions *simultaneously*. To examine connections under the prism of their functional contribution enables two dimensions of connectivity to be diagnosed. First, it diagnoses the appropriateness of the intensity of coupling's of *existing* connections. Second, it tracks the potential *absence* of functionally necessary connections, such as the connection between the public and politics for the performance of the function of the public's orientation. These purely functional probes do an important job in the critical assessment of political systems, but they do not suffice for the diagnosis of their democratic quality. The normative distinctiveness of democracy, through the multiple principles enacting it, is also crucial for the assessment of systemic connections.

I contended in Chapter 6 that connections themselves do not enact principles. Just as connections do not perform functions but only enable/facilitate their performance, connections only enable and facilitate the enactment of principles by connected practices. For instance, when performing the function of orientation (e.g., more particularly agenda-setting), a mini-public (as a practice) can enact the principles of inclusion and representation *if* it is properly connected to the broad public (e.g., via random selection). Accordingly, it is not the connective method of random selection that enacts representation and inclusion, but the mini-public itself. However, this connection is crucial to that end: without it, there is no way the mini-public could enact these principles. Another practice of selection such as designation would not have the same effect in terms of the enactment of principles, although it could contribute to enact other principles such as expertise. The quality of couplings is thus not assessed with democratic principles, but with the six variables characterizing the variety of mutual couplings. However, in addition to the need for appropriate couplings to perform specific functions, it is essential to investigate how couplings contribute to the enactment of democratic principles in parts of the system. Hence, the important question to be asked is: *Which coupling intensity enables/facilitates or impedes/restricts the enactment of some specific democratic principles within the coupled parts?*

Although, generally speaking, connections do not enact democratic principles, there is perhaps an important exception to that. As Saward stresses (2021: 136), connections can be more or less *visible*. Visibility (or close concepts such as publicity, transparency, etc.) is a democratic principle that is often in trade-off with others (e.g., with deliberation, see Chambers 2005). Visibility is taken as such when assessing the operation of specific systems (e.g., parliament, politics), and in some cases there might be good reasons to restrict visibility. But when it comes to *connections* between systems, I am inclined to agree that there must be a "wider visibility of specific institutional connections" (Saward 2021: 136). This also rejoins Bächtiger & Parkinson's claim regarding deliberative systems; such a system "*connects*, processes, and weighs different claims and reasons (which themselves take the form of memes) in a *visible* way" (2019: 108, emphases mine). I follow the authors in the importance of visibility within a democratic system.

The way I understand it in this framework is basically functional; people must be able to see what happens (i.e., function of observation) in order to accept it or criticize it if need be (i.e., function of justification).

While visibility should ideally be maximal across the system, I nonetheless accept that some venues and circumstances can legitimately call for closed-door operations (parliamentary commissions, executive agencies, audit procedures, emergency situations). Accordingly, visibility cannot be taken, analytically speaking, as a democratic principle that *a priori* trumps every other; it can be traded-off in some circumstances in favor of other democratic principles (e.g., deliberation, efficiency, precaution). However, I take the requirement of visibility to be always applicable to *connections*: people must be able to observe, not what occurs in *every* part of the system, but how the system as a whole operates, that is, how its different parts are connected in a complex architecture. I do not see any example where the visibility of stabilized connections could prevent the political functions from being performed and other democratic principles from being enacted. I therefore suggest that the broad stabilized connections between systems (pictured as spaces or steps) must be *visible* by the entire public. Put differently, people must be aware of the mechanisms of connections between the democratic system's parts. Consequently, *visibility* would be an additional normative criterion applying especially to all connections. This leads to an additional analytical question: *To what extent are the structural couplings between the system's parts visible by the public as a whole?*

5. The minimal justifiability of political arrangements

After the description of the shape of the political system in terms of differences and connections, the next task is to tackle its assessment in democratic terms. In other words, we now have to apply the normative layer to the reality revealed by the descriptive layer. To start with, I stress the importance of the *justifiability* of political arrangements in terms of democratic principles for the diagnosis of democratic systems. In his pragmatic conception, Fung contends that "we need not (initially, at any rate) look into the reasons—the ways that this policy process respects political equality, accountability, or secures desirable outcomes—that might justify these arrangements" (2012: 612). He argues instead that these arrangements "are justified according to their capacity to solve problems" (ibid.: 613). By reading Fung's position through the framework developed here, I agree that *part* of the justification of political arrangements depends on their capacity to perform political functions appropriately, and this is captured by the above questions tracking the core (mis-)functioning of the system. *Political* problems are thus related to the (mis-)performance of political functions by practices, and we can consider which functionally equivalent practice better performs a particular political function. But if we are to interrogate the *democratic* quality of political arrangements, problems necessarily regard the democratic principles that they enact or fail to enact. As Saward notes commenting Fung's account, the crucial question is not merely "what works," but "what works with respect to what values" (2021: 25). Consequently, the justifiability (and thus the diagnosis) of political arrangements depends on both their *functional* and *normative* strengths and weaknesses.

Accordingly, once that we have mapped the functioning of a political system, the first question to be asked regarding its democratic quality is: *Whether political arrangements are minimally justified or justifiable according to the criteria of reciprocity and generality* (see Chapters 5 and 6). This question applies both to the broad architecture of political systems and the more specific practices constituting this architecture. It examines whether the existing configuration of the political system (mapped with the questions highlighted above) *is* or *could be* supported or rejected by justifications that are reciprocal and general. Ideally, if *actual* justifications sustaining a systemic architecture (or a specific part of it) do exist, their assessment has to be prioritized. The criteria of reciprocity and generality are directly applicable to assess *actual* justifications.

Things get more complicated when actual justifications are missing, and it is likely that they would be absent in many contexts under diagnosis. In these cases, we have to rely on hypothetical justifiability, by asking: *Could this political arrangement be justified by reciprocal and general justifications?* For example, the broad absence of functional differentiation between the political and religious systems, in countries such as Iran or Saudi Arabia, could hardly be justified by both reciprocal and general claims towards members of religious minorities which are nevertheless subject to this normative order. This illustration is obvious, but in most cases the answers to this question are much less clear-cut. For instance, is the practice of unregulated donations to electoral campaigns and candidates by private and anonymous actors justifiable reciprocally and generally? Supportive claims such that it enhances political freedom and diversity of candidates *a priori* respect both reciprocity and generality. But simultaneously, claims to oppose this practice, such that it only benefits candidates defending a particular range of interests and even that it makes elected candidates indebted to their donors, also *a priori* respect reciprocity and generality. Therefore, some features of political systems (like this practice) cannot be directly ruled out by the test of *minimal* justifiability. This test primarily identifies political arrangements that are obviously not democratic in that they cannot be supported by reciprocal and general justifications. In that, it is a *minimal* filter. However, the question of minimal justifiability secondarily casts light on the practices that require further investigation in order to determine whether they serve or undermine the democratic quality of a specific political system.

6. The justifiability of the trade-offs in the practices' enactment of democratic principles

It is among the multiple political practices that pass the test of minimal justifiability that diagnosis displays its more critical potential. We are now investigating the democratic quality of specific parts of the system, such as the parliament or elections. We are here trying to assess: *To what extent particular minimally democratic practices are contextually appropriate and should be preferred to a range of functional equivalents?* The pivotal elements in this assessment are the enactment of some democratic principles instead of others and the justifiability of the trade-offs they embed considering the compensatory relationships they might have with other practices.

As a reminder, political systems potentially enact multiple principles, and parts of the system (represented as spaces or steps) enact different principles (and with variable degrees of saliency). Indeed, the democratic principles enacted by the parliament are likely to differ from the ones enacted by, say, practices of direct democracy, such as popular initiatives or referendums. Once that we have mapped the systems and practices at play in a broader system, we can ask the question: *Which democratic principles are actually enacted in the elements under investigation?*[115] For example, we can observe that the practice of a participatory budgeting process effectively enacts the principles of

---

[115] This question echoes Saward's, which asks: "What has a presence in X now, with regard to the requirements of the democratic minimum?" (2021: 114), although its range is broader by questioning the enactment of all democratic principles (what Saward labels ordering principles).

participation, citizen engagement, and empowerment, but poorly performs on enacting deliberation and expertise. Of course, the practice of participatory budgeting, like any other democratic practice, does not have to enact *all* the possible democratic principles. But the actual enactment of *some* principles instead of others must be interrogated in relation to the democratic principles that might be *expected* for this practice.

As a reminder, the principle of inclusion (as a general expectation of democratic systems) is expected to be enacted by *all* democratic practices. However, this enactment can (and in some cases *must*) be traded-off with other democratic principles: absolute and overarching inclusion is not functionally possible in a democratic system and would prevent the enactment of other democratic principles. Normatively speaking, what matters is the justifiability of *exclusion*. Therefore, we must confront the trading-off of inclusion in favor of other democratic principles to the test of justifiability by asking: *Is the trading-off of inclusion in practice X justified/justifiable by reciprocal and general reasons?* This leads to sharp questions such as: is this trade-off functionally necessary (i.e., is it practically impossible for this particular practice to combine all the expected democratic principles and still perform its specific function) *and* is this trade-off compensated/balanced in a venue that both performs the same function and is appropriately connected with it? When the answers to one of these questions is "no," then we have identified a democratic *problem*: the trade-off under analysis is unjustified and needs to be "corrected." To correct the trade-off means redesigning the practice in question towards the enactment of further expected democratic principles, *or*, balancing the trade-off within another practice enacting the traded-off democratic principle(s), performing the same function and adequately coupled with it.

Besides inclusion, which is expected in every political venue of a democratic system, other democratic principles (e.g., participation, accountability, deliberation, epistemic advancement) are instead particularly expected for *some* practices. Ideally, democratic practices would feature *all* of the democratic principles. But this ideal is hardly achievable in real-life settings because the enactment of some democratic principles impedes other principles from being enacted as well. The "full menu" of democratic principles is often not possible. Therefore, we cannot expect every democratic principle to be enacted perfectly in every location of the democratic system. In some venues, some democratic principles will be salient at the detriment of others. When assessing a part of the system, we thus have to consider: *Which democratic principles could be expected to be saliently enacted by a particular practice?*

We now have to identify which democratic principles could be saliently expected for a political practice. If we recall Chapter 6, practices are oriented towards two different kinds of goals: functional goals and normative expectations. The first orientation to each practice is its function. These include broad functions such as those related to the political subsystems, but also more specific functions such as agenda-setting (as a subfunction of "orientation"), expertise, conflict-management, and many other detailed political tasks to be undertaken when performing broad political functions. But democratic principles such as deliberation or participation are not *goals* independently of a political function to be performed. They are *additional expectations* for the performance of a specific function. For instance, the function of agenda-setting can be expected to enact deliberation, and thus a deliberative mini-public aiming to propose issues to be tackled by further political venues becomes an appropriate practice. Of course, when a democratic problem such as the lack of deliberation within agenda-setting is identified, to strengthen deliberation as a democratic expectation can become the goal of a "corrective" practice like a mini-public. But still, this practice must be oriented towards the function of agenda-setting and perform it in order for this practice to potentially strengthen deliberation *in* agenda-setting.

The distinction of functional goals and normative expectations is crucial to identify what makes a practice contextually desirable or problematic in a particular system. Indeed, in order to fit a democratic context, a practice has to fulfill both some functional goals and some normative expectations. Granting that a particular practice does effectively perform a specific function (e.g., selection of political performers), we can turn towards the normative analysis regarding *how democratically* this practice performs this function. With the practice's functional orientation/limitation, we can detect more clearly its actual trade-offs between democratic principles, assess their justifiability in terms of possible compensatory relationships within the same function, and target the democratic principles to be enhanced in priority within clear functional limits. Therefore, the distinction between the functional and normative goals of a practice provides an analytical orientation towards the specific principles that might be expected for specific goals (functions). Indeed, functions as specific goals orient towards the potential democratic principles that could regulate *how* that aim is reached. For example, if the aim is to build expertise on an important issue, the expected principles would first of all be epistemic advancement and deliberation. If the aim is instead conflict-management, the salient expectations would be respect and recognition. These examples illustrate how the function calls for the saliency of some principles over others. The questioning of which democratic principles could be expected provides cues on how existing trade-offs could be justifiable and which alternative enactment should be favored.

However, if the functional goal provides an orientation towards what *could be* expected, it does not determine which democratic principles are *actually* expected. At the end, the saliency and priority of some democratic principles over others is itself a matter of democratic choice, hence of citizens' preferences. Indeed, the democratic quality of political practices relies not only on their enactment of democratic principles but also on the justifiability of *these* democratic principles instead of others. Put differently, it does not suffice, normatively speaking, for a political practice to enact democratic principles, it also requires the enactment of the democratic principles that are *actually* saliently expected. Again, if actual claims regarding the expectations around the saliency and priority of some democratic principles do exist in the political system, these claims and their justification must be assessed in light of the criteria of reciprocity and generality. Often, such specific claims are unlikely to have a widespread existence (unless well-settled democratic practices of reflexive diagnosis already exist). Therefore, more general demands can be taken as useful indicators of the expected democratic principles. For instance, we could wonder with Saward (2021: 117): "What changes of institutional configurations or reforms are advocated in X, and with what degrees of support or opposition?" Such a question can bring emphasis on the democratic principles that are seen as particularly necessitating (greater) enactment, in addition to what citizens see as problematic and in need of change.

With these insights on the *actually* expected principles, we can assess whether the actual practices enact appropriate sets of democratic principles. Again, we have to wonder: *Is the trade-off between democratic principles justified/justifiable by reciprocal and general reasons; is the trade-off functionally necessary; and is it compensated in a connected venue performing the same function.* These three questions lead to the identification of context-specific democratic problems. If one of their answers is "no," we then have identified a democratic problem that can be solved either by reshaping the practice in question towards the enactment of further democratic principles *or* by balancing the trade-off within another practice performing the same function and adequately coupled with it.

7. The normative comparison of functionally equivalent practices

With a clear view on which political arrangements and practices are contextually problematic, and why they are so, we can finally turn towards the aim of comparing the merits of diverse solutions, that is, in systemic terms, the normative comparison of functionally equivalent practices (e.g., different practices for the selection of political performers). As a reminder, at this point we have identified a practice that performs a function, for example, the function of selection of political executives performed by the practice of periodic direct majoritarian elections. This practice, let's say, effectively enacts the democratic principles of representation and participation but fails to enact deliberation. We have also noticed that this trade-off is not compensated by other practices that contribute to the same function, such as a widespread public debate on the respective merits of the candidates for office or a deliberative mini-public that broadly publicizes its reasoned assessment on the matter. One solution emerging from this situation is to design and institutionalize such a deliberative mini-public. Then by "adding" this new political venue and connecting it appropriately (here, with the public), we attempt to balance this normative trade-off. A second kind of solution is to look for a functionally equivalent practice where this trade-off is *absent*. Concretely, such a practice would enact *all* the expected democratic principles (in this example representation and participation, *and* deliberation). If such a practice is available, its normative superiority is straightforward. In that case, such a practice should *replace* the practice of majoritarian elections.

A third possible scenario is more complex. Let's assume that we cannot find a practice able to enact simultaneously all the expected democratic principles and nor can we "add" a balancing practice. We thus have to change the existing practice slightly in order to make it more democratic (yet not perfectly democratic). Accordingly, in reforming the practice, we have to replace an existing unsatisfactory trade-off between democratic principles, with a better trade-off. Let's say that the practice of periodic direct majoritarian elections enacts a trade-off that is not satisfactory because, besides representation, deliberation is also saliently expected in the political context under investigation. A more satisfactory trade-off would allow more room for deliberation within this practice. A greater enactment of deliberation becomes the normative orientation for the reform of this practice. If what appears to be saliently expected for this function is representation and deliberation instead of citizen participation, the indirect election of political executives by a representative *and deliberative* body would be a functional equivalent that is normatively superior to direct election. The lack of citizen participation could thus be compensated for by the direct elections of political representatives, in charge of electing political executives. In this scenario, the normative comparison of functionally equivalent practices leads to the *division* of one practice (direct majoritarian elections of political executives) into two complementary and balancing practices (direct elections of political representatives + indirect elections of political executives).

These three different scenarios illustrate how the diagnostic tool can serve to frame and problematize a situation of democratic deficit and discuss the democratic merits of alternative solutions. For now, I envision three possible routes for the improvement of democratic practices in a systemic vein: to *add* and connect a practice in order to balance a normative trade-off, to *replace* an existing practice with a functionally equivalent practice where the trade-off is absent, and to *divide* an existing practice into two complementary practices, appropriately sequenced and coupled.

This illustration attempts to imagine how the suggested diagnostic material could be used to discuss the democratic merits of different political arrangements. In order to highlight its potential added value, I will briefly contrast it with another theoretical frame that compares the merits of functional equivalents in democratic terms. In Warren's framework (2017, see Chapter 2), the generic theoretical strengths and weaknesses of practices are highlighted. For instance, the practice of deliberation is very effective at connecting preferences to collective will and agendas, and generating epistemic and ethical goods (Warren 2017: 46). Therefore, the practice of deliberation is crucial to perform the function of collective agenda and will formation, contrary to the practice of voting that is not good at fostering will-formation. But this theoretical comparison does not provide much light on the relative strengths and weaknesses of particular practices *in their systemic context*. If one is to use this framework to identify actual problems, one cannot go much further than noticing that some "democratic functions" (as Warren labels them) are not performed by the appropriate practices. In Warren's account, generically speaking, collective decision-making must be performed by voting and representing rather than deliberating. But we cannot see, for instance, that in a specific context where democratic principles such as accountability and epistemic advancement are particularly expected, collective decision-making should nevertheless enact saliently *these* democratic principles. Such a situation could justify, for example, the practice of a designated technocratic body that would enact accountability and epistemic advancement in performing decision-making. In Warren's account, such an outcome cannot emerge from the analysis because practices are theoretically and rigidly attributed to their respective function(s).

Accordingly, the main difference and alleged added value of my framework over Warren's is that the former specifically enables us to "understand the strengths and weaknesses of each kind of practice from a democratic perspective" (ibid.: 45), both in terms of functions and democratic principles, and does so with a sensitivity towards what is contextually expected and justified. Furthermore, it allows us to identify trade-offs and envision compensatory relationships within the same function, and to target much more clearly which democratic principles must be saliently enacted compared to others and why. As a consequence, the proposed framework and guidelines for diagnosis is potentially more fine-grained, subtle, and sensitive to context and citizens' expectations. As such, it could (with major further developments) provide a more critical and practical orientation to efforts of democratic (re-)design.

Diagnosis of democracy and democratic diagnosis

These guidelines for the diagnosis of democratic problems in political systems are suggestive and broadly sketched. They form the contours of *a* diagnostic tool, a possibility of structured problematization of democratic systems among others. The particular shape of the suggested diagnostic guidelines emerges from the (re-)construction of a systemic perspective on democracy (see Chapter 6). These guidelines illustrate how the systemic lens is helpful for the diagnosis of democratic shortcomings. Indeed, they provide *a* perspective on what problems are and a common semantic to identify, frame, and discuss these. Moreover, I have suggested that diagnosis must be systemic in nature; while some political practices are intrinsically problematic (obviously non-democratic), most are problematic in context and in relation with other practices. Finally, I claimed that the critical and systematic diagnosis of democratic problems of political systems is valuable for democracy as an ideal and for democracies as empirical realities. In the following section, I clarify and justify this claim in highlighting what are the *needs*, practical *means*, concrete *possibilities*, and main *aims* of this diagnostic tool within democratic systems.

Diagnostic needs

The systemic lens has brought some insights: political systems constantly change, their shape is highly contingent, and they do attempt to steer their own shape-shifting. Political systems do observe themselves through the structural presence of (and variable connections with) *a public*. In systemic terms, modern political systems feature *self-thematization* and *self-reflexivity*; they produce and connect communications (including communications about themselves), and they self-describe and self-legitimize through some principles (generally, but not necessarily, *democratic* ones). Sociologically speaking, modern political systems do problematize themselves or some of their parts; they do "criticize" themselves or parts of themselves.[116] Normatively speaking, the question is *how* they do that. Once again, the practice of *justification* is pivotal here. For Forst, critique is a practice of justification that necessarily occurs in social contexts (see Chapter 5). The practice of critique targets existing normative orders, practices, and narratives of justifications. People do question and criticize the power structures by which they are affected or subjected, and the

---

[116] The phenomenon of self-thematization and self-reflexivity is *inevitable* insofar as a political system exists. The shift of its code from government/governed to government/opposition greatly increases the opportunity and "normalcy" of *critical* self-thematization. The anti-democratic practice of political repression has the purpose and effect of impeding by force opportunities of critical self-reflection.

justifications/reasons that sustain them. By doing so, they raise a normative claim to justification and justifiability; social systems (as normative orders for Forst), and their structures and operations, *must* be justified. The normative right and duty to justification emerge from the practice of critique of existing justifications.

By having at its core this right and duty to justification, *democracy* (as a particular political system) demands collectively binding decisions *and its own practices of justifications* to be justified. It thus recursively implies the necessity of critique in order to target and challenge its current practices of justification. As a practice of justification *itself*, critique must be justified too. Accordingly, the particular practices of critique can be more or less justified in democratic terms. There is therefore a symbiotic relation between critique and democracy: democracy requires justified critique, and critique calls for *democratic* practices of justifications.

Diagnosis, as I label it, is a particular kind of critique. Democratic critique must remain open-ended and include multiple critical forms (e.g., social movements, civil disobedience, critical art). In contrast, diagnosis is a much more limited and oriented kind of critique; it is a *structured* and *guided* critique. It targets specific problems and identifies them through a pre-established and justified diagnostic strategy. I do not mean here that any diagnostic strategy should follow the guidelines suggested above, only that diagnosis is a specific way of undertaking critique because of its *systematic* and *organized* character. As such, the critical task of diagnosis could be to some extent institutionalized and proceduralized within a democratic system. As claimed in Chapter 6, the ultimate normative horizon for a democratic system is to be democratically self-justified, self-diagnosed, and self-corrective. To get closer to this ideal, democratic systems would benefit from venues where self-justification, self-diagnosis, and self-correction can unfold. Actually, my point is that since a democratic system inherently requires the critique of its own practices of justification, venues for this reflexive critique *must* exist, and some of them must be secured and stabilized by procedures. In some of these venues, the practice of critique would benefit from being structured and guided to a variable extent: such venues would be locations of *self-diagnosis*.

As a necessary element of the functioning of a democratic system, the practice of self-diagnosis itself must be democratic. Democratic systems demand venues for the *democratic diagnosis* of their own democratic pathologies. The *diagnosis of democracy* must ultimately be performed through *democratic diagnosis*. A practice of diagnosis is democratic (just like any other democratic practice) by enacting democratic principles in the best way possible, supported by compelling justifications and connected appropriately to other parts of the democratic system. The target of democratic diagnosis is first and foremost the current shape of the political system in order to pinpoint its democratic shortcomings. But by its need to be democratic as well, the practice of diagnosis is thus recursively subject to diagnosis itself. Ultimately, the task of diagnosis would also target the obstacles and opportunities of democratic diagnosis within democratic systems (thus the absence of locations for critical systematic diagnosis can itself be considered as a democratic deficit to be corrected), the existing diagnostic tools themselves (the guiding structure), and the democratic character of the specific venues of democratic diagnosis.

Practical diagnostic means

Regarding the concrete *means* to perform democratic diagnosis, the practice of meta-deliberation comes directly to mind as the best way to perform it (see Chapter 6). Indeed, democratic meta-deliberative venues aimed at reflective institutional design (Landwehr 2015; Landwehr & Schäfer 2023) represent good candidates for performing democratic diagnosis. As a complex reflexive activity, the diagnosis of democratic systems would arguably benefit from some facilitated meta-deliberation. Two concrete empirical examples are akin to a process of democratic diagnosis. First, the *Bürgerrat Demokratie* in 2019 was a unique democratic experiment that gathered 160 citizens randomly selected from all around Germany to answer the question: "Whether and in what form our proven parliamentary representative democracy can be supplemented by further elements of citizen participation and direct democracy" (Participedia 2024). With the practice of deliberation at its core, this citizens' assembly produced twenty-two recommendations to strengthen German democracy. Although Fleuss (2023) takes this experiment as an example of "challenging the rules of the game," the framing of the question invites participants to envision complementary devices rather than problematizing/challenging existing ones, which would be the focus of a democratic diagnosis. Second, the

Citizens' Assembly on Democracy in the UK gathered sixty-seven citizens online to draw the contours of what the UK democratic system should look like (Renwick et al. 2022). This deliberative process was more aspiration-driven than problem-driven, in that it did not focus on what the *current problems* in the UK's democratic system are. Although they are not proper examples of democratic *diagnosis*, these two experiments certainly contribute to the broader aim of improving democracy, and by doing so place the practice of deliberation at their core.

Deliberation is certainly pivotal to the performance of democratic diagnosis, but it cannot *a priori* exhaust all the possibilities of performing diagnosis within democratic systems. Other practices could contribute to the overall diagnostic effort. For instance, the broad consultation *Un pays pour demain* ("A country for tomorrow"), launched by the Belgian federal government in 2020, combined an online consultation with several discussion groups to question citizens' expectations in terms of democratic structures and preferences for democratic reforms (Un pays pour demain 2023). Other possible means are mentioned by Geissel, as examples of "continual quality-monitoring and adaptation" (2023: 57). She mentions existing means, such as election committees "responsible for revealing potential misconduct, mistakes and frauds of one institution or actor" (ibid.). However, she insists that their evaluative scope is limited and does not target the whole democratic system. Another example, the *Democratic Audit*, evaluates the democratic quality of political systems by including citizens' evaluations and assesses opportunities for democratic improvements. This measurement tool certainly pinpoints democratic shortcomings, but it is not "embedded in the democratic setup" (ibid.). Geissel calls instead for the institutionalization of a public agency, the "Committee for Monitoring and Evaluation" (ibid. 60). With an aim akin to democratic diagnosis (i.e., continuous quality assessment and adaptation), this agency would check the appropriateness of existing practices to fulfill the democratic preferences of citizens and report flaws in doing so. Arguably, all of these experimented or suggested means could contribute to a various extent to the overall task of democratic diagnosis.

I do not aim to propose here how exactly democratic diagnosis should be realized in practice, as there are probably multiple possibilities and there is room for contextual particularities across the varieties of democratic systems. The practical horizon of democratic diagnosis is open-ended and everything is still to be created. Creativity, testing, failures, and continuous innovation will be necessary to realize it. None-theless, I suggest that democratic diagnosis can be taken as an essential democratic *function*, deriving from the broad function of justification, which can be dispersed across the democratic system and be performed by diverse practices in several venues, enacting various democratic prin-ciples. As with any other function, democratic diagnosis can be per-formed through more or less democratic practices. In a democratic system, the task of diagnosis would ideally be distributed among several venues, and citizens would have multiple opportunities to contribute to it. Citizens themselves, in collaboration with civil society organizations, academic experts, administrative personnel, political representatives, and possibly other actors, would undertake the diagnosis of *their* own democratic system. Moreover, in order to legitimize democratic diagno-sis as a necessary democratic task, and to ensure its impact on the dem-ocratic system, it would need to be institutionalized in some venues.

So far *specialized* venues of democratic diagnosis do not exist. Con-sequently, such specialized venues of democratic diagnosis could be implemented and tested in the same way deliberative mini-publics and other democratic innovations have spread in the last decade: often through hybrid formats designed by academic experts, civil society organizations, and/or political authorities, with ordinary citizens as their main actors. In democratic systems now facing important chal-lenges (e.g., France, UK, Italy), the acute need for democratic transfor-mation could benefit from experimenting prior efforts of democratic diagnosis, in order to identify areas of necessary reforms and to legit-imate the focus on certain problems. The specific forms of such ven-ues of democratic diagnosis would not be that different from existing democratic innovations, *only the purpose is*. Possible forms include a constitutional convention of randomly selected citizens, special com-mittees made of political representatives, expert panels, broad online public consultations, and various other forms yet to be invented. More-over, the performance of democratic diagnosis in complex democratic systems cannot be restricted to a single venue; it requires the com-plex articulation of different venues of diagnosis. A *system of democratic diagnosis* must be developed. Accordingly, I call for an effort of demo-cratic innovation focusing on the agenda of democratic diagnosis. The horizon of this democratic agenda is open-ended, it could take multi-ple and diverse forms. My claim is that such an agenda is *necessary* and must be tackled on its own by democratic systems.

Diagnostic possibilities

In most political contexts, the ambitious agenda of democratic diagnosis is unlikely to become part of political reality in the near future. Where venues of *democratic diagnosis* do not or cannot exist (for whatever reasons), the pivotal task of *diagnosis of democracy* remains essential. The specific problems of democratic systems still need to be detected in order to develop appropriate solutions. Hence, where diagnostic venues for citizens are absent, the diagnosis of political systems is the responsibility of political performers: the state through its administrative resources, civil society organizations, political parties, the parliament, the executive, and so on. However, their respective interests and partial perspectives may restrict their reflexivity and even willingness to perform such a diagnosis. A special kind of observer can, though, process enough complexity to perform the diagnosis of political systems: "experts" such as political scientists. They can provide a detailed and justified answer to the question of: *What are the problems here?*, which emerges from an explicit diagnostic strategy. Their respective answer would still only be *one* perspective, but a justified and tractable one emerging from a robust and transparent framework. Somehow, the limitedness of the subjective perspective of the "diagnostic expert" on her object of diagnosis is compensated for by the transparency of her frame and process of analysis. Of course, there would be disagreements among experts on the diagnosed problems, but a shared diagnostic strategy would provide a common ground for the structured and constructive confrontation of these disagreements. This is why a diagnostic *framework* is useful: it enables other observers to criticize the way existing diagnoses were conducted.

As an external observer, the political scientist in her office attempts to diagnose a political system that can only be fully observed from within (see Chapter 3). In order to do so, the researcher has to "observe the internal observers," that is, the different actors of the political system under investigation, the public in particular. By doing so, the "diagnostic expert" must include in her analysis the perspectives internal to the political context under diagnosis. In particular, the diagnostic framework suggested above requires her to consider internal perspectives under the forms of *actual justifications* and salient *normative expectations* for political arrangements. These two empirical elements are the pivotal features for the diagnosis of democratic systems: they orient the focus on what people *actually* expect in a political context, and why and how they justify these expectations. In the end, what is a democratic problem or not relies on the contextual expectations and justifications of citizens and not on "objective" pointers. Of course, the suggested diagnostic guidelines question the extent of fulfillment of a few democratic preconditions and the minimal justifiability of democratic practices. On these two grounds, basic democratic problems can be identified without including citizens' perspectives. However, most of the operative work of these diagnostic guidelines is to uncover the features of existing political systems (e.g., sequences of practices, connections, normative trade-offs) and reach a position where experts and citizens can interrogate whether these features are problematic and justify why. A "diagnostic expert" can propose a *theoretical* justification of what is problematic, but it must at best be sensitive to *citizens' preferences*.[117] Diverse methodological approaches (surveys, interviews, experiments) can contribute to fuel the "expert-diagnosis" with citizens' preferences, and ideally with the justifications sustaining these.

Expert diagnoses are, of course, insufficient for a democratic system: they cannot replace venues of *democratic* diagnosis. However, in a systemic perspective and even though they are not democratic themselves, their contributions can nevertheless be valuable for the sake of democracy's contextual enhancement. Indeed, the diagnosis of democracy by experts performs the political function of observation and enacts the democratic principles of epistemic advancement. Moreover, it can produce a diagnosis of democracy that, if considered by the system under analysis, can contribute to its improvement. Nothing is *a priori* preventing diagnosis from being performed by experts. In some cases, experts might even be the only actors in a position to undertake it. Indeed, the "expert-diagnosis" of democratic problems is always *appropriate* and *possible*. One can always diagnose

[117] Geissel offers a strong case for considering citizens' preferences in the (re-)design of democratic systems (2023: 34–43). Her case combines both normative (democracy as self-governing, legitimacy, inclusive responsiveness, political equality, and accountability) and empirical reasons (enhanced stability, increased democratic quality, political satisfaction, democratic revitalization). These reasons are complementary with the ones advanced in my framework: the functional necessity for political systems of self-observation and orientation by the public, and democracy normatively grounded on the right to justification. The sensitivity to citizens' preferences concretely opens the possibility that: "Some communities might not want a 'deliberative system' [...] others might like the agonist model, [...] others might be much more satisfied with direct democracy" (ibid.: 6).

from one's university office the countless democratic shortcomings of China or Russia as political systems. What is not always possible is *democratic* diagnosis, that is, the diagnosis of a political system by its citizens themselves through democratic means. Even in strict authoritarian systems such as Russia or China, a diagnosis of democratic problems could be useful and appropriate. Not only for the researcher that wishes to pinpoint the major multiple and interconnected democratic failures of these regimes, but also for the citizens of these countries, who wish to problematize the specific complexity of these regimes beyond their daily personal experiences of domination and political oppression, and identify concrete possibilities for transformation in democratic terms. This is *a fortiori* the case for political systems that are democratic on paper, but with a worrying tendency towards authoritarianism (e.g., India, Hungary, Brazil). These examples are limiting cases of the possibility and appropriateness of both "expert-diagnosis" and democratic diagnosis. The point is that the reflexive critique of a political system over itself is an essential democratic function; its fulfillment through structured democratic practices (i.e., democratic diagnosis) is always *valuable* although not always *possible*.

In contrast, both "expert-diagnosis" *and* democratic diagnosis are always appropriate and possible for allegedly more developed and stabilized democratic systems, including national ones, of course (e.g., Switzerland, Germany, US, etc.) but also supranational ones such as the EU. Indeed, *a priori*, no democratic system is perfect, and all are perfectible. Even if one democratic system turns out to be absolutely perfect, and perfectly matches the expectations of its citizens, we have yet to reach that happy conclusion. As such, both "expert-diagnosis" and democratic diagnosis are particularly appropriate and possible in *already-democratic somehow* contexts, where a fine-grained diagnostic tool becomes especially useful and enlightening. In these contexts, "expert-diagnosis" and democratic diagnosis can likely be combined in "hybrid" experiments, bringing together academic expertise and citizen participation.

Democratic diagnosis is always oriented by a frame, yet that does not prevent flexibility in the task, with continuous adaptations of the diagnostic frames and the diagnostic processes. The frame that I have suggested certainly has its own strengths and flaws. As presented, it is too complex and abstract to serve as a pragmatic orientation to citizens and political performers in their diagnostic enterprise. But in the face of the widespread use of the systemic semantic in daily life by citizens themselves, I am quite convinced that the systemic lens would be enlightening to most people. The frame of systems differentiation is a complex analytical simplification of the functioning of democratic systems. But it is undoubtedly one that is intuitive enough (to some extent) to be made understandable for anybody. The proposed diagnostic guidelines are a starting point for developing more appropriate tools for diagnosis and for framing them in more didactic terms. Democratic diagnosis requires us to find an appropriate balance between analytical robustness and widespread practical accessibility and usability for citizens.

Diagnostic aims

Democratic diagnosis aims to structure the critical self-observation of the political system. As such, the democratic necessity of diagnosis directly impacts the function of *observation* by the public. While in a modern political system the public critically observes politics and the administration, democratic diagnosis proposes lens with which to do so; it offers a method for targeting problems and reading them with a common language. Schematically, the injunction in favor of democratic diagnosis would be to say: "Citizens, identify the problems in the functioning of *your* democratic system. Here are some tools to do so." If democracy is to be a continuously self-corrective system, democratic diagnosis is certainly a necessary task, as well as one that has to be undertaken by citizens themselves. Such an *immanent critique* is intrinsically part of what democracy is. If democratic systems are constantly evolving and in need of improvement in the face of changing complex environments, there should always be people raising claims that the way we practice democracy here and now is problematic because of X or Y reason, and that we could do better here and there.

The aim of a diagnostic tool is not to produce an "objective" answer to the question of what is problematic, sorting out the "right" diagnostic among multiple perspectives in that regard. The aim is instead to provide a structured and maximally neutral context in which to confront these perspectives. The diagnostic tool is a meta-perspective to orient conflicting perspectives towards a constructive debate through a common language in which disagreements over democratic problems can be clearly formulated, reciprocally and generally justified, and productively confronted. A structured way of diagnosing political reality can serve as the grounds for a collective problematization that is transparent on how it proceeds, precisely in order to better isolate genuine sources of disagreement on what is actually problematic. Accordingly, a diagnostic frame does not aim to produce "objectively" good *answers*, but to ask good *questions* and to collectively confront diverse possible answers, to the extent they are supported by reciprocal and general justifications.

The purpose of democratic diagnosis is to structure this democratic debate for its contextual unfolding, by providing a flexible common semantic from which disagreements can emerge and be constructively confronted. A rationale for it derives directly from the constructivist tenet of systems theory: a social system constructs its own reality and rationality by observing itself. The public (i.e., citizens) are the main internal observers of the political system and the source of its immanent critique. But "the public" is a differentiated subsystem only in its capacity of observing the whole political system; it is composed of countless and overlapping social systems and groups that inevitably have multiple and conflicting perspectives on the political system. Consequently, there will necessarily be an irreducible plurality of perspectives regarding what the democratic problems of a political context are. Different people and groups can experience the same political system very differently, facing diverse challenges and articulating various grievances, some specific to their own reality (socio-economic factors or individual and collective identities are here determinant). Hence, their respective individual and collective agency within the system is different: some have more agency than others in the political system. Exclusionary structures and dynamics (based notably on identity, gender, race, religion, sexuality, socioeconomic conditions) within political systems are major targets of diagnosis as well. A genuinely *democratic* process of diagnosis must include marginalized voices and be an opportunity to voice their grievances towards the functioning of the political system. *Plurality* and *differences* are at the core of democratic diagnosis: plurality and differences of perspectives, experiences, grievances, preferences, sensibilities, and expectations towards the functioning of a specific democratic system.

A process of democratic diagnosis aims at the emergence, explicit framing and justification, and constructive confrontation of these differences. Such a process, as a shared experience of democracy, can represent a fruitful context in which to build shared perceptions of the democratic system under the prism of its problems. Moreover, a process of democratic diagnosis is also an opportunity for citizens to build, develop, or revise their expectations towards democracy. By collectively questionning what they find problematic and why, they can indirectly discover and express what they actually expect from democracy and for what reasons. Democratic diagnosis can thus represent a fertile ground for the construction, expression, and "refinement" of citizens' preferences (Geissel 2023) about democracy and the justifications supporting these. It pushes citizens to build and justify their preferences regarding concrete trade-offs, where democratic principles (to which all can adhere as abstract ideas) are actually in conflict. Democratic diagnosis ultimately asks the question: *Which trade-offs between democratic expectations do we find problematic and which ones do we prefer instead?*

Besides the *identification* of the specific problems of a democratic system, democratic diagnosis also contributes to the *legitimation* of problematic priorities, and hence to further efforts at designing and legitimizing appropriate solutions. Indeed, if citizens agree on the need to tackle certain issues, it legitimizes the sustained research for solutions for these specific problems. The agenda of democratic diagnosis assumes that if people disagree on solutions, it is often because they do not agree on what the problems are. By displacing the debate towards problems rather than solutions, democratic diagnosis seeks to establish commonality on *what is problematic*, as shared grounds for the process of deciding collectively on *what is the best solution*.

Democratic diagnosis hence invites citizens who believe that *nothing* is problematic in their democratic system to justify why; citizens who believe that *everything* is problematic to explain and justify what in particular is problematic and why, and citizens who believe that *something* in particular is problematic to justify why, and how their eventual proposed solution(s) actually answer this problem. Accordingly, democratic diagnosis could challenge three quite rigid positions. First, citizens who we could label "democratic conservationists," who are convinced that existing representative democracy is democracy *tout court*, works perfectly fine, and that there is no point in democratic innovation. Second, citizens who are disappointed about democracy (for whatever reasons) and call for other types of political systems.

Relatedly, citizens holding that there is a general and widespread conspiracy and that the "system" works for the benefit of a group of powerful people plotting behind the scenes. Third, citizens who are convinced they know what the problem in their democratic system is (who are often also enthusiasts towards a specific solution). This includes populists, convinced that political elites are corrupt and that the solution is a providential leader representing the "real people" without many intermediaries. It also includes citizens who are enthusiastic for a specific democratic innovation, such as randomly selected citizens' assemblies, sometimes perceived as the perfect solution to the crisis of representative democracy.

All these positions exist, to variable extents, in most contemporary democracies. The agenda of democratic diagnosis takes them all seriously. In particular, those who articulate the existence of problems within democratic systems cannot be ignored, whether such problems are real or not. These positions are expressed in the public sphere, but it is systematically distorted, fragmented, and polarized, and citizens are prone to manipulation, disinformation, and indoctrination. In response, democratic diagnosis invites citizens to partake in a *structured* debate, which is ideally exempt from these detrimental features of the public sphere. Through a guided and structured process of collective problematization, it invites citizens, regardless of their prior positions on the matter, to identify together what actual problems are faced by their democratic system, potentially including these pathologies of the public sphere and the features conducive to them. This debate is demanding: *epistemically*, in asking citizens to investigate the complexity of existing democratic systems and to build informed and justified positions about what is problematic or not; and *normatively*, in demanding reciprocal and general justifications for citizens' positions. Democratic diagnosis is a structured debate where these diverging positions are expressed and confronted *differently* than in the public sphere, hence potentially more productively.

To summarize this section, the diagnostic tool proposed here is potentially *for everybody*. The suggested diagnostic guidelines are common questions that both experts and citizens could ask themselves when attempting the diagnosis of a political system in democratic terms. Whether expert-driven, citizen-driven, or under hybrid forms, all these paths of diagnosis should be explored. For the expert diagnosis, methodological tools can be developed to that aim. For the hybrid and citizen-driven forms, democratic innovations can be designed. The task of diagnosis should be a joint effort after all. The diagnostic capacities of multiple actors must be improved for that venture. As Fung puts it: "Citizens and public leaders should be on the lookout for deficits in their democratic institutions [...] [and] should master the democratic craft of judging and implementing a wide range of alternative decision-making procedures that mark improvements upon the quality of our collective decision making" (2012: 622). In addition, solutions can pose new problems, hence diagnosis must be a *continuous* task (as democratic innovation is for Fung and democratic design is for Saward). Much work remains to be done in that endeavor. Democratic theorists can contribute to it if they endorse the challenge of diagnosis, as I urge them to do.

Conclusion

Reaching a solution depends largely on the diagnosis of what the problem is. In some ways, a big part of the solution relies upon the robustness of the diagnosis of the problem. What democratic theory (also) needs to undertake now is to develop some tools to do so. We democratic theorists have not yet carried out enough critical work to understand the potentiality of democratic systems in context and the obstacles to it. Here is a suggestion of a tool to help us do so. I insist on the speculative, suggestive, and forward-looking character of this chapter. It proposes a *programmatic agenda*, a challenge for the development of democratic theory and practice. The developed tool itself is merely illustrative of the complexity of this endeavor. This diagnostic tool undoubtedly lacks clarity, consistency, and exhaustiveness. It is likely that the chronological ordering and the conceptual articulation between its guiding questions will have to be revised. Clearly there is much work to be done, clearly it is a contestable and imperfect suggestion. It is not a detailed *metric*, but it might encapsulate some grounds for further development. It now requires development, testing, and recursive refinements. Nonetheless, perhaps what is of most value here is the *attempt* to develop such a tool, and the *injunction* for that endeavor, because the task of diagnosis is critically important for any democratic system.

In the current circumstances of increasing social complexity and widespread backlash towards the liberal-representative kind of democracy, symptoms such as populism or abstentionism might be manifest, but the exact *problems* faced by particular democratic systems are much less obvious. Consequently, one thing that democracies need today is collective and critical contextual diagnoses of their own functioning and obstacles to democratic improvement. The agenda of democratic diagnosis aims to put collective and structured critique at the core of democracies, to push these systems to problematize not only *societal* but also *political* issues, and do so in tackling the full complexity of democratic systems.

This agenda is congruent with two recent major developments in democratic theory that could enrich, complement, or challenge the specific agenda of democratic diagnosis. One is Fleuss's *radical proceduralism* (2021), an innovative philosophical position in the debate regarding substance versus procedure as the source of democratic legitimacy, stating that only inclusive democratic procedures ground legitimacy. From a different debate and approach, she reaches a similar conclusion to the one I reached with my endorsement of a systemic perspective: the need for citizens to "challenge the rules of the democratic game." It is encouraging to notice that different aims, perspectives, and justifications led to similar propositions, and further mutual engagement could develop this common agenda. The second is Geissel's prospective future towards *thriving democracies* (2023) and concrete institutional proposals to realize this. Grounded in the principle of self-governing, it demands that "citizens and communities decide how they want to govern themselves" and hence be "the creators, authors and owners of their democracy" (ibid.: 4). The agenda of democratic diagnosis fits comfortably within this normative horizon. In suggesting that we problematize reflexively the actual shape of democratic systems and by offering analytical tools grounded on a systemic perspective to do so, democratic diagnosis could be a necessary step towards this democratic horizon.

Conclusion

This book tentatively sketched a picture of what *democracy as a system* could be. What comes out of this attempt is *one* depiction of democratic systems. This theoretical analysis was a journey into democracy's complexity with *system* for orientation. The destination of this journey and the routes taken were not fully known at the moment of departure. Only the horizon was perceptible: the genuine interrogation of *what is a democratic system*. To answer this question, I reversed the perspective currently at play in the systemic turn in (deliberative) democratic theory. I wondered, not what makes democracy a system, but what makes a system a democratic one. I questioned democracy from and through a systemic perspective, instead of questioning systems from a democratic perspective.

Democracy through a systemic lens

This shift of perspective led to unexpected paths and areas of knowledge. That was precisely the objective: to challenge both my own presuppositions and a few others at play in the current debate on deliberative and democratic systems. This goal pushed me to tackle in particular the complexity of Niklas Luhmann's systems theory. This was not merely a matter of theoretical choice: one cannot pretend to interrogate social systems without confronting Luhmann's paradigm. While I expected to find within it the stability of determining structures, I instead encountered contingency and processes of differentiation. I took seriously Luhmann's radical constructivist approach, notably because the centrality of *contingency* and *processes* resonates deeply with the central issue of context-sensitivity and pushes towards a kind of democratic proceduralism. However, Luhmann's theory was mainly useful in its provision of a comprehensive and context-sensitive framework for the sociological understanding of political systems as fruitful grounds for the identification of what makes democracy distinctive. His theory may be full of misleading assumptions and misplaced conclusions, but his effort and success in systematization is undeniable. It is a complete conceptual system coherently articulating several distinctions to make sense of social complexity. In that sense, it is a differentiated conceptual system that can serve as a transversal antagonist to other conceptual systems, including democratic theory in general, and the nascent democratic systems approach in particular. As such, it can play the role of a powerful critical probe: a sound and challenging perturbation to many settled assumptions. This perturbation, if taken seriously as I hope I have, allows the self-observation of democratic theory through external critical lenses.

The systemic perspective was thus used as a conceptual lens to see with *some* clarity. This lens enabled contrasts and shades to be distinguished within the complexity of democratic systems. Through this lens, some meaning took shape, and new questions and insights came to light. The systemic perspective allowed me to take as a conceptual system a current debate in democratic theory, some of whose latent structures, insights, and shortcomings I was then able to tentatively thematize. It provided common analytical tools for me to observe different conceptual systems (e.g., deliberative democracy, Forst's theory, Warren's problem-based approach, Saward's democratic design), and therefore *systematize* to some extent *a* debate in rearticulating their respective contributions. While the above discussion is certainly not the state of the debate in democratic theory, it may be a debate to come. Actually, the main claim of this book is that it *should* be a debate to come: the theoretical framework of democratic systems should be the topic of in-depth discussion. The development of a *democratic systems approach* should be a priority on the academic agenda, through an interdisciplinary effort integrating all streams of democratic scholarship and normative models of democracy. By its inherent overarching and abstract nature, a systemic approach to democracy has such an integrative potential. It could provide the theoretical grounds and conceptual language for a productive confrontation of various perspectives on democracy, by structuring the expression of disagreements on specific points *all along the way* from ontological and epistemological postulates to normative positions, methodological tools, and propositions of institutional design.

In order to propose a structure of debate for the construction of a democratic systems approach, I first attempted to *clear the theoretical grounds* of a particular debate current in democratic theory, that of deliberative and democratic systems. This literature took "systems" mainly as an enlightening metaphor in order to refocus on the "big picture" of democracy's complexity. As highlighted in Chapter 1, democratic theorists have not sufficiently tackled the challenge of conceptualizing democracy *as a system*. They have provided accounts of deliberative and democratic systems, but they have insufficiently confronted the core theoretical assumptions upholding their diverging conceptualizations. Moreover, they remain unclear on *how* they arrived at the specific content proposed in their respective accounts, regarding both the descriptive and normative dimensions. In order to challenge their assumptions, I reconstructed the abstract questions that need to be answered in order to reach their answers (and potentially *other* answers) regarding the architecture, functioning, and normative orientation of democratic systems. These six questions focus on the nature of the parts in the system, their analytical clustering in distinct ensembles, the connections between these parts, the boundaries of the system, the normative criteria to assess the quality of the system, and the application of these criteria. In addition, I suggested that in conceptualizing these six dimensions, democratic theorists must be aware of and explicit on how *context-sensitive* their conceptual, analytical, and normative categories are. This reconstruction of the latent issues of the debate generated a proposition of *structuration* for this debate, a necessary step towards the clarification of the theoretical grounds of democratic systems.[118]

As discussed in Chapter 2, a few major contributions (Warren 2017; Bächtiger & Parkinson 2019; Saward 2021) expanded and improved the initial accounts of the systemic approach in democratic theory, in targeting more specifically the theoretical core of what democratic systems are and could be. Nonetheless, through a close reading of these works, it appeared to me that on the one hand, the respective results were unsatisfactory and perfectible, and on the other hand, the lack of confrontation between these maintained a situation of insularity of their respective conceptions and some indeterminacy regarding the presuppositions, normative assumptions, and analytical categories at play in the debate. These crucial contributions, I suggested, have not been directly confronted because of their distinct aims and emphases. However, as they

[118] By setting the debate at this level of abstraction, I relied upon distinctions between some concepts: systems/environment, action/communication, structures/processes, descriptive/normative, power/justification, functions/practices/principles, political/democratic/deliberative, and critique/diagnosis. By contrasting concepts, we can conceive their distinctive meaning and create complex articulations between them. Although there may certainly be other ways to proceed, this strategy is one that has led to *some* insights.

are diverse perspectives on the theoretical core of democratic systems, and as they respectively embed crucial insights into parts of this theoretical core, this direct confrontation uncovered their main commonalities and divergences regarding the essential features of democratic systems. However, beyond what they commonly shared, the merits of their diverging propositions were not indisputable as each was persuasive in its own way. Consequently, I concluded it was impossible to sort out their respective strengths and weaknesses, and to develop an overall conceptualization of democratic systems on their sole grounds, without the help of an *external challenge* to democratic theory.

As the object was deliberative/democratic *systems*, this challenge was naturally looked for in Chapter 3 within the complex apparatus of *systems theory*. I took the challenge seriously, by considering what this perspective (Luhmann's in particular) had to offer. One could consider that I pushed this consideration too far, landing on a kind of *radical* systemism, or worse on a dogmatic Luhmannism. Hence one may simply read the propositions that emerge from it as insular and biased by this radical systemic perspective. But I do not think that this book must be read solely as a "Luhmannian systems theory" perspective on democratic theory. Indeed, Luhmann's theory is already an impressive interdisciplinary effort that shares a lot with multiple seminal authors (Husserl, Parsons, Weber, Durkheim, Simmel, Hegel, Goffman, Kelsen, Simon, Merton, and even Habermas, etc.).[119] Accordingly, my positioning within Luhmann's perspective is not so insular. It does not claim that Luhmann's is the "best" theory of social systems and the most fruitful route to question democratic theories. It claims instead that it is a sound and powerful transdisciplinary contribution providing a reliable *heuristic tool* to simultaneously interrogate both the complexity of democratic *systems* and that of democratic *theory*. Luhmann's systems theory provides a perspective, a strategy for questioning, and a detailed semantic that apply both to the object under observation (democratic systems) and to the conceptual system operating this observation (democratic theory). The "method" itself is systemic, as it examines separate yet connected concepts under the prism of their

---

[119] Furthermore, it is in a way surprising that most contemporary critical streams of thought have bluntly ignored this "grand theory" that articulates several of their own assumptions. As Kim (2015: 355) notes: "It is striking that systems theory's resolute commitment to difference, contingency, posthhumanism and postfoundationalism has not found much resonance in recent theoretical developments within political theory that have been increasingly guided by a similar constellation of ideas and orientations."

function in a theoretical apparatus. Moreover, it is systemic in that it produces a conceptual system open to external perturbations and willing to take every contribution on board to strengthen itself.

In that regard, other welcome approaches are challenging the systemic lens as allegedly more fit to explore the complexity of democratic realities. One is the nascent *democratic assemblage approach* (Felicetti 2021; Asenbaum 2022b). In contrast (*they claim*) to the systemic approach, democratic assemblage emphasizes the "messiness" and contingency of democratic architectures, the unpredictability of their transformation rather than stable continuity, the spontaneous emergence of new connections and practices, and the agency of human and non-human actors in the democratic assemblage process. This approach opposes in particular the expectation of "synergy" for systemic interactions (Felicetti 2021). Democratic systems, they alert us, are not harmonious ensembles of designed institutions operating in synergy: they also feature conflict and disruption. Moreover, relying on a "flat ontology," they urge us to "overcome the exclusion of non-humans" (such as animals, plants, objects, and natural events) from democratic theory and practice, since these agents participate within democratic assemblages (Asenbaum 2022b: 250). A second and similar challenger is the *deliberative ecologies approach* "advocating a move beyond the systemic approach" (Mendonca et al. 2024: 2). Although it specifically targets the *deliberative* systems approach (and not the nascent *democratic* systems approach), its "relational critique" is nonetheless potentially relevant. It targets mainly the functionalism[120] of the systemic approach, which allegedly includes oversimplifying social life, linearizing complex and recursive interconnections, homogenizing units of analysis, conceiving "actors and political arenas through fixed, universal, aprioristic categories, roles and functions," and not acknowledging "the open-ended dynamic of discursive flows" (ibid.). They advocate instead an ecological approach as comprehensive, relational, "sensitive to the complexity, the heterogeneity, and the dynamics of the political world" (ibid.: 4).

These two challenging approaches could potentially foster the development of an overarching analytical apparatus of democratic complexity. They position themselves as *alternatives* to the systemic

---

[120] The systemic approach is here, as often, criticized as *functionalist*. However, this recurrent critique generally relates to Parsonian *structural functionalism* and Easton's theory, reducing systems theory to it, without any consideration of Luhmann's paradigm.

approach, highlighting the importance of features allegedly absent from it (complexity, emergence, contingency, agency, dynamism, change, recursivity, conflict). If these approaches are able to articulate these core concepts, *as the systemic approach actually does*, but in a better way, they could be robust and appealing alternatives. To do so, they would have to provide a better account of democracy, combining a *conceptual articulation* of parts-whole, structures-processes-agency, stability-transformation, complexity-unpredictability, and contingency-universality; an *analytical apparatus* to navigate complex and dynamic democratic realities and map context-sensitive political arrangements; and a *normative horizon* built upon and articulated with their conceptual and analytical frameworks. They could, in a complementary spirit, challenge *some parts* of the systemic approach too, by proposing better conceptualizations or new crucial dimensions (such as the importance of non-human agents). Both the alternative and complementary paths are welcome to foster the debate, but I invite these approaches to *also* consider systemic propositions built upon Luhmann's systems theory, and not only contrast their approach with the "strawman" of Parsonian structural functionalism. They may well be surprised at how many "alternative" assumptions they share with such a democratic systems approach and identify more precisely their specific challenges and/or added values.

That being said, the systemic lens may not, after all, be the best way of meeting the challenge of understanding democracy's complexity, but it does provide *a* picture of the same thing we are all looking at from distinct perspectives. If all the possible perspectives illuminate *one part* of democracy's complexity, so too does the systemic perspective. Perhaps the part it casts light on is the doomed effort of humans to complexify, systematize, rationalize, order, and regulate things in a contrived and abstract apparatus, *ad nauseam* sometimes. But if this effort brings *some* clarity and generates new meanings, by bringing to bear *some* analytical power and critical potential, maybe it is nevertheless valuable.

Problematizing democratic systems

This reengagement with systems theory provided pivotal resources in Chapter 4 to understand political systems as differentiated systems of communication, with power as a communicative medium. In particular, systems theory offered a reliable guide, an analytical anchor to uncover contextual differences along common features: *functions*. The use of functions as an analytical lens enables us to envision variable practical possibilities for performing political tasks, and to track these when attempting to describe contextual political realities. This functional orientation suggests a few common features of differentiation that shape the broad specificity of existing political contexts: external differentiation (from societal and political environments), internal differentiation (vertical and horizontal), differentiated inclusivity, and so on. These categories of differentiation can be used to *map* the broad contours of any political system, whether local, regional, national, international, supranational, or transnational. By focusing the analytical distinction of political systems onto their functional features, this strategy of representation is exempt from normative presuppositions on how what political systems *should* look like. Although it is true that this proposed frame of reference for political systems historically emerged from the contingent Western perspective on social reality, it shall not be seen as a definitive and rigid scheme for the mapping of political realities. For instance, the internal differentiation of political systems (in politics, administration, and the public) does not represent a universal and timeless picture of how political systems are necessarily internally structured. But it serves as a *counterfactual reference* to question how contemporary political systems are *actually* structured, both through variations of this internal differentiation and through possible other forms of differentiation. Besides its analytical strengths, I suggested that this representation and mapping strategy unfortunately come with a strong limitation: the intended normative indeterminacy of Luhmann's framework.

To bypass this stalemate, I attempted in Chapter 5 a deviation from Luhmann's theory that nevertheless remained broadly compatible with its sociological grounds and systemic tenets. From his conceptualization of power, I reached (through Habermas) Forst's theory of noumenal power. This contemporary seminal piece regarding the nature of power is appealingly connected by Forst to his normative theory of justification, as he argues that relations of power are ultimately relations of justification, since power always displays justification to motivate acceptance. From this descriptive understanding of justification, Forst builds a normative orientation for appropriate justification: its reciprocal and general character. In face of my acceptance of these normative grounds, one can rightly see here a foundational-ist move (although that is debatable since these grounds emerge from Forst's reconstruction of the critical and moral dimensions inherent in the practice of justification). As with any grounds, these are con-testable. But what I deemed particularly appealing here is their simul-taneous *minimality* (reciprocity and generality are quite minimal yet essential expectations for "good" justification), *pervasiveness* (they apply to each relation of power/justification occurring in a normative order), and *flexibility* (these criteria demand a *form* of justification, not a specific *content*). As such, they constitute good candidates for the "universal" core and normative orientation of a *democratic procedural-ism* that opens the door for a "diagnostic-evaluative pluralism" where some contextual normative expectations can be at play in various nor-mative orders but that are still in need of reciprocal and general jus-tification. Perhaps the important outcome of this discussion is not so much the proposed content of *this* twofold normative layer combining universal criteria of justification and context/system-specific norma-tive expectations. What is of importance instead is a renewed insis-tence in theorizing such a *twofold* articulation for the normative core of democratic systems, in order to ground democracy's normative dis-tinctiveness while allowing its contextual fulfillment through variable forms that can themselves be assessed on their own, yet without fall-ing into a relativist impasse.

From these normative grounds, I argued in Chapter 6 that what makes democracy's distinctiveness is its specific function of justifica-tion, a pervasive expectation towards all the operations (that is, com-munications) of the political system if they are to be democratic in kind. In order to develop the critical potential of this function in a democratic system, I relied on a reconceptualization of the theoreti-cal core of democratic systems along the conceptual *functions/practic-es/principles* triad. The main added value of this threefold distinction is that it articulates common political *functions* (as analytical focal ref-erences) with various *practices* performing these while enacting some democratic *principles*. This conceptualization enables the contextual justifiability of particular practices to be problematized while distin-guishing their functional goal (*what needs to be done*) from the demo-cratic principles they can enact (*how this should be done*). By avoiding the conflation of these two kinds of goals, this distinction encourages us to identify more clearly the democratic principles that are enacted (or not) by practices, while emphasizing their unique critical bite. Moreover, I argued that if democratic systems require the constant justification of their practices, the enactment of *some* specific democratic principles instead of others in cases of trade-offs is also subject to this burden of justification, such that the contextual choice of democratic ends to be prioritized remains to some extent a *democratic* one. If one disagrees with this assertion, it then transforms into a question: *If we agree that democratic principles can and sometimes must be traded-off in some democratic venues, to what extent and how must these trade-offs themselves be decided democratically?*

In Chapter 6, I also took position on the use we could (and I think *should*) make of the analytical categories of "deliberation" and "deliberativeness" when assessing and diagnosing democratic systems. My point was that by taking deliberation and deliberativeness as clear-cut analytical distinctions, we can better locate and push forward their critical bite, in contrast (yet in complementarity) with all the other democratic expectations to be satisfied in a complex political system. In different locations of a democratic system, the deliberative expectations are likely to vary depending first on the function they attempt to regulate. Is deliberation or deliberativeness expected for the function of *orientation* through formal agenda setting or opposition, the function of *elaboration of decision premises* by the executive, the function of *selection of political performers* through public election or within a political party, the function of *legislation* by a large body of representative or an executive agency, the function of *implementation* through the coordination and planning it requires, or recursively for the function of *observation* by the public through a reflexive critique on the system? Depending on which function is at stake, the practical possibilities for deliberation and the specific need for deliberativeness will be different; randomly selected mini-publics could contribute to some of these functions, so could expert panels, parliamentary committees, a high executive and her councillors, party caucuses, social movements, and others. And in all these diverse venues, the deliberative expectations would face *other* democratic expectations that must be enacted *as well*, and thus could require trade-offs.

Hence, my point here is only an analytical one: in order to reach this analytical position where we can problematize a practice both in functional and normative terms, we need these clear-cut analytical distinctions. Functions/practices/principles is a pivotal distinction, deliberative/democratic principles is another. In addition, distinguishing deliberation from other democratic expectations (e.g., inclusion, participation, representation) keeps deliberation's unique critical aspiration operative in a diagnostic framework. Accordingly, my position regarding deliberative democracy and more specifically the deliberative systems approach is simple and trivial: we share the same normative horizon, as I think all models of democracy ultimately do (representative democracy, participatory democracy, epistemic democracy, or any adjective preceding democracy). My only suggestion here is *how* we can use these adjectives to fulfill as best as possible and with subtlety their respective critical aspirations towards our common normative horizon of *democratic systems*. The only thing I did here was to articulate our common normative horizon of "democracy" through a systemic conceptual and analytical apparatus in order to strengthen our capacity to problematize this horizon and to diagnose the specific problems that distance us from it. Overall, this book does not challenge existing accounts of both deliberative and democratic systems, it only uses their crucial contributions to propose a challenge: let's develop a conceptual and analytical apparatus for the tasks of problematization and critical diagnosis of democratic systems.

Finally, I argued in Chapter 7 that with such a conceptualization of democratic systems, characterized by a sociologically grounded descriptive layer capable of mapping the specificities of political realities, and a flexible normative layer to assess these, we could attempt to build the theoretical foundations of a diagnostic framework for the detection of contextual democratic problems. Such a diagnostic tool could be useful for operating a guided and organized critique of democratic systems, both from external political observers (such as political scientists) and political actors (including citizens). Moreover, and this claim is stronger, I claimed that *if* (and this is a big "if") we conceive democratic systems as I did in the 250 previous pages, their normative apex is to be self-justified, self-diagnosed, and self-corrective. Hence the strong claim of the book is the following: democratic systems require a reflexive and justified critique, and they would benefit from venues of democratic diagnosis to operate this democratically. If democratic systems do so, I think that we can still "hope that democracy will be the means [...] to overcoming the pathologies that otherwise in society get reproduced through democracy" (Forst 2021: video).

Regarding potential contributions: is this book a *normative* contribution to the debate in democratic theory? I am not sure, it is tentatively an *analytical* contribution, as it tries to clear some theoretical grounds. It is true that it relies on some normative claims; in particular, it rests on the normative grounding of reciprocal and general justification as the normative core of democratic systems. That normative core is contestable, but a normative orientation for democracy, whatever it is, was necessary for the task of proposing a comprehensive framework of democratic systems. Nevertheless, I think that this suggested overall theoretical framework could still be of value for someone advocating an *alternative* normative core of what democracy is/ should be. Indeed, one can still rely on the descriptive layer for the mapping of political systems, and then apply one's own normative criteria for the assessment of their democratic quality. In addition, one can still find inspiration from the guiding questions for the task of diagnosis, even with other normative criteria. Furthermore, this book also takes position towards normativity itself in democratic theory; by "delaying its treatment" (as Saward 2019 puts it) and largely restricting its importance in the effort of democratic theorizing, we are reminded that what is at stake is not only democratic "principles and norms" but also the functional necessities of constant adaption to complex environments. In that vein, one can even see the democratic need for *reflexive critique* as being a functional need. As such, is my suggestion for developing democratic diagnosis a *normative claim* or a *functional necessity* for democratic systems? Perhaps it is both.

After all, this book is just a *theoretical thread*. It is a *complex* thread, in that it demands effort and openness to challenge. It is also a *deep* thread, in that it asks foundational questions and suggests answers at the abstract level of the core of democratic systems and democratic theory. This thread puts only some pieces together, in a particular order. Regarding these pieces, the thread articulates a few pieces (systems, communication, power, justification, normativity, democracy, deliberation), coming from diverse perspectives and interrogations. Through *systems theory* it tackles some elements of social theory, organization theory, communication theory, interactionism, epistemology, and phenomenology. Through *Habermas and Forst* it incorporates critical theory, some Kantianism, some moral constructivism. Through *democratic theory* the thread is oriented by interrogations on democratic and deliberative systems and by concerns of diagnosis and ultimately design. In a sense, it is a *transdisciplinary* thread, an exploratory journey. It may be over-interpretative on some points, understanding their meaning in a way perhaps not always faithful to their original meaning. But I have tried to use all these contributions in a constructive manner, by making small deviations from several theories and combining them in a creative way, in order to produce a thread that *somehow* displays the complexity of democracy, or part of its complexity. Because this thread is so long, deep, and complex, it exposes itself to criticism on many fronts; but that it is the point of this thread, to serve as a *heuristic* tool to identify where it is wrong and needs to be corrected. Therefore, the overall conclusion is not "it's complex" nor that "it depends," but a proposition on *how* it is complex and how we can do justice to this complexity by attempting to reduce it; and *how* and to what extent it depends and how we can embrace the variation in our efforts of democratic theorizing. In short, this thread just proposes or reminds us of an agenda: let's *also* make democratic theory a heuristic and diagnostic system in our joint efforts at making democracy a critical and emancipatory system.

Present challenges and future paths

This book was an *attempt* to sketch a complex theory of democratic systems. As it is, the suggested framework of democratic systems contains various flaws and limitations. Regarding the flaws, it is obvious that it is too complex and abstract. These flaws were perhaps avoidable, but only to a limited extent: the purpose of this book was to debate some deep-rooted core premises of democratic theory, and that requires abstract and complex theoretical work. Moreover, the proposed conceptual system is already a *reduction* of the complexity of democratic systems, which aims as best it can to *mirror* this complexity; there was thus a balance to be found between unintelligible complexity and simplistic reduction. Further theoretical work is required to reach this middle ground and develop it into a more appropriate and operative *democratic systems approach* combining:

1. A context-sensitive analytical apparatus to *observe* existing democratic systems in all their complexity and contingency (exempt from the normative bias of models' perspectives) and *map* the multiple differentiated and interacting elements (agents, practices, spaces, moments, levels of governance, functions, principles)

composing existing democratic systems, and their relations/imbrications with other social systems (economy, academia, mass media, etc.).

2. Methodological tools to *assess* the democratic performance/quality of existing democratic systems (local, regional, national, supranational, transnational, functional such as schools or companies), *diagnose* their specific problems calling for democratic solutions (reforms or innovations), and *design* appropriate solutions (new practices, new connections, new sequences) answering these specific shortcomings.

3. The *design and experimentation* of accessible tools and democratic venues to perform, as well, the above tasks with political actors, citizens in particular.

Regarding the limitations, one is that the proposed framework of democratic systems relates to several *debates* in democratic theory (e.g., procedure versus substance, universalism versus contextualism) and *approaches* (e.g., realism, agonism, pragmatism, standpoint theory) regarding which it does not explicitly take position. Arguably, this tentative theory of democratic systems falls somewhere within these debates and could articulate a position regarding these. But these debates were not the targets of this book. Similarly, it is likely that several approaches to democratic theory can challenge many assumptions of this framework, or maybe agree on some. However, there was no room here to anticipate their *potential* criticisms, and this book did not intend to position itself regarding their *indirect* challenges (such as the agonist criticism towards deliberative democracy). That will eventually be the object for future debates, which I hope will be driven by constructive convergences towards a metamodels approach rather than by sterile models' defense.

Another limitation is more internal; the suggested guidelines for the diagnosis of democratic problems do not constitute a detailed *metric* ready to be used as such. This essential work remains to be done. In addition, the main limitation is clearly that these guidelines are not followed by an empirical illustration and "testing" of their critical potential. This theoretical apparatus now faces the double challenge of applicability: first, under the form of *expert diagnosis* to assess whether the suggested diagnostic guidelines are actually helpful in the identification of democratic problems; second, under the form of *democratic diagnosis*, through the experimentation of innovative democratic venues where political actors and citizens collectively problematize their democratic system through these guidelines. The task of diagnosis itself, independently from the suggested guidelines and maybe relying on much better ones, would benefit from empirical testing and recursive refinements. Democratic scholars must now endorse an interdisciplinary agenda of developing robust and maximally neutral diagnostic tools in order to identify democratic problems.

The construction of this diagnostic agenda is also a challenge for democratic theorizing. It interrogates the respective role(s) of democratic theorists and citizens within the diagnostic process. This challenge resonates with recent calls to *democratize* democratic theorizing by including citizens' perspectives and theorize with transparency (Asenbaum 2022c; Fleuss 2021). This challenge also permeates the normative horizon of *self-governing* democracies (Geissel 2023). In contrast to philosophically justified grand normative visions of democracy, Geissel insists that citizens are to continuously (re-)shape their own democratic system. Hence, she posits self-governing as the normative core of democratic systems and calls for a democratization of the debate on what democracy should look like. This crucial debate is not only relevant for democratic theorists or professional politicians, it directly concerns citizens as well. It thus confers a normative expectation upon citizens: that they contribute to the ongoing effort of improving democratic systems. If democratic theorists do not sketch grand normative visions of what ideal democratic systems should look like, then what is/are our role?

While citizens have a central role to play in deciding the democratic architecture through which they govern themselves, democratic theorists can "help" (Mansbridge 2014), "support," and "inspire" (Geissel 2023) this normative enterprise. They can contribute to it by "helping communities to identify the best way to govern themselves" (ibid.: 5), for instance, in facilitating open-ended conversations about it (Fleuss 2021). Ultimately, the specific agenda of democratic diagnosis shares the same aim: develop guiding tools (not final prescriptions) to empower and support citizens as they decide themselves, collectively and democratically, on which democratic features they favor. Democratic diagnosis specifically does so in guiding citizens in the *problematization* of their own democratic system and the design of appropriate solutions. The role of democratic theorists is to help citizens locate and understand problems, to enable them to solve these in the best possible way, not to provide ready-made solutions. It assumes that democratic problems and solutions are not matters of *philosophical* justification but of *political* justification. This is particularly the case regarding the multiple trade-offs between the democratic expectations present within democratic systems. As a reminder, no practices or institutional architectures can be democratically perfect; complex democratic systems are composed of multiple democratic trade-offs, privileging the enactment of some democratic principles over others. The role of democratic theorists is to shed light on these trade-offs. They should act as wise guides to the difficult choices citizens must make regarding how to *settle* these trade-offs, not settle them on behalf of citizens. Philosophical arguments can guide citizens, but it is ultimately upon their expectations and justifications that *democratic* choices on the shape of their democratic system are made. The best democratic scholars can do is to support them with humility in their constant task of problem identification and design of imperfect solutions. To do so, they can:

1. *Develop guiding tools* to diagnose the specific problems of democratic systems and expose existing trade-offs between democratic expectations.
2. *Design innovative democratic venues* for the collective problematization and (re)construction of the democratic ideal, and continuously refine these through co-design with political actors, citizens in particular.
3. *Participate in the democratic diagnosis effort* by supporting citizens' problematization, within these venues, at some steps of the process.

Finally, this book poses a challenge to existing democratic systems: if everything works perfectly and no effort towards democratic reform or innovation is necessary, let's reach this comforting conclusion together through a robust process of democratic diagnosis. If something is wrong, or simply could be improved, let's together identify exactly what through a robust process of democratic diagnosis. In both cases, democratic diagnosis is necessary.

Contemporary societies face major challenges: we are living in "diabolical times" (Bächtiger & Dryzek 2024) and the near future does not look bright. We struggle to envision how we could reverse this destructive path. The "system" (broadly understood) seems fixed and impossible to reform through its existing tools. Calls from various political streams to completely *change the system* are not surprising, and some are frankly frightening. The challenge for contemporary democratic systems is to show that the system can change *from within*, that it can display self-critical tools for deep and reasonably quick transformation in order to tackle the life-threatening challenges of our time. We have to collectively question and potentially revise the "rules of the game" (Fleuss 2021), if we hope to continue playing together. To do so, democratic systems *need* to institutionalize permanent self-perturbation, a critical feedback loop, and constant self-problematization. This is exactly what venues of democratic diagnosis could do. Mansbridge recently wrote that in the face of our democratic crisis: "The goal should be to devise forms of democracy that retain the organizing capabilities and critical thrust of today's adversary democracies but introduce greater capacities to think together for the common good" (2023: 13). Processes of democratic diagnosis would sort out what we must retain from existing democratic systems (arguably, much is valuable) and what must be changed, through a critical thrust aimed at strengthening our capacities to think *and act* together for the common good. She concludes: "In this crisis, democratic innovation is not a luxury" (ibid.). As part of the process of democratic innovation, nor is democratic diagnosis.

Concluding remarks

How to summarize the main meaning of this book? What is the "take home message"? It depends for whom. Some might find interest in specific parts of this conceptual system, others with the whole. While each part matters on its own, their articulation into a complex whole produces an emergent and quite basic assertion: the social phenomenon of democracy must be understood as a complex system, whose fulfillment unfolds within a functionally limited perimeter of variable possibilities that embed specific problems and seeds for solutions. We therefore need to systematically and continuously diagnose the particular democratic problems of political systems. Framed as an injunction: let's target problems in addition to solutions (if not primarily), and let's focus on the opportunities for people to problematize their own political system. In the end, the outcome of this book is merely a broad meta-commentary on democratic theory and democratic practice; we do not undertake enough diagnostic work on democratic systems, both in academia and in politics. It may sound trivial, but I think it remains a crucial message. To borrow Fung's words: "Rather than trying to describe what lies at the end of the path of inquiry, the [...] [systemic] conception of democracy sketched above maps out the first few steps in that journey and provides a method of inquiry with which to follow it. Now it is time to take those steps and see what lies ahead" (2012: 624). My modest contribution in that regard, if there is any, is a complex yet justified call (or perhaps only a reminder) to undertake the task of diagnosis, and a few suggestions to do so. My genuine hope is that this book can contribute to the task of diagnosing democratic problems, for whoever tries to do so, political actor, academic expert, or ordinary citizen.

To conclude, does the above discussion make sense? Is it meaningful? Maybe not. It has nonetheless tackled meaningful contributions; it has tried to grasp their complexity, often reducing it, in order to rearticulate parts of their meaning in an alternative conceptual apparatus. Although the proposed conceptual system is certainly not a faithful and authoritative depiction of political complexity, my hope is that it nevertheless represents a complex and ordered possibility for multiple deviations. If the justified negation of communications creates new meanings, I hope to have proposed quite a few contestable assumptions to generate further meaningful divergences, *including my future own*. One has to start somewhere, and the suggested theoretical framework is a proposed beginning, not a definitive assertion. Its value does not merely depend on the alleged correctness of this theoretical apparatus but on the extent of its potential for self-correction. The robustness of this conceptual system will rely, as Luhmann puts it, on its capacity to "itself recognize which of its assumptions it has to change or differentiate if it is to be able to recast those facts in its own theoretical language" (1986: 7). If there is a goal I wish to have reached here, that it is most definitely the one. The final question remains as to whether this book is a meaningful contribution. It is a perturbation at best, to the few conceptual systems it may encounter on its brief and limited path. It will be a challenge, I hope, for those who genuinely wonder what democracy is and could be.

Bibliography

ADAMS, Kevin, HESTER, Patrick T., & BRADLEY Joseph M. (2013) "A Historical Perspective of Systems Theory," in KRISHNAMURTHY, A., & CHAN, W. K. V (Eds.) *Proceedings of the 2013 Industrial and Systems Engineering Research Conference.*

AGAZZI, Evandro (1978) "Systems Theory and the Problem of Reductionism," *Erkenntnis*, 12(3): 339–358.

AHLERS, Anna (2021) "The Rise of Complexity: Internal Differentiation of Political Systems," in AHLERS, Anna, KRICHWESKY, Damien, MOSER, Evelyn, & STICHWEH, Rudolf (Eds.), *Democratic and Authoritarian Political Systems in 21st Century World Society: Volume 1 – Differentiation, Inclusion, Responsiveness*. Bielefeld: Bielefeld University Press.

ALBERT, Mathias (2016) "Luhmann and Systems Theory," *Oxford Research Encyclopedias: Politics.*

ARNOLDI, Jakob (2001) "Niklas Luhmann: An Introduction," *Theory, Culture and Society*, 18: 1–13.

ASENBAUM, Hans (2018) "The End of Democratic Theory? A Challenge to the Problem-Based Approach," Paper Presented at the Participatory and Deliberative Democracy Conference, September 5–7, 2018, London.

ASENBAUM, Hans (2022a) "Beyond Deliberative Systems: Pluralizing the Debate," *Democratic Theory*, 9: 87–98.

ASENBAUM, Hans (2022b) "Democratic Assemblage," in DAVIDIAN, Anne, & JEAN-PIERRE, Laurent (Eds.) *What Makes an Assembly? Stories, Experiments, and Inquiries*, London: Sternberg Press.

ASENBAUM, Hans (2022c) "Doing Democratic Theory Democratically," *International Journal of Qualitative Methods*, 21: 1–12.

BACHTIGER, André, NIEMEYER, Simon, NEBLO, Michael, STEENBERGEN, Marco, & STEINER, Jürg (2010) "Disentangling Diversity in Deliberative Democracy," *Journal of Political Philosophy*, 18 (1), 32–63.

BACHTIGER, André, & BESTE, Simon (2017) "Deliberative Citizens, (Non)Deliberative Politicians: A Rejoinder," *Daedalus*, 146(3): 106–118.

BACHTIGER, André, & PARKINSON, John (2019) *Mapping and Measuring Deliberation: Towards a New Deliberative Quality*, Oxford: Oxford University Press.

BACHTIGER, André, & DRYZEK, John (2024) *Deliberative Democracy for Diabolical Times: Confronting Populism, Extremism, Denial, and Authoritarianism*, Cambridge: Cambridge University Press.

BARALDI, Claudio, CORSI, Giancarlo, & ESPOSITO, Elena (2021) *Unlocking Luhmann: A Keyword Introduction to Systems Theory*, Bielefeld: Bielefeld University Press.

BARALOU, Evangelia, WOLF, Patricia, & MEISNNER, Jens O. (2012) "Bright, Excellent, Ignored: The Contribution of Luhmann's System Theory and Its Problem of Non-Connectivity to Academic Management Research," *Historical Social Research / Historische Sozialforschung*, 37(4): 289–308.

BAXTER, Hugh (1987) "System and Life-world in Habermas's Theory of Communicative Action," *Theory and Society*, 16: 39–86.

BAXTER, Hugh (2011) *Habermas. The Discourse Theory of Law and Democracy*, Stanford: Stanford University Press.

BECKENKAMP, Martin (2006) "The Herd Moves? Emergence and Self-organization in Collective Actors," in *Preprints of the Max Planck Institute for Research on Collective Goods*, Bonn, 2006/14.

BENHABIB, Seyla (2015) "The Uses and Abuses of Kantian Rigorism. On Rainer Forst's Moral and Political Philosophy," in BENHABIB, Seyla, FLYNN, Jeffrey, FRITSCH, Matthias, and FORST, Rainer. Review Symposium: The Right to Justification by Rainer Forst. *Political Theory*, 43(6): 777–792.

BERMEO, Nancy (2016) "On Democratic Backsliding," *Journal of Democracy*, 27: 5–19.

BERTALANFFY, Von, Ludwig (1972) "The History and Status of General Systems Theory," *The Academy of Management Journal*, 15(4): 407–426.

BESCH, Thomas (2020) "Forst on Reciprocity of Reasons: A Critique," *The Southern Journal of Philosophy*, 58(3): 357–382.

BESTE, Simon (2016) "Legislative Frame Representation: Towards an Empirical Account of the Deliberative Systems Approach," *The Journal of Legislative Studies*, 22(3): 295–328.

BOLTANSKI, Luc, & THEVENOT, Laurent (1991) *De la Justification. Les Economies de la Grandeur*. Paris: Gallimard.

BORCH, Christian (2005) "Systemic Power: Luhmann, Foucault, and Analytics of Power," *Acta Sociologica*, 48(2): 155–167.

BORNE, Elisabeth (2022) *Séminaire Gouvernemental*, Paris, August 31, 2022.

URL: https://www.youtube.com/watch?v=Em5efA8OBls&t=5s (consulted September 15, 2022).

BOSWELL, John, & CORBETT, Jack (2017) "Why and How to Compare Deliberative Systems," *European Journal of Political Research*, 56(4): 801–819.

BOSWELL, John, ERCAN, Selen, & HENDRIKS, Carolyn (2016) "Message Received? Examining Transmission in Deliberative Systems," *Critical Policy Studies*, 10(3): 263–283.

BOURGNE, Patrick (2017) "

BRENNAN, Jason (2016), *Against Democracy*, Princeton: Princeton University Press.

BRUNCZEL, Balazs (2010), *Disillusioning Modernity: Niklas Luhmann's Social and Political Theory*, Frankfurt-am-Main: Peter Lang.

BUNGE, Mario (2000) "Systemism: The Alternative to Individualism and Holism," *Journal of Socio-Economics*, 29: 147–157.

BUNGE, Mario (2004) "How Does It Work? The Search for Explanatory Mechanisms," *Philosophy of the Social Sciences*, 34(2): 182–210.

BURALL, Simon (2015) "Room for a View: Democracy as a Deliberative System," *InvolveUK*.

BUZAN, Barry, & ALBERT, Mathias (2010) "Differentiation: A Sociological Approach to International Relations Theory," *European Journal of International Relations*, 16(3): 315–-337.

CANEY, Simon (2014) "Justice and the Basic Right to Justification," in FORST, Rainer (Ed.) *Justice, Democracy and the Right to Justification: Rainer Forst in Dialogue*. London: Bloomsbury Academic.

CASTELLS, Manuel (1996), *The Rise of the Network Society*, Malden, MA: Blackwell.

CHAMBERS, Simone (2005) "Measuring Publicity's Effect: Reconciling Empirical Research and Normative Theory," *Acta Politica*, 40: 255–266.

CHAMBERS, Simone (2012) "Deliberation and Mass Democracy," in PARKINSON, John, & MANSBRIDGE, Jane (Eds.) *Deliberative Systems: Deliberative Democracy at the Large Scale*. Cambridge: Cambridge University Press.

CHAMBERS, Simone (2015) "Democracy and Critique: Comments on Rainer Forst's Justification and Critique: Towards a Critical Theory of Politics," *Philosophy and Social Criticism*, 41(3): 213–217.

CHAMBERS, Simone (2017) "Balancing Epistemic Quality and Equal Participation in a System Approach to Deliberative Democracy," *Social Epistemology*, 31(3): 266–276.

CHERNILO, Daniel (2002) "The Theorization of Social Coordinations in Differentiated Societies: The Theory of Generalized Symbolic Media in Parsons, Luhmann and Habermas," *British Journal of Sociology*, 53(3): 431–449.

CINALLI, Manlio, & O'FLYNN, Ian (2014) "Public Deliberation, Network Analysis and the Political Integration of Muslims in Britain," *British Journal of Politics and International Relations*, 16(3): 428–451.

COPPEDGE, Michael (2023) "V-Dem's Conceptions of Democracy and Their Consequences," The Varieties of Democracy Institute Working Papers, 2023 (135): 1–31.

COPPEDGE, Michael, GERRING, John, ALTMAN, David, et al. (2011) "Conceptualizing and Measuring Democracy: A New Approach," *Perspectives on Politics*, 9(2): 247–267.

CURATO, Nicole (2015) "Deliberative Capacity as an Indicator of Democratic Quality: The Case of the Philippines," *International Political Science Review*, 36: 99–116.

CURATO, Nicole, & BOKER, Marit (2016) "Linking Mini-publics to the Deliberative System: A Research Agenda," *Policy Sciences*, 49(2): 173–190.

CURATO, Nicole, BOKER, Marit, & MIN, John B. (2019) *Power in Deliberative Democracy: Norms, Forums, Systems*, London: Palgrave Macmillan.

CURATO, Nicole, DRYZEK, John, ERCAN, Selen, HENDRIKS, Carolyn, & NIEMEYER, Simon (2017) "Twelve Key Findings in Deliberative Democracy Research," *Daedalus*, 146(3): 6–13.

DALLMANN, Hans-Ulrich (1998) "Niklas Luhmann's Systems Theory as a Challenge for Ethics," *Ethical Theory and Moral Practice*, 1: 85–102.

DAHL, Robert A. (1989) *Polyarchy: Participation and Opposition*, New Haven: Yale University Press.

DALTON, Russel (2004) *Democratic Challenges, Democratic Choices: The Erosion of Political Support in Advanced Industrial Democracies*, Oxford: Oxford University Press.

DEAN, Rikki, RINNE, Jonathan, & GEISSEL, Brigitte (2019) "Systematizing Democratic Systems Approaches Seven Conceptual Building Blocks," *Democratic Theory* 6(2): 41–57.

DEAN, Rikki, & GEISSEL, Brigitte (2018) "Defining Democracy: From a Problem-Based to a Modular Approach," Paper for the ECPR General Conference, August 24, 2018, Hamburg, Germany.

DEAN, Rikki, BOSWELL, John, & SMITH, Graham (2020) "Designing Democratic Innovations as Deliberative Systems: The Ambitious Case of NHS Citizen," *Political Studies*, 68(3): 689–709.

DENT, Eric B., & UMPLEBY, Stuart A. (1998) "Underlying Assumptions of Several Traditions in Systems Theory and Cybernetics," in TRAPPL, Robert (Ed.) *Cybernetics and Systems '98*, Vienna: Austrian Society for Cybernetic Studies.

DRYZEK, John (2009) "Democratization as Deliberative Capacity Building," *Comparative Political Studies*, 42: 1379–1402.

DRYZEK, John (2010) *Foundations and Frontiers of Deliberative Governance*, New York: Oxford University Press.

DRYZEK, John (2011) "Global Democratization: Soup, Society, or System?," *Ethics and International Affairs*, 25(2): 211–234.

DRYZEK, John (2016) "Symposium Commentary: Reflections on the Theory of Deliberative Systems," *Critical Policy Studies*, 10(2): 209–215.

DRYZEK, John (2017) "The Forum, the System, and the Polity: Three Varieties of Democratic Theory," *Political Theory*, 45(5): 610–636.

DRYZEK, John, & STEVENSON, Hayley (2013) "Democratizing Global Climate Change: A Deliberative Systems Approach," Paper Presented for Presentation the 8th Pan-European Conference on International Relations, September 18–21, 2013, Warsaw.

DRYZEK, John, & STEVENSON, Hayley (2014) *Democratizing Global Climate Governance*, Cambridge: Cambridge University Press.

DRYZEK, John, BACHTIGER, André, CHAMBERS, Simone, et al. (2019) "The Crisis of Democracy and the Science of Deliberation," *Science*, 363 (6432): 1144–1146.

DUBE, Richard (2017) "Niklas Luhmann et l'observation empirique du droit: communication, fonction, code et programme," *Droit et société*, 96: 381–400.

EASTON, David (1953) *The Political System: An Inquiry into the State of Political Science*, New York: Alfred A. Knopf.

ECHEVERRIA, Gabriel (2020) *Towards a Systemic Theory of Irregular Migration: Explaining Ecuadorian Irregular Migration in Amsterdam and Madrid*, IMISCOE Research Series.

ELSTUB, Stephen, & McLAVERTY, Peter (2014) *Deliberative Democracy: Issues and Cases*, Edinburgh: Edinburgh University Press.

ERCAN, Selen, HENDRIKS, Carolyn, & BOSWELL, John (2018) "Reforming Democracy in Disconnected Times: A Deliberative Systems Approach," Paper presented at European Consortium of Political Research Joint Sessions, Nicosia, April 10–14, 2018.

ERCAN, Selen, HENDRIKS, Carolyn, & DRYZEK, John (2019) "Public Deliberation in an Era of Communicative Plenty," *Policy & Politics*, 47: 19–39.

ERMAN, Eva (2016) "Representation, Equality, and Inclusion in Deliberative Systems: Desiderata for a Good Account," *Critical Review of International and Political Philosophy*, 19(3): 263–282.

ERMAN, Eva (2022) "The Boundary Problem of Democracy: A Function-sensitive View," *Contemporary Political Theory*, 21: 240–261.

FEARON, James (1998) "Deliberation as Discussion," in ELSTER, Jon (Ed.) *Deliberative Democracy*, Cambridge: Cambridge University Press.

FELICETTI, Andrea (2021) "Learning from Democratic Practices: New Perspectives in Institutional Design," *The Journal of Politics*, 83(4): 1589–1601.

FELICETTI, Andrea, NIEMEYER, Simon, & CURATO, Nicole (2016) "Improving Deliberative Participation: Connecting Mini-publics to Deliberative Systems," *European Political Science Review*, 8(3): 427–448.

FERRARESE, Estelle (2004) "Niklas Luhmann et l'opinion publique : l'autre de l'espace publique," *Cahiers Internationaux de sociologie*, 116: 97–115.

FERRARESE, Estelle (2015) "La justice, une formule de contingence. La tentation politique de Niklas Luhmann," in SOSOE, Lukas (Ed.) *Le droit - un système social*, Hildesheim: Georg Olms Verlag.

FLEUSS, Dannica (2021) *Radical Proceduralism: Democracy from Philosophical Principles to Political Institutions*, Leeds: Emerald Group Publishing.

FLEUSS, Dannica (2023) "Challenging the "Rules of the Game": The Role of Bottom-Up Participatory Experiments for Deliberative Democracy," in BUA, Adrian, & BUSSU, Sonia (Eds.) *Reclaiming Participatory Governance: Social Movements and the Reinvention of Democratic Innovation*, London: Routledge.

FLYNN, Jeffrey (2004) "Communicative Power in Habermas's Theory of Democracy," *European Journal of Political Theory*, 3(4): 433–454.

FLORIDIA, Antonia (2018) "The Origins of the Deliberative Turn," in BACHTIGER, André, DRYZEK, John, MANSBRIDGE, Jane, & WARREN, Mark (Eds.) *The Oxford Handbook of Deliberative Democracy*, Oxford: Oxford University Press.

FORST, Rainer (2001) "The Rule of Reason: Three Models of Deliberative Democracy," *Ratio Juris*, 14(4): 345–378.

FORST, Rainer (2007) "First Things First: Redistribution, Recognition and Justification," *European Journal of Political Theory*, 6(3): 291–304.

FORST, Rainer (2011a) "The Ground of Critique: On the Concept of Human Dignity in Social Orders of Justification," *Philosophy and Social Criticism*, 37(9): 965–976.

FORST, Rainer (2011b) "The Power of Critique", *Political Theory*, 39: 118–123.

FORST, Rainer (2011c) *The Right to Justification: Elements of a Constructivist Theory of Justice*, New York: Columbia University Press.

FORST, Rainer (2014) "Justifying Justification: Reply to My Critics," in FORST, Rainer (Ed.) *Justice, Democracy and the Right to Justification: Rainer Forst in Dialogue*, London: Bloomsbury Academic.

FORST, Rainer (2015a) "Noumenal Power," *The Journal of Political Philosophy*, 23(2): 111–127.

FORST, Rainer (2015b) "The Right to Justification: Moral and Political, Transcendental and Historical Reply to Seyla Benhabib, Jeffrey Flynn and Matthias Fritsch," in BENHABIB, Seyla, FLYNN, Jeffrey, FRITSCH, Matthias, & FORST, Rainer. Review Symposium: The Right to Justification by Rainer Forst. *Political Theory*, 43(6): 822–837.

FORST, Rainer (2017) *Normativity and Power: Analyzing Social Orders of Justification*, Oxford: Oxford University Press.

FORST, Rainer (2018) "Noumenal Power Revisited: Reply to Critics," *Journal of Political Power*, 11(3): 294–321.

FORST, Rainer (2021) "The Meanings of Democracy – Melissa Williams, Rainer Forst & Zhao Tingyang in Conversation," *Video discussion presented by the Thomas Mann House and Goethe-Institut China*.

FORTIER, Michael (2013) "Niklas Luhmann: la réalité des médias de masse," *Lectures [En ligne]: Les comptes rendus*, mis en ligne le 26 juin 2013, URL: http://journals.openedition.org/lectures/11826 (consulted February 3, 2022).

FOUCAULT, Michel (1979) "Naissance de la biopolitique 2: Cours au Collège de France," URL: https://www.youtube.com/watch?v=6of1lFoE_40 (consulted December 12, 2021).

FUNG, Archon (2012) "Continuous Institutional Innovation and the Pragmatic Conception of Democracy," *Polity*, 44(4): 609–624.

GARCIA AMADO, Juan A. (1989) "Introduction à l'œuvre de Niklas Luhmann," *Droit et société*, 11–12: 15–52.

GASTIL, John, KNOBLOCH, Katherine & REITMAN, Tyrone (2015) "Connecting Micro-Deliberation to Electoral Decision Making: Institutionalizing the Oregon Citizens' Initiative Review," in COLEMAN, Stephen, PRZYBYLSKA, Anna, & SINTOMER, Yves (Eds.) *Deliberation and Democracy: Innovative Processes and Institutions*, New York: Peter Lang.

GEISSEL, Brigitte (2023) *The Future of Self-Governing, Thriving Democracies: Democratic Innovations By, With and For the People*, London: Routldege.

GILGEN, Peter (2012) "System – Autopoiesis – Form: An Introduction to Luhmann's 'Introduction to Systems Theory,'" in LUHMANN, Niklas, *Introduction to Systems Theory*, Cambridge: Polity Press.

GOODIN, Robert (2005) "Sequencing Deliberative Moments," *Acta Politica*, 40(2): 182–196.

GOSEPATH, Stefan (2021) "Equality," *The Stanford Encyclopedia of Philosophy* (Summer 2021 Edition), ZALTA, Edward N. (Ed.) URL: https://plato.stanford.edu/archives/sum2021/entries/equality/ (consulted September 1, 2022).

GUY, Jean-Sebastien (2019) *Theory Beyond Structure and Agency: Introducing the Metric/Nonmetric Distinction*, London: Palgrave Macmillan.

GUZZINI, Stefano (2001) "Another Sociology for IR? An Analysis of Niklas Luhmann's Conceptualisation of Power," Paper prepared for the 42nd Annual convention of the International Studies Association in Chicago, February 21–25, 2001.

HABERMAS, Jürgen (1987) *The Theory of Communicative Action, Volume 2: Lifeworld and Systems, A Critique of Functionalist Reason*, Boston: Beacon Press.

HABERMAS, Jürgen (1996) *Between Facts and Norms: Contributions to a Discourse Theory of Law and Democracy*, London: Polity Press.

HENDRIKS, Carolyn (2016) "Coupling Citizens and Elites in Deliberative Systems: The Role of Institutional Design," *European Journal of Political Research*, 55: 43–60.

HENDRIKS, Carolyn, ERCAN, Selen, & BOSWELL, John (2020) *Mending Democracy: Democratic Repair in Disconnected Times*, Oxford: Oxford University Press.

HERTIG, Stephan, & STEIN, Lars Stein (2007) "The Evolution of Luhmann's Systems Theory with Focus on the Constructivist Influence," *International Journal of General Systems*, 36(11): 1–17.

HOLDO, Markus (2020) "Meta-deliberation: Everyday Acts of Critical Reflection in Deliberative Systems," *Politics*, 40: 106–119.

HOLMES, Stephen, & LARMORE, Charles (1982) "Translators' Introduction," in LUHMANN, Niklas, *The Differentiation of Society*, New York: Columbia University Press.

JASKE, Maija, & SETALA, Maija (2020) "A Functionalist Approach to Democratic Innovations," *Representation*, 56(4): 467–483.

JONSSON, Magnus (2015) "Democratic Innovations in Deliberative Systems: The Case of the Estonian Citizens' Assembly Process," *Journal of Public Deliberation*, 11: 1–29.

KERVEGAN, Jean-François (2003) "Quel est le sens de 'l'autonomie du droit'? A propos du débat Habermas/Luhmann," in RENAULT, Emmanuel & SINTOMER, Yves (Eds.) *Où en est la théorie critique?*, Paris: La Découverte.

KIM, Joohyung (2015) "The Social and the Political in Luhmann," *Contemporary Political Theory*, 14(4): 355–376.

KING, Michael, & THORNHILL, Chris (2003) *Niklas Luhmann's Theory of Politics and Law*, New York: Palgrave MacMillan.

KNODT, Eva (1994) "Toward a Non-Foundationalist Epistemology: The Habermas/Luhmann Controversy Revisited," *New German Critique*, 61: 77–100.

KNODT, Eva (1995) "Foreword," in LUHMANN, Niklas, *Social Systems*, Stanford: Stanford University Press.

KNOPS, Andrew (2016) "Deliberative Networks," *Critical Policy Studies*, 10(3): 305–324.

PARKINSON, John (2016) "On Scholarly Metaphors, or, what is Deliberative about Deliberative Democracy," Paper Presented at the ECPR Joint Sessions, Pisa, April 24–28, 2016.

PARKINSON, John, & MANSBRIDGE, Jane (2012) *Deliberative Systems: Deliberative Democracy at the Large Scale*, Cambridge: Cambridge University Press.

PARKINSON, John (2018) "Deliberative Systems," in BACHTIGER, André, DRYZEK, John, MANSBRIDGE, Jane and WARREN, Mark (Eds.) *The Oxford Handbook of Deliberative Democracy*, Oxford: Oxford University Press: 432–446.

PARKINSON, John (2019) "Deliberation as Meaning-making," Paper presented at the European Consortium of Political Research General Conference, Wrocław, September 2019.

PARKINSON, John (2020) "The Roles of Referendums in Deliberative Systems," *Representation*, 56(4): 485–500.

PARKINSON, John, DE LAILE, Sebastian, & FRANCO-GULLIEN, Nuria (2020) "Mapping Deliberative Systems with Big Data: The Case of the Scottish Independence Referendum," *Political Studies*, 70(3): 543–565.

PARSONS, Talcott (1951) *The Social System*, London: Routledge.

PARSONS, Talcott (1969) *Politics and Social Structure*, New York: Free Press.

PARTICIPEDIA (2024) "Germany's Citizens' Assembly on Democracy (Bürgerrat Demokratie)," URL: https://participedia.net/case/5806 (consulted March 23, 2024).

PICKEL, Andreas (2011) "Systems Theory," in JARVIE, Ian C., & ZAMORA-BONILLA, Jesus (Eds.), *The SAGE Handbook of the Philosophy of Social Sciences*, London: Sage Publications.

POLI, Roberto (2010) "The Complexity of Self-reference: A Critical Evaluation of Luhmann's Theory of Social Systems," *Quaderno 50 del Dipartimento di Sociologia e Ricerca Sociale de l'Universta di Trento*.

PRZEWORSKI, Adam (1999) "Minimalist Conception of Democracy: A Defense," in SHAPIRO, Ian, & HACKER-GORDON, Casiano (Eds.) *Democracy's Value*, Cambridge: Cambridge University Press.

RABAULT, Hugues (1999) "Hommage à Niklas Luhmann. L'apport épistémologique de la pensée de Niklas Luhmann : un crépuscule pour l'Aufklärung ?," *Droit et Société*, 42–43: 449–465

RABAULT, Hugues (2015) "La réalité comme artefact : le constructivisme sociologique de Niklas Luhmann," *Droit et société*, 89: 207–218.

RASMUSSEN, Jens (1998) "Constructivism and Phenomenology: What Do They Have in Common, and How Can They Be Told Apart?," *Cybernetics & Systems*, 29(6): 553–576.

RENWICK, Alan, SCOTT, Kaela, RUSSELL, Meg, CLEAVER, James, & OSBORNE, Frances (2022) *Report of the Citizens' Assembly on Democracy in the UK: Second Report of the Democracy in the UK after Brexit Project*, London: The Constitution Unit.

REY, Felipe (2023) "The Representative System," *Critical Review of International Social and Political Philosophy*, 26(6): 831–854.

ROSENBERG, Morris (1954) "Some Determinants of Political Apathy," *Public Opinion Quarterly*, 18(4): 349–366.

ROTTLEUTNER, Hubert (1989) "A Purified Sociology of Law: Niklas Luhmann on the Autonomy of the Legal System," *Law & Society Review*, 23(5): 779–798.

SAFFON, Maria Paula, & URBINATI, Nadia (2013) "Procedural Equality, the Bulwark of Equal Liberty," *Political Theory*, 41(3): 441–481.

SAWARD, Michael (2003) "Enacting Democracy," *Political Studies*, 51: 161–179.

SAWARD, Michael (2010) *The Representative Claim*, Oxford: Oxford University Press.

SAWARD, Michael (2019) "Theorizing about Democracy," *Democratic Theory*, 6(2): 1–11.

SAWARD, Michael (2021) *Democratic Design*, Oxford: Oxford University Press.

SAYER, Andrew (2005) "Reductionism in Social Sciences," Paper for workshop on "Challenges to Dominant Modes of Knowledge: Reductionism," December 16–17, 2005, Paris.

SAYER, Andrew (2010) "Reductionism in Social Sciences," in LEE, Richard E. (Ed.) *Questioning Nineteenth-Century Assumptions about Knowledge, II: Reductionism*, New York: State University of New York Press.

SCANLON, Thomas (2018) *Why Does Inequality Matter?*, Oxford: Oxford University Press.

SEIDL, David, & BECKER, Kai H. (2010) "Organizations as Distinction Generating and Processing Systems: Niklas Luhmann's Contribution to Organization Studies," *Organization*, 13: 9–35.

SETALA, Maija (2017) "Connecting Deliberative Mini-publics to Representative Decision-making," *European Journal of Political Research*, 56(4): 846–863.

SIMON, Herbert (1982) *Models of Bounded Rationality. Volume 1: Economic Analysis and Public Policy*, Cambridge, MA: MIT Press.

SMITH, William (2016) "The Boundaries of a Deliberative System: The Case of Disruptive Protest," *Critical Policy Studies*, 10(2): 152–170.

SORENSEN, Eva, & TORFING, Jacob (2007) *Theories of Democratic Network Governance*, New York: Palgrave MacMillan.

SPENCER-SMITH, Richard (1995) "Reductionism and Emergent Properties," *Proceedings of the Aristotelian Society*, 95: 113–129.

STEENBERGEN, Marco, BACHTIGER, André, SPORNDLI, Markus, & STEINER, Jürg (2003) "Measuring Political Deliberation: A Discourse Quality Index," *Comparative European Politics*, 1: 21–48.

STEINER, Jürg (2008) "Concept Stretching: The Case of Deliberation," *European Political Science*, 7(2): 186–190.

STICHWEH, Rudolf (2011b) "Niklas Luhmann," in RITZER, George, & STEPNISKY, Jeffrey (Eds.), *The Wiley-Blackwell to Major Social Theorists*, Hoboken, NJ: Blackwell Publishing.

STICHWEH, Rudolf (2011b) "Systems Theory," in BADIE, Bertrand, BERG-SCHLOSSER, Dirk, & MORLINO, Leonardo (Eds.) *International Encyclopedia of Political Science*, New York: Sage Publications.

STICHWEH, Rudolf (2021) "Individual and Collective Inclusion and Exclusion in Political Systems," in AHLERS, Anna, KRICHWESKY, Damien, MOSER, Evelyn, & STICHWEH, Rudolf (Eds.) *Democratic and Authoritarian Political Systems in 21st Century World Society: Volume 1 – Differentiation, Inclusion, Responsiveness*, Bielefeld: Bielefeld University Press.

THALER, Richard, & SUNSTEIN, Cass (2008) *Nudge: Improving Decisions about Health, Wealth and Happiness*, New Haven: Yale University Press.

THOMPSON, Dennis (2008) "Deliberative Democratic Theory and Empirical Political Science," *Annual Review of Political Science*, 11:497–520.

THORNHILL, Chris (2006) "Niklas Luhmann: A Sociological Transformation of Political Legitimacy?," *Distinktion: Journal of Social Theory*, 7(2): 33–53.

THORNHILL, Chris (2008a) "On Norms as Social Facts: A View from Historical Political Science," *Soziale Systeme*, 14: 46–67.

THORNHILL, Chris (2008b) "Niklas Luhmann, Carl Schmitt, and the Modern Form of the Political," *European Journal of Social Theory*, 10(4): 499–522.

THORNHILL, Chris (2011) "Political Legitimacy: A Theoretical Approach between Facts and Norms," *Constellations: An International Journal of Critical and Democratic Theory*, 18(2): 136–169.

UN PAYS POUR DEMAIN (2023) "Rapport," URL: https://unpayspourdemain.be/pages/rapport.html (consulted March 22, 2024)

VALENTINOV, Vladislav, HIELSCHER, Stefan, & PIES, Ingo (2016) "Emergence: A Systems Theory's Challenge to Ethics," *Systemic Practice and Action Research*, 29(6): 597–610.

VALENTINOV, Vladislav (2019) "The Ethics of Functional Differentiation: Reclaiming Morality in Niklas Luhmann's Social Systems Theory," *Journal of Business Ethics*, 155: 105–114.

VANDERSTRAETEN, Raf (2002) "Parsons, Luhmann, and the Theorem of Double Contingency," *Journal of Classical Sociology*, 2: 77–92.

VINCENT, Jean-Marie (1999) "La société de Niklas Luhmann," *Cahiers Internationaux de Sociologie*, 107: 355–367.

WAGNER, Gerhard (2012) "Function and Causality," *Revue internationale de philosophie*, 259: 35–53.

WALZER, Michael (1999) "Deliberation and What Else?," in MACEDO, Stephen (Ed.) *Deliberative Politics: Essays on Democracy and Disagreement*, New York: Oxford University Press.

WARREN, Mark (2007) "Institutionalizing Deliberative Democracy," in ROSENBERG, Shawn W. (Ed.), *Deliberation, Participation and Democracy: Can the People Govern?*, London: Palgrave Macmillan.

WARREN, Mark (2008) "Citizen Participation and Democratic Deficits: Considerations from the Perspective of Democratic Theory," in DeBardeleben, Joan, & Pammett, Jon (Eds.) *Activating the Citizen.*,London: Palgrave Macmillan.

WARREN, Mark (2017) "A Problem-Based Approach to Democratic Theory," *American Political Science Review*, 111: 39–53.

WARREN, Mark (2023) "Democracy and the Corruption of Speech," *Political Studies Review*, 22(2): 289–297.

Acknowledgments

The writing of this book would not have been possible without the support of several people and organizations. I warmly thank the Swiss National Science Foundation for granting me eighteen months for international mobility to the Universities of Warwick and Maastricht. I would also like to thank the Schmidheiny Foundation for granting me eleven months of financial support to finish the writing of my thesis. I am also indebted to the University of Geneva, in particular the Department of Political Science and International Relations, the Institute of Citizenship Studies, and the Faculty of Social Sciences, for continuous and diverse forms of support along this book journey. I am also grateful to Epistémé Editions, in particular Lucas Giossi and the proof-reader, for their amazing editorial work. I thank as well the Swiss National Science Foundation for supporting the Open Access version of this book.

My intellectual debts are countless: here I name only a few of those who helped me develop this book. For their feedback, suggestions, criticisms, opportunities, and enthusiast support, in conferences or discussions, I would like to thank Alice el-Wakil, Frank Hendriks, Claudia Landwehr, André Bächtiger, Sonia Bussu, Nino Junius, Julian Frinken, Ian O'Flynn, Nadia Urbinati, Cristina Lafont, Annabelle Lever, Julia Jakobi, Palle Bech-Pedersen, Samuel Hayat, Pierre-Etienne Vandamme, Arild Ohren, Antonin Lacelle-Webster, Maija Setälä, Elisa Minsart, Laurent de Briey, Vincent Jacquet, Rikki Dean, Jonathan Rinne, Clementina Gentile Fusillo, Melisa Ross, Hans Asenbaum, Dannica Fleuss, Ricardo Mendonça, Bruno Magalhaes, Hannah Schoch, Esma Baycan-Herzog, Yoann Della Croce, Serkan Seker, Basel Mansour, Elisa Banfi, Jérôme Grand, Quentin Borgeat, Simon Hug, Emanuela Ceva, Pascal Sciarini, Frédéric Varone, and Marco Giugni. I warmly thank Bernard Reber for reading and providing comments on my PhD thesis. My thanks also go to Andri Heimann for in-depth discussions and promising horizons on the political agenda of democratic diagnosis. Special thanks go to Julien Vrydagh for his careful reading, constructive suggestions, stimulating discussions, and exciting collaborations on the development of the democratic systems approach and the democratic diagnosis agenda.

I am profoundly grateful to those people who directly supported my PhD journey. My sincere thanks go to John Parkinson for the huge positive impact he had on my work and for the honor of having him as a juror. All my gratitude goes to Michael Saward for having accompanied my work with great openness and enlightening guidance and for the privilege of having him as a juror. I sincerely thank Nenad Stojanovic for his sound and challenging comments on my thesis and his trust these past years while working together. Finally, I want to express my deepest gratitude to my PhD supervisor and mentor Matteo Gianni: this book would not exist without his constant support, trust, and wisdom on both an intellectual and human level.

On a more personal note, I am forever indebted to my friends, in particular Igor, Anastasia, and Mike for their non-academic yet clever support and remarks. My heartfelt thanks go to my family, in particular my sister Sarah and my parents, Giovanna and Pedro, for their care and emotional support throughout this journey.

Victor Sanchez-Mazas
Geneva, May 2024

About the author

Victor Sanchez-Mazas is a political researcher from the University of Geneva. He is a member of the Institute of Citizenship Studies and of the Department of Political Science and International Relationships. His research focuses on democracy and stands at the intersection of theory and applied research. In collaboration with public collectivities, he designs and implements several projects of democratic innovation in Switzerland. These practical experiments stem from his theoretical work and inspire it. Through this back-and-forth between theory and practice, Dr. Sanchez-Mazas aims to combine the theoretical grounds with concrete possibilities for democratic transformations of contemporary societies.

His PhD thesis defended at the University of Geneva in October 2022 is the basis of the present book.

Achevé d'imprimer en novembre 2024 par Corlet Imprimeur - 14110 Condé-en-Normandie
Dépôt légal : novembre 2024 - N° d'imprimeur : 24110477 - Imprimé en France